MW00782489

NAPOLEON'S MERCENARIES

By the same author

Napoleon's Soldiers: The Grande Armee of 1807
as Depicted in the Paintings of the Otto Manuscript

Napoleon's Army 1807–1814
as Depicted in the Prints of Aaron Martinet

NAPOLEON'S MERCENARIES

Foreign Units in the French Army
under the Consulate and Empire, 1799–1814

Guy C. Dempsey, Jr

GREENHILL BOOKS, LONDON
STACKPOLE BOOKS, PENNSYLVANIA

In memory of
Jean M. Dempsey (1922–1996)
and
Guy C. Dempsey, Sr (1920–2001)

Napoleon's Mercenaries
First published 2002 by Greenhill Books, Lionel Leventhal Limited, Park House, 1 Russell Gardens, London NW11 9NN
and
Stackpole Books, 5067 Ritter Road, Mechanicsburg, PA 17055, USA

British Library Cataloguing in Publication Data
Dempsey, Guy C.
Napoleon's mercenaries: foreign units in the French Army under the Consulate and Empire, 1799–1814
1. France. Armee – History – 19th century 2. Foreign enlistment – France – History – 19th century 3. Mercenary troops – France – History – 19th century 4. France – History – Consulate and Empire, 1799–1815
I. Title
355.3'1'0944'09034

ISBN 1-85367-488-5

Library of Congress Cataloging-in-Publication Data available

Designed and edited by Roger Chesneau
Printed and bound in Great Britain by MPG Books Ltd, Victoria Square, Bodmin, Cornwall

Front endpapers: (left) a Sbire, one of Prince Borghese's mounted Guards, and a grenadier and voltigeur from the Légions Piémontaises; (right) a mounted chasseur, voltigeur, officer and grenadier of the Légion Portugaise.
Back endpapers: (left) a grenadier of the Régiment de Catalogne, an officer and grenadier from the Légion Irlandaise, and grenadiers from the Régiment Joseph-Napoleon and Régiment d'Illyrie; (right) troops from the Swiss regiments, the Régiment d'Isembourg and the Bataillon du Prince de Neufchatel.
The endpapers are plates by Noirmont and Alfred de Marbot.

Contents

Illustrations

Between pages 160 and 161

Foreword

I began writing this book more years ago than I care to remember when I first had the perverse thought that it might be more interesting and challenging to study the identifiable units of foreigners that served in Napoleon's armies rather than the Emperor's more mundane French troops. I have subsequently amassed a vast amount of information on my chosen topic by work in some of the great libraries of the world, including the Library of Congress, the British Library, the London Library, the New York Public Library and the Sterling Library at Yale University. I also tackled relevant primary sources at the National Army Museum in London, the Museum of the Army in Paris, the French National Archives in Paris, the Anne S. K. Brown Military Collection in Providence, Rhode Island, and, most importantly, the French Army Archives at Vincennes. The great challenge in finishing this book has been to put aside the thrill of the hunt for new information in favour of the less obvious pleasure of organising and synthesising the information I already have in hand. (Since one can never have too much information, however, I encourage readers to contact me via the publisher of this work if they have relevant primary source information to contribute.)

I have been fortunate to have had many informal collaborators for this work, but unlucky in that two of the most important of these are no longer with us—Andrew Zaremba and John Elting. At the risk of naming too few of the others, I would particularly like to thank the following individuals for the contributions, large and small, that they have made over many years to my knowledge of Napoleon's foreign troops: Giancarlo Boeri, Piero Crociani, Manfred Ernst, Massimo Fiorentino, Markus Gärtner, Peter Harrington, J.-P. Loriot, Yves Martin, George Nafziger, Jonathan North, Frédéric Pouvesle, Albert Rigondaud, Dr Jean Sarramon, Edmund Wagner and all the patient individuals who work on interlibrary loan requests at the Rye Free Reading Room and in the Westchester County Library System. I would also like to acknowledge the debt I owe to Alain Pigeard, whose superb research, refelected in his many published books and articles, has made completion of this work easier than would otherwise have been the case. The present work has also benefited in innumerable ways from the existence of the two Napoleon Series on the Internet (www.napoleonseries.org and www.napoleon-series.org), so I would also like to express my thanks to the founder of the first one, Fons Libert, the people who keep them running and those who contribute to their content.

As for the largest debts of gratitude I owe with respect to this book, my publisher, Lionel Leventhal, has earned a close second place by giving me a chance to write on this somewhat rarified topic and then enduring patiently a plethora of missed deadlines. First place, however, goes to my wife, Nancy, and my three daughters, Katie (a fellow night owl), Elizabeth and Laura, whose lives have been disrupted in many small ways by my avocation.

Guy C. Dempsey, Jr

Author's Note

This volume uses the accepted French spelling for all personal and unit names because it is written from the point of view of the French military establishment. It should be pointed out, however, that these French versions were often far from accurate, particularly in the case of individual names in non-Romance languages, such as those of Polish soldiers.

The sources cited in shorthand form in the text are all listed, with full details, in the Bibliography.

G.C.D.

Napoleon's Mercenaries: An Overview

This book is about the mercenaries who served in the French armies of the Napoleonic wars, the distinctive units of foreign soldiers of fortune who fought for money (and a variety of other motives) alongside the regiments of native Frenchmen who formed the bulk of Napoleon's forces. In the terminology of the time, these units were broadly and simply categorised as *troupes étrangères* (foreign troops) to distinguish them from both the line and light regiments of the French regular army and from the other, French-manned, auxiliary formations (such as the Guard of Paris and the gendarmes) that were also 'outside the line' of battle, or '*hors ligne*'. At their worst, these mercenaries were mere 'hirelings'—cannon fodder of doubtful quality and loyalty to be used only to spare better troops from some militarily or medically dangerous service. At their best, however, they were consummate practitioners of the profession of arms ready to fulfil their contract of service honourably at the risk of life and limb long after those fighting for more classically noble motives might have quit. Their collective story, which has never been told in its entirety, constitutes a fascinating chapter in the Napoleonic epic because of the diversity of little-known personalities and events it encompasses.

It should be recognised from the outset that this book does not attempt to deal with all the non-French elements associated with the French Army of the Napoleonic era. Allied armies, whether those of other Bonaparte family kingdoms such as Westphalia and Naples or those of client states such as Bavaria and the other members of the Confederation of the Rhine, are beyond its scope, as are the many 'regular' French army units that were composed of men conscripted from territories outside the natural boundaries of France that came to be absorbed into the French Empire by conquest or treaty, such as the 112th Line Regiment formed exclusively with Belgians from the nine departments carved out of the old Austrian Netherlands.[1] The focus is, instead, just on those particular foreign military formations that (a) were integral units of the French Army during Napoleon's political reign from 1799 to 1814, (b) were intentionally and exclusively recruited by voluntary enlistment from populations that were not politically part of France when the unit was formed, (c) were paid by the French Treasury and (d) fought under a French flag or standard (if the unit had one at all).

[1] N. to Berthier, 14 Fructidor Year XI (1 September 1803), Nap. *Corr.*, No 7062, Vol. 8, pp. 509–10.

One might quibble about some of the nuances of these criteria, but they do capture the main elements which were recognised at the time as distinguishing the *troupes étrangères* from other kinds of units: they were composed of volunteers (as opposed to conscripts) who had made a conscious choice to serve in the armed forces of France rather than those of their own homeland. Indeed, it was precisely in order to emphasise this reality that Napoleon chose to give most of these units distinctive names such as the 'Irish Legion' and the 'Joseph Napoleon Regiment', stressing their non-French origins. The chronological cut-off has been included in order to limit coverage to only those units that were in existence while Napoleon was in control of the French government and thus able to affect the formation or dissolution of particular units.

The main difficulty with these criteria comes from the second element, because the continuing physical expansion of the borders of France throughout the period under study made a mockery of traditional European boundaries. For instance, the 2nd (or Dutch or Red) Light Horse Lancers of the Imperial Guard would seem to be a classic 'foreign' unit. Nonetheless, the regiment has not been included in this volume because it was not in fact formed until after Holland had been dissolved as an independent state and incorporated into the French Empire, so for the whole of its existence it was recruited exclusively from 'citizens' of France (in the grandest imperial sense of that geographical concept). The 1st (or Polish) Regiment of Light Horse Lancers of the Guard is included, however, because it was recruited exclusively from Poles and the Duchy of Warsaw was never annexed to France. On the other hand, the 4th, 7th and 9th Polish line infantry regiments that served with the French armies in Spain during much of the Peninsular War are not included because they carried standards of the sovereign Duchy of Warsaw even when they were being paid by France, and were thus allied units rather than true *troupes étrangères*. The Croat regiments are an especially odd case. Their home territory was ceded to Napoleon after the 1809 war against Austria, but it was never legally integrated into the French Empire, so they never became involuntary Frenchmen and still qualify for inclusion.

The existence of the *troupes étrangères* in Napoleon's armies represented the continuation of a long French tradition of use of mercenaries. By the start of the Revolution, France had been employing distinct units of foreign mercenaries in her armed forces for at least 700 years.[2] The Bourbon monarchs of the eighteenth century had followed this practice in a particularly aggressive (and successful) fashion through their many wars, a fact that accounts for the appearance in French military history of such formations as the Irish and Swiss Brigades that distinguished themselves at Fontenoy in 1745, the Royal Italian Regiment that helped capture Minorca in 1756, the Duke of Lauzun's Legion of Foreign Volunteers that fought for American independence at Yorktown in 1781 and numerous regiments of foreign hussars. It also accounts for the inclusion in the French Army establishment for 1791 of eleven Swiss,

---

[2] For the origins of the practice, see Fieffé, Vol. 1, pp. 3–7.

eight German, three Irish and one Belgian line infantry regiments, in addition to the Swiss Guards of Louis XVI and approximately eight cavalry regiments with a significant foreign element.[3] The foreign aspect of these units was proudly advertised by giving them uniforms of various colours that set them apart from the white-coated regular French army units.

During the course of 1791, however, all the foreign units came under suspicion for potential pro-Bourbon loyalty and, consequently, for potential counter-revolutionary attitude as well. After the officers of the Nassau and Royal German regiments published a declaration of hostility to the National Assembly, that body responded with a decree dated 21 July that eliminated all special status previously granted to foreign troops:[4]

> The 96th Regiment of Infantry, previously known as the Nassau Regiment, and the other units previously designated by the title of German, Irish or Belgian ['Liègoise' in original] regiments of infantry are all part of the French Army. In consequence, they are not entitled to any special distinctions and they will henceforth wear the same uniform, have the same discipline and will be treated with respect to pay, appointments and funding in the same manner as other French troops.

Relations between the foreign units and the forces of the Revolution deteriorated from that point as many non-French officers and men joined the flood of emigrés leaving the country. France's declaration of war against Austria, Prussia and Great Britain in April 1792 caused further distress for the foreign units and led to the mass defection of the Conflans (Saxon) Regiment of Hussars on 9 May and of the Royal German Regiment on 13 June.[5] On 16 June the Swiss regiment Watteville declined to renew its contract and returned to Switzerland.[6] Such developments deepened distrust and dislike of all the mercenaries, including the Swiss (who had not been covered by the 1791 decree), and set the stage for the massacre of the Swiss Guards at the Tuileries on 10 August. The rest of the Guards and the remaining seven Swiss line regiments were formally disbanded on 20 August 1792.[7]

Even as it was doing away with the mercenary units inherited from the deposed monarchy, however, the French government was starting to promote the inclusion of foreigners in the French Army as a matter of revolutionary policy. For instance, a decree dated 2 August 1792 promised both financial and non-financial rewards to any individual foreign soldier who might choose to desert and join the forces of revolution in their struggle against monarchical oppression.[8] In addition, the French military establishment formed whole new units of non-Frenchmen (such as the Belgian and Batavian [Dutch] Legions formed in 1792 and 1793, respectively) whenever it felt it

[3] A list of all the regiments of the French Army for that year can be found in Liliane and Fred Funcken, *The Lace Wars* (2 vols, London, 1977).
[4] Fieffé, Vol. 1, pp. 380–1.
[5] David Johnson, *The French Cavalry 1792–1815* (London, 1989), Introduction, pp. 4–5.
[6] Fieffé, Vol. 1, p. 398.
[7] Fieffé, Vol. 1, pp. 398–406.
[8] Fieffé, Vol. 2, pp. 5–8.

could foment unrest and promote French interests by doing so. The subversive nature of these policies exemplifies why the nations arrayed against France in the First Coalition felt so threatened by their Jacobin foe.

As a result, by the time of the *coup* of 18 Brumaire (9 November 1799), the armies of France had come to include a noticeable number of units with distinctly foreign-sounding names, such as the Battalion of Piedmont Patriots, the Maltese Legion and the Guides of Omar. Some of these had been created by Napoleon himself, so when he took control of the French government through his position as First Consul, it came as no surprise that his attitude towards the use of mercenary forces was favourable. In this area of endeavour, however, like so many others, he was able to refine and improve on the work of his predecessors to develop an approach to the use of foreign troops that was uniquely his own. That approach was, above all else, defined by his endless need for soldiers to serve as the foundation for his essentially military regime.

Looking back on his career from the perspective of St Helena, Napoleon is said to have remarked that 'a soldier like me requires 100,000 men a year.'[9] (Remarkably, modern scholarly analyses of the loss of life in the Napoleonic Wars support the conclusion that this rough estimate–suggesting a total of 1.4 million French military deaths for the fourteen years Napoleon was in power–is not far from the mark, although possibly a little on the high side.)[10] Whatever the exact number, it is certainly true that, from the very start of his start of his rule, Napoleon was acutely aware that he required a steady supply of fighting men for his armies and that foreign troops were a significant component of the resources he called upon to meet this need.

First and foremost, of course, Napoleon obtained his manpower from the machinery of conscription that had been created by the Revolution and that was subsequently refined by him via the improvement of governmental bureaucratic efficiency at the local level. It is generally reckoned that just over 2,000,000 men were conscripted between 1804 and 1814–a number which, of course, includes many non-Frenchman who became subject to conscription because there homelands were incorporated into the French Empire by conquest.[11] The next most important source of soldiers was alliance with other powers, which produced a record number of soldiers for the Grand Army in 1812 when Napoleon was able to obtain contingents for the Russian campaign even from such reluctant allies as Prussia and Austria.[12] The next source was French

[9] Emmanuel Las Cases, *Memoirs of the Emperor Napoleon* (London, 1936), Vol. 4, Pt 3, p. 119.

[10] Estimates of the French military loss of life during the Napoleonic Era have ranged from a high of 5,260,000 to a more reasonable consensus of approximately one million. The time periods and the methodologies of the various studies which have been attempted are summarised in brilliant fashion by Jacques Houdaille, 'Pertes de l'Armée de Terre sous le Premier Empire, d'après les Registres Matricules', *Population*, No 27 (1972), pp. 27–50.

[11] A. Meynier, 'Levées et Pertes des Hommes sous le Consulat et l'Empire', *Revue des Études Napoléoniennes*, Vol. XXX (1930), pp. 26–51 at 26.

[12] A pro-forma 1812 order of battle for the armies of all of the technically independent allied states that were ruled directly by Napoleon or one of his relatives can be found in Margueron's *Campagne de Russie* (4 vols, Paris, 1897–1906), Vol. 1, pp. 37–9.

TABLE 1: INFANTRY STRENGTH, 1800–1812

Category	April 1800	August 1805	March 1809	January 1812
Total infantry	598 (100%)	452 (100%)	641 (100%)	784 (100%)
Guard	n/a	4 (1%)	20 (3%)	47 (6%)
Line and Light Infantry	472 (79%)	86 (85%)	474 (74%)	585 (75%)
French *hors ligne* (13%)	78 (10%)	45 (11%)	72 (6%)	50
Troupes étrangères	48 (8%)	17 (4%)	75 (12%)	103 (13%)

citizens serving other than by way of conscription, a category which covers true volunteers (a relatively small number) and all the men serving in the French auxiliary units that were part of the *troupes hors ligne*. The foreign troops were the last of these sources.

It is very difficult to make a precise calculation of the relative importance of the manpower contribution made by foreign mercenaries to the strength of the French Army over the whole of the period in question, but a reasonable indicator in terms of order of magnitude can be found in the figures compiled by General Belhomme for his history of French infantry. His categorisation of foreign troops does not line up perfectly with the precise criteria used in this work, but he provides sufficient detail about his computations to allow for rough adjustment of his figures to reflect the viewpoint of this study. Table 1 shows the adjusted strength totals from Belhomme (expressed in thousands rounded to the nearest whole number) for the infantry units of the French Army at certain selected dates.[13] By way of comparison, the figures compiled by Belhomme for the number of infantrymen fielded by Napoleon's vassals and allies in the same years are: 1800–24,000; 1805–78,000; 1809–290,000; and 1812–296,000 (not counting the contingents from Austria, Prussia or Denmark). Since Belhomme's calculations do not include cavalry, artillery or engineers, the number of *troupes étrangères* was actually larger in absolute terms for each year noted, but their percentage contribution to the total strength of the whole French Army was smaller because of the very small number of foreign units other than infantry.

Since these figures represent annual snapshots of strength, they do not reflect the total cumulative number of *troupes étrangères* that may have served in the French Army during the whole of the period. The best information available on that score is that

[13] Belhomme, Vol. 4, pp. 220–1, 314, 436 and 531–3.

TABLE 2: MANPOWER LOSSES, 1804–1814

Outcome	Frenchmen		Foreigners	
	Extrapolated nos (000s)	%	Extrapolated nos (000s)	%
Died in combat	87.5	4.6	22	4.0
Died in hospital	303	16	69	12.5
Taken prisoner	384	20.4	153	27.9
Struck for long absence	242	12.8	68	12.4
Deserted (pre-April1814)	180	9.6	100	18.1
Discharged (pre-April 1814)	243	12.9	46.5	8.5
Present with unit 1814	421	22.3	91	16.5
Promoted officer	26.5	1.4	0.5	0.1
Sub-total	**1,888**	**100.0**	**550**	**100.0**
Fate unknown	127.5	6.3	94.5	14.7
Total	**2,015.5**		**644.5**	

presented by an innovative 1972 statistical study of Napoleonic service records.[14] The study, based on an examination of a one-in-five-hundred sample from regimental rosters from 1804 to 1814, focuses on the outcome of the military career of each soldier as noted in the regimental matriculation rolls. Unfortunately from the point of view of this work, the study does not distinguish between foreigners in regular army units and those in the *troupes étrangères*. Despite that problem and the general need for caution in interpreting statistics from a small sample, the results of the study are nevertheless still instructive. They support the conclusions that death in combat was the least significant peril for Napoleonic fighting men and that there were noticeable differences between the typical fate of a foreign soldier and that of a native Frenchman (see Table 2). These figures also provide some supporting evidence for the derogatory conclusions that *troupes étrangères* were more prone than native French troops to surrender and to desertion.

The *troupes étrangères* added a tremendous human diversity to the ranks of Napoleon's armies in the form of unusual characters with exotic backgrounds, such as Colonel Papas-Oglou of the *Chasseurs d'Orient*, who started as a Mameluke admiral and ended up a French officer, and Captain Samuel Ulan, the Lithuanian of Tatar descent who chose to exile with Napoleon over life as a subject of the Russian Czar. The individual mercenaries we can know best today are those who left memoirs. As a result, we can consider the military history of the period from the point of view of the class-conscious Miles Byrne of the Irish Legion, the libidinous Captain Friedrich of the

[14] Jacques Houdaille, 'Pertes de l'Armée de Terre Sous le Premier Empire d'Après les Registres Matricules', *Population* (1972), pp. 27–50.

Isembourg Regiment, the peripatetic Rifleman Maempfel, who served in the Prussian, French and British Armies, or the stalwart Heinrich von Brandt, a German serving in the Vistula Legion who helps to illustrate the fungible nature of nationality in a world only on the cusp of discovering true nationalism. We can learn about other individuals from snippets in the histories of their units. For instance, Alfred Guye's monograph on the Neufchatel Battalion enables us to identify Marc Warnery (sometimes spelled 'Varnéry') as the individual who probably holds the record for serving in the most foreign units. Warnery, a native of Switzerland who was born in 1776 and who is noted in one inspection report as a zealous officer who spoke three languages, first enlisted in the Helvetian Demi-brigades, then transferred in 1806 to the *Pionniers Blancs*. After a stint in the Legion of the North, he joined the Neufchatel Battalion, where he served in the Voltigeur and Carabinier companies prior to his disappearance in Russia.[15]

One cannot help regretting, however, that we cannot learn more about such tantalising characters such as Jan and Vincent Konopka, the brothers who led the Vistula Legion Lancers to their extraordinary triumph at Albuera in 1811, or Kosmas Stephanis from Smyrna, the 161st individual inscribed on the rolls of the Mamelukes of the Guard, who served in the Greek Legion, joined the Mamelukes as an NCO, earned the Legion of Honour in 1806, was stripped of his rank in 1809 and finally was killed at Bautzen in 1813. Language barriers and lack of written records pose a particular hurdle to learning more about the men who served in Balkan units such as the Provisional Croatian Regiment or the Albanian Regiment.

The mercenary element in Napoleon's armies was not confined to the lower ranks. In fact, foreign-born generals constituted nearly 6 per cent of the total number of senior officers employed in the French armies from 1792 to 1814. According to Alain Pigeard's monumental study of French Army leadership, no fewer than 190 foreigners (broken down as follows in terms of their national origins) reached the rank of General during that period:[16]

33	Germans	26	Swiss	26	Poles
24	Dutch	22	Belgians	21	Italians
14	Irish	7	Canadians	5	Portuguese
4	Austrians	3	Russians	3	Americans
2	English	2	Serbians	1	Spanish
1	Dane	1	Venezuelan		

These generals were an extremely diverse lot. A few, such as the Irishman Arthur O'Connor (1767–1852), achieved their rank solely through political or ideological influence and never commanded troops in combat. The Venezuelan Francisco de Miranda (1756–1816) did see some fighting, but he is certainly more famous for his

[15] The information about Warnery comes from Guye, p. 56.
[16] Alain Pigeard, *Les Étoiles de Napoléon*, pp. 764. Napoleonic colonels of foreign origin made up nearly 12 per cent of the total. Quentin, p. 12.

part in the South American independence movement than he is for any involvement in the Napoleonic Wars. General Antoine Henri Jomini (1779–1869), a Swiss, was a brilliant student of war but he ignobly deserted the French cause in 1813. Most of these officers, however, were competent professional soldiers who fairly earned the right to have their names inscribed on the Arc de Triomphe. Numbered among the latter were such famous Napoleonic military leaders as Jan Henryk Dabrowski (1755–1818) (better known in France as Dombrowski), a Pole who fought with the French from 1796 to 1814; Jean Louis Ebénézer Reynier (1771–1814), a mercurial Swiss who held important commands in Egypt, Italy and Spain; Herman Wilhelm Daendels (1763–1818), a Dutch lawyer who served as Governor-General of the Dutch East Indies and still managed to be present at the crossing of the Beresina; and Prince Charles Frederick Louis Maurice of Isenburg (1766–1820), who raised his own regiment for service in the French Army. One of these foreign generals, Prince Joseph Antoine Poniatowski (1763–1813), even achieved the highest military title possible when he was named as a Marshal of France during the Battle of Leipzig in 1813, although he enjoyed that honour for less than forty-eight hours before his death on 19 October.

Despite this demonstrated tolerance for foreigners in command positions in his armies, Napoleon nevertheless had an unwavering prejudice against the use of foreign officers in sensitive staff positions and even against their transfer to other foreign regiments. In 1806 he refused to allow officers from the Tour d'Auvergne and Isembourg Regiments to serve as adjutants or aides-de-camp.[17] The next year he rejected a proposal to put a Battalion Chief from the Isembourg Regiment in command of the Albanian Regiment: 'Do not propose any promotions for officers of the Isembourg and La Tour d'Auvergne Regiments. Nominate only men who have always served with us.'[18] He apparently had a particular concern that the officers of those two regiments were all 'adventurers' who could not be trusted to be properly loyal to France or to himself—but his concern was at times more general than that.[19] For instance, he often indicated that he did not want to have foreign troops stationed in important fortresses.[20] Napoleon even severely criticised Marshal Soult for having sent the trophies of the Battle of Albuera to Paris in the custody of a 'foreigner'.[21]

From an economic point of view, the *troupes étrangères* were an expensive luxury. Recruitment of mercenaries involves not only the payment of an initial premium to seal the transaction, but also the payment of an additional premium over time in the form of enhanced pay and privileges and special uniforms. They even involved additional

---

[17] Decision of 15 August 1806, Nap. *O&A*, No 3538, Vol. III, p. 138. When Marshal Perignon made a request in 1811 to have Lieutenant Esclignac of the '*1er Régiment Prussien*' assigned to him as ADC, Napoleon reiterated his view that officers of foreign corps were unsuitable material for such sensitive post. (Nap. *O&A*, No 4521, Vol. 3, p. 387.)

[18] Decision of 3 November 1807, Nap. *O&A*, No 3756, Vol. 3, p. 188.

[19] N. to Minister of War, 15 November 1810, Nap. *O&A*, No 4362, Vol. 3, pp. 344–5 at 345.

[20] Decision of 26 April 1811, Nap. *O&A*, No 4557, Vol. 3.

[21] N. to Berthier, 23 August 1811, Nap. *Corr.*, No 18078, Vol. 22, p. 436.

cost because they required payment of wages on a reasonably regular basis—a radical notion in Napoleonic times. Unlike the ordinary conscripts in the rank-and-file of the Grand Army, foreign troops actually had some leverage to enforce their demands. As Napoleon's Swiss troops were heard to proclaim on at least one occasion during the period while striking for pay: 'No money, no Swiss.' The high cost of foreign troops was never far from Napoleon's mind, judging from the following typical passage in an 1810 letter about the Prussian Regiment:[22]

> These foreign regiments don't render me any useful service and yet they cost a lot; this situation cannot be allowed to continue given the cuts I want to make in military spending.

Napoleon seems to have had three reasons why he thought the extra expense of the foreign units justifiable on the whole, although not all the reasons were applicable to all the formations. First, as had been the case during the Revolution, foreign units could be used for political as well as military purposes. Several of the units (such as the Irish Legion or the Albanian Regiment) were composed of individuals from territories controlled by powers at war with France. By their existence alone, they served as an inspiration for internal dissension in the enemy regime and created a subversive threat to the enemy by providing persuasive evidence that co-operation with the French was preferable to resistance to them. Units of this type often showed excellent spirit and enthusiasm in battle because they expected that their efforts would be rewarded by Napoleon with some improvement of their national political fortunes.

The second advantage of foreign units was that they could be used as a repository for unemployed soldiers from defeated enemy armies who might otherwise pose a threat to domestic peace and tranquillity. A good example in this regard is the Prussian Regiment raised from Prussian prisoners of war and disbanded soldiery after the Battles of Jena and Auerstadt. In this case, the extra expense was justified as a means of avoiding both the costs of maintaining the prisoners and the costs of the civil unrest which might ensue if the men were left to their own devices.

The last advantage of employing foreign troops was the most cynical and practical: they could be used instead of loyal and reliable units of native Frenchmen in less desirable and (for the most part) more unhealthy posts and duties around the French Empire. This was not a new approach invented in Napoleonic times, since one of the main historical reasons for the existence of mercenaries has always been the desire of the hiring power to spare its own native sons from danger, but Napoleon was particularly skilled in putting it into practice and was not reluctant to give public expression to his intentions in this regard. Writing in 1811 to his Minister of War about the need to assign foreign units to garrisons in Holland, the Emperor concluded:[23]

---

[22] N. to Minister of War, 22 September 1810, Nap. *Corr.*, No 16941, Vol. 21, p. 140.

[23] N. to Minister of War, 19 October 1811, Nap. *P&T*, No 6271, Vol. 4, pp. 740–1. It should be noted that the modern Foreign Legion is valuable to governments of France for precisely this reason, since it enables them to deploy troops in international crises without concern for public relations because it will not be Frenchmen who come home in coffins.

> It has become important to organise promptly the Irish and Prussian foreign regiments. . . . I attach a great importance to having these two regiments, comprising at least six battalions, guarding the islands of Zealand and Holland, because these locations are so unhealthy that French troops I send there are destroyed; and I want to spare my line regiments that burden. . . . You must take this assignment very seriously because successful completion will spare the lives of many Frenchmen.

If Prince Metternich, the Austrian diplomat, can be believed, Napoleon may actually have thought that his practice of sacrificing his foreign troops in place of French units was a source of his popularity with the French people. Writing of an interview he had with Napoleon at Dresden in the summer of 1813, Prince Metternich recorded that Napoleon made the following provocative statements:[24]

> 'You are no soldier,' said he [Napoleon], 'and you do not know what goes on in the mind of a soldier. I was brought up in the field, and a man such as I am does not concern himself much about the lives of a million men.' [Footnote of Metternich: 'I do not dare to make use here of the much worse expressions employed by Napoleon.'].... Napoleon recovered himself, and with calmer tones said to me the following words, no less remarkable than the former: 'The French cannot complain of me; to spare them I have sacrificed the Germans and the Poles. I have lost in the campaign of Moscow three hundred thousand men, and there were not more than thirty thousand Frenchman among them.'

The numbers quoted are too low by a significant margin both in absolute and percentage terms, but there is still an important degree of truth to the words. Indeed, one of the main reasons for the miraculous rebirth of the Grand Army in 1813 was the fact that so many French battalions had been spared the Russian campaign. One might expect Metternich to be a biased witness, but his testimony cannot be entirely disregarded because the attitude recorded is consistent with Napoleon's actual employment of his foreign troops. One anonymous mercenary expressed his awareness of this attitude in the following terms: 'Unhappy the Emperor's foreign troops, who are invariably employed upon every disagreeable and unprofitable duty.'[25]

Napoleon's specific actions with respect to his foreign troops varied considerably over the term of his reign. The period from his accession to power to the Peace of Amiens was basically a time of consolidation during which very few new foreign units were created (although a number saw France for the first time when the Army of Egypt was repatriated) and some were dissolved. With the renewal of hostilities in 1803, Napoleon embarked on a systematic attempt to build up the number of foreign troops, with particular emphasis on those units identified with specific nationalities. This effort resulted in such developments as the reorganisation of the Polish Legions, the formation of the Irish Legion and the hiring of four regiments of Swiss. Next, the succession of wars from 1805 to 1809 highlighted the need for as much organised

[24] C. Metternich, *Memoirs of Prince Metternich* (5 vols; reprint New York, 1970), Vol. 1 (1773–1815), p. 190.
[25] This remark was recorded by a British officer who had been captured at the Battle of Talavera. Charles Boothby, *A Prisoner of France* (London, 1898), p. 234.

manpower as possible while providing a steady supply of new foreign recruits in the form of defeated enemy armies. During this period, the units formed, such as the Prussian and Westphalian Regiments, were intended primarily as vehicles for recycling enemy soldiers who might otherwise have become a nucleus for resistance to the French.

After 1809, however, Napoleon found it was less expensive to turn foreigners into Frenchmen by the annexation of new territories than it was to maintain them in their own independent units, so from that year onward the number of units dwindled even though the number of soldiers they provided continued to climb until 1812. The Valais Battalion lost its independent existence after its homeland was annexed to France, while the Hanoverian Legion was disbanded when the expansion of the Empire to the Elbe coupled with the growth of the Westphalian Army left it terminally short of new recruits. During this period Napoleon also began to strip away the special national distinctions of the regiments he retained—hence his renaming of the Tour d'Auvergne, Isembourg, Irish and Prussian formations as the 1st to 4th Foreign Regiments. The Emperor also became liable to deploy different battalions of the same foreign unit in different locations. For example, by 1810 the sixteen battalions of Swiss troops were spread all over Europe:[26]

> The [Swiss] battalion with the Army of Catalonia will be completed by a detachment of 400 men from the two battalions that are at Marseilles and Toulon. After that has been achieved, of the four Swiss Regiments, there will be four battalions at Naples, three in Spain (two at Valladolid and one in Catalonia), two at Marseilles and Toulon, two on the island of Walcheren and two in the 13th Military Division.

This period also saw an increase in the indiscriminate recruiting of prisoners of war to fill out foreign units—another development that undermined their uniqueness and, more importantly, their military effectiveness. Under then-prevailing ethical standards, there was no opprobrium attached either to the French recruiting efforts or to the acceptance of such offers by the foreign prisoners, but the recruits produced by this methodology were hardly model soldiers. Even the ethnic purity of the Polish and Swiss regiments was affected by this trend, so much so that Napoleon felt the need to remind the Minister of War that this was not a desirable result:[27]

> . . . repeat the order to the Majors of the Regiments of the Vistula that they should admit only Poles and reject all Russians and Germans; these Regiments should be composed exclusively of men who can speak Polish.

Because the rest of Europe was at peace, the largest component of the prisoner population was formed by Spaniards, with nearly 50,000 captives of that nationality incarcerated in France in December 1811 alone.[28] Faced with the prospect of war with

[26] N. to Minister of War, 5 August 1810, Nap. *Corr.*, No 16763, Vol. 21, pp. 20–2 at 20.
[27] Letter of N., 11 March 1812, Nap. *Corr.*, No 18571, Vol. 23, pp. 305–6 at 305.
[28] Aymes, pp. 170–1.

Russia, Napoleon canvassed a number of different suggestions in early 1812 as to how he could best mobilise that manpower to serve his interests. Some of the units that resulted from that initiative (such as the *Sapeurs Espagnols*) are chronicled in this work, but other ideas never came to fruition. For instance, Napoleon briefly considered the creation of a Spanish cavalry regiment, but ultimately rejected that idea on the basis of cost.[29] He also considered the direct incorporation of Spaniards into his regular army units in modest proportions such as ten or twelve for each company of the artillery train.[30] Although he never carried through on a proposal to recruit 10 per cent of every infantry company from Spaniards, he did try to organise one full infantry battalion of Spaniards for each of his three regiments of refractory conscripts and to give those units distinctive uniforms emphasise their special character:[31]

> The Spaniards to be incorporated into the Battalion of the Belle-Île Regiment will wear the light infantry uniform worn by the men of that unit. Those who will be incorporated into the Walcheren and Île-de-Ré Regiments will wear line infantry uniforms. In each case, however, they will have blue cuffs and blue lapels with yellow piping so that they can be easily distinguished from all French soldiers.

These plans were ultimately not fully realised, owing to the difficulty of distinguishing true volunteers in the prisoner population from men enlisting simply to escape captivity. As Napoleon explained to his military bureaucrats:[32]

> My intention is that we should not enrol any Spanish prisoner other than one who is volunteering of his own free will and we should not fool ourselves into thinking that men enlisted on any other basis will become submissive soldiers when they reach the front. Your letter has accordingly caused me to decide that the only units recruited from Spanish prisoners that should be kept are the battalion of sappers, the company of workers and the cadre of the Walcheren battalion.

The huge losses in the Russian campaign eliminated many of the foreign units as viable combat forces and the process of recruiting those that did survive back to full strength was usually an exceedingly lengthy process. Meanwhile, the crisis in Napoleon's use of foreign troops occurred in the autumn of 1813. As the armies of the Seventh Coalition mobilised against Napoleon after the summer armistice, many of his previously staunchest allied and foreign units turned against him. The Croatian troops fell apart when the Illyrian provinces were invaded, Bavaria and Naples defected in exchange for favourable treatment from the Coalition and, worst of all, the Saxons abandoned the French on the battlefield at Leipzig. Even though the problems related mostly to erstwhile allied contingents, these defections convinced Napoleon that foreign troops of any sort were not generally to be trusted:[33]

---

[29] Note for Count Daru, Nap. *Corr.*, No 18529, Vol. 23, pp. 257–9 at 257.
[30] *Ibid.*, p. 258.
[31] N. to Minister of War, 11 March 1812, Nap. *Corr.*, No 18570, Vol. 23, pp. 304–5 at 305.
[32] N. to Minister of War, Nap. *Corr.*, No 18670, Vol. 23, p. 388.
[33] Note for Count Daru, 15 November 1813, Nap. *Corr.*, No 20893, Vol. 26, pp. 427–8.

> We have reached a point where we cannot count on any foreigners. To do anything else would be extremely dangerous for us. . . . These units must be turned into pioneers and must be kept away from posts on the frontier and in our fortresses.

He assigned Count Daru the task of creating a 'serious' proposal for disarming all the offending units in order to make their weapons and equipment available for use by more loyal forces. The proposal was presented and ratified on 25 November 1813.

The 25 November decree cut a large swathe through the foreign and allied troops still serving with the French Army in the aftermath of Napoleon's defeat at Leipzig. Napoleon evidently felt that his Polish and Swiss troops would remain loyal no matter what circumstances might arise, but almost all the other units of *troupes étrangères* were affected. The decree disbanded the following units:[34]

1. *Régiment de Prusse* (4th Foreign)
2. *Régiment d'Illyrie*
3. *Chasseurs Illyriens* (and the related Provisional Croatian Regiments)
4. *Hussards Croates*
5. *Régiment Joseph-Napoléon*
6. *Légion Portuguais*

In each of these cases, the decree provided that the surviving soldiers would be herded into one or more battalions of 'pioneers' or 'workers' who wielded picks and shovels rather than muskets but who were still subject to military discipline. His stated objective was to free up the weapons and equipment of the foreign units for use by more loyal French forces: '[t]he weapons gathered in the course of these disbandments will be used to provide arms for the French Army.'[35]

The 25 November decree dealt with other units as well. First, it included a general purge of soldiers of German or Illyrian origin from the 1st, 2nd and 3rd Foreign Regiments (formerly the *Régiment de La Tour d'Auvergne*, the *Régiment Isembourg* and the *Régiment* or *Légion Irlandais*, respectively; Articles 2, 3 and 7). It also disbanded all the Spanish units raised by Joseph Napoleon during the years of his ill-fated reign, many of which had been attached to the French Army during the evacuation of Spain at the end of 1813 (Articles 11–14). Finally, it specified that all the Rhine Confederation troops still with the French armies under Soult near the border with Spain should not only be disarmed but also put under guard as prisoners of war (Article 16). This last provision backfired, however, when the Frankfurt and Nassau battalions in Soult's army learned of their intended fate before they could be disarmed and thereupon defected *en masse* to the British.[36]

---

[34] This author has not found the complete text of the 25 November decree in any printed collection of Napoleon's correspondence, but its contents can be reconstructed from sections quoted in secondary sources such as Fieffé and the volumes by Boppe.

[35] 25 November Decree, Article 17.

[36] Sauzey, Vol. VI, pp. 247–53.

The 25 November decree was a drastic solution to the perceived problem of foreign troop disloyalty and it took a heavy toll on the spirits of the many foreign soldiers who intended to remain true to their obligations. These men were professional soldiers for whom disarmament was a significant disgrace, and that injury was exacerbated by the insult of being incorporated into pioneer units whose very name emphasised their shame. One senior officer in charge of the formation of such a battalion reported:[37]

> . . . the label of 'pioneers' . . . has produced despair among the officers, NCOs and men; ancient grenadiers and soldiers covered with wounds received in the last campaigns complain bitterly about the unfairness of being given this name as recompense for their services and they say proudly that they will not pick up tools instead of weapons.

A number of foreign officers and men, acting with or without official sanction, attached themselves to French units to continue to serve the Emperor, but many more simply absented themselves from the Army without leave, taking the decree as a very obvious sign that their services were no longer required.

A study such as this must inquire as a final matter about the overall military performance of Napoleon's foreign troops, but there is no easy answer to that question. On the debit side of the ledger, many units failed to provide any valuable service in return for Napoleon's investment. The worst of the lot was probably the *Régiment de Prusse*, which was humiliated in action both on Walcheren Island in 1809 and at the Almaraz bridgehead in 1812, but even the vaunted Swiss had a low point when a battalion of the 3rd Swiss Regiment surrendered to a mixed Portuguese and Spanish force in 1810, losing its imperial Eagle in the affair. The Illyrian Chasseurs melted away through desertion when they were finally needed to defend their homeland. The many *Bataillons Étrangers* and units of foreign pioneers consumed plentiful pay and rations, but contributed little other than physical presence in return.

Other foreign troops were among the finest fighting units in the French Army and had splendid service records. One thinks immediately of the remarkable courage displayed by the Swiss Regiments at Pultusk and at the Beresina in 1812 and the brilliant exploits of Colonel Jan Konopka and his lancers of the Vistula Legion at the Battle of Albuera in 1811. The exotic appearance of the Mamelukes struck fear into such disparate enemies as the Russian Horse Guards at Austerlitz and the Spanish mob at Madrid during the 2 May 1808 uprising, while the more pedestrian-looking Irish Legion assured its own place in Napoleonic history by its stout-hearted behaviour at the last stand of General Puthod's division near Löwenberg in October 1813. The Provisional Croatian Regiments had their finest hour at Pultusk in 1812, while elements of the Portuguese Legion helped Oudinot win his marshal's baton at Wagram in 1809.

Napoleon himself never voiced an explicit opinion on this subject, yet it seems obvious that the foreign troops he valued and trusted the most were the Poles. They

[37] Report of General Tilly, 14 January 1814, quoted in P. Boppe, *Les Espagnols*, p. 165, n. 1. See, generally, A. Pigeard, 'Les Pionniers'.

served him faithfully in all his campaigns and, as epitomised by the glorious (but unnecessary) charge of the *Chevau-Légers Polonais* at Somosierra in 1808, never questioned his orders. His failure to resurrect their lost nation as an independent state was a great betrayal of that faith on his part, but he tried to make it up to them in the end. In his articles of abdication, Napoleon recognised that his was not the only fate being decided at the time, and he stipulated that the Poles should not suffer because of their loyalty to him:[38]

> *Article 19*: In recognition of their honourable service, all the Polish troops who are presently serving in the armies of France shall be free to return to their homes, conserving their arms and baggage. Polish officers, NCOs and men will all have the right to retain the decorations that have been accorded them as well as all related pensions.

Napoleon made some use of foreign troops during his short-lived reign in 1815. Although the detailed organisation of the foreign troops in the French Army during that period is outside the self-defined scope of this study, the information in Appendix C demonstrates that, even after his experience in 1813, Napoleon still believed in the value of forming distinctive foreign units with some claim to homogeneity of national origin.

[38] Grabowski, p. 262.

4ME RT SE

Unit Descriptions

Artillerie Septinsulaire

(Septinsular Artillery)

Date of Creation 1 January 1808. (Bucquoy, *Troupes Étrangères*, p. 140.)
Circumstances of Creation The name of this unit refers to the seven major islands (Corfu, Paxos, Ithaca, Santa Maura [Leucadia], Cephalonia, Zante and Cerigo) of the Ionian archipelago, which had been formed into a state called the Septinsular Republic prior to 1807. No information has been found that gives details of the formation of this particular unit, but the name suggests that it may have been in existence during that prior regime.
Composition Two companies of foot artillery.
Commanders *1810*: Captain Nicolas Vlatas, who was taken prisoner by the British at the capitulation of Santa Maura in 1810. (Savant, *Les Grecs*, p. 387.)
Operational History No specific information found, but the information about the unit's commander suggests that at least a detachment of the unit was present during the British attack on Santa Maura.
Final Transformation Disbanded in 1814.
Uniforms This unit is said to have worn the same uniforms as French foot artillery of the line. (Bucquoy, *Troupes Étrangères*, p. 140.)
Standard No information found, but it is interesting to note that the Septinsular Republic, which gave its name to the unit, had a blue flag decorated with a yellow Venetian lion. (This flag is illustrated on the following Web page: www.crwflags.com/fotw/gr-ion.html.)

Artillerie Suisse

(Swiss Artillery; also known as the *Garde-Côtes Suisses*[(Swiss Coast Guard])

Date of Creation This artillery unit was created by an order dated 30 Germinal Year XI (20 April 1803). (Reproduced in *Journal Militaire* for Year XI, Pt 2, pp. 89–90.)
Circumstances of Creation The order that created the Swiss artillery company was concerned generally with reorganising some of the smaller military units of the

Helvetian Republic and turning them into formations that could provide more effective support to the French armies (see, for example, the separate entry for the *Chasseurs à Cheval Helvétiques* formed at the same time).

Composition This company-size unit had the following strength:

1	First Captain
1	Second Captain
1	Lieutenant
1	Second Lieutenant
1	Sergeant-Major
1	Sergeant
1	Fourrier
4	Corporals
4	Artificers
24	1st Class Cannoneers
56	2nd Class Cannoneers (including one carpenter and one metal worker)
2	Drummers
97	

Commanders *1805*: Captain Burnand. (Champeaux, *État Militaire An XIII*, p. 93.)

Operational History This Company seems to have served in a coastal defence role at Cherbourg during the whole of its existence.

Final Transformation The Company was absorbed into the 1st Swiss Regiment some time after February 1806. (Note dated 26 February 1806, Nap. *O&A*, No 3347, Vol. 3, p. 96.)

Uniforms No direct information found. A note from Napoleon to his Minister of War refers to the fact that 'The company of Swiss Coast Guards at Cherbourg lacks jackets; see that some are issued right away.' (Note of 2 Messidor Year XI [21 June 1803], Nap. *O&A*, No 1284, Vol. 2, p. 56.)

Standard No information found.

Bataillon Allemand

(German Battalion; also known as the *Bataillon de Déserteurs Autrichiens* [Battalion of Austrian Deserters] and the *1er Bataillon Étranger* (1st Formation) [1st Foreign Battalion])

Date of Creation 21 Fructidor Year VII (9 September 1799).

Circumstances of Creation A unit of this name was first organised at Bordeaux to make military use of deserters from the armies of Austria and its allies. (Belhomme, Vol. 4,

p. 205.) Two years later another unit, referred to as the *Bataillon de Déserteurs Autrichiens*, was formed for the same purpose by an Order of the Consuls dated 7 Pluviose Year IX (27 January 1801): 'There will be formed a Battalion of Austrian deserters. All the commissioned officers and half of the non-commissioned officers will be French.' (The Organisational Order is reproduced in the *Journal Militaire* for Year IX, Pt. 1, p. 358.) Belhomme states that the 1801 order 'expanded the German Battalion', but the 1801 order does not in fact mention the earlier unit. (Belhomme, Vol. 4, p. 241.) Nevertheless, the two units do seem to have been combined in some fashion around this time because, subsequent to early 1801, only one such unit can be traced. However, both original unit names (as well as some other designations) seem to have been used indiscriminately to refer to the combined force.

Composition The 1799 formation was organised into five companies, each consisting of three officers and 124 soldiers. The establishment of the 1801 unit was set at 'one thousand men, to be organised in the same manner as a French battalion.' (1801 Organisational Order.)

Commanders *1799 Unit*: Battalion Chief Boyer. (Fieffé, Vol. 2, p. 54.) *1801 Unit*: No information found.

Operational History In 1801 the Battalion was attached to the Observation Corps of the Gironde, a force formed by Napoleon to assist his Spanish Bourbon allies in a campaign he was urging them to wage against Portugal. The Spanish actually launched a half-hearted invasion of the neighbouring kingdom in the spring of 1801, but Charles IV allowed his chief minister, Manuel Godoy, to earn the title 'Prince of Peace' by quickly negotiating a mutually face-saving peace treaty at Badajoz in June. This development frustrated Napoleon's original plans for the Observation Corps, so he decided to use its constituent parts in some of his other schemes.

As a result, after some garrison duty in French towns and at Salamanca in Spain, the 813-man-strong Battalion was embarked at Cadiz on 18 January 1802 as part of a contingent of reinforcements for the ill-fated French force attempting to re-establish order on the island of Saint-Domingue. (Auguste, *Participation Étrangère*, p. 128; *Journal Militaire* for Year X [1802–03], Pt 1, p. 237, further confuses the nomenclature issues relating to this battalion by referring to the '1er Bataillon étranger . . . embarqué à Cadix'.) It was thrown into action almost immediately upon its arrival and drew surprising praise for its performance from one officer (Letter of Jean Marie de Villaret to Decrès quoted in Auguste, *Participation Étrangère*, p. 130):

> A German battalion that spearheaded the assault was repulsed three times at the foot of the ditch and sustained a most deadly fire with the calm and cool intrepidness that characterises these foreign soldiers.

An Order of Battle for the Army of Saint-Domingue in the spring of that same year records that the *Bataillon Allemand* had a strength of 617 men and was serving (along with the 30th, 31st and 38th Demi-brigades) in the division commanded by General

Edmé Étienne Desfourneaux. (Leclerc, *Lettres*, Item LXI, p. 152.)

Final Transformation The German Battalion had been so ravaged by combat casualties and by yellow fever by November 1802 that it was dissolved and its few survivors were incorporated into the 11th Light Demi-brigade. (Poyen, p. 321.)

Uniforms The Organisational Order for the 1801 unit specifies that '[T]his battalion will be dressed in green.' A modern watercolour of a soldier of this battalion by Henri Boisselier in the French Army Museum Library in Paris depicts a figure wearing a bicorne hat and an entirely green light infantry-style uniform. (Darbou.)

Standard No information found.

Bataillon de Déserteurs Allemands

(German Deserter Battalion; see also *3e Bataillon de Déserteurs Étrangers* [3rd Foreign Deserters Battalion] and *2e Bataillon Étranger* [2nd Foreign Battalion])

Date of Creation This Battalion was created by a Consular Order dated 2 Thermidor Year X (21 July 1802).

Circumstances of Creation 'There will be formed a battalion composed of German deserters.' (Article 1 of the Order, Nap. *Corr.*, No 6197, Vol. 7, p. 528.) The Order specifies that the Battalion was to be organised at Cremona. This unit was the third formation of foreign deserters created in 1802, so it was sometimes known as the *3e Bataillon de Déserteurs Étrangers*.

Composition The Battalion was to have the same organisation and pay rates as an equivalent French formation. (Article 2 of Consular Order.) All the officers had to be French, but no Frenchmen were permitted to serve as rank-and-file soldiers.

Commanders *1802:* Battalion Chief Bechaud. (Fieffé, Vol. 2, p. 54.)

Operational History In 1803 the Battalion was the subject of a detailed letter from Napoleon to Berthier (N. to Berthier, 20 Pluviose Year XI [9 February 1803], Nap. *Corr.*, No 6574, Vol. 8, p. 203):

> The First Consul desires you, Citizen Minister, to write to General Murat to invite him to take all necessary actions to complete recruitment of the battalion of foreign deserters now forming at Cremona to its full establishment of 600 men. He may, if necessary, allow Poles, Swiss and even Italians to join the battalion. This unit thus offers the means to isolate all the troublesome soldiers that might otherwise disturb the tranquillity of Italy.

The letter ends by stating that the Battalion must be in Genoa by 20 Ventose (11 March) ready to embark for foreign service.

Final Transformation Belhomme, who refers to this unit exclusively as the *3e Bataillon de Déserteurs Étrangers*, says that the Battalion was sent to Saint-Domingue from Genoa on 9 February and Fieffé reaches the same conclusion. (Belhomme, Vol. 4, pp. 258 and 265; Fieffé, Vol. 2, p. 54.) Belhomme also reports that the unit was incorporated into the *Légion du Cap* in Saint-Domingue by an order dated 2 May 1803. (Belhomme, Vol. 4, p. 270.) Based on the letter from Napoleon quoted above, however, Belhomme's embarkation date cannot be correct, but that does not necessarily invalidate the rest of his information. The French Army archives, on the other hand, indicate that 'the Battalion of German Deserters created by an order dated 2 Thermidor Year X and concentrated at Cremona' was transformed into the *2e Bataillon Étranger* (2nd Foreign Battalion; see separate entry) that remained in existence until 1813. (Index to SHA Carton X[h]2 in Ministry of War, *Inventaire*, p. 239.) Given the loose use of terminology for all these 'miscellaneous' foreign units, it is possible that all these sources are correct, since part of the Battalion could have ended up in the Caribbean while another part could have served as the nucleus for the 2nd Foreign Battalion.

Uniforms The Organisational Order specifies that the Foreign Deserters were to have iron grey uniforms and captured Austrian weapons. A letter was sent eight days after the order asking for permission to add *lie-de-vin* (dark purplish-red) to the uniform as a facing colour, but no reply to that letter has been found. (SHA Carton X[h]2.)

Standard No information found.

Bataillon de Déserteurs Autrichiens

(Austrian Deserter Battalion)

See *Bataillon Allemand* (German Battalion).

Bataillon de Patriotes Piémontais

(Piedmont Patriots Battalion)

Date of Creation 10 Thermidor Year VII (30 July 1799).

Circumstances of Creation The Austro-Russian reconquest of northern Italy in the spring of 1799 forced many francophile residents of the former Kingdom of Piedmont to flee to France. A particularly heavy concentration of these refugees ended up in Savoy, where they were formed into a battalion to guard the pass of Mont Cenis. (Belhomme, Vol. 4, p. 203.)

Composition This Battalion consisted of nine companies, but no information has been found concerning their composition.

Commanders No information found.

Operational History No information found.

Final Transformation The Battalion was incorporated into the *Légion Italienne* on 10 Prairial Year VIII (30 May 1800) (see separate entry). (Belhomme, Vol. 4, p. 227.)

Uniforms No information found.
Standard No information found.

Bataillon de Piombino

(Piombino Battalion; also known as the *Bataillon Félix*)

Date of Creation The Principality of Piombino and the Piombino Battalion were both formed pursuant to a decree dated 27 Pluviose Year XIII (16 February 1805).
Circumstances of Creation When Napoleon named his brother-in-law, Felix Bacciocchi, to be the ruler of the tiny principalities of Lucques and Piombino, he also required him to form a coastal defence battalion for the purpose of garrisoning the fortress of Piombino. (Marmottan, 'Piombino', p. 513.)
Composition Article VIII of the Organisational Decree for the Principality specifies that the Battalion was to have five companies of 80 men each. (Marmottan, 'Piombino', p. 513.) The Battalion also had a band.
Commanders *Creation to final transformation:* Jean Jacques François Siméon (1765–?), a Swiss who had served in the French Bourbon armies. He had met Elisa Bonaparte when he was stationed in Corsica in 1797. (His portrait can be found in Marmottan, 'Piombino', p. 512.)
Operational History The Piombino Battalion was taken on to the French military payroll almost as soon as Elisa took up the throne of Piombino. No information has been found about its activities apart from the description of one naval skirmish featuring the Battalion that appears in Marmottan, 'Piombino', p. 520.
Final Transformation The unit was disbanded after the fall of Napoleon.
Uniforms The uniform consisted of a blue vest with sleeves (possibly with sky blue piping), white trousers, grey overcoat and a shako. (Marmottan, 'Piombino', p. 519.)
Standard The Battalion carried a standard ornamented with an Eagle. (Marmottan, 'Piombino', p. 517.)

Bataillon du Prince de Neufchatel

(Prince of Neufchatel's Battalion)

Date of Creation 11 May 1807.
Circumstances of Creation The Principality of Neufchatel was ceded by the King of Prussia to Napoleon in a treaty dated 15 December 1805 and then was given by Napoleon to his valued chief of staff, Marshal Louis Alexandre Berthier, on 30 March 1806. (Guye, pp. 21–3.) Little more than a year later, the Emperor decided that Prince's new subjects should provide an infantry battalion for use in his armies and, not surprisingly, the Prince of Neufchatel graciously agreed.

Composition The Battalion was organised pursuant to a decree dated 11 May 1807. (Reproduced in Guye, pp. 34–5.) The unit consisted of a staff of eight individuals and six companies of infantry (including one of grenadiers and one of voltigeurs). Each company had three officers, fourteen NCOs, two drummers, a sapper and 140 privates. Recruiting was restricted to natives of the Principality of Neufchatel, the Republic of Valais and the cantons of Switzerland. Marshal Berthier was given the honour of nominating all officers of the Battalion during his lifetime.

By an Imperial decree dated 27 August 1808, Napoleon added a combined artillery and engineer company to the Battalion. (Quoted in Guye, p. 70.) The composition of the new company included 32 artillerymen manning two six-pound cannon, sixteen sappers and sixteen train soldiers.

Commanders *Formation to 9 December 1811*: Battalion Chief Jean Henri de Bosset (1762–1812). (See portrait in Guye, p. 25.) His only prior military experience was in the Neufchatel artillery company, but he made himself very useful to Berthier at the outset of the new Prince's reign. He left the Battalion when he was promoted to the rank of Adjutant Commandant (equivalent to a Colonel). He died from an illness contracted while he was serving in an administrative post in the captured city of Smolensk in 1812. *11 December 1811–21 February 1814*: Battalion Chief Charles Frédéric d'Andrié, Vicomte de Gorgier (?–1814). Gorgier, 'a magnificent specimen reputed to be one of the handsomest men in the French Army', commanded the Carabinier company of the battalion from its inception. (Memoir of Robert, quoted in Guye, p. 191.) He was promoted to be chief of staff of General Michel Marie Pacthod's Division and was killed just over a month later when that unit was defeated at Fère-Champenoise on 25 March. He was not replaced in the Battalion.

Operational History The Battalion was slowly organised at Besançon during the course of 1807. By the end of the year Napoleon was so frustrated with the lack of progress that he threatened to have the Battalion combined with the Valais Battalion in order to make one decent-sized unit. He was prevailed upon to be patient, but the Emperor decided that the unit could be of more use in the interim stationed on the coast of France. Accordingly, the Battalion was transferred to Havre in Normandy in April 1808, and it remained there until early 1809. The Battalion saw no action during this period, but it suffered losses nevertheless—three men discharged for medical reasons, three sent back to Swiss Regiments as deserters, 26 dead in hospital from disease and 41 lost to desertion. The total strength of the unit on 28 December 1808 was 25 officers and 762 men. (Guye, p. 82.)

The Battalion was called to the Grand Army in 1809 to provide protection for Imperial headquarters, but it did not reach Austria until after the Battle of Aspern/Essling. It was assigned to the bridgehead of the French Army during most of the Battle of Wagram, but it apparently sortied forth near the end of the fighting on 6 July and saw some action in the same sector where General Antoine Charles Louis Lasalle was killed. (Guye, p. 96.)

In early 1810 the Battalion was transferred to Spain, where it spent the next two years as part of the Army of the North combating guerrilla chiefs such as El Merino, Mina and Julian Sanchez. (Guye, pp. 108–9.) The tasks of the unit fell into three main categories: (a) guarding convoys, (b) foraging and (c) taking part in punitive expeditions. (Guye, p. 112.) The unit was at first based at Burgos under the command of General Jean Marie Pierre François Lepaige Dorsenne of the Imperial Guard. Later, it was stationed at Salamanca under General Paul Thiébault.

Although the Battalion was regularly and routinely involved in action with the enemy during this period, only a few of its combats are worthy of special note. In the summer of 1810 the Battalion participated in the siege of Ciudad Rodrigo, but it never entered Portugal. It was then assigned to General Michel Marie Claparède's division of the 9th Corps formed to protect the rear of the Army of Portugal. In March 1811 Captain de Gorgier of the Battalion had two important successes against Don Julian Sanchez, but on the 21st of that same month the Battalion was ambushed at Bivisqua by 500 men hidden in a village. (Schaller, p. 131.) In addition to taking casualties, the unit lost 23 men captured.

It appears that the Battalion faced the British Army on two occasions. In April 1811 it may have skirmished with British troops as Claparède's division advanced to cover the return of Marshal Masséna's defeated army. Five months later, the Battalion was in a combat division commanded by General Thiébault that took part in a French raid into Portugal. On 27 September 1811 the unit, including its artillery company, went into action against the Fusilier brigade of the British Army at Aldea da Ponte. The village changed hands several times, but the French ultimately prevailed in this relatively minor skirmish (Letter of de Bosset quoted in Guye, p. 136):

> On 27 September the Battalion conducted itself well in action against the English at Aldea Puente [*sic*]. Perrot had his cheek pierced by a ball. The brave lad had himself bandaged and then returned to the ranks. Preudhomme had his leg broken by a cannon ball that just missed throwing me to the ground. . . . Our poor surgeon, Mon. Maréchal, had his calf taken off by a ball as his was ministering to wounded men in the ranks, and after he was bandaged,he went on to aid 60 more men from various units. . . . It was only discipline and coolness under fire that enabled the Battalion to get out of a difficult situation and prevented us from suffering more, for our losses amounted to six killed and eighteen wounded, including the three officers mentioned above.

The losses from casualties, sickness and desertion were constant and they were compounded at times by the expiration of enlistments, since the volunteer soldiers of the Battalion were permitted to go home when their four-year commitment ended. (Guye, p. 140.) Nevertheless, the unit managed to keep up a reasonable strength via drafts from Neufchatel as well as occasional enlistment of miscellaneous Swiss found in the Peninsula. When the unit was reviewed after it was recalled from Spain in 1812, the inspecting officer was surprised to find the unit in relatively good condition (Guye, p. 147):

> The men of the Battalion of the Prince of Neufchatel are generally of a good age and a good physique for making war. They all have a vigorous air about them that indicates that the fatigues of 27 months of difficult campaigning in Spain have not left them worn out.

The Battalion did not leave Spain until the end of March 1812, so it missed the start of the Russian campaign. In a typical feat of marching for the period, however, it travelled essentially directly from Salamanca to Smolensk, arriving at its destination on 7 October with a strength of 661 officers and men. (Guye, pp. 159 and 170.) (At least one officer had travelled faster than that, because Captain Jeanrenaud of the Artillery company is noted as having been wounded at Borodino on 7 September.) The men of the Battalion were thus present in the city when their former commander, Colonel de Bosset, died there on 29 October. The whole Battalion participated in his funeral cortège. (Guye, p. 166.)

The retreat from Russia began for the Battalion on 14 November 1812 with the evacuation of Smolensk. Although it had seen no combat, the strength of the Battalion was already down to 483 officers and men. (Guye, p. 170.) On 17 November the Battalion was involved in heavy fighting at Krasnoi as Napoleon desperately sought to clear a path for the troops following behind him. The unit suffered cruelly from artillery fire. Captain Jeanrenaud was wounded again, Commandant de Gorgier had his horse killed underneath him and Paymaster Lieutenant August Borel and 30 men were captured by Russian cavalry along with the unit's cash box. (Guye, p. 172.) The unit was still recognisable on the last day of the Beresina crossings but was disbanded thereafter. When Commandant de Gorgier assembled what was left of the Battalion at Insterburg on 19 December he found he had thirteen officers and exactly seven men. The fate of the others who left Smolensk one month earlier breaks down as shown in Table 3 (Guye, pp. 174–5).

Marshal Berthier had to resort to conscription to fill the ranks of the Battalion for 1813, but, even with that measure, it was not ready for action until after the summer armistice. (Guye, p. 182.) On 13 July 1813 there were 115 men of the Battalion serving at headquarters and 388 men at the unit depot at Besançon. (Guye, p. 184.) The Battalion was assigned to escort Berthier's headquarters throughout the autumn campaign and thus avoided any serious combat until the last day of the Battle of Leipzig. (Article 15, Order dated 14 September 1813, Nap. *1813*, No 443, pp. 163–4.) It was

TABLE 3: LOSSES, OCTOBER–DECEMBER 1812

	Officers	Men
Killed in action	1	35
Wounded and abandoned	–	57
Killed by cold or privation	6	139
Missing	5	220

subjected to heavy artillery fire on 18 October, purportedly from Saxon artillery that had gone over to the enemy, and suffered two officers killed and four wounded. (Memoir of Robert quoted in Guye, p. 198.)

The Voltigeur company of Neufchatel Battalion fought with the rearguard during the retreat from Leipzig. On one occasion, the unit's *cantinière* was attacked and wounded by a Cossack, but she managed to kill her assailant with a pistol she always carried and returned triumphantly to the Battalion mounted on a captured enemy horse. (Guye, p. 199.) Many of the surviving men of the Battalion were stricken by sickness as they passed through Mainz, and those who remained fit were either re-assigned to the Battalion depot or scattered throughout the army. The unit therefore had no organised presence with the army for the campaign of 1814, although individual soldiers may have attached themselves to the Élite Headquarters Company that was also associated with Marshal Berthier. The depot company of the Battalion served through the siege of Besançon, although it did suffer from desertions. (Guye, pp. 215–17.)

Final Transformation The last 64 officers and men were formally disbanded on 19 June 1814. (Guye, p. 223.)

Uniforms The distinctive yellow uniform of the Neufchatel Battalion is relatively well-documented thanks to unit memoirs and surviving officer artefacts and portraits. (See, generally, A. Nicole, *Histoire du Canari Abraham Nicole* [Locle, 1876], and Rigo, *Le Plumet*, No U12 [*Bataillon de Neufchatel 1807–1809–1812*].) The uniform jacket had short tails, silver buttons (marked with the words 'Bataillon Neufchatel' in the centre and surrounded by the words 'Empire Français' above and a laurel wreath below) and red lapels, cuffs, cuff flaps, collar and turnbacks; the trousers were white and there were black, below-the-knee gaiters. (Guye, pp. 44–5, based on Nicole.) The carabiniers wore bearskins (without plates) and red epaulettes, while the voltigeurs and centre companies wore shakos and, respectively, green and white epaulettes. The silver shako plate was in the shape of a shield topped by a crown and decorated with an imperial eagle. (Blondieau, p. 26.)

The uniforms of the officers can be studied from a jacket of Commandant de Bosset which is now in the Army Museum in Paris and from existing portraits of several officers, including one of Captain Louis de Brun painted by Louis Boilly, one of the most celebrated painters of the day. (The portraits of Brun, Captain Abraham Henri Petitpierre of the Carabiniers and Lieutenant Charles Henri Bobillier are reproduced—in black-and-white only—in the text to Jurgen Olmes, *Heere der Vergangenheit* Plates Nos 88 and 89 [Frankreich, *Das Bataillon des Fürsten von Neufchatel (1807–14)*...]; that of Brun only appears in both Marmottan, p. 176, and Guye, p. 137.) Based on this evidence, it seems that officers had the same basic uniform as their men, albeit with longer tails on their jackets. The only exception is that Commandant de Bosset's jacket has white turnbacks, trimmed red (with an unusual silver ornament that appears to be two crossed batons of a French Marshal) and no cuff flaps. For full dress, officers wore at first an unusual form of felt hat with the brim folded up only in front (the so-called 'chapeau à la Henri IV') with a cockade held by one strip of white lace and a floppy black plume. (Marmottan, p. 179.) For service wear, the headdress was the shako or bearskin. The officers wore gorgets and are said to have had black waist-belts worn without a belt plate, but a white waist-belt with buckle is clearly visible in the portrait of Captain Petitpierre. (*Ibid.*)

The only real point of controversy about the dress of the Battalion concerns the exact shade of yellow that was used, since archival sources refer to the unit being issued with 'chamois', or buff, cloth. (Marmottan, p. 180.) The jacket of de Bosset in the French Army Museum is golden yellow, while that in the portrait of Brun has a brownish cast. Given the instability of the dyes then available, it is probably the case that the uniforms of the Battalion could represent a wide range of shades. It is nevertheless quite surprising to find an eyewitness in 1813 stating that the uniforms were orange-red in colour (E. D'Odeleben, *Rélation Circonstanciée de la Campagne de 1813 en Saxe* [2 vols, Paris 1817, Vol. 1, p. 197]):

> Bonaparte [*sic*] had accorded him [Berthier] the special distinction of having his own personal guard made up of soldiers from the Principality of Neufchatel. They were distinguished by the bad taste of their uniforms, for without doubt one will never again see a force of light infantry in short jackets the colour of crayfish ['écrevisses', or 'krebsbutterfarben,' in the original German text] with red cuffs.

The Battalion's uniform appeared for the first time at Imperial headquarters at Tilsit in 1807 well before the Battalion was properly organised. Carabinier Sergeant Pierre Lichty was dressed in the proposed uniform and sent to Marshal Berthier so that he could give his blessing to the choices made. (Guye, pp. 127–8.) The Marshal was apparently pleased with the result and may have enjoyed the fact that his unit would be instantly recognisable because no other unit in the Grand Army had yellow jackets. Having a noticeable uniform was, however, not always an advantage (Guye, p. 45):

> The yellow colour of the uniform of the infantry struck everyone who saw the Neufchatel soldiers and never failed to provoke some heckling and mockery from soldiers of other units. The Swiss called them 'canaries', the French called them the 'serins' [birds] and later, in Spain, the inhabitants referred to them as 'amarillos', 'pasidos' or 'canarios'.

In contrast, the uniform of the specialists in the artillery company formed in 1808 was a blue jacket (with varied facings, yellow piping and vertical pockets), blue vest, blue trousers and red epaulettes. The artillerymen had blue lapels, red cuffs and yellow collars; the sappers had yellow lapels, black cuffs and blue collars; and the men of the train had blue lapels, iron grey cuffs and yellow collars. (Guye, p. 72.)

The Battalion was apparently well administered from the point of view of its clothing because, even after the unit's long service in Spain, its uniforms were generally found to be in good condition when it was inspected at Bordeaux in early 1812. (Guye, p. 149.) The only exception was that the headwear of the unit was 'very worn, especially the bearskins of the Carabiniers'. New issues of shakos and bearskins were made shortly thereafter. (Guye, p. 151.) Some paintings in the Museum of Art and History of Neufchatel that are attributed to an artist named Beck give some additional details of how the unit looked when it passed through Leipzig shortly thereafter on its way to Russia. (See reproductions in Rigo, *Le Plumet*, U12.) In one, a Carabinier has epaulettes with white crescents and white piping along the entire perimeter of the shoulder strap, and he is wearing short black gaiters with red trim and a tassel. In another, a Voltigeur has similar yellow trim on his epaulettes, a tall green plume on top of a pompom on his shako and white overalls worn over white gaiters. Beck depicts the artillerymen of the Battalion with yellow instead of red cuffs and red cords and tufted pompons on their shakos.

The Beck paintings also depict a sapper of the Battalion. The bearded figure is wearing the uniform of a Carabinier, including a bearskin with red cords and a plume. He has the crossed-axes badge of his function in red on both sleeves, a white apron and an axe belt ornamented with a silver grenade and silver crossed axes. The red turnbacks of his jacket have yellow/chamois grenade ornaments. (This figure is reproduced in Rigo, *Le Plumet*, No 191.) Based on archival research, it seems likely that Battalion drummers were issued with new Imperial livery green uniforms about this time. (Marmottan, p. 180.)

A private in the Battalion has left an interesting account of the preparations for an Imperial review that took place at Dresden in August 1813 (Narrative of François Robert, Guye, p. 193):

> 'Berthier, are your Canaries ready for action?'
>
> 'Almost, Sire.'
>
> 'I will review them.'
>
> 'When it pleases Your Majesty.'
>
> 'Tomorrow with the Young Guard. Place them on the right of the line.'
>
> 'Yes, Sire.'
>
> The Battalion was very excited when this news was announced. Weapons were polished, belts were whitened, yellow ochre was used to cover the spots on our jackets, chalk of Spain for the stains on our trousers and vests. Finally the great day arrived. Our appearance was magnificent—the fur bonnets of the grenadiers, the green plumes of the centre companies and the yellow plumes of the voltigeurs all made for an excellent effect.

Standard Abraham Nicole, a soldier of the Battalion, noted that his unit had a special flag when it left Havre on 1 April 1809 (quoted in Marmottan, p. 180):

> This was the first time that our colour was unfurled. While waiting to receive a colour just like the one carried by units entitled to Eagles, the Commandant had arranged, on orders from Berthier, for the manufacture of a small flag of tricolour serge which had the following words on both sides: 'Bataillon du Prince de Neufchatel'.

No information has been found as to whether the Battalion subsequently received an official ensign.

Bataillon Expéditionnaire Piémontais
(Piedmontese Expeditionary Battalion)

See *Tirailleurs du Po.*

Bataillon Italique
(Italic Battalion)

Date of Creation 1 June 1799. (Belhomme, Vol. 4, p. 193.)
Circumstances of Creation This Battalion was formed from the soldiers from Cisalpine Army units who had sought refuge in France after the victories of the Russians and Austrians under Marshal Suvorov during the spring campaign of 1799. (Humbert, p. 63.)
Composition The Battalion had 900 men divided into nine companies, eight of Fusiliers and one of Grenadiers. In early 1800 the strength of the Battalion was increased by the addition of a 'brigade' of student engineer officers and two companies composed exclusively of Cisalpine Army NCOs. (Humbert, p. 63.)
Commanders *Creation to disbandment:* Battalion Chief Giovanni Torduti.
Operational History The Battalion saw service only in non-combat areas, being assigned first to watch the Col de Tende pass through the Alps and then to participate in the occupation of the Valais canton. (Humbert, p. 63.)
Final Transformation In June 1800 the Battalion was used to form the core of the 1st Line Demi-brigade of the re-formed Cisapline Republic Army. (Humbert, p. 63; Belhomme, Vol. 4, p. 231.)
Uniforms The uniform was the same as that for French line infantry except that the jacket had a green collar and green cuffs. (Humbert, p. 63.)
Standard No information found.

Bataillon Polonais
(Polish Battalion)

Date of Creation The Polish Battalion was formed pursuant to an Imperial order dated 14 September 1813 (reproduced in Nap. *1813*, No 443, pp. 163–4).
Circumstances of Creation The short-lived Polish Battalion was improvised by Napoleon as a means to entice veteran Polish soldiers to continue in his service as members of the Imperial Guard.
Composition Article 12 of the Organisational Order includes reference to some other battalions being formed at the same time for the Imperial Guard that were to have 800 men, but is silent on the size of the Polish Battalion itself. (Nap. *1813*, No 443, p. 164.) The order does specify, however, that the men for the Battalion were expected to be at least 23 years old and to have had at least two year's military service. (Nieuwazny, p. 9.)

Commanders *Formation to 20 (?) October 1813:* Major Stanislas Kurcyusz (1784–?), a veteran of the campaigns of 1807, 1809 and 1812 and holder of the Legion of Honour and the Polish decoration Virtuti Militari. (Nieuwazny, p. 12.) One of Napoleon's Polish staff officers calls him 'a good and brave officer'. (Grabowski, p. 104.)

Operational History The Polish Battalion was brigaded during its short existence with a battalion of Saxon Guards in French pay in the 2nd Old Guard Division commanded by General Philibert Jean Baptiste François Curial. The unit went into action for the first time on 16 October, fighting against the Austrians on the right flank of Napoleon's position at Leipzig alongside the Poles of Poniatowski's 8th Corps. The Battalion fought well again on the 18th, then retreated before the last bridges were blown on the 19th. Unfortunately, the morale of the unit was very fragile. During the retreat many of the men deserted and, it is said, the commander let himself be captured. Nevertheless, the remnants of the Battalion fought at Hanau on 30 and 31 October under Captain Stanislas Smett. (Nieuwazny, p. 14.)

Final Transformation When the unit was inspected at Mainz on 5 November 1813 it was obvious that the Battalion had been through some hard fighting because there were only fifteen officers and 82 men present out of all those that had started the campaign less than three weeks earlier. These survivors were amalgamated into the *3ème Éclaireurs de la Garde* (see separate entry). (Nieuwazny, p. 14.)

Uniforms The initial plan Napoleon had in mind for the Battalion was that it would wear Polish-style uniforms with bearskin caps. (Organisational Order, Article 13.) The colours of the uniform were probably supposed to be those of the Fusilier Grenadiers of the Guard—blue jacket, blue collar, white lapels , red cuffs and turnbacks and white cuff flaps and epaulettes. However, given the short time available for the organisation of the Battalion, it is possible that many of the men simply wore the jackets from their parent units. There were not enough bearskins available to carry out that part of Napoleon's plan, so instead, for the sake of uniformity, the Poles received an issue of shakos of the sort used by the Saxon Guard on campaign when they were not wearing their own bearskins. (It is unclear, however, whether the bearskins were abandoned entirely or whether they were worn in the field by the few soldiers lucky enough to have them.) The uniform was completed with blue overalls and grey overcoats. Officers wore bicorne hats and blue single-breasted jackets with gold epaulettes. (These uniform details come from the memoirs of a soldier of the Saxon Guard quoted in Nieuwazny, p. 13.)

Standard No information found, but the unit is unlikely to have had one.

Bataillon Septinsulaire

(Septinsular Battalion)

Date of Creation 13 September 1807.

Circumstances of Creation This unit was raised on the island of Corfu and seems to have been formed from the debris of a local military that had been originally raised when the Republic of Venice ruled the Ionian Islands prior to 1798. (SHA Carton X[l] 37; Belhomme, Vol. 4, p. 383.)

Composition This single-battalion unit initially had a strength of six companies of 150 men each, who were to be recruited exclusively from natives of the Ionian Islands. The size of the Battalion was increased to nine companies by a decree dated 1 January 1808, but the number of men per company was reduced to 100. (Belhomme, Vol. 4, p. 390.) The difficulty of finding native Ionians to join the unit eventually led to the enlistment of Italians, Neapolitans, Dalmatians and even Austrian prisoners. (Pigeard, *L'Armée*, p. 472, and Fieffé, Vol. 2, p. 154.) There was even a proposal made to incorporate Spanish prisoners into the unit, but this was rejected by Napoleon, who pointed out that they might consume precious rations and the betray the French at the first opportunity. (N. to Minister of War, 21 September 1810, Nap. *Corr.*, No 16939, Vol. 21, p. 289.)

Commanders *Creation to 1811*: Battalion Chief Lorenzo Pieri (Fieffé) or Pierris (Bucquoy). These are perhaps one and the same person as the Colonel Laurent Piéris (1744–18??) mentioned by still another source as having been the commander of an unspecified battalion of infantry in the forces of the Septinsular Republic in 1804. (Savant, *Les Grecs*, p. 318.) Despite his age, Colonel Piéris was given the command of the island of Cephalonia in 1809, which he surrendered to the British without firing a shot three months later. He was returned on parole to Corfu, and finally retired from service due to age and infirmity in 1811. *1811 to disbandment:* Commandant Garzonis (Savant, *Les Grecs*, p. 204).

Operational History This unit was used exclusively for the occupation and defence of the Ionian Islands. It is mentioned only once in Imperial correspondence of the period and then only in a negative context: 'The Septinsular Battalion does not serve a very useful purpose but it does involve a large expense.' (N. to Minister of War, 6 October 1810, Nap. *O&A*, No 4316, Vol. 3, p. 332.) At the end of 1811 Camille Delladecima, a captain in the Battalion and one of its original Venetian officers, was sent to Paris to make the case why the unit should not be dissolved. He was unsuccessful in his task but, at the same time, he promoted his own career by obtaining an appointment to the staff of General Bertrand in Illyria. He accompanied his general for the whole of the campaign of 1813 in Germany, although he was captured at the Battle of Leipzig just after having been made a commandant of the Legion of Honour. (Savant, *Les Grecs*, pp. 204–6.)

Final Transformation The Battalion was disbanded in 1812, the remnants being incorporated into the *Sapeurs Ioniens* (see separate entry). (Index for SHA Carton X[l]37 in France, *Inventaire*, p. 239.)

Uniforms Belhomme states that the unit had dark blue uniforms with sky blue facings (Vol. 4, p. 383)—a conclusion echoed, with additional detail, by the text accompanying Card No 7 of Bucquoy Card Series No 129 ('La Division des Îles Ioniennes'), which adds the information that the unit wore a light infantry-style uniform and had cuff flaps. Unfortunately, neither that information nor the information about two other versions of the uniforms also given by Bucquoy can be traced back to any primary source. Chartrand reports that archival research by Roger Forthoffer located only references to red and (dark?) blue cloth on the inventories for the unit. (Chartrand, *Napoleon's Army*, p. 128.)

Standard Charrié (p. 172) states unequivocally that the Battalion received neither an Eagle nor a flag.

Bataillon Valaisan

(Valais Battalion)

Date of Creation The unit was formed by an Imperial decree dated 12 Vendémiaire Year XIV (4 October 1805). (*Journal Militaire* for 1805, Pt 3, pp. 297–300.)

Circumstances of Creation The Valais Battalion which served with the French Army from 1805 to 1811 ultimately owed its brief existence to the two salient geographic characteristics of the Valais (Wallis) canton of Switzerland—the Great St Bernard and the Simplon Passes through the Alps. Once Napoleon identified the strategic importance of those avenues to Italy during the Marengo campaign, he did not want the territory to fall under hostile control, but neither could he annex it outright at that stage of his power. Napoleon solved his dilemma by the political expedient of providing enthusiastic encouragement to an indigenous Valaisan independence movement that culminated in 1802 with the Valais breaking away from the other cantons of the Helvetian Confederation and establishing itself as an independent republic enjoying the formal protection of France. (Schaller, p. 101.)

The new Republic of Valais thus owed its very existence to Napoleon, and he ultimately exacted payment for that debt in late 1805 when he called upon the Republic to provide him with a unit of Valais troops to serve in his armies. It is remarkable to find that Napoleon was devoting attention to such a relatively insignificant matter at the same time as he was completing the encirclement of an Austrian Army at Ulm, but that in fact was the case. On 4 October 1805 he issued a detailed decree setting forth the specifications for a new battalion to be recruited exclusively from citizens of the Valais Republic. These specifications were incorporated with only a few minor changes into a bilateral agreement between the Republic and France that was signed by the Grand Bailiff Augustini of Valais on 14 October and ratified by Napoleon on 1 November. (A copy of the agreement, labelled a 'Capitulation', can be found in SHA Carton X[l]14. It differs slightly in content from the version of Napoleon's original decree printed in the *Journal Militaire*.)

Composition The sixteen articles of the Valais Capitulation constitute an intricate and detailed mercenary contract. The Battalion was to be composed of a staff corps (including such specifically enumerated individuals as a surgeon-major, a master tailor, a master shoemaker, a master gaiter maker, a master gunsmith, a fencing master and a chaplain) and five infantry companies, including one of grenadiers, giving a total strength of 661 officers and men. The recruits were to be volunteers only, between 18 and 40 years old, having a minimum height of 5 feet 2 inches. They were to be enlisted for a term of four years.

With respect to pay, allowances and equipment, it was contemplated that the Valais Battalion would be on the same footing as a battalion of French line infantry, but it was also accorded several special distinctions. In common with other Swiss troops in the French Army, the Battalion was given a red uniform, but, more importantly, it was also allowed to institute its own systems of military justice and religious observances. In addition, the commander of the Battalion was given the right to correspond directly with the Minister of War on all matters affecting the unit. Finally, the Battalion was exempted from service in French colonies.

Commanders *10 July 1806–16 February 1810*: Charles Joseph Marie Louis de Bons (1756–?), an officer who had served in the Bourbon regime's Courten Regiment. As a practical matter, he ceased to command the Battalion after having been severely wounded on 16 August 1808 at Gerona in Spain. *20 February 1810–16 September 1812*: Pierre Joseph Blanc (1769–1850), a soldier who began his career in the Army of Piedmont and was made Adjutant-Major of the Valais Battalion in 1807. He took effective command of the unit from the time of the injury to Battalion Chief Bons, although he was not actually promoted to the rank of Battalion Chief until 20 February 1810. (A miniature portrait of Blanc is reproduced in colour in Martin, 'Le Bataillon Valaisan', opposite p. 321.)

Operational History If Napoleon was hoping that the agreement with Valais would result in an immediate addition for his forces, he was soon disappointed because the mustering of the Valais Battalion ultimately proved to be a lengthy and frustrating process. The first six months of the Battalion's existence was occupied almost exclusively by acrimonious discussions between the French Minister of War and the Valais authorities concerning the appointment of officers to the Battalion. Even after Commandant de Bons was appointed *Chef de Battalion* of the unit in July 1806 and recruiting began in earnest, the process still went very slowly. The basic problem seems to have been a genuine shortage of native Valaisans constituting the pool of potential recruits, since the relatively small population of Valais already provided the bulk of the men for the Swiss Régiment de Preux in Spanish service, as well as a 600-man National Guard for home service. Napoleon was finally forced in early 1807 to agree both to lower the minimum height requirement and to reduce the strength of each company from 129 to 83 men in order to hasten the recruiting process. (Schaller, p. 124.) At the same time, however, he delivered an ultimatum to the Valais authorities, threatening to disband the Battalion and abrogate his treaties with them if the unit was not completely organised by 1 May. (N. to Minister of War, 6 March 1807, Nap. *Corr.*, No 11946, Vol. 14, p. 387.)

As a result of these expedients, by 4 May 1807 the effective strength of the Battalion had risen to nearly 500 men and by August of that same year it had become sufficiently well organised to be mustered into service. Contemporary inspection reports indicate that the appearance of the Battalion's rank and file was impressive: 'The men of the battalion are very good looking and very tall; the company of Grenadiers is superb.' (Report of General Louis Antoine Pille quoted in Martin, 'Le Bataillon Valaisan', p. 325.) The inspectors also found praise for the officers of the Battalion. One of the typical entries in a report dated 9 December 1807 evaluating all the officers (SHA Carton X[l]14) is as follows: 'Étienne Eyer—an intelligent and brave officer who handles his company very well. Speaks both French and German.'

The active service of the Valais Battalion began and ended in the province of Catalonia in eastern Spain. When the Spanish people rose against the French in May 1808 there were some 12,000 French troops in that region under the command of General Duhesme, and this force soon found itself cut off and beleaguered in the Barcelona area by the aroused populace. Napoleon realised that these troops had to be reinforced, but this had to be achieved in a way which would not detract from the primary French military effort in central Spain. The solution he adopted was to organise a relief force under the command of his aide-de-camp, General Honouré Charles Michel Joseph Reille (1775–1860), that was composed only of units such as the Valais Battalion that would not be missed by the Grand Army.

As a result, when the Valais Battalion arrived at Perpignan on the Spanish frontier on 13 July 1808, it was, despite its lack of combat experience, one of the best units in Reille's division. (Report of Commandant de Bons quoted in Martin, 'Le Bataillon Valaisan', p. 325–30.) The others were a motley assortment: two battalions of the 113th Line (which had been formed that year upon the annexation of the Duchy of Tuscany); five provisional battalions made up from companies taken from the depots of no fewer than 20 separate regiments; a battalion of National Guards of the 'Pyrénées Orientales' Department; a battalion of the 5th Legion of the Reserve from Grenoble; and several companies of gendarmes. The cavalry consisted only of two squadrons of Tuscan Dragoons and one provisional squadron each of cuirassiers and chasseurs. (Oman, Vol. 1, p. 320.) The whole amounted to just under 8,400 men.

Despite this ill-assorted force, Reille achieved remarkable success at his appointed task. Making frequent use of the Valais Battalion, he succeeded in clearing the main route south from France. In the course of this advance, the Battalion saw its first combat action when a grain convoy it was escorting was ambushed by guerrillas on 15 July while it was negotiating a narrow pass that caused one classics-minded officer to think of the Battle of Thermopylae. (Clemenso, *Souvenirs*, p. 28.) The commander of the convoy made special mention of the bravery and steadiness of the Valais men as they faced harassing fire from the enemy for a total of twelve hours. (Commandant de Bons' Report.) On 24 July 1808 Reille's corps linked up with Duhesme's forces before the Spanish fortress of Gerona, the most significant site of Spanish resistance in Catalonia.

The Battalion was assigned to a brigade commanded by General Dominique Joba (1759–1809).

The city of Gerona is divided in two by the River Onaf, and consequently any besieging force is likewise compelled to divide itself to institute an effective blockade. The French initially possessed only the bare force necessary to accomplish this task, and their strength was soon reduced by hard service in the siege trenches, the unhealthy situation of their camps and a general lack of provisions to a point where the blockade was incomplete. The Valais Battalion suffered particularly severely from the heat and skimpy rations, and by 16 August it had been reduced to an effective strength of only 235 men present under arms. (Commandant de Bons' Report.) Unfortunately, on that day the Spanish garrison launched a surprise sortie from the fortress which was supported by a simultaneous advance by a Spanish force outside Gerona. The first line of French troops was broken and routed, and when the Valais Battalion attempted to stem the tide de Bons was wounded in the right thigh and the Battalion was in turn put to flight. The French eventually rallied, and the Battalion even participated in a counter-attack which re-took part of the siege works that had been lost. At nightfall, however, the French had no choice but to order a retreat. Duhesme retired to Barcelona, while Reille withdrew to Figuières. Quarter-Master Hyacinthe Clemenso thought that the entire French force would have been captured if the Spaniards had manoeuvred more intelligently. (Clemenso, *Souvenirs*, p. 29.) As it was, the Battalion lost twelve killed and 22 wounded (including three officers). (Commandant de Bons' Report.)

In the wake of the repulse at Gerona, the war in Catalonia settled into a pattern which was to become bleakly familiar to the French and their allies in the years ahead. The *somatenes* and *miqueletes* of Catalonia, as the local guerrilla forces were called, displayed throughout the Peninsular War a uniquely fierce and persistent resistance which was only occasionally moderated by a local French triumph. In the early autumn of 1808 they harried the French with particular vigour, and every foraging expedition, reconnaissance or convoy outside the cities controlled by the French meant a full-scale expedition for the Valais Battalion and the other units in Reille's command. Moreover, the French were short of clothing, transport and equipment and their ranks were thinned by dysentery and rheumatic afflictions.

Napoleon's response was finally to send some experienced troops to the province in the form of two veteran divisions from the Army of Italy under Marshal Gouvion St-Cyr, who assumed command of the entire Catalonian theatre of war. With this reinforcement the French were able to take the offensive once more, and in November 1808 the Valais Battalion found itself part of a force besieging the fortress of Rosas on the Catalonian coast. The siege was an eventful one, with the extremely active defence by the Spanish garrison being stiffened by sailors and marines landed from English ships in the harbour. The covering force under St-Cyr held off potential relief forces, however, and on 5 December 1808 the Spanish commander, O'Daly, was forced to surrender.

The Battalion was left in garrison at Rosas while the rest of the French Army waged a brilliant campaign against the Spanish regular forces in Catalonia which culminated in the relief of Barcelona and the victory of Valls on 25 February 1809. This paved the way for a spring campaign aimed at reducing Gerona once and for all, and on 5 May 1809 the French once again broke ground before that fortress. The immediate siege force was provided by Reille's old division, including the Valais Battalion, reinforced by German units from Berg, Würzburg and Westphalia and, ultimately, another division composed of Italian and Neapolitan troops. Oman's version of the order of battle of the French forces at this siege of Gerona (Vol. 3, p. 525) does not list the Valais Battalion, but the detailed description of the services rendered by the Battalion during the siege that is contained in Schaller (pp. 125–9) provides convincing evidence of its presence.

The second Spanish defence of Gerona from May to December 1809 is less well known than the defence of Saragossa, but it was no less epic a struggle. Over half the garrison fell during the siege, but that figure tells only part of the story, for approximately 6,000 people out of a total urban population of some 14,000 also perished. The siege was no less perilous for the French, however, whose total casualties during the siege may have amounted to over 13,000 men. For the Valais Battalion, the siege was a slow, gruelling experience which cost it over one-third of its strength. Nevertheless, the Battalion endured the entire siege and played a significant role in repulsing the final sortie of the Spanish on 7 December 1809. Ironically, after the surrender, an officer of the Battalion discovered that his brother-in-law, an officer in one of the Swiss Regiments recruited by the Spanish Bourbons, had been serving in the Gerona garrison. (Clemenso, *Souvenirs*, pp. 29–30.)

When the city formally surrendered on 10 December the primary military task of the Valais Battalion again became one of pacification and of forays against the guerrilla bands which dominated the countryside. We have few details of this monotonous but deadly service, but we do know that Lieutenant Tabin was killed in a skirmish on 10 April 1810. The operational base of the Battalion was changed from time to time during the summer of 1810, but its role always remained the same. (Clemenso, *Souvenirs*, p. 30.) In October, Lieutenant Dufour was wounded in action against 'brigands' on the 10th, while Captain Boudet, the Quarter-master of the Battalion, was wounded and captured along with all of the unit's records on the 18th. (*Ibid.*; Martinien states that 2nd Lieutenant Clemenso was also wounded on the 18th, but his memoirs do not mention such an occurrence.) This type of warfare was as deadly as it was unglamorous, and by the end of the year the Battalion was again reduced to just over 200 men despite the fact that it had been receiving constant drafts of reinforcements from Valais as well as a thin but steady stream of recruits from Swiss soldiers who had been captured while serving in the Spanish armies. (SHA Carton X[l]14.)

Final Transformation The ultimate fate of the Valais Battalion was eventually decided not by the Spanish guerrillas but rather by the Valais Republic's erstwhile protector.

On 12 November 1810 Napoleon cavalierly determined that an independent Valais no longer suited his purposes and he accordingly annexed Valais to the French Empire as the Department of the Simplon Pass. In a formal ceremony on 12 December the remnants of the Battalion were paraded at Junquera and asked to swear allegiance to their new master. The report of the French general conducting the ceremony specifies, perhaps with a touch of poetic licence, that 'the men of the Battalion unanimously repeated "We swear it! Long live the Emperor!" with the enthusiasm which characterizes the loyalty of these brave solders.' (Report of General François Gilles Guillot [1759–1818], quoted in Martin, 'Le Bataillon Valaisan', on p. 332.)

In February 1811 the Battalion was withdrawn from Spain to be refitted and brought up to strength, and shortly thereafter it learned that it was to become the third battalion of a reconstituted 11th Regiment of Light Infantry, that number in the light infantry arm having been vacant since 1803. The other battalions of the regiment were provided by the Corsican Tirailleurs and the *Tirailleurs du Po* (see separate entry), both of which also lost their special status in the French Army at that time. Owing to the administrative problems of raising the new regiment, however, the Battalion was not formally disbanded until 16 September 1811, at the depot of the 11th Light at Wesel in Germany. Even though the Battalion had ceased to exist, however, Valais soldiers continued to serve valiantly under the flag of France in the ranks of the new regiment during the campaigns of 1812, 1813 and 1814. Napoleon did grant the unit one last favour: he agreed to honour the original four-year voluntary enlistments for all the men whose terms expired after the Battalion was incorporated into the 11th Light. (Decision of 22 October 1811, Nap. *P&T*, No 6287, Vol. 4, p. 748.)

Uniforms There are three primary sources of information about the uniforms of the Valais Battalion, all of which confirm that the unit wore red, line infantry-style jackets with white collars, cuffs, cuff flaps and lapels, trimmed with thin red piping: (a) a miniature portrait of Chef de Bataillon Blanc from the waist upward (reproduced in a colour facsimile in Martin's article, and (b) two Battalion uniform coats (described and reproduced photographically in Pigeard, 'Le Bataillon Valaisan'). One coat (from the Museum of Sion) is that of a Grenadier officer; the other (from the Vaudois Military Museum) is that of a Grenadier corporal. (The latter coat was also documented by Bucquoy in his 1927 article on the Battalion and in his series of cards on the same subject [Series 166, Card 3].)

The surviving officer's coat and the coat represented in the miniature have virtually identical features down to the gilt buttons and the horizonal red pockets with white piping in the coat-tails. In the portrait, Blanc's lapels have straight bottoms and leave his vest exposed. The Battalion Chief is wearing massive gold epaulettes and holding a black shako with gold cords, fittings and lace trim top and bottom and a partially visible gold plate in front that may be in the shape of an eagle. The shako also has a black visor that is apparently attached to gold bosses on the side and is surmounted by an extraordinarily tall white plume. The Battalion Chief is wearing a red swordbelt with gold trim and short brown gloves. The officer coat has white turnbacks that have no red indentation at the bottom and that are decorated with embroidered gold grenades mounted on red backgrounds.

The Grenadier corporal coat is also quite similar except that the buttons are white metal rather than gilt. The buttons themselves are decorated with the initials 'BV' in the centre and the legend 'Empire Française' around the circumference. (The initials are in script on the buttons of the officer's coat.) The coat is adorned with white, fringed epaulettes and has two diagonal aurore stripes just above the flap, which itself has three buttons. The turnback ornament in this case is a grenade with a white circular body, outlined in red, and a red 'burst'.

There are a number of secondary sources (including, most particularly, paper soldiers from the Wurtz Collection and later sources based on those soldiers) that present other and additional details about the uniforms of the Battalion that are simply incorrect. A good example of available misinformation is that reported in great detail in a variety of sources concerning the uniforms of the Voltigeurs of the Battalion. In fact, there is no evidence that the Battalion actually ever had a Voltigeur company; on the contrary, both the original Decree organising the Battalion and an inspection report from 1810 refer only to the grenadiers and four other companies, labelled in the Inspection Report simply as companies 1 to 4. It seems likely that the artists who painted the figures in the Wurtz Collection simply assumed that there must have been a Voltigeur company and illustrated an example accordingly.

Since no primary descriptions of the uniforms of the drummers and musicians of the Battalion have been found, those presented in secondary sources must be treated with suspicion even though those positions certainly existed. With this caveat, the Bucquoy card series does contain a plausible illustration of a Fusilier drummer based on a paper soldier from the Carl Collection (which generally earns higher marks for reliability than the Wurtz Collection). The relevant figure wears a blue jacket with the same white lapels, collar, cuffs and cuff flaps, but it also displays on each shoulder a red 'swallow's-nest' shoulder ornament below a white shoulder strap. All these features a trimmed with a thick line of yellow lace.

Standard Pierre Charrié has expressed the opinion that the Battalion received neither an Eagle nor a flag, but there are several pieces of information that are inconsistent with that view. (Charrié, p. 169.) With respect to the possibility that the unit had a colour, Charrié himself notes that the table of organisation called for a colour-bearer (*porte-drapeau*), and we know that the position was ultimately filled since Joseph Louis Rappaz, the first colour-bearer, is noted as having been killed in action in July 1808. (Clemenso, *Souvenirs*, p. 28 and note 52.) As for the possibility that the Battalion had an Eagle, it is known that in May 1807 General Louis Antoine Montchoisy (1747–1814), commander of the 28th Military Division, wrote to the Minister of War mentioning that delivery of 'the Eagle that will guide the Battalion to victory is eagerly awaited', thus acting as if a decision had already been made. The Minister might have ultimately have decided to withhold the Eagle, but it was not in fact unique for a single battalion. Moreover, on 11 May 1810 *Sous-Lieutenant* Ignace Tabin, whose brother had been mortally wounded in a clash with guerrillas the month before, was officially appointed as Eagle-bearer of the Battalion (*porte-aigle*, and not merely *porte-drapeau*). (Martin, 'Le Bataillon Valaisan', p. 325; the date of Tabin's appointment–which is not specified in Martin–is given as 11 March by Charrié, but the date in the archives is 11 May.)

Bataillons de Déserteurs Étrangers (Nos 1–3)

(Foreign Deserter Battalions [Nos 1-3])

1st Foreign Deserter Battalion

Date of Creation 2 Germinal Year X (23 March 1802).

Circumstances of Creation The Organisational Decree created two Battalions of Foreign Deserters, the 1st to be organised at Genoa in Italy. (Belhomme, Vol. 4, p. 250.)

Composition The Organisational Decree called for the Battalion to have five companies. (Belhomme, Vol. 4, p. 250.) Its establishment was increased to ten companies of 100 men each on 21 Messidor Year XI (10 July 1803), then reduced back to five companies of 120 men each on 1 May 1805. (Belhomme, Vol. 4, pp. 274 and 300.)

Commanders No information found.

Operational History After being formed in Italy, the 1st Battalion was transferred to Elba in 1803 and then on to Corsica in 1805.

Final Transformation This Battalion is mentioned in the official order of battle for the French Army for Year XIII (1804–05) but disappears from the official records by August 1805. (Champeaux, *État Militaire*, p. 106; 'Armed Forces of the Empire' for 16 Thermidor Year XIII [14 August 1805], reproduced in Alombert & Colin, Vol. 1 [Document Annexes et Cartes], pp. 3–34.)

Uniforms No information found.

2nd Foreign Deserter Battalion

Date of Creation 2 Germinal Year X (23 March 1802).

Circumstances of Creation The Organisational Decree created two Battalions of Foreign Deserters, the 2nd to be organised at Alexandria in Italy. (Belhomme, Vol. 4, p. 250.)

Composition The Organisational Decree called for the Battalion to have five companies. (Belhomme, Vol. 4, p. 250.) On 21 Messidor Year XI (10 July 1803) the establishment of the 1st Foreign Deserter Battalion was increased to ten companies of 100 men each. (Belhomme, Vol. 4, p. 274.)

Commanders No information found.

Operational History The battalion was organised on the Italian mainland but was transferred to Elba in July 1803. (Belhomme, Vol. 4, p. 274.)

Final Transformation The Battalion is mentioned in the official order of battle for the

French Army for Year XIII (1804–05) but disappears from the official records by August 1805. (Champeaux, *État Militaire*, p. 106; 'Armed Forces of the Empire' for 16 Thermidor Year XIII [14 August 1805], reproduced in Alombert & Colin, Vol. 1 [Document Annexes et Cartes], pp. 3–34.)
Uniforms No information found.
Standard No information found.

3rd Foreign Deserter Battalion

See *Bataillon de Déserteurs Allemands.*

Bataillons Étrangers (Nos 1–4)

(Foreign Battalions [Nos 1–4]; see also *Bataillons de Déserteurs Étrangers* [Foreign Deserter Battalions])

1st Foreign Battalion

Date of Creation 2 Germinal Year X (23 March 1802).
Circumstances of Creation This unit was formed at Havre in the 14th Military Division by an order dated the same day as that forming the first two Battalions of Foreign Deserters. By August 1805 it had become a unit consisting mainly of natives of countries other than France and had taken on the designation '*1er Bataillon Étranger*'. (SHA Carton X[h]1.)
Composition The 1st Battalion was formed as a depot battalion for deserters (both French and non-French) from foreign armies. The strength of the Battalion ebbed and flowed as men were organised and equipped and then shipped to colonial posts in groups of 50, so it had the strength of only a single company when it was transferred to Cherbourg in 1806. It then slowly expanded again (and was sometimes referred to as the '*1er Bataillon de Déserteurs Étrangers*'). A third company was added in 1808, and the unit was then completely reorganised, by an order dated 16 July 1809, to consist of a staff and six companies of chasseurs. (SHA Carton X[h]1.)
Commanders *1802–09*: Captain Commandant Joseph Thierry Étienne. (SHA Carton X[h]1.) *1809–12*: Battalion Chief Foulon de Doué, who had served with the La Tour d'Auvergne Regiment. (SHA Carton X[h]1.) *1812*: Battalion Chief Poncelet. (Fieffé, Vol. 2, p. 54.) **1813:** Battalion Chief Pacaud. (Fieffé, Vol. 2, p. 54.)
Operational History After being based on the coast of the English Channel from 1802 to 1810, the 1st Foreign Battalion was posted to garrisons in Holland. Although reports speak of heavy desertion from the unit because of Holland's unfavourable climate and the imposition of strict discipline, it still had a strength of 23 officers and 939 men (including 799 present for duty) on 10 April 1812. (SHA Carton X[h]1.) The Battalion was posted to the forts of the Helder in 1812 and 1813, where it finally saw action against a variety of enemies. Captain A. M. Muller was wounded in a 'fight with

smugglers', while Lieutenant Blussard became a casualty in an 'affair' involving small English naval craft. All its officers during these years received reasonable fitness reports, but at least one had an exceptional background. Jean Pierre Amiet (b. 1770) was a Frenchman who had voluntarily joined the French Army in 1791 in a burst of Revolutionary zeal, then fought in Italy and Egypt and received a Sabre of Honour. (Lievyns, Vol. 1, p. 460.) He transferred to the Battalion in 1806 from the Battalion of Chasseurs of the Orient.

Final Transformation The Battalion was dissolved at Antwerp on 19 December 1813, at which point many of the men deserted rather than be re-formed in to a pioneer unit. (SHA Carton X[h]1.) The rest of the men were split between the pioneer force then being formed and the *3ème Régiment Étranger* (see separate entry).

Uniforms No information had been found except for two small points. First, the unit had blue, white and a small amount of red cloth in its stores; second, the inspection reports from 1808 note that the Battalion was 'well dressed'.

Standard No information found.

2nd Foreign Battalion

Date of Creation 1803.

Circumstances of Creation This Battalion was formed on the island of Elba in 1803 through the combination of the *Bataillon de Déserteurs Allemands* with some separate *Compagnies de Déserteurs Étrangers* (see separate entries). The unit was initially called the *2ème Bataillon d'Infanterie Étranger*, but it had no identifying number in the *État Militaire* for Year 13 (1804–05). It became the 2nd Foreign Battalion for once and for all some time after the reorganisation of the 1st Foreign Battalion in 1809 (see separate entry).

Composition By 1805 the Battalion had a strength of 29 officers and 847 men, including drummers, organised in six companies (SHA Carton X[h]2). A carabinier company was proposed for the Battalion as early as 1806, but none was created until 1809, when the 6th company was converted to that status. The archival records of the Battalion reveal that most of its officers had been in the regular army but had retired because of wounds limiting their ability to engage in active campaigning. (SHA Carton X[h]1.)

Commanders *15 June 1803–3 September 1808*: Battalion Chief Felix Victor Emmanuel Charles, Baron de Wimpffen (1778–1813). He was elected second-in-command of a battalion in the French Army when he was only 14 years old, but he was wisely suspended from that position before he could exercise any actual authority. He next appeared as an aide-de-camp to his father, General François de Wimpffen, but retired after his father's death in 1800. He left the Battalion when he was transferred to the 13th Line. *?–1812*: Battalion Chief Edouard Martin, who ultimately transferred to command of the 1st Colonial Battalion. (SHA Carton X[h]2.) *1813*: Battalion Chief Bérard. (Fieffé, Vol. 2, p. 54.)

Operational History The 2nd Foreign Battalion served on Elba from 1803 to 1806. It was then posted for some time to Corsica, but eventually was reassigned to Elba by

1809. In May of that year, a hundred or so men of the Battalion manning a small fort on the island of Pianosa (near Elba) repulsed an British attack, losing their commander, Captain Delu, in the process. The British returned in greater strength in June, captured the garrison and blew up the fort. It is perhaps an indication of the perceived military value of the Battalion that the British simply put their prisoners ashore on Elba rather than going to the trouble of transporting them to a more enduring captivity in England. (Davin, p. 30.) The unit also suffered an officer casualty defending against a British assault on the Fiumicino Tower near Rome in 1812. In 1813 one officer was wounded on the Italian mainland at Civita Vecchia and another in Corsica.

Final Transformation The 2nd Foreign Battalion was in Rome along with two battalions of the Isembourg Regiment when the Decree of 25 November 1813 was put into effect. All the non-Frenchmen in that force were collected into a new unit called the 2nd Pioneer Battalion, while the remaining French citizens were reformed into a new 1st Battalion (plus two extra depot companies) for Isembourg. (Carle, 'Dernier Jours', p. 58.) At the time of its demobilisation, the 2nd Foreign Battalion had the following composition (SHA Carton X[h]2):

61	Frenchmen	46	Italians	10	Dutchmen
210	Austrians	35	Prussians	39	Russians
11	Swiss	6	Spaniards	101	Poles
1	Swede	75	Rhine Confederation natives		

Uniforms The unit is assumed to have worn the same grey uniforms as the German Deserter Battalion with which it was formed. By 1805 the uniform included shakos, jackets, Hungarian-style vests and Hungarian-style breeches, although all of this clothing and equipment was in poor condition. (SHA Carton X[h]2.)

Standard No information found.

3rd Foreign Battalion

Date of Creation 3 September 1809.

Circumstances of Creation As a result of the influx to France of numerous prisoners of war and deserters from the armies that fought against Napoleon in 1809, the Minister of War proposed that the Emperor should 'form a 3rd battalion of foreign soldiers, to be composed of six companies, like each of the two existing battalions of this type.' (Nap. *P&T*, No 3529, Vol. 3, p. 218.) The proposition was approved by Napoleon on 3 September. The initial cadre for the new battalion was provided by excess soldiers from the 2nd Foreign Battalion then stationed on Elba.

Composition The battalion consisted of six companies, one of which was designated carabiniers. (SHA Carton X[h]2.)

Commanders **?–1811:** Battalion Chief Drujon. On 7 September 1811 Napoleon asked

General Clarke to give him a report on this officer 'about whom I only hear bad things'. (Nap. *P&T*, No 6131, Vol. 4, pp. 664–5.) Napoleon also expressed a preference for finding a 'good officer' in Corsica to take charge of this Battalion. **?–1813:** Battalion Chief Salles, who was killed in action at the defence of Livorno on 14 December 1813.
Operational History The Battalion was organised on Elba, where it remained until 1811, when it was posted to Corsica. It was stationed at Livorno in 1812, then split between Livorno and Elba for 1813 and 1814. One officer is listed as having been wounded 'by Portuguese brigands' on 13 July 1812—a circumstance that is almost impossible to explain given the location of the Battalion and the fact that no French units were anywhere near Portugal at that time. Lieutenant Franceschetti was wounded on Elba on 20 May 1813, while one officer was killed and three were wounded defending the city of Livorno in December 1813.
Final Transformation Napoleon exempted the Battalion from the general dissolution of foreign units he ordered at the end of 1813: 'We can leave the 3rd Foreign Battalion on the island of Elba; I am assured that this Battalion is not bad.' (N. to Minister of War, 1 December 1813, Nap. *O&A*, No 6266, Vol. 4, p. 367.) It was still on the island at Porto-Ferrajo in April 1814, and was disbanded thereafter. (SHA Carton X[h]2.)
Uniforms A drawing by E. Fort in the Print Room of the French National Library is annotated with a manuscript note (presumably by the artist) giving a description of the clothing of the Battalion. (BN Oa 501 pet fol, Fort, *Troupes Allemandes*.) The description, which is noted as having come from a Report from the Minister of War to Napoleon dated 19 December 1810 that can be found in the National Archives of France, is as follows:

> The 3rd Foreign Battalion needs to be completely re-uniformed; that means for each man we must acquire 1.22 metres of dark sky blue cloth, 0.158 metres of imperial blue cloth for the facings; 1.49 metres of white *cadis* for the turnbacks and lining of the coat-tails; 22 big buttons and 8 medium; vest of white *tricot*; two small white metal buttons; white *tricot* trousers; .25 metres of dark sky clue cloth for a forage cap; beige cloth overcoat; shako, cartridge box, shoulder-belt . . .

The drawing by Fort interprets this information as leading to a uniform jacket for the 3rd Battalion which had relatively short tails, sky blue light infantry-style lapels with dark blue piping and dark blue collar, cuff-flap and cuff piping. The figure in the drawing is wearing breeches with black gaiters reaching to just below the knee.
Standard No information found.

4th Foreign Battalion

Date of Creation March 1810.
Circumstances of Creation This unit was formed in order to make use of soldiers who had been serving in units of the Vatican army that were being disbanded. (Belhomme, Vol. 4, p. 470.)

Composition The unit had the same composition as the other three Foreign Battalions.
Commanders No information found.
Operational History No information found.
Final Transformation No information found.
Uniforms No information found.
Standard No information found.

Bataillons Francs de l'Île d'Elbe

(Volunteer Battalions of the Island of Elba)

Date of Creation 23 Germinal Year XI (13 April 1803).
Circumstances of Creation Napoleon created two Battalions by this name in order to provide a force to defend the island of Elba in the event of a renewal of hostilities with Britain. (Belhomme, Vol. 4, p. 268.)
Composition Each Battalion consisted initially of four companies of 100 men each. They were composed exclusively of inhabitants of Elba except that four men in each unit (including the Battalion Chief) had to be French. After the renewal of war between France and Britain an extra company was added to each Battalion and they were authorized to enlist foreign and French deserters from official depots. (Belhomme, Vol. 4, p. 268.) On 28 February 1805 the two Battalions were combined into one unit composed of eight companies. (Belhomme, Vol. 4, p. 297.)
Commanders According to the Champeaux's *État Militaire Pour An XIII*, the commander of the 1st Battalion in 1805 was Battalion Chief Duchoqué. That publication regrets that it was unable to locate a list of officers for the 2nd Battalion.
Operational History The only information found as to the operations of the Battalion are the details of the officer casualties listed in Martinien. Lieutenant Vallet was mortally wounded on 20 August 1809 while manning a battery at Porto Longone. Lieutenant Mante was wounded on 26 September 1809 in action against English small boats. Captain Dérosier was wounded on 3 January 1810 without any information as to circumstances. Captain Rutigny and 2nd Lieutenant Bicais became casualties in action against 'Sicilian corsairs' on 12 August 1810, while Lieutenants Pisani and Pezzella were hit resisting a British landing party on 2 May 1813.
Final Transformation In the summer of 1810 the Minister of War proposed that the Volunteer Battalion of Elba be disbanded. Napoleon tentatively approved the proposal and suggested that the officers might be transferred to the *Régiment de la Méditerranée* while the men could be sent to the Foreign Battalion in Corsica. (Decision of 19 August 1810, Nap. *O&A*, No 4261, Vol. 3, p. 317.) On 1 September the Battalion was ordered to cease enlistment of soldiers who were not natives of Elba and was renamed the *Bataillon de Gardes Nationaux de l'Île d'Elba* (National Guard Battalion of the Island of Elba). (Belhomme, Vol. 4, p. 482.) The Battalion was still in existence (albeit with a

strength of only four companies) when Napoleon became the ruler of the island in 1814. (Belhomme, Vol. 4, p. 665.)

Uniforms No information found.

Standard Charrié (p. 172) states that the distribution of 1804 model colours to these Battalions was approved by Berthier on 16 June 1804.

Bataillons Liguriens

(Ligurian Battalions)

Date of Creation March 1799.

Circumstances of Creation The Republic of Liguria (formerly the city state of Genoa) was called upon to provide three battalions of infantry for the French war effort in March 1799. (Belhomme, Vol. 4, p. 191.) These units served with the French Army until July 1801. (Belhomme, Vol. 4, p. 231.) After the breakdown of the Peace of Amiens, Napoleon sent a Franco-Italian corps under General St-Cyr to occupy the city of Taranto in the heel of the Italian peninsula. On 10 May 1803 the 1st and 2nd Ligurian Battalions of the Line were designated to form part of that force. (Belhomme, Vol. 4, p. 272.)

Composition In July 1805 the 1st Battalion had nine companies with a total strength of 32 officers and 632 other ranks. (Decision of 1 August 1805, Nap. *P&T*, No 148, Vol. 1, pp. 66–7.)

Commanders No information found.

Operational History The Ligurian Battalions served the French faithfully in 1799, when they were involved in the Battle of the Trebbia, and again in 1800 when they fought bravely during the siege of Genoa. The two Battalions that joined St-Cyr's expeditionary force in 1803 had become so reduced by attrition by April of 1804 that the rank-and-file of the 2nd Battalion was then amalgamated with that of the 1st and the cadres of the 2nd were sent home to recruit. A new 2nd Battalion returned to Taranto in September 1804 (Belhomme, Vol. 4, p. 288), but it appears that the two units at Taranto were again amalgamated into a single battalion in early 1805.

Final Transformation After the Ligurian Republic was annexed by France at the beginning of July 1805, there was no reason to keep the Battalions as a separate force. By means of an order dated 15 Messidor Year XIII (2 July 1805), Napoleon decreed that all Ligurian troops would be combined into a single light regiment of two battalions. (This decree is mention in a later decision dated 1 August 1805–Nap. *P&T*, No 148, Vol. 1, pp. 66–7.) The first battalion of the new regiment was formed from the nine companies of Ligurian troops then at Taranto. The second battalion was formed from all other Ligurian troops, who were moved from Genoa to Grenoble to reduce opportunities for desertion. Sometime after 1 August 1805 the new regiment was designated the 32nd Light Infantry Regiment of the French Army.

Uniforms No information found.
Standard No information found.

Chasseurs à Cheval Aragonais

(Mounted Chasseurs of Aragon; also known as
the *Volontaires Aragonais à cheval* [Mounted Volunteers of Aragon])

Date of Creation November 1811.
Circumstances of Creation This mounted unit was formed spontaneously by Benito Falcon, the *alcalde* (mayor) of the town of Gelsa, to fight back against the depredations of loyalist guerrillas. (Sorando Muzas, Section 1.)
Composition The unit consisted initially of one company of cavalry formed at Bechite with a maximum strength of 60–70 men. This unit was brought under the same administrative command as the *Fusiliers Aragonais* (see separate entry) by a decree dated 1 July 1812. A second company was decreed at the same time, but it was probably never fully formed.
Commanders **1st Company**—*Formation to final transformation:* Captain Benito Falcon (1769–?), who deserted to the loyalist guerrillas in 1812. **2nd Company**—*Formation to final transformation:* 2nd Lieutenant Francisco Ballejo, who had served with the *Fusiliers Aragonais* (see separate entry).
Operational History No information found.
Final Transformation The companies suffered from such significant attrition, particularly in the form of desertions, after the French defeat at Salamanca that by 5 September 1812, there was only one soldier present and ready for action. (Sorando Muzas, Section 1.)
Uniforms No information found.
Standard No information found.

Chasseurs à Cheval Helvétique

(Helvetian Mounted Chasseurs)

Date of Creation 30 Germinal Year XI (20 April 20 1803).
Circumstances of Creation This unit was formed from the Hussars of the Helvetian Legion (see separate entry for *Legion Helvétique*) that had been part of the armed forces of the Helvetian Republic. (SHA Carton X[l] 46[b].)
Composition This company-size unit had the following strength (Order of 30 Germinal An 11 [20 Apri 1803] printed in *Journal Militaire* for Year *XI*, Pt 2, pp. 89–90):

1	First Captain	1	Sergeant-Major	2	Trumpeters
1	Second Captain	2	Sergeants	108	Chasseurs
1	Lieutenant	1	Fourrier		
2	Second Lieutenants	8	Corporals		

Commanders Captain Lottaz. (Schaller, p. 40.)
Operational History No information found.
Final Transformation The Helvetian Chasseurs were incorporated into the 19th Mounted Chasseurs on 21 April 1804. The unit had a strength of three officers and 49 men as of that date. (SHA Carton X[l] 46[b].)
Uniforms Given that the Helvetian Chasseurs were the military descendants of the Helvetian Legion Hussars, it is not surprising that they wore a hussar-style uniform. As depicted in R. Knötel's print of a *'Jäger zu Pferd der Helvetischen Legion 1803'* (*Uniformenkunde*, Vol. 17, No 24), reconstructed from a drawing 'in the Basel Historical Museum', the uniform consisted of a conical black shako with a red wing, trimmed yellow, and a feather plume in traditional Swiss colours (green, red and yellow, from bottom to top); a green dolman with three vertical rows of buttons connected with yellow lace; red collar and cuffs, trimmed yellow; green breeches, trimmed yellow; and black boots.

Equipment and horse furniture, including sheepskin saddle cloth, were the same as for any French line Chasseur. (See also Bory, *Régiments Suisses*, Illustration No 7.) The yellow metal buttons were marked with the initials 'CH' for '*Chasseurs Helvétiques*'. (SHA Carton X[l] 46[b].) In 1987 the Musée des Suisses à l'Étranger in Geneva displayed a green dolman with five vertical rows of buttons linked with yellow lace braid that may have belonged to a trooper of this unit.
Standard No information found.

Chasseurs à Cheval Ioniens

(Ionian Mounted Chasseurs)

Date of Creation This unit was formed by a decree dated 13 December 1808, confirming a provisional organisation approved on 27 November 1807. (Organisational Decree, Nap. *Corr.*, No 14557, Vol. 18, p. 115.)
Circumstances of Creation Fieffé reports that the unit was formed from a cadre taken from the 25th Mounted Chasseurs serving with the French Army in the Kingdom of Naples (Fieffé, Vol. 2, p. 154), but the Organisational Decree states that the unit was to recruited by means of voluntary enlistments of natives of the 'Seven Islands' (Ionian Islands).
Composition The strength of the unit in its provisional form was one squadron of cavalry, but the organisation was reduced to a single company of 128 officers and men by the December 1808 decree. The structure was the same as for a company of French line Chasseurs.
Commanders Squadron Chief Lastour. (Pigeard, *L'Armée*, p. 450.)
Operational History No information found.
Final Transformation Evacuated to France in 1814 with the rest of the French garrison

of Corfu, the remnants of this unit were incorporated into the 6th Lancers at Lyon, 12 September 1814. (Index for SHA Carton X[l]37 in France, *Inventaire*, p. 239.)
Uniforms The 1808 Organisational Decree prescribes that the unit will 'retain' the same uniform as the 25th Regiment of Mounted Chasseurs, namely a green jacket with *garance* (dark red) facings, but with buttons bearing the inscription 'Chasseurs Ioniens'.
Standard No information found, but it is unlikely that such a small formation ever had a standard.

Chasseurs à Pied Grecs

(Greek Foot Chasseurs)

Date of Creation 10 March 1808. (A. Boppe, *L'Albanie*, p. 229.)
Circumstances of Creation This unit was formed from Greek refugees found in the Ionian Islands when they came under French rule after the Treaty of Tilsit.
Composition Eight companies, including three élite, with an effective strength of 951 men, all under the command of a Battalion Chief. (A. Boppe, *L'Albanie*, p. 229.)
Commanders No information found.
Operational History No information found.
Final Transformation Incorporated into Régiment Albanais (see separate entry) 1 July 1809.
Uniforms No information found.
Standard No information found.

Chasseurs Catalans

(Catalonian Chasseurs)

Date of Creation April/May 1812.
Circumstances of Creation This unit was a company-strength formation composed of deserters from the Spanish armies fighting the French in Catalonia. (Mercador Riba, p. 223.)
Composition The unit was initially a single company, but the establishment had doubled by 1813. (Mercador Riba, p. 223.)
Commanders *Formation–?:* Captain Andrés Quintana. (Mercador Riba, p. 223.) *?–Final transformation:* Captain Rigault. (Notes of Dr Jean Sarramon.)
Operational History No information found.
Final Transformation The unit was disbanded in January 1814. (Notes of Dr Jean Sarramon.)
Uniforms No information found.
Standard No information found.

Chasseurs Croates

(Croatian Chasseurs; see also *Chasseurs Illyriens*)

Date of Creation This unit was formed by a decree of 24 January 1811. (Belhomme, Vol. 4, p. 495.)

Circumstances of Creation The French administration in Illyria formed the so-called *Chasseurs Croates* as an expedient to permit it to have Croatian troops available for local defence needs without having to mobilise any single Regiment of *Chasseurs Illyriens* (see separate entry). The local French commander, Marshal Marmont, wanted to raise a total of four battalions, but Napoleon cut him off at two in order to save money (N. to Minister of War, 24 January 1811, Nap. *Corr.*, No 17294, p. 367). Each Battalion of Croatian Chasseurs was consequently constructed with detachments from the Battalions of Illyrian Chasseurs already in existence that were made available for active service for six months at a time. (Belhomme, Vol. 4, p. 495.)

Composition These Battalions had the same organisational structure as the Illyrian Chasseurs.

Commanders No information found.

Operational History No information found.

Final Transformation The Battalions were disbanded in February 1813. (Belhomme, Vol. 4, p. 606.)

Uniforms No information found.

Standard No information found.

Chasseurs de L'Ampurdan

(Chasseurs of L'Ampurdan; also known as
the *Chasseurs du Lampourdan* and the *Miqueletes de Don Pujol*)

Date of Creation This unit was formed in September 1810 and then regularised by an order of General Louis Baraguey d'Hilliers dated 5 October 1810. (Mercador Riba, p. 221.)

Circumstances of Creation The unit was formed from deserters from the Spanish guerrillas fighting against the French in Catalonia. (Rousseau, p. 267.) The unit was based in the Ampurdan region of Catalonia around the city of Figueras.

Composition The initial version of this unit was a single company of 60 men commanded by two officers. The establishment was expanded to a strength of 150 men by an order dated 11 December 1810. (Mercador Riba, p. 221.) On 9 September 1813 the composition of the unit was as follows (SHA Carton C[8]371):

1 Commandant
2 Captains

2	Lieutenants
5	2nd Lieutenants
3	*Maréchaux des Logis Chef*
10	*Maréchaux des Logis*
3	Fourriers
19	Brigadiers
10	Drummers and Trumpeters
168	Chasseurs

Commanders *Formation to final transformation:* Captain, then Commandant (with the rank of Battalion Chief), José Pujol, also known as Don Pujol. Pujol, a smuggler with a grudge against the Spanish government, was a small man whose face was ravaged with smallpox scars. (Lamon, pp. 51–2, n. 1.) According to Martinien's work, he was wounded in action four times, once each year from 1810 to 1813.
Operational History The Chasseurs had a reputation for ferocious behaviour directed equally towards the enemy and the local civilian population. In the latter category, the Chasseurs were accused at different times of robbery, rape, pillage and despoliation of churches. (Mercador Riba, p. 222; Rousseau, pp. 267–70.) Apart from Don Pujol, three officers of the Chasseurs were wounded in combat: 2nd Lieutenant Irondy on 18 November 1812 at Montserrat; Lieutenant Aigueviva on 9 July 1813 at the Chapel of la Salud; and 2nd Lieutenant Calvet on 15 November 1813 in defence of a convoy.
Final Transformation At the end of 1813 the Chasseurs were combined with the other companies of *Miqueletes Catalans* (see separate entry) to form the *Chasseurs Étrangers*.
Uniforms A Swiss soldier serving in Catalonia made note of the dress of Don Pujol in 1813: 'His uniform, like that of his soldiers, was a blue velour *carmagnole* jacket with large blue velour overalls. He and the cavalrymen in his unit wore shakos, but the men on foot wore hats *à la Henri IV* (i.e., with the brim turned up in front).' (Lamon, pp. 51–2, n. 1; see also Bueno, plate 61.)
Standard No information found.

Chasseurs d'Orient

([Middle] Eastern Chasseurs)

Date of Creation 17 Nivôse Year X (7 January 1802).
Circumstances of Creation This unit was formed by a decree of the First Consul in order to provide employment for the survivors of the *Légions Coptes and Grecques* (see separate entries) who had accompanied the French back to France from Egypt. Article 1 of the decree specified that: 'All Greeks, Copts, Egyptians and Syrians who served with the French Army in the Middle East will be formed into a battalion having as many companies of 80 men each as may be necessary to accommodate demand. It will be

organised and paid in the same manner as a battalion of light infantry.' (Nap. *Corr.*, No 5915, Vol. 7, p. 359.)

Composition An order of 21 Fructidor Year X (8 September 1802) set the establishment of the Chasseurs as a staff and ten companies, one of which was designated as an élite company of Carabiniers. (A. Boppe, 'Chasseurs', p. 18.) (There is no evidence that the Chasseurs ever had a Voltigeur company.)

Commanders *Creation to February 1813*: Colonel Nicholas Papas-Oglou (1758–1819), the commander of the *Légion Grecque* (see separate entry). He was away from the Chasseurs from mid-1805 to the end of 1806 (in Constantinople), from 1807 to 1809 (serving as a liaison to Ali Pasha of Janina) and again for much of 1812 (in command of a garrison on the Balkan coast opposite Corfu). *February 1813 to disbandment:* Colonel Gabriel Sidarious (1765–1851), who had been the last commander of the *Légion Copte* (see separate entry) founded by his uncle, General Jacob. Whenever Colonel Papas Oglou was on detached service, Sidarious was in actual command of the Chasseurs.

Operational History Organisation of the new unit proceeded very slowly. Its exotic recruits did not take well to new military customs and discipline in what was for them a foreign country. The desertion rate was, as a result, exceptionally high, as was the rate at which men were found to be unfit for service and were relegated to the depot of refugees in Marseilles. By 1806, the effective force of the Battalion was only 288 officers and men instead of the regulation 1,000 men. (A. Boppe, 'Chasseurs', p. 19.) While recruiting went on at the Battalion's depot in Marseilles (later transferred to Toulon), a small detachment did win an unusual battle honour for the Chasseurs. One hundred men were embarked with the Toulon fleet for service as marine infantry and they must have set sail, because Martinien's compilation records that two Captains of the Chasseurs were wounded (one mortally) at the Battle of Trafalgar. (Alombert & Colin, *1805*, Vol. 1 [Annex], p. 31.) The prospect of service with the Navy, however, may have been another reason why the Chasseurs had trouble recruiting and retaining soldiers.

Despite the weakness of the unit, Napoleon decided to employ the Chasseurs on active service in 1806 as part of the force sent by him to occupy the Balkan territory of Dalmatia ceded by Austria after the War of the Third Coalition. When General Lauriston was besieged in Ragusa (Dubrovnik) in the autumn of 1806 by a Russian expeditionary force and its Montenegrin allies, the Chasseurs played a prominent role in the relief expedition mounted by General Molitor, with Colonel Sidarious and Captains Harigli, Samathraki and Kiriaco winning the cross of the Legion of Honour for their exploits. (Savant, *Les Grecs*, p. 297.) The hard campaign reduced the unit to the skeletal size of seventeen officers and 60 NCOs and men. (Return of 20 November 1806, A. Boppe, 'Chasseurs', p. 22.)

At this juncture, Colonel Papas-Oglou re-joined the unit, but only long enough to realise that he needed to find more recruits if he was to have a military command in more than name only. In early 1807 General Marmont, the military governor of

Dalmatia, sent him, along with two officers of the Battalion, on a diplomatic mission to promote relations with Ali Pasha of Janina, the governor of Albania for the Ottoman Empire, and, if possible, to enlist Greeks residing in Ottoman territory for the Battalion. (Savant, *Les Grecs*, p. 297–8.) The mission was successful in the short run on the first count, but was terminated abruptly by news of the Treaty of Tilsit, which shifted France from being an ally of the Turks to being an ally of the Russians. This change helped the Chasseurs because they were consequently able to obtain recruits from a corps of Greek volunteers that had fought with the Russians from 1806 to 1807, but which was disbanded in early 1808. (Haptzopoulos, pp. 432–4.)

Over the next few years the Chasseurs were shifted from garrison to garrison in the Balkans and were only sporadically engaged in combat against Monenegrin and Albanian foes. In April 1809 the unit was transferred to Corfu, where the only action was occasional service in batteries firing on English ships, although this was still dangerous enough to give rise to a number of officer casualties. Since the potential Greeks recruits on Corfu had already been formed into their own unit (see separate entry for *Chasseurs Grecs*), the strength of the unit continued to diminish, falling from 293 men in 1810 to 104 in 1812. (A. Boppe, 'Chasseurs', p. 116, n.1.) The breakdown of the latter number by national origin gives a good sense of the diversity of the Chasseur population:

18	Frenchmen	15	Egyptians	1	German
17	Dalmatians	4	Italians	1	Maltese
14	Greeks 'from the Archipelago'	1	Hungarian		
		1	Pole		
30	Greeks 'from the Ionian Islands'	1	Serb		
		1	Neapolitan		

The lack of meaningful duty was certainly harmful to morale. Lieutenant Antoine Sarandis is a somewhat mysterious but colourful figure who began his military service as an unofficial member of the staff of General Lasalle. He was by his commander's side when Lasalle was killed at the end of the Battle of Wagram. In recognition of his services and because of his Greek origins, he was eventually given a commission with the Chasseurs. Sarandis became so bored with his inactivity that he wrote directly to the Minister of War in 1811 asking for more active duty. When that letter went unanswered, he simply left on a furlough from which he never returned. (Savant, *Les Grecs*, p. 334.)

The strength of the Chasseurs continued to fall until February 1813, when the remaining Chasseurs received orders to leave Corfu and join the garrison of Ancona in Italy. They left without their Colonel, since Papas-Oglou chose instead to take command of the important post of Parga on the Balkan mainland opposite Corfu. The Chasseurs suffered another blow when some thirty men from the unit fell into the hands of the English when one of the transports carrying them from Corfu to Italy was captured. This loss and other attrition meant that Colonel Sidarious had only 33 men under his command by August 1813. (A. Boppe, 'Chasseurs', p. 117.)

Final Transformation With the fall of the Empire, the depot of the Chasseurs was moved to Lyon, and the unit was dissolved in that city in September 1814. (A. Boppe, 'Chasseurs', p. 126.)

Uniforms The uniform of the Chasseurs was set by Napoleon himself in an order dated 21 Fructidor Year X (8 September 1802) which specified that the unit was to be dressed the same as any unit of French light infantry. Given the remoteness of its postings, it is unlikely that the Chasseurs ever received the 1812 uniform.

Standard According to Hatzopoulos, a standard of this unit can be found in the National Historical Museum of Greece in Athens. (Hatzopoulos, p. 428, n. 6.) Unfortunately, it appears that the flag referred to is in fact one from a unit of the same name that served with the French Army contingent at Salonika in Greece during the First World War. (Correspondence with the curator of the National Historical Museum, December 2000.)

Chasseurs Illyriens (Nos 1–6)

(Illyrian Chasseurs [Nos 1-6]; see also
Régiments Provisoires Croates [Croatian Provisonal Regiments])

Date of Creation October 1809.

Circumstances of Creation 'Illyrian Chasseurs' was the name given by Napoleon to the six regiments of frontier (or *Grenz*) infantry of the Austrian Army that he acquired under the terms of the Treaty of Vienna signed on 14 October 1809. As part of that peace settlement, the Hapsburgs ceded to France both a swath of Balkan territory encompassing portions of the regions known to the Austrians as 'Civil Croatia' and 'Military Croatia' as well as the indigenous Croatian military forces found there. The French gave the area the classical name of the Province of Illyria and re-christened the local regiments involved with the following titles (P. Boppe, *La Croatie Militaire*, p. 12):

1st Chasseurs or Regiment of Lika
2nd Chasseurs or Regiment of Ottochatz
3rd Chasseurs or Regiment of Ogulin
4th Chasseurs or Regiment of Sluin
5th Chasseurs or 1st Banat (or Glina) Regiment
6th Chasseurs or 2nd Banat (or Petrina) Regiment

These units existed because the frontier regions of the Austrian Empire bordering on Turkish territory had historically been settled by colonists who exchanged military service for Imperial protection. In the wake of the Vienna Treaty, Napoleon chose to leave the traditional arrangements in place and took the relevant units into his army as a continuing frontier defence force, despite the fact that some of them had in fact fought against the French that year.

Composition Because these Regiments had a dual military and civil role in the districts they represented, their composition was unusual. For military purposes, each Regiment had a peacetime strength of two battalions of six companies each, but this was typically doubled in time of war, as had been the case during the 1809 campaign. There is no specific mention of élite companies for the battalions, but each company did have 20 Chasseurs specially armed with carbines. (Report of the Minister of War, 14 November 1810, quoted in P. Boppe, *La Croatie Militaire*, Appendix J, p. 200.) Since they also discharged some non-military responsibilities, however, each of the Regiments also had some unusual non-combatant personnel attached to its establishment as 'Extra Personnel', including Catholic priests, forest rangers, customs officers and 'clock repairmen'. (A complete list of personnel is set forth in P. Boppe, *La Croatie Militaire*, Appendix B, pp. 164–5.) Some of the more traditional military personnel, such as the Regimental surgeons, also had dual military and civilian duties.

Commanders All of the 1809 commanders of these Regiments chose to remain in Austrian service, so a new slate of colonels had to be appointed:

Regiment of Lika (No 1) *28 December 1809–26 October 1811*: Marc Slivarich von Heldenbourg (1762–1838), a Major in the Regiment while it was in Austrian service, was the only senior officer holdover to the French regime. He was appointed to command of the 1st Provisional Croatian Regiment (see separate entry) on 26 October 1811 and ultimately became a general in the French Army. He was not formally replaced.

Regiment of Ottochatz (No 2) *3 January 1810–17 April 1810*: Colonel Louis Henri René Meynadier (1778–1848), who, after three months of indecision, chose to remain as an ADC to General Martin Vignolle of the Army of Italy rather than take up command of this Regiment. *17 April 1810–8 July 1812*: Pierre Winter (1759–1817), who was allowed to retire in 1812 because of serious physical infirmities. *12 August 1812–23 February 1813*: Robert de Gordon (1781–1815), a native of South Africa who had served in the Dutch Army at Capetown, Surinam (where he was captured by the English) and Java. He was called away to command the 3rd Provisional Croatian Regiment (see separate entry). He was not formally replaced.

Regiment of Ogulin (No 3) *28 December 1809–26 August 1811*: Baron Joseph Serrant (1767–1827), who served until he was transferred to command of the 8th Light. *26 August 1811–9 August 1812*: Xavier Holevatz (1763–?), who served until he was transferred to command of the Regiment of Sluin. He was apparently an extremely good officer, but he was transferred because he was a native of the Ogulin district and it was considered preferable for him to command a Regiment in which he did not have any family ties. (Report of General Bertrand, 14 December 1811, set forth in P. Boppe, *La Croatie Militaire*, Appendix N, pp. 222–3.) He was not formally replaced.

Regiment of Sluin *27 May 1810–9 August 1812*: Jacques Robert Souslier, Baron de Choisy (1772–1826), a former emigré and ADC to Marshal Marmont. Since he had only served in cavalry regiments prior to this appointment, he was not particularly successful as the commander of an infantry unit and he left to become a staff officer (*Adjutant-Commandant*). *9 August 1812 to disbandment (?)*: Xavier Holevatz (1763–?), who transferred from command of the Regiment of Ogulin. He was originally slated to command the 2nd Provisional Croatian Regiment, but was replaced by Colonel de Gordon, who could speak better French, before the Regiment was formed. The entry for this officer in Quentin does not have any information relating to his career after this appointment.

1st Banat Regiment *30 December 1809–1 October 1811*: Étienne Joly (1771–1850), who left to take command of the 3rd Provisional Croatian Regiment (see separate entry) and ultimately became a Brigade General. He was not formally replaced.

2nd Banat Regiment *28 December 1809–1813*: Jacques Jean Marie François Boudin, Count de Tromelin (1771–1842), another former emigré who had actually been attached to the naval command of Sir Sydney Smith while that officer was supporting Turkish resistance to Napoleon's invasions of Egypt and Syria. He left to serve with the Grand Army and was apparently not replaced.

Operational History The hardest aspect of the transition from Austrian to French service was the linguistic one, since the men spoke Croat and were accustomed to receiving orders in German, while the new French officers generally spoke only their own language. That problem was overcome by creating a special commission to translate instructional material into the local language and by arranging an exchange programme sending Croatian officers to serve temporarily in French regiments while delivering French NCOs to each battalion of Chasseurs. (P. Boppe, *La Croatie Militaire*, pp. 33–4.)

Napoleon was aware of the favourable military reputation won by the Croatians during their service in the Austrian Army and he hoped to find a way to use them militarily himself. Because of the unusual composition of the Regiments themselves, however, he decided he could not bring them to the Grand Army as integral units. Instead, he formed different combinations of service battalions of the Regiments into provisional units available for active campaigning. (See separate entry for *Régiments Provisoire Croates*.) These expedients, which ultimately involved eight different complete battalions plus drafts out of the total strength of twelve battalions of Chasseurs, left the units remaining in Croatia in a weakened condition and barely able to perform their frontier defence functions. (P. Boppe, *La Croatie Militaire*, p. 104, n. 1.) Each Regiment of Illyrian Chasseurs contributed 300 men every six months to form active-duty battalions to provide garrisons for Zara (now Zador), Ragusa (now Dubrovnik) and Karlstadt (Karlovac). (Belhomme, Vol. 4, p. 464.) Fortunately, they were never tested by anything more than minor raids by Turkish and Montenegrin foes, although a skirmish against some of these 'brigands' did cost the Ogulin Regiment three wounded officers (including Colonel Serrant) on 16 March 1810 at Zerzatz.

Some new challenges arose in 1813 as British naval activity in the Adriatic increased. After occupying the island of Lissa, the British began an active campaign of coastal raiding which occasionally brought them into contact with the Illyrian Chasseurs. For instance, a company of the second battalion of the 1st Banat Regiment repulsed a British landing force of 200 men at Fasana on 13 February 1813. (P. Boppe, *La Croatie Militaire*, p. 74.) As the year wore one, however, the morale of the units began to fail as news of the disasters in Russia spread through the region. Desertion increased markedly and, in one instance, French troops had to organise a punitive expedition in July to deal with a particularly aggressive band of deserters from the 2nd Banat Regiment who were disturbing the peace near Novigrade. (P. Boppe, *La Croatie Militaire*, p. 77.)

Final Transformation The entry of Austria into the war against Napoleon at the end of the summer armistice proved to be a final blow from which the Illyrian Chasseurs were unable to recover. The Croats were apparently reluctant to fight against their former Hapsburg comrades-in-arms, and, as Austrian troops began to occupy their home territories, the stream of deserters became a flood. For instance, by the end of September the Ogulin Regiment had been reduced to a mere ten officers and 51 men. (Report of Major Baudisson, P. Boppe, *La Croatie Militaire*, p. 84, n. 1.) There were some exceptions, of course–such as the case of Lieutenant Count Charles Pierre de Taulignan, quartermaster of the second battalion of the 1st Banat Regiment, who saved the paychest in his charge by fighting his way (at the cost of seven of the ten men of his escort) through the British and Austrian forces that combined to capture Fiume (now Trieste) on 23 August (P. Boppe, *La Croatie Militaire*, p. 80, n. 1)–but they were relatively rare.

The Croats who were isolated in French garrisons after the Austrian offensive performed no better. General Joseph Montrichard, the commander of Ragusa, reported in October: 'Our position has been critical; today it is even worse. The Croats continue to desert daily on all sides notwithstanding the precautions I have taken . . . ' (P. Boppe, *La Croatie Militaire*, p. 83.) A local resident in Ragusa noted the same phenomenon (Stulli Diary, 2 September [October?], quoted in Bjelovucic, p. 142):

> During the month of September, when it was known of the outbreak of war between Austria and France and the entrance of the Austrians into Croatia, the Croats of the 4th Regiment of the garrison of Ragusa did not cease deserting to the enemy. The Croats of the 3rd at Cattaro did the same thing. The small boat of the English brig 'Il Saraceno' was continuously busy bringing these deserters to Mezzo and then to Lissa and Fiume.

Desertion ultimately was the least of the worries the Croats created for French commanders, since in many cases the behaviour of the Croats included mutiny as well as active treason. At Cattaro, a battalion of the Ogulin Regiment refused to work on improving the defences. (P. Boppe, *La Croatie Militaire*, p. 87.) At Perasto, the Croats played a decisive role in forcing the French commander to surrender by physically

TABLE 4: ILLYRIAN CHASSEUR DISTINCTIONS, 1809

Unit	Collar & Cuffs	Buttons
1st Chasseurs (Lika)	Violet	Yellow
2nd Chasseurs (Ottochatz)	Violet	White
3rd Chasseurs (Ogulin)	Orange	Yellow
4th Chasseurs (Sluin)	Orange	White
5th Chasseurs (1st Banat)	Vermillion	Yellow
6th Chasseurs (2nd Banat)	Vermillion	White

menacing the other units in the garrison and waving flags of surrender from the walls. (Report of Commandant Calmain, 14 October 1813, quoted in P. Boppe, *La Croatie Militaire*, p. 85.) Finally, in the worst case, '[a] band of Croatian deserters, commanded by English officers' was credited with capture of the town of Stagno on 1 November. (Report of Prince Eugene Beauharnais, 21 November 1813, quoted in P. Boppe, *La Croatie Militaire*, p. 85, n. 2.)

The Illyrian Chasseurs thus had effectively ceased to exist by the end of 1813, although some officers apparently fought on with their French comrades. In particular, Lieutenant Delarue of the 4th (Sluin) Regiment and Lieutenant Cazin of the 5th (1st Banat) Regiment are both reported as having been wounded in the defence of Ragusa on 9 January 1814.

Uniforms The Chasseurs at first retained the uniforms they had worn in Austrian service in 1809. This uniform consisted of a brown jacket (which had replaced the traditional Hapsburg white coat in 1808) and medium blue trousers. The facing and button colours from 1808 were as shown in Table 4 (P. Boppe, *La Croatie Militaire*, p. 15, n.1).

By an Order of Marshal Marmont dated 28 December 1809, however, the Chasseurs were required to adopt French cockades and rank distinctions and to replace or modify all aspects of their clothing and equipment which reflected their Hapsburg origins (e.g., yellow and black piping and Imperial Austrian eagles and ciphers). (P. Boppe, *La Croatie Militaire*, Appendix E, pp. 175–6.)

Napoleon wanted to be very frugal in dealing with the dress of the Illyrian Chasseurs: 'I do not see the necessity to spend a lot of money to dress 14,000 men who will never serve anywhere but in their own home territory and who are already sufficiently dressed for that duty.' (Imperial decision of 22 April 1811, Napoleon *P&T*, No 6046, Vol. 4, p. 618.) Nevertheless, the uniforms of the Chasseurs were completely redesigned by a another decree of Marmont, now the Governor-General of Illyria, dated 22 May 1810 (P. Boppe, *La Croatie Militaire*, Appendix E, pp. 176–8):

> Article 1: The uniform of the Croatian regiments will hereafter be national blue in colour, with the same colour trousers, white vest, Hungarian *brodequins*, a French-style shako and a beige overcoat.

> Article 2: The buttons and ornaments will be of white metal, as will the epaulettes and sword knots of the officers. The buttons will be the same as those for French light infantry and will bear the number of the regiment.

'*Brodequins*' were apparently laced boots extending above the ankle. Authorisation of this non-standard footwear was a concession to local custom: 'If they are accustomed to wearing *brodequins*, why not leave well enough alone?' (Decision of 22 April 1811, Napoleon *P&T*, No 6046, Vol. 4, p. 618.)

The Regiments were distinguished by having different facing colours on their collars, cuffs and turnbacks, as shown in Table 5. The facing colour for the 4th Regiment (Sluin) was changed to *aurore* (light orange) by a subsequent decree dated 3 June. (P. Boppe, *La Croatie Militaire*, Appendix E, p 178.) Due to the fact that the Croatian regiments traditionally had non-commissioned officers with the rank of 'Vice-Corporal', but no Sergeant-Majors, the decree specified that all under-officers would be upgraded to the next highest rank in the French Army for the purposes of determining their rank distinction (e.g., Vice-Corporals became corporals and Sergeants became Sergeant-Majors).

The original decree gives some other important details about the new uniform. First, Article 6 states that the style is to be same as that of the then current Austrian uniforms. Second, Article 5 specifies that, while the Colonels of the units should try to introduce the blue uniforms as quickly as possible, 'until the use of the new uniforms is established, the NCOs and men are authorised to wear *black* coats and white trousers [emphasis added]'. This practical detail may reflect the fact that it might be harder to find blue cloth to make new uniforms than it would be to dye the brown uniforms to black.

On a related uniformological note, Marmont also established French-style uniforms for the officerships he created within the Government of Illyria to administer and manage his indigenous army. They all wore dark blue single-breasted jackets with nine buttons and were distinguished by different facings and details. For instance, aping the French Engineering Corps, the Illryian engineers had black collars and cuffs, red piping and lining, gold epaulettes and buttons, blue vests and trousers and

TABLE 5: ILLYRIAN CHASSEUR FACINGS, 1910–1818

Unit	Collar, Cuffs and Turnbacks
1st Chasseurs (Lika)	Red
2nd Chasseurs (Ottochatz)	Crimson
3rd Chasseurs (Ogulin)	Yellow
4th Chasseurs (Sluin)	Violet
5th Chasseurs (1st Banat)	Sky blue
6th Chasseurs (2nd Banat)	Green

Hungarian boots. Illyrian Staff Officers, on the other hand, had blue collars cuffs and turnbacks, gold epaulettes and buttons and white vests and trousers. (Decree of 17 June 1810, P. Boppe, *La Croatie Militaire*, Appendix E, pp. 179–80.)

Although the Provisional Croatian Regiments formed from 1811 onward and composed of men from the Illyrian Chasseurs wore green, light infantry-style uniforms (see 'Uniforms' section of separate entry for *Régiments Provisoires Croates*), the blue uniforms of the Illyrian Chasseurs who remained in Croatia were never modified, despite the fact that the Minister of War formally proposed in June 1813 that the standard blue uniform should be adopted for all Croat soldiers (*ibid.*) It is possible, however, that some of the old Austrian uniforms came back into use in 1813, because some primary sources report that brown uniforms were worn by Croatian reinforcements coming to the Grand Army. (See Pegau MS, 14 February 1813, in R. Knotel, *Mitteilungen*, Vol. 15, No 4 [1908], p. 1 [brown uniforms with red 'cuffs']; Forthoffer, *Fiches Documentaires*, No 50 [brown uniforms with yellow facings]; and Freiberg MS, Plate 44, in R. Knotel, *Mitteilungen*, Vol. 17, No 8 [1912], p. 29 [brown uniform with red facings].)

Standard The organisational tables for these Regiments call for colour bearers, but no information has been found about the regimental colours they might have carried. There is a little flag, or *fanion*, in a Viennese collection that may have been an informal standard of the Ogulin Regiment. The item is a small white banner mounted on a staff adorned with an iron spearpoint finial. The flag bears the diagonal inscription '3e Illyrien 1er Bat.' (Charrié, p. 172.) (This cannot belong to the Illyrian regiment, because there was only a single unit by that name—see separate entry for *Régiment d'Illyrie*.) Other battalions of Illyrian Chasseurs may have carried similar flags.

Chevau-légers Belges du Duc d'Arenberg

(The Duke of Arenberg's Belgian Light Horse)

Date of Creation This unit was formed by a decree dated 30 September 1806 that authorised Duke Prosper Louis, the ruler of the small principality of Arenberg, to form a light cavalry regiment for service in the French Army under the name of the Belgian Light Horse. (Couvreur, p. 563.)

Circumstances of Creation Napoleon's intent in forming the Belgian Light Horse Regiment was to exploit the aristocracy of the old Belgian provinces of the Hapsburg empire as another source of manpower for his armies. To set the proper tone, he conferred command of the unit on a representative of one of the most noble families from that area and he specified that all the men of the Regiment had to be natives of the French departments that had been created from the former Hapsburg lands. The success of this recruiting effort can be judged by the fact that 27 of the first 40 officers were nobles. (Bucquoy, *Cavalerie Légère*, pp. 176–7.)

Composition The Regiment had a staff and four service squadrons, each of which was composed of two companies with four officers and 112 other ranks. (Rigo, 'Ameil', p. 29.) The principality of Arenberg was a member state of the Confederation of the Rhine, and in January 1807 Napoleon authorised the Duke to incorporate into the Regiment as a fifth squadron the small contingent of horsemen that he was obligated to contribute to the Confederation. (Bucquoy, *Cavalerie Légère*, p. 178.) This contingent had to be paid, clothed and fed by the Duke. It was, however, given a French squadron commander (Squadron Chief Jean Augé) from Alsace to make it easier for the men to acclimatise to French service. (Rigo, *Le Plumet*, Plate No U33.)

Commanders *Creation to disbandment*: Prosper Louis, Duke of Arenberg (1784–1861), the reigning prince of that small state. He was just 21 years old when he received command of the Regiment, and Napoleon was sufficiently pleased with his services to leave him in command when the unit was taken into the French Army. He was captured by the British during the action at Arroyo del Molinos in Spain on 28 October 1811.

Operational History It took many months to find enough volunteers to fill the Regiment and it took even longer after that to organise the unit for active service because most of its officers and men had not seen prior military service. To speed things up, Napoleon gave the unit a tough, veteran Major to assist the Duke with the organisation of the unit. Unfortunately, this officer, Auguste Jean Ameil, was so obtuse that he did not realise that Napoleon specifically wanted the Regiment to have an ethnic identity and in February of 1807 he complained about that circumstance (Couvreur, p. 566):

> The Regiment of Light Horse is composed exclusively of men born in Belgium. These men have formed in the unit a sort of Belgian nationalist spirit. Walloon language and customs prevail.

Ameil even went so far as to suggest that this situation could be corrected by the incorporation some 150 Frenchmen into the unit. Berthier quickly sent the following reply on behalf of the Emperor (Couvreur, p. 566):

> It was the Emperor's intention that this Regiment be recruited exclusively from inhabitants of the new departments and this political objective has happily been fulfilled. Under the eyes of the Emperor, and surrounded by French units, this new Regiment will quickly emulate the spirit of our brave fighting men.

The Emperor did make one important change: the Duke was ordered to incorporate into the Regiment the squadron of cavalry that constituted the entire military force of the principality.

In the spring of 1807, 450 officers and men of the Regiment, divided into three squadrons, were brigaded with the 3rd Dutch Hussars in a polyglot corps formed under the command of Marshal Brune for service along the Baltic coast of Prussia and Swedish Pomerania. The Regiment suffered its first officer casualty in March, but it did not see any noteworthy action until August, when it crossed swords with a regiment of Swedish Light Dragoons on the 5th of the month near Anclam. (Rigo, *Le Plumet*, U33.)

After the surrender of Stralsund, the Regiment was assigned to the command of Marshal Bernadotte, then governor of the city of Hamburg. At this juncture, the Regiment mustered 35 officers and 892 men. (Rigo, *Le Plumet*, U33.)

The Belgian Light Horse remained in northern Germany for the next year (except for 2nd Lieutenant Gérard, who was on detached service in Constantinople as an ADC to the French ambassador, General Horace Sébastiani). (Decision of 29 January 1808, Nap. *O&A*, No 5428, Vol. 4, p. 69.) The stay was relatively uneventful until August 1808, when the Regiment was called upon to help subdue the units of the Spanish expeditionary corps in Denmark under the Marquis de la Romana that had not been able to take ship with the British Navy and return to Spain. (Rigo, *Le Plumet*, U33.) Shortly thereafter, the Regiment received its own orders for Spain. (Decision of 19 October 1808, Nap. *P&T*, No 2375, Vol. 3, p. 497.)

Final Transformation The Belgian Light Horse Regiment was transformed at the stroke of pen into the 27th Regiment of Mounted Chasseurs by a decision of 29 May 1808. The Regiment continued in French service under that designation until 1814.

Uniforms The available information about the uniforms of the Belgian Light Horse is both straightforward and confusing at the same time. It is straightforward because the diligent research of Messrs Bucquoy, Thomas, Benigni and Rigo shows conclusively that the Regiment started out wearing a chasseur-style uniform featuring a single-breasted jacket and ended up wearing a hussar-style uniform complete with dolman and sabretache. It is confusing, however, because there is no definite information about the timing and circumstances of that transition.

The backdrop for discussion of the uniforms of the Regiment is the fact that Napoleon intended that the unit would operate at a lower cost than the average regiment of French light cavalry. The Organisational Decree consequently specifies that the men were to have only one coat, were to ride small (and thus less expensive) horses and were to have a inexpensive saddle with saddle pads instead of a full saddle cloth. (Bucquoy, *La Cavalerie Légère*, p. 180.) The Duke, it seems, had other, more ambitious plans for his Regiment, and this tension between the desires of the commander and the desires of the military bureaucracy recurs throughout the units history. For instance, with respect to the horse furniture, as early as December 1806 the Duke was advertising in a Liège newspaper for black sheepskin saddlecloths, although there is no indication that he ever acquired enough of them to make a general distribution. (*Ibid.*, p. 181.)

The Organisational Decree for the Regiment is not very clear as to the details of the chosen uniform (*ibid.*, p. 180): 'The uniform will be the same as that for [French] Mounted Chasseurs except that the choice of colour will be made by the Colonel.' A subsequent letter from the Minister Dejean provides the missing details (*ibid.*):

> The Regiment will have for its uniform a dark green jacket; amaranth collar, cuffs, trim and lining; horizontal pockets; yellow buttons; overalls in the same colour as the jacket; hussar boots; and for the headwear, a shako.

Dejean also indicated that all rank insignia and lace distinctions would be yellow (or gold, as the case might be).

There has been some controversy over the years as to the exact style of the initial uniform jacket that was worn by the Regiment in accordance with this decree. Some say it was a long-tailed garment with lapels open over the stomach and angled at the bottom; others say it was a single-breasted coat with abbreviated tails like the short-tailed, so-called 'Kinski' jacket that became very popular from 1809 onward. Research this century has discovered conclusive evidence that both views are correct. On the one hand, bills from uniform suppliers to the Colonel indicate that he ordered (and presumably wore) the type of long-tailed coat with lapels that would have been typical for line Chasseurs officers at the time the Regiment was formed. (Bucquoy, *La Cavalerie Légère*, p. 183.) On the other hand, an inspection report dated 19 December 1807 demonstrates that each man had a *habit veste*, a vest with sleeves, a pair of overalls with buttons up the side seam (*charivari*), an overcoat with cape, Hungarian boots, a shako or bearskin and a fatigue cap. (Rigo, 'Ameil', p. 30.)

No matter what the style of this initial uniform, the Regiment soon began to wear hussar-style clothing. The evidence supporting this point takes the form of some paintings from the so-called Hamburg Manuscript (or Manuscript of the 'Bourgeois of Hamburg'), one of the best primary sources for the study of Napoleonic military uniforms, that must have been painted in the years 1806 and 1807 because those were the only years that the unit was anywhere near Hamburg. Rigo suggested in a 1975 article that the hussar uniforms might have been worn by the Arenberg Contingent that was incorporated into the Regiment in January 1806, then asserted that conclusion as a fact fifteen years later in the text to *Le Plumet* No U33. The best supporting evidence for his view is the fact that the captions to the relevant paintings in the Hamburg Manuscript all refer to 'Arenberg's Cavalry' and not the 'Belgian Light Horse'. That position seems to be fully refuted, however, by a letter from a Captain D'Éstournelle, the clothing officer for the Regiment, that was found by Colonel Bucquoy and that seems to provide conclusive evidence that the men of the Arenberg Contingent incorporated into the Regiment wore the same uniform as the rest of the men except for Arenberg cockades (yellow with a red centre) and sabretaches decorated with the three golden flowers of the Arenberg coat of arms. (*Ibid*., p. 182.) The true explanation for the hussar uniform is probably very mundane and probably has to do simply with the Duke trying to procure the most attractive uniforms possible for a unit whose very existence depended on voluntary enlistments, and he re-clothed the Regiment squadron by squadron as and when resources were available to do so.

Whatever the explanation for the coexistence of all these disparate facts, the Hamburg figures provide authentic information about the dress of the Regiment and need to be described in full:

Hamburg MS Painting No 59: 'Chasseurs and an Arenberg Cavalryman'. Although the caption is somewhat ambiguous, it seems possible that this picture depicts three soldiers from the Regiment (as opposed to one figure from the Regiment and two from some other unspecified regiment of Chasseurs) and therefore illustrates both the chasseur dress and the hussar dress side by side. Since two figures have the same uniform, it is possible to determine logically from the caption that the other figure wearing a dark green dolman with three rows of buttons connected by yellow braid with red collar and pointed cuffs, both trimmed with yellow, is intended to be the 'Arenberg Cavalryman'. His head is covered by a black shako ornamented only with a regulation tricolour pompom and he is wearing green overalls with yellow buttons down the outside seam of the overalls. His shoulder-belt and waist-belt both seem to be tan in colour, but there is no sign of a sabretache.

The other two figures are dressed in dark green single-breasted jackets with short tails that feature red pointed cuffs (with two buttons), red piping down the front, red turnbacks without ornaments and green collars with a small red patch (decorated with a silver button) on either side of front opening. The far left figure, busy filling his pipe, has silver buttons and fitted green overalls with a double red stripe down the side. He is also wearing an unusual form of green fatigue cap with brim and an oversize, flat round crown with red trim. Judging from what appears to be a strip of lace on his forearm, the last cavalryman is intended to be an NCO and he has been depicted wearing a shako that does not have a front plate but does have white cords (with a white raquette hanging off the right side), two bands of white around the top (the upper wider than the lower) and a tricolour cockade (coloured red, yellow and blue [?] reading from the outside to the inside) surmounted by a circular yellow pompom with a yellow centre. He is also wearing green hussar breeches with spear-point decorations on the thigh. There are no visible buttons down the front of the jacket, but this may simply be a mistake of the artist.

Although the facing colour of the Regiment was amaranth, a pinkish red, the facings of all the figures in this painting are the same shade of bright red.

Hamburg MS Painting No 60: 'Trumpeter of Arenberg Cavalry'. This picture features a very unusual figure wearing the same style of hussar dress with overalls as the figure in the prior painting but with the dolman being pinkish-red in colour with green braid and green collar and cuffs trimmed with yellow. The uniform is completed by an unusual headdress that looks most like the upper half of a regulation pinkish-red czapska with a brim and some yellow trim on the bottom edge. His hat has a large French cockade and a short length of green cord with a green raquette hanging off the right side. The figure is mounted on a white horse with black leathers, a white sheepskin saddle cloth and a green portmanteau with red trim and a red spread eagle at each end.

Hamburg MS Painting No 61: 'Carabinier of the Arenberg Cavalry Regiment'. This soldier of the élite company is wearing the same uniform as the hussar-style figure in Painting No 59 except that it is topped off by an enormous busby with red cords, bag (with yellow trim) and a red plume. He is also mounted and has the same horse and horse furniture as the Trumpeter.

The use of a hussar uniforms by the Regiment is documented by two other primary sources. The first is a naive painting by Andreas Ornstrup in the Danish Royal Library that depicts an officer of the Regiment in a busby with a red plume and bag and gold cords, a green pelisse with grey fur trim, gold braid and red shoulder straps trimmed gold, long green trousers with gold Austrian knots and the hint of a black sabretache. The other source is an 1806 portrait of an officer named Louis Charles Van der Burch in a pelisse that is reproduced in Couvreur, p. 569.

The shakos shown in the Hamburg MS do not have plates, but it seems that the Regiment may at some point had such an ornament with a special Regimental design. The evidence is a picture in Blondieau's book of a diamond-shaped plate featuring crowned eagle with outstretched wings over a small set of the initials 'C.-L. B.' (for '*Chevau-Légers Belges*'). (Blondieau, p. 27.) The same source also mentions a plate with the same initials surmounted by a crown.

Standard The 27th Chasseurs is said to have had one 1804 Model colour and Eagle received 'at an unknown date'. This may have been given to the unit while it was still the Belgian Light Horse. (Charrié, p. 223.)

Chevau-légers Lanciers de la Garde (No 1)

(Light Horse Lancers of the Guard [No 1])

See *Chevau-légers Polonais de la Garde*.

Chevau-légers Lanciers de la Garde (No 3)

(Light Horse Lancers of the Guard [No 3])

Date of Creation The unit was formed by an Imperial decree dated 5 July 1812 (reproduced in Dundulis, pp. 281–3).

Circumstances of Creation The 3rd Light Horse Lancers were created by Napoleon in order to take advantage of the martial enthusiasm of the population of ancient state of Lithuania when he freed it from Russian rule at the start of the 1812 campaign. To provide potential volunteers the best possible incentive to come forward, he decided that he would give the ethnic Poles of Lithuania the same 'honour' he had given to the Poles of Poland in 1807, namely the privilege of contributing a regiment to his own Imperial Guard.

Composition The Organisational Decree called for the creation of a regiment with a staff and five squadrons, each consisting of two companies of four officers and 120 men. (Articles 3 and 4.) Napoleon's ambitious plans called for admission to the Regiment to be limited to Polish (and specifically not Lithuanian) landowners and sons of landowners between the ages of 18 and 40 who could furnish at their own expense a horse and clothing and equipment of the prescribed model. (Article 5; see also Dundulis, p. 282)

Commanders *Formation to final transformation:* Brigade General Jan Konopka, the former commander of the *Lanciers de la Légion de la Vistule* (see separate entry) and then Major of the 1st (Polish) Light Horse Lancers of the Guard, was designated to command the new regiment by a decree dated 5 July 1812. (Reproduced in Dundulis, p. 283.) The Majors of the Regiment were Colonels Casimir Tanski and Joseph Chlusowicz, formerly commander of the 2nd Regiment of the Vistula Legion.

Operational History Napoleon's aspirations for this Regiment seem to have been realised for the most part, so there were a high percentage of aristocrats in its ranks. In particular, the Regiment recruited heavily from the students of the University of Vilna, who had been disappointed in their hope of providing a university honour guard for Napoleon. (Dundulis, p. 212; Chelminski, p. 233.) Napoleon took an active interest in the formation of the unit and made extra funds available to assist with fitting out the men, but things still proceeded rather too slowly from his point of view. Nevertheless, by early October two squadrons of the Regiment, led by General Konopka himself, were ready to join the main armies.

The combat history of this detachment was unexpectedly short and disastrous (see, generally, Chelminski, pp. 233–4). Although he is said to have been warned that a large Russian force was hunting for him, Konopka, who was under orders to reach Minsk as soon as possible, chose a leisurely itinerary that included a stop in the town of Slonim, where his family home was located. The column was even accompanied by Konopka's wife and those of Generals Dombrowski and Zayonchek. When Major Tanski objected to this behaviour, he was summarily dismissed and sent back to the Regimental depot.

At dawn the next day, 19 October, Konopka and his men were attacked by a force under Russian General Czaplic consisting of two regiments of foot chasseurs, the Pavlograd Hussars, a regiment of Cossacks and twelve pieces of horse artillery. Judging from the evidence of that Konopka, Chlusowicz and sixteen other officers were wounded (including one mortally), the Regiment put up a spirited resistance, but the outcome was unfavourable. The Russians captured Konopka himself, thirteen officers, 235 NCOs and men and the regimental treasury. Amazingly, the three wives escaped by crossing a river on a raft while their frustrated Cossack pursuers looked on.

General Langeron, a French emigré serving in the Russian Army, records in his memoirs that Konopka failed to post any sentinels and send out any patrols while he was at Slonim. He concludes that such an oversight was so inexplicable on the part of such an experienced officer that it lends credence to a theory that Konopka had overspent the regimental funds and saw no way out of scandal other than to let himself be captured. (Langeron, p. 28.)

Final Transformation The men who escaped from Slonim and those still forming at Grodno comprised a force of about 500 men. These remained under the command of

Major Tanski until they were incorporated into the 1st Light Horse Lancers by a decree dated 12 March 1813.

Uniforms According to its Organisational Decree, the 3rd Regiment was supposed to wear the same uniform as the 1st, or Polish, Lancers of the Guard, except that the buttons of the 3rd were to be yellow metal rather than white (Article 9). This meant that the lace of the Regiment was also yellow instead of white (gold instead of silver in the case of the officers). The wealth of the men recruited for the Regiment contributed to uniforms of very fine quality. General Langeron declared in his journal that the unit 'was composed for the most part of young men from the grandest families of Lithuania and Volhnya; it is impossible to give an idea of the richness and elegance of their uniforms and the beauty of their horses.' (Langeron, p. 23.)

Standard Regnault (p. 186) notes that one Russian source (Heckel) claims that the Eagle of the 3rd Lancers was captured at Slonim. He refutes that claim with the statement that no Eagle was granted to the Regiment prior to the action at Slonim. He also points out that neither the original report of General Czaplic nor that of his superior, Admiral Chichagov, mentions anything about a standard, which would presumably have been an important highlight if a capture had occurred. Andolenko (p. 193) comes to the same conclusion using most of the same facts, but he also bases his argument on the conclusion that the Eagle trophy attributed by the Russians to the 3rd Guard Lancers was in fact the Eagle of the 3rd Light Horse Lancers of the Line.

Chevau-légers Polonais de la Garde

(Polish Light Horse of the Guard; also known after 1809 as the *Chevau-légers Lanciers Polonais*)

Date of Creation The unit was created by a decree dated 6 April 1807 (Chelmisnki, pp. 223–5).

Circumstances of Creation The creation of the Polish Light Horse of the Guard satisfied two important Napoleonic objectives: it tapped into the patriotic fervour of an oppressed people to promote French goals; and it associated the new Bonaparte dynasty with some of the oldest aristocratic families in Europe. By all accounts, the rank-and-file of the Regiment were just as much aristocrats as the officers, a circumstance that in fact made the regiment hard to discipline and train. (Masson, pp. 286–7.)

Composition The Regiment of Light Horse was initially divided into a staff and four squadrons of two companies each. (Organisational Decree, Article 2.) A unique feature was that the Regiment had a 'Colonel Commandant' and two French Majors chosen from the Guard in addition to four squadron chiefs. (Organisational Decree, Article 4.) The Regiment was recruited exclusively from landowners and sons of landowners between the ages of 18 and 40 who could defray the cost of their own uniforms, equipment and horses. (Organisational Decree, Article 5.)

The establishment remained the same until 12 March 1812, when a fifth squadron was added. (Decision, Nap. O&A, No 5791, Vol. 4, p. 213.) The Regiment was reorganised on 12 March 1813 to incorporate the remains of the 3rd Light Horse Lancers and the Lithuanian Tatars. This gave the unit a strength of six squadrons (three forming part of the Old Guards and three of the Middle Guard), plus the company of Tatars (which also qualified as part of the Middle Guard). As Napoleon's need for cavalry increased, a seventh squadron was added by a decree dated 25 June 1813. On 9 December 1813 the Regiment was reduced to four squadrons and the excess officers and men were used to form the *Régiment d'Éclaireurs à Cheval de la Garde No 3* (see separate entry). The Tatars were attached to the 3rd Scouts.

Commanders *Formation to final transformation:* General Vincent Corvin Krasinski (1782–1856). The Polish Light Horse was one of the few Napoleonic units to preserve the same commander during the entirety of its existence. Like many of his peers, Krasinski fought against the partitioning powers in 1792–94, but, unlike many, he chose to remain in Poland when the fighting ended rather than to go into exile. He eagerly embraced the French cause when the latter arrived in Warsaw in December 1806, and he was commissioned as a colonel of one of the new cavalry regiments formed by Dombrowski at that time. He found favour with Napoleon because of the prominence of his family, and was appointed to be colonel of the Polish Light Horse on 7 April 1807; he preserved that command even after he was promoted to the rank of Brigade General on 16 December 1811 and then General of Division on 28 November 1813. (For a description and depictions of his uniform, see Rigo, *Le Plumet*, Print No 25, 'Garde Impériale, 1er Régiment de Chevau-légers Lanciers Polonais, Colonel Major 1813'.) He was wounded at Borodino, Freyburg and Arcis-sur-Aube in 1813–14. He was also the nominal author of the manual adopted by the French Army in 1811 to teach cavalry how to handle lances. (See *Essai sur le Maniement de la Lance* [Paris, 1811].)

After Krasinski's first promotion, the Regiment was typically commanded in the field by one or more of its Majors, all of whom ranked as Colonels of the line:

Antoine Charles Bernard Delaitre (1776–1838), who commanded the Mameluke squadron before joining the Polish Light Horse and who became Colonel of the 7th Mounted Chasseurs on 27 January 1811.

Pierre Dautancourt (1771–1832), a consummate organiser who was named Brigade General on 28 November 1813 but nevertheless remained with the Poles.

Jan Konopka (see separate entry for *Chevau-Léger Lanciers de la Garde No 3*).

Prince Dominque Radziwill (1786–1813), who joined the unit on 27 October 1812 from command of the Polish 8th Lancers he had raised at his own cost. He died unexpectedly on 11 November 1813, apparently from internal injuries suffered at, but not recognised as serious during, the Battle of Hanau. His portrait can be found in Tranié, p. 124.

Jean Leon Hippolyte Kozietulski (1781–1821). The Polish Light Horse was the first and only unit he served in, although he did act as Major of the affiliated *Régiment d'Éclaireurs à Cheval de la Garde* in 1814. His portrait can be found in Tranié, p. 38.

Jean Paul Jerzmanowski (1779–1862), who had served in both the Polish Legions and the Grand Army before joining the Light Horse as a Captain. He became a Squadron Chief in February 1811 and a Major only on 15 March 1814. He was the commander of the Elba Squadron of Polish Lancers that accompanied Napoleon into his first exile and later fought at Waterloo. His portrait can be found in Tranié, p. 157.

Operational History Except for a few individual officers and men, the Regiment did not play a role in the 1807 campaign. The 1st and 2nd Squadrons were organised sufficiently to proceed to France in September 1807, but the 3rd Squadron was unable to follow until January 1808. (Masson, p. 286.) The Regiment was posted to Chantilly and dazzled the local civilians wherever it went. Its stop-over in France was brief, however, since Napoleon decided to give his newest force some campaign experience by attaching the Light Horse to the forces sent to deal with the ruling family of Spain. The unit entered Spain early enough to be present at the insurrection of 2 May at Madrid, when Colonel Krasinski was wounded and thus became the unit's first casualty.

The unit's first formal experience of battle (and three officer casualties) came at the Battle of Medina del Rio Seco on 14 July 1808, when a force under Marshal Bessières routed the Spanish Army of Galicia. This action cleared the way for Napoleon's brother, Joseph Bonaparte, to proceed to Madrid to become enthroned as the King of Spain. Unfortunately, owing to the Spanish victory at Bailen that occurred only a short while later, Joseph's stay in his capital was extremely brief, as was that of the Poles: by the beginning of August they were back at the Ebro River, waiting for revenge.

The arrival of the veterans of the Grand Army and of the Emperor himself changed the balance of Peninsular affairs dramatically in favour of the French when the French counter-offensive began at the beginning of November. Although much of the Army viewed the unit with disdain because it had gained a position in the Imperial Guard without earning it, the Poles were deployed at headquarters on escort duty. In light of the weak resistance being put up by the Spanish armies, they did not at first see any action, but that circumstance changed abruptly on 30 November 1808 at the pass of Somosierra through the Guadarrama mountains on the road to Madrid. This was the last important geographic obstacle between Napoleon and the Spanish capital and the Spaniards had consequently pulled together a force of some 12,000 regulars and militia with sixteen pieces of artillery to make a stand at the summit.

Napoleon knew that his victorious veteran army could clear the position easily and began the day with a traditional infantry advance along both shoulders of the pass. By late morning, however, he had become irritated at the lack of progress. When Colonel (later General) Hippolyte Marie Guillaume Piré, one of Marshal Berthier's aides-de-camp, reported back that it was 'impossible' to proceed faster, the Emperor lost his temper. What happened next illustrates both the folly and the grandeur of war: Napoleon turned to the single squadron of Polish Light Horse then serving as his personal escort (which happened to be the 3rd Squadron, composed of the 3rd and 7th companies) and ordered them to break through the heart of the enemy position.

(Niegolweski, p. 11.) The possibility of success was extremely slight, but, like a later band of cavaliers in a similar position, Squadron Chief Jean Kozietulski and his men of the 3rd Squadron of the Light Horse understood that it was not their job to 'reason why'. They simply formed into a column of fours and set off up the pass, accompanied by General Pierre Montbrun and Colonel Piré. (The best source of information about the charge is Niegolewski's monograph on the subject, but the collection of first-hand accounts of the action found in Balagny, Vol. 3, pp. 429–60, is very helpful, as is the historiography of the action presented in Kujawski, pp. 64–179.)

The Spanish position consisted of four separate artillery batteries arrayed at intervals along the single road leading to the summit of the pass, each one of which was flanked by supporting infantry (see map in Kujawski, p. 158). The strength of this formidable position was further enhanced by the fact that the road crossed a number of mountain rivulets, so the attacking force was periodically forced to navigate narrow bridges along the way. It was just after having crossed the first of these that Kozietulski went down when his horse was killed and his leaderless men took temporary refuge from the enemy fire in a fold in the road. Napoleon was now in an even worse mood because enemy skirmishers had sent a few shots in his direction, so he had no patience when he received word of this rebuff. Even though some of his generals still argued for a change of orders, the Emperor simply exclaimed: 'It is impossible that my Guard could be stopped by armed peasants'. (Ségur, Vol. 1, p. 429.) He then called on one of his staff officers, Count Philippe de Ségur, to ride forward and reiterate his order to the Poles to charge home immediately at all costs. There was no ignoring the message carried by Ségur. Trumpets blaring, the Light Horse squadron, now led by Captain Jean Dziewanowski, came racing out of its covered position shouting 'Forward, long live the Emperor!' (Niegolewski, pp. 27–8.) The behaviour of the Light Horse under such circumstances elicited a backhand compliment from Colonel Marbot: 'The Poles have only one good quality, but that they possess to the fullest measure—they are very brave.' (Marbot, p. 275.)

Miraculously, the charge succeeded. Each battery exacted a price, but none was able to stop the impetus of the Poles. As the men in front fell, the ones behind took their place, sabring Spanish gunners as they went. The Spanish infantry peppered the column from the flank, but seems to have been stunned by the audacity and speed of the attack. This was not a controlled charge; it was, rather, a disorganised race to the summit of the pass in which only speed mattered. At one point Lieutenant Rowicki called out to his comrade André Niegolewski: 'Stop my horse—I have lost control.' Niegolewski replied: 'Give him his head!' (Niegolewski, p. 30.) Captain Dziewanowski was struck down after the third battery by a cannon ball that killed his horse and broke his leg. Ségur, the only Frenchman who participated in the charge (Montbrun and Piré having detached themselves at some point), got to within thirty paces of the last guns, but was then shot in the side and forced to dismount and take cover behind some rocks by the side of the road. (Ségur, Vol. 1, p. 432.) At last, however, Lieutenant Niegolewski,

Maréchal des Logis Sokolowski and a handful of troopers reached the summit of the pass and scattered the defenders of the fourth battery. Their moment of triumph was, however, neither sweet nor long.

As he reined in his exhausted and wounded horse for the first time since the start of the charge, Lieutenant Niegolewski asked his NCO about the whereabouts of the rest of his men. 'They are dead,' came the grim reply. The Lieutenant soon noticed some enemy artillerymen starting to rally, so he led his men against this new threat. Sokolowski was killed and the troopers scattered in this fight, so Niegolewski found himself alone when his horse was killed and he fell to the ground, unable to defend himself. He later recalled the vivid memory of having two Spaniards put their muskets to his head and fire, but he miraculously survived those shots and the nine bayonet wounds that followed. His ordeal ended only when the remaining Spaniards were chased away by the arrival of the rest of the Light Horse Regiment and some squadrons of the Guard Chasseurs that Napoleon had launched up the pass in the wake of the first heroic band. (Niegolewski, pp. 30–1.) Napoleon himself arrived at the summit before Niegolewski was evacuated and awarded the grievously wounded officer a Legion of Honour decoration on the spot. (Niegolewski, p. 33.)

Niegolewski's testimony, backed by accounts of other eyewitnesses, confirms that men of the 3rd Squadron actually reached their objective, but the human price of that triumph was high, although perhaps not as high as one would expect given the difficulty of the task. The 3rd Squadron probably mustered between 125 and 150 men at the start of the day, not including officers. (Balagny, Vol. 2, p. 424, n. 2.) Of these, 57 were killed or wounded by enemy fire, while 24 more were injured in falls. (Balagny, Vol. 2, p. 422.) Of the seven other Polish officers who took part in the charge, three were killed outright (Lieutenants Rowicki, Rudowski and Kryzanowski) and four were wounded, including one mortally (Captain Dzieswanowski). There are no figures available as to the losses suffered by the Spanish defenders, but in any event their morale was shattered, as evidenced by the fact that the trailing squadrons of Guard cavalry hardly suffered any losses at all during their transit of the pass. The Spaniards subsequently turned upon their own leaders and killed the General who had been in command of the position.

Napoleon never explained why he decided to assign the men of the 3rd Squadron such a foolhardy and dangerous task. Perhaps he was testing the Poles; perhaps he was indulging in the whim of an absolute ruler to demonstrate his power of life and death over his subjects. In any event, what he gave the Light Horse in return was lasting fame. As the next Bulletin declared (Bulletin of the Army of Spain, 2 December 1808, Nap. *Corr.*, No 14524, Vol. 18, pp. 87–8, at 88):

> The action [at Somosierra] was decided by a charge made by General Montbrun at the head of the Polish Light Horse of the Guard, a charge which was as brilliant as any ever made and in which the Light Horse regiment covered itself with glory and proved conclusively that it was worthy of being part of the Imperial Guard.

The Poles remained in Spain only a little longer than Napoleon, which means that they participated in the capture of Madrid and then the commencement of the chase after Sir John Moore's army at the end of December. They were ordered back to Paris at the beginning of February for rest and re-fitting (N. to Bessières, 11 February 1809, Nap. *Corr.*, No 14770, Vol.18, p. 258):

> You have received the order to send to Paris all of my Polish Light Horse, which I wish to reorganise. The zeal that they showed in Spain has made me decide to take an interest in this corps, which has need of a definitive organisation.

One of the points that interested the Emperor was that of the unit's armament. The Poles had traditionally been associated with the lance as a weapon of war, and most of the cavalry formed for the Duchy of Warsaw had been organised as lancers (also known in German as 'uhlans'). The Light Horsemen, however, were initially armed only with sabres, pistols and carbines. When he returned from Spain, Napoleon decided that he wanted to have lancers in the French Army as well, so he issued orders for the Polish Light Horse to armed and trained with lances as soon as they returned from the Peninsula. (N. to General Walther, 26 February 1809, Nap. *Corr.*, No 14819, Vol. 18, p. 291.) There is no indication, however, that this order was carried out before the Light Horse departed for the campaign against Austria.

The Light Horse saw little action during the fighting in Bavaria during the early stages of the 1809 campaign. They were, however, fully engaged at the main battles of Aspern/Essling and Wagram. Only part of the unit participated in the former action, but it still lost one officer and six men killed and one officer and 30 men wounded. (Tranié, p. 56.) The whole Regiment was present at Wagram, where one officer and some twelve men were killed and twelve officers and 80 men were wounded (one of the officers mortally).

On 6 July 1809, the last day of Wagram, the Poles found themselves charging the uhlans of Schwarzenberg and the Dragoon of La Tour. Major Delaitre was very near-sighted and had failed to see that a charge on the nearer of the enemy units would put leave the Regiment's flank exposed to the other. Squadron Chief Kozietulski, of Somosierra fame, compensated for the error in time and the Poles routed the enemy cavalry, capturing 150 men and the regimental commander, Prince Auersberg. One observer theorised that the Austrian prisoners had given up easily because they were conscripted Poles who welcomed an opportunity to escape Hapsburg service. (Chlapowski, pp. 185–6.)

It is often written that the Poles were given their lances in honour of their victory over the uhlans but, as noted above, Napoleon had already made that decision before the campaign started. The primary source that supports the more colourful story can be found in J. M. Chevalier, *Souvenirs des Guerres Napoléoniennes* (Paris, 1970), the memoirs of a Guard Chasseur:

> There, the Poles and my regiment made a brilliant charge. We overthrew a regiment of uhlans . . . It was a pleasure to see our brave Poles, who were not at that time armed with lances, seize the lances of the Austrian lancers and use them against their former owners.

In any event, in the weeks and months following the unit's return to France at the of 1809, the Poles received their new armament and were re-designated '*Chevau-légers Lanciers*'. When the Dutch Light Horse Lancers were added to the Guard in 1810, the designation 'First' was added to the regimental title.

At the start of 1810 Napoleon apparently gave serious thought to returning to the Peninsula to finish the subjugation of Spain and Portugal for once and for all. That event never came about, of course, but the mere possibility led to two squadrons of Lancers under Major Delaitre being detached in April 1810 for service in the Peninsula as part of a Guard cavalry brigade under General Louis Lepic. During their eighteen months of Peninsular exile, the Poles were engaged primarily in anti-guerrilla service in northern Spain while the rest of the Regiment, which stayed in Paris, dealt with nothing more strenuous than the celebrations associated with Napoleon's marriage and then, a year later, with the birth of his son. The detachment in Spain was present at the Battle of Fuentes de Oñoro on 3–5 May 1811, but a lack of orders at a crucial stage of the action prevented the Guard cavalry from playing any significant role in that action.

All the squadrons of the Regiment were reunited for the Russian campaign. The memoirs of Squadron Chief Desiré Chlapowski provide first-hand details of the services of the Light Horse in that campaign, which were invariably more painful than glorious. With respect to the 'easy' part of the campaign before Borodino, he writes of skirmishes with Cossacks, bad weather, dysentery and lack of forage for the horses. In particular, he noted that the Cossacks had longer lances than the Poles, 'but did not handle them as well'. (Chlapowski, p. 259.) At Borodino, the Regiment had to endure enemy artillery fire all day long, but never executed a charge.

After Borodino, the Poles were generally brigaded with the Dutch Lancers of the Guard under the command of General Edouard Colbert. Chlapowski recalls, perhaps with some bias, that the Poles were more proficient at their duties than the Emperor's Dutchmen and, in particular, were better able to contend with sudden attacks by Cossacks. After a post of the Red Lancers was surprised and captured, Colbert made certain that the men from the two regiments were paired for outpost duty. (Chlapowski, p. 272.) General Colbert once even tried to use the failings of the Dutch Lancers as a ploy to defeat a force of Cossacks (Chlapowski, pp. 283–4):

> The Dutchmen were less adroit than our men and did not know how to defend themselves against Cossacks. Every time they were in the rearguard they would lose a few men, and the Cossacks were becoming increasingly bold in attacking them.
>
> One day General Colbert ordered a squadron of Poles to swap their white cloaks for blue Dutch ones. The Poles were then left as the rearguard of the brigade in the early morning before it grew light in order to bait the Cossacks into action. When the Cossacks arrived on the scene they saw the blue cloaks and advanced courageously and

> quickly, thinking that they faced only Dutchmen. But as soon as our squadron advanced confidently to meet them, they recognised their error and retreated, crying 'These are Poles!'

The Poles were used exclusively as escorts for Napoleon during the retreat, so they did not fight in any of the major engagements. They did, however, see some hard fighting, as was the case when a cloud of Cossacks surprised the Emperor's entourage on 25 October. The duty squadron of Poles under Kozietulski, reinforced by a handful of staff officers, barely managed to protect the Emperor until reinforcements arrived to chase the Cossacks away. (Chlapowski, pp. 281–2.) The most important service the Poles provided in the end was the escort for the first leg of Napoleon's journey when he abandoned his army to return to Paris. According to Chlapowski, 422 officers and men were still with the Regiment when it re-crossed the Niemen River at the end of the retreat. This was more men than could be found in the other four cavalry regiments of the Guard combined. (Chlapowski, pp. 298–9.)

Given the overall shortage of cavalry in the French Army following the Russian campaign, the Poles of the Guard were required to play an extraordinarily active role in the fighting in 1813. For a start, the veteran core of the regiment was supplemented by the amalgamation of the *3e Chevau-légers Lanciers* into the 1st Regiment on 22 March (Pigeard, *Troupes Polonaises*, p. 27) and a draft of 500 survivors from General Dombrowski's division of the army of the Grand Duchy of Warsaw. These expedients enabled Napoleon to field ten squadrons, or two full regiments, of Polish Lancers, and he made liberal use of them in the absence of other experienced cavalry. (Chlapowski, p. 305.) At the Battle of Bautzen, for instance, the Poles were used to escort the Emperor at daybreak, reinforce the main battle line during the day and then send out patrols at night to protect the French infantry from attacks by the superior Allied cavalry. (Grabowski, p. 57.)

In the autumn campaign, the Poles particularly distinguished themselves at the Battles of Dresden, Leipzig and Hanau. They also had success in smaller actions. Shortly after the Battle of Kulm, the Polish Light Horse encountered the Prussian hussar regiment commanded by the son of Marshal Blücher. When the younger Blücher imprudently advanced ahead of his unit, he was captured by a *Maréchal des Logis Chef* from the Lancers. The Emperor wanted to give the NCO the Legion of Honour for the feat, but General Krasinski refused, saying that the soldier was unworthy since he had robbed Colonel Blücher of his watch and medals. (Grabowski, pp. 119–20.) Captain Ambroise Skarzynski, an officer known for his extraordinary strength and courage, distinguished himself on two occasions. Once he challenged a Cossack officer to single combat and dispatched him with a single sabre stroke; another time, he was chasing a better mounted enemy officer and resorted to throwing a lance like a javelin in order to bring down his quarry. (Grabowski, pp. 182–3; his portrait appears in Tranié, p. 141.)

The split of the Polish Lancers into two units in December 1813 (see separate entry on the *Éclaireurs*) did nothing to diminish the use of the Poles in action in 1814. At Château-Thierry, one Polish squadron captured an entire Prussian battalion. At Montereau they cleared a bridge at the gallop and dispersed an enemy force. They accomplished that same feat at Berry au Bac, this time led by newly promoted Squadron Chief Skarzynski, who grabbed a Cossack lance and used that weapon in preference to his sabre. The men from the depot of the Regiment even furnished a detachment that joined in the defence of Paris on 30 March. (Tranié, pp. 129, 134 and 143–4.)

Final Transformation After Napoleon abdicated, the Poles were released from duty, but a fair number volunteered to accompany the Emperor to Elba. He formed these volunteers into the Elba Squadron, which provided the core of the reorganised regiment that fought in the Waterloo campaign.

Uniforms The most complete and reliable treatment of the distinctive blue and light crimson uniforms of the Polish Light Horse is that provided by Lucien Rousselot's trilogy of plates on the unit—No 47 on the rank-and-file, No 65 on the Trumpeters and No 75 on the officers. Two useful adjuncts to that source are the contemporary illustrations in Pétard's 'Lancier Polonais' (including a colour reproduction of Martinet's print of the magnificent kettle drummer of the Regiment) and the many portraits in Tranié. Rather than compete with such information, this study will deal with the uniforms of this unit by providing a translation of a detailed description of the subject written in 1848 by General Joseph Zaluski, an officer who served in the Light Horse. His description, which is the most comprehensive discussion of uniforms ever committed to writing by a Napoleonic veteran, is as follows (quoted in Vanson, 'Chevau-légers', at pp. 16–19):

> In the beginning, when the volunteers who formed the unit had more taste for elegant uniforms than they had military experience, two versions of uniform were adopted—a white one for parades and a dark blue one for service wear. For officers, there were also two versions of service dress—*grande tenue* (full dress) and *petite tenue* (ordinary dress). Full dress featured a Polish-style jacket, or 'kurtka,' while ordinary dress featured a French-style jacket or frock coat. Ordinary dress could also include a surtout [single-breasted jacket] for an officer or a vest for a trooper, not to speak of overcoats and other complementary items of clothing. . .
>
> Everyone in the Regiment wore a Polish bonnet (czapska [*sic*]) of ribbed crimson cloth with a yellow metal shako plate in the shape of a half sun with a silver centre decorated with a golden letter 'N' surmounted by a golden crown.
>
> All the trim on the czapska was silver for officers, mixed silver and crimson for non-commissioned officers and white for Corporals and private soldiers. The same held true for epaulettes and aiguilettes; these latter were a distinctive feature of the uniforms of Guard cavalry units and gendarmes.
>
> The edging of the visor, the chinscales and other metallic accessories were silver for officers and silver plate for the troops. On parade, everyone wore superb white plumes of ostrich or cock feathers. Superior officers up to the grade of Squadron Chief (inclusive) had a crimson velvet czapska with silver trim and a plume of heron feathers.

On the march, all these frills disappeared or were covered over except for the epaulettes and aiguilettes. In such circumstances, the czapska was covered with black waxed cloth.

These same czapski were worn on parade with white kurtkas with crimson lapels richly embroidered with silver thread and crimson trousers with silver stripes.

For balls, the French-style jackets were also white with crimson facings and the same embroidery as the kurtka.

The marvellous white uniforms were adopted while half the Regiment was still in Warsaw and before it had its first combat experience in Spain at Madrid on 2 May1808 and at [Medina del] Rio Seco on 14 July. Once it became clear that the unit would spend more time on campaign and at war than it would in salons and at court, the splendid white uniform was abandoned and replaced for parade dress by on consisting of a dark blue kurtka with crimson facings and dark blue trousers with crimson stripes. The lapels of all grades of officer were ornamented with a fine silver embroidery . . . [in the form of three thin parallel silver lines and a fourth wavy line around the mid-stripe]; while those of NCOs and simple troopers had a small line of silver lace. For parades, the lapels were folded back and closed over the wearer's chest and stomach by hooks; officers wore a sash of silver and crimson silk. For service and travel wear, the lapels would be arranged to hide the facing colour, and overalls lined with leather were worn. As part of these changes, crimson trousers came to be worn only by superior officers and only as an optional item.

All belting, that is to say the sabre belt, the cartridge box belt, etc., was of white leather that was carefully tended. These objects were made of silver cloth lined with red moroccan leather for officers. The cloaks and surtouts of officers were made of dark blue cloth; their fatigue caps were square-shaped, crimson *confederatkas* [a Polish headdress made popular during the uprising of the Confederation of the Bar] trimmed with black fleece. The cloaks for the troopers were white with crimson collars and their fatigue caps were the standard French type in the three 'Polish' colours.

In the early days of the unit, the trumpeters were dressed entirely in crimson with silver and white trim but, much later, they received white czapskas with red plumes and white kurtkas with crimson facings; the other details of their uniforms were the same as for the other ranks. They rode white horses with crimson saddle cloths ornamented on each side in front with a crowned 'N' and in the rear with a crowned eagle. The rest of the regiment used blue saddlecloths trimmed with crimson with the same ornaments in silver for officers and white for the troopers.

The leatherwork of the regiment's bridles and harnesses was decorated with metal ornaments and the portmanteaus were crimson.

This ensemble of uniforms had an impressive effect, particularly when the regiment was massed for reviews. No other regiment of the Guard looked quite so striking. . . . The appearance of the regiment became even more attractive when it began to carry lances with decorative white and crimson pennons.

There are several surviving examples of uniforms of the Polish Light Horse in the Polish Army Museum in Warsaw. The most important for research purposes are a full uniform of a Light Horse officer with crimson trousers and one of an NCO. (The best photograph of the latter uniform can be found in Zygulski, p. 192; Pigeard, *Troupes Polonaises*, p. 25 has photographs of both, but the colour is poor.) There is also a fascinating child-size officer's uniform that was made for the son of General Krasinski.

(Zygulski, p. 195; see also the portrait of Krasinski's son wearing this uniform that appears in Tranié, p. 74.)

A number of regimental czapkas have survived as well. Based on that evidence, it seems that the first model of czapka worn by the Light Horse was taller and had a different plate than later versions. (Compare Zygulski No 84 with Nos 82, 83 and 86–88.) It is also possible to see the difference between the elegant headwear of senior officers and the less well constructed czapkas of regimental privates. (See, for example, photographs of General Krasinski's czapka in Gembarzewski, p. 310; the original is now in the Sikorski Institute in London.) Zaluski's recollections also provide interesting detail about the cockade worn by the Poles on their czapkas (quoted in Vanson, 'Chevau-légers', at p. 19):

> Since we were entirely in the pay of the French Army, our regiment wore French cockades. However, in memory of the Confederation of the Bar, we all put Maltese Cross ornaments, our national emblem, on the cockades. These crosses were silver for officers and white metal for other ranks.

The Polish Army Museum also has an example of the type of soft cap worn by Light Horse officers when they were off duty. (See illustration in Zygulski, p. 194.) Some members of the Light Horse made temporary use of a very unusual headdress during the short time the unit spent in Spain. On 30 December 1808 a detachment of Light Horse captured some 40 busbies ('very beautiful fur caps') from the 10th Hussars of Sir John Moore's British army in Spain. These were immediately distributed to the men whose czapskas were especially dilapidated and worn happily by the recipients until the Light Horse returned to France. (Balagny, Vol. 4, p. 33, n. 1, citing notes of General Dautancourt.)

Standard Despite the special interest taken by Napoleon in the Regiment of Light Horse, the unit did not receive an Eagle (with an 1804-pattern colour) until 30 June 30 1811, and then it received only one. (Tranié, p. 172 and Charrié, p. 181; see also Rigo, *Le Plumet*, Plate No 36, 'Garde Imperial: 1er Régiment de Chevau-légers Lanciers, Étendard 1811–1813'.) The text of the colour referred to the '*Chevau-Légers Lanciers*'. In April 1813 the colour was replaced with one of the new 1812 pattern. There is no primary source that provides information about the number and identity of the battle honours of the Regiment listed on the colour. (Tranié, p. 173.) Neither the Eagle nor this later standard were carried in action during 1813 or 1814. (Tranié, p. 173.) Perhaps because of this restriction, the Light Horse seems to have carried some unofficial flags, or fanions, on campaign. One of these, designated the Colonel's fanion, was a white silk swallow-tail pennon the same size and shape as those for the troop. It was decorated with a white Polish eagle on a crimson six-pointed star in a light blue circle on the obverse and a silver 'N' on a five-pointed star in a crimson circle within a light blue circle on the reverse. The central medallions were also adorned with numerous legends in Polish. (See illustration in Tranié following p. 159.)

Compagnies de Déserteurs Étrangers

(Foreign Deserter Companies)

These ephemeral units were created over a fifteen-month period from 1803 to 1804. In general, no specific information has been found about the fate of these Companies, but Napoleon once expressed the view that such independent companies of foreign deserters should ultimately be combined into battalions of five companies each, so it is likely that they were all incorporated into other, larger units. (N. to Berthier, 6 Thermidor Year XI (25 July 1803), Nap. *Corr.*, No 6939, Vol. 8, pp. 414–15 at 415.)

1st Company

Date of Creation This unit was created by an order dated 3 Messidor Year XI (22 June 1803). (Index to SHA Carton X[h]1 in France, *Inventaire*, p. 220.)

Circumstances of Creation The Company was organised at Genoa. (*Ibid.*)

Composition No information found.

Commanders Captain Ursleur. (*Ibid.*)

Operational History This Company was moved the island of Elba by an order dated 15 Fructidor Year XI (2 September 1803). It was initially combined with the 2nd Foreign Battalion on Elba, but the Company eventually regained independent status pursuant to an order dated 21 Vendémiaire Year XII (14 October 1803).

Final Transformation No information found.

Uniforms No information found.

Standard No information found.

2nd Company

Date of Creation This unit was created by an order dated 3 Messidor Year XI (22 June 1803). (Index to SHA Carton X[h]1 in France, *Inventaire*, p. 220.) It was not actually organised, however, until the 1er Jour Complémentaire Year XI (18 September 1803).

Circumstances of Creation This Company was organised at Cremona. (*Ibid.*)

Composition No information found.

Commanders Captain Ostievka. (*Ibid.*)

Operational History This Company was moved the island of Elba by an order dated 15 Fructidor Year XI (2 September 1803). It was initially combined with the 2nd Foreign Battalion on Elba, but the Company eventually regained independent status pursuant to an order dated 21 Vendémiaire Year XII (14 October 1803). (*Ibid.*)

Final Transformation No information found.

Uniforms No information found.

Standard No information found.

3rd Company

Date of Creation This unit was created by an order dated 6 Frimaire Year XII (20 November 1803). (Index to SHA Carton X[h]1 in France, *Inventaire*, p. 220.)
Circumstances of Creation The Company was organised at Cremona. (*Ibid.*)
Composition No information found.
Commanders Captain Strazewski. (*Ibid.*)
Operational History No information found.
Final Transformation No information found.
Uniforms No information found.
Standard No information found.

4th Company

Date of Creation No information found.
Circumstances of Creation No information found.
Composition No information found.
Commanders Captain Brodin. (Index to SHA Carton X[h]1 in France, *Inventaire*, p. 220.)
Operational History No information found.
Final Transformation This Company was incorporated into the 2nd Foreign Battalion on Elba pursuant to an order dated 15 Thermidor Year XII (3 August 1804).
Uniforms No information found.
Standard No information found.

Compagnies Franches Cantabres

(Volunteer Cantabrian Companies)

Date of Creation 9 April 1813.
Circumstances of Creation These units were created pursuant to a decree of General Bertrand Clausel, acting in his capacity as commander of the French Army of the North operating in the north of Spain, for service in the three provinces (Alava, Guipuzcoa and Vizcaya) comprising the 4th Military Government of the French occupation forces. (Aliana, pp. 75–7.) Enlistment was limited to natives of the relevant provinces, which also had to pay for the cost of raising these units.
Composition Clauzel's decree called for the creation of eight companies of volunteer infantry: two in Alava (one at Vitoria and the other at Salvatierra); three (including one of coast guards) in Guipuzcoa (one at Bargara, another at Tolosa and the coast guard company at Guetaria); and three companies (including one of coast guards) in Vizcaya (two at Bilbao and the coast guards at Portugaleto). (Organisational Decree, Article 3.) Each company was to be commanded by a Captain and composed of 149 officers and men.

Commanders No information found.
Operational History No information found.
Final Transformation No information found.
Uniforms Articles 5 and 9 of the Organisational Decree provide full details of the uniforms of these companies:
Coast Guard Companies: Shako; blue '*habite-veste*' and overalls; scarlet collar, cuffs and piping; yellow metal buttons marked with an anchor; and equipment as for the *Artillerie de la Marine*. (See Bueno, Plate 46.)
Infantry Companies: Shako; brown '*habite-veste*' and overalls; lapels, collar and cuffs of provincial facing colours (Alava–*aurore*; Guipuzcoa–field green; Vizcaya–scarlet); white metal buttons decorated with the provincial name; and equipment as for Spanish light infantry. (See Bueno, Plate 45.)
Standard No information found.

Demi-brigades Helvétiques (Nos 1–6)

(Helvetian Demi-brigades [Nos 1-6])

Date of Creation November 1798.
Circumstances of Creation The Directory of France passed a law on 30 November 1798 permitting the French Army to recruit an auxiliary corps of 18,000 volunteer Swiss soldiers. (Belhomme, Vol. 4, pp. 181-2.) The corps was organised into six so-called 'Helvetian' Demi-brigades, uniformed, equipped and paid for by the French government.
Composition Each Demi-brigade had three battalions, and each battalion had nine companies.
Commanders
1st Helvetian Demi-Brigade *Creation to January 1800:* No information found. *January 1800–20 August 1805:* Colonel François Dominique Perrier (1746-820).
2nd Helvetian Demi-Brigade *Creation to May 1799:* No information found. *May 1799–6 May 1805:* Colonel Béat Louis de Watteville, who was removed from command because of unspecified irregularities. *6 May 1805 to disbandment:* Louis Clavel, who had been the colonel of the 3rd Swiss line battalion incorporated into the 1st Demi-brigade in 1803 (Schaller, p. 27) and who went on to command the 4th Battalion of the 1st Swiss Regiment (see separate entry).
3rd Helvetian Demi-Brigade *Creation to January 1800:* No information found. *January 1800 to disbandment:* Colonel Raguettly (1756-1812), who started his military career as a cadet in the Bourbon Regiment. He became the commander of the 1st Swiss Regiment (see separate entry).
4th–6th Helvetian Demi-brigades No information found.
Operational History The Helvetian Demi-brigades were formed relatively quickly and

were assigned for 1799 to General (later Marshal) Masséna's Army of Switzerland. On 1 August 1799 the Grenadier companies of the 1st and 2nd Demi-brigades were combined into the 7th Battalion of an élite, all-Grenadier division formed by Masséna (Belhomme, Vol. 4, p. 204.) that fought in the Second Battle of Zürich along with the rest of the 1st and 2nd Demi-brigades and a detachment of the 4th. The special Grenadier division was disbanded in December.

In January 1800, just after Napoleon came to power, the number of Demi-brigades was cut in half. The 1st and 2nd Demi-brigades were combined to form the new 1st Demi-brigade, while the 3rd and 4th Demi-brigades and 5th and 6th Demi-brigades underwent similar amalgamations. This process resulted in some unemployed soldiers, and these were formed into four battalions (three line and one light) that were then transferred back into the pay of the Swiss government as a small national army. (Belhomme Vol. 4, p. 213.) Following this reorganisation, the Demi-brigades were assigned to the General Sainte-Suzanne's division of the Lower Rhine of the Army of the Rhine, with an average strength over 700 men per unit. (Picard, *Hohenlinden*, p. 391.)

After peace came to the Continent in 1801, the Helvetian Demi-brigades served in a number of scattered garrison locations. In January 1803, attrition forced another reorganisation. Ironically, this time the January 1800 methodology was reversed and the units of the Swiss national army that had been created from the Demi-brigades were used to bring them back to acceptable strength. The 3rd Swiss line battalion was incorporated into the 1st Demi-brigade, the light battalion became part of the 2nd Demi-brigade and the 1st and 2nd line battalions were transformed into the 3rd battalion of the 3rd Demi-brigade. (N. to Berthier, 20 Germinal Year XI (10 April 1803, N. *Corr.*, Vol. 8, No 6677, pp. 274–5 at 274.)

The 1st Demi-brigade subsequently spent a lot of time on the Atlantic coast, which explains how several companies from that unit came to be pressed into service as marines on board the vessels *Algésiras* and *Achille* for the naval campaign of 1805. They first sailed to the Caribbean, where 100 of their number were added to the garrison of Guadeloupe, then returned to Europe to participate in the Battle of Trafalgar. The claim that a Swiss musketball was the one that struck down Admiral Nelson must be ignored, however, because neither of the two ships named above was in action against HMS *Victory* at the relevant time. (Schaller, p. 26.)

One Swiss source states that the 2nd Demi-brigade served in General (later Marshal) Jean Lannes' vanguard division during the Marengo campaign, but no other source has been found to corroborate this possibility. (Schaller, p. 27.) The 3rd Demi-brigade spent a number of years in Corsica, from which location its 1st Battalion was shipped to Saint-Domingue on 20 January 1803. Only eleven men returned from that ill-fated expedition.

Final Transformation The Helvetian Demi-brigades were incorporated into the 1st Swiss Regiment in 1805. (See separate entry on *Régiments Suisses*.)

Uniforms The first uniform of the Demi-brigades was a blue jacket with red facings and yellow buttons, worn with a bicorne hat, blue vest and trousers, and black gaiters and belts. (Belhomme Vol. 4, p. 182.) By 1800 the prescribed dress had become more colourful and had the following details (*État Militaire pour An XI*):

> National Blue coat; yellow lapels and cuffs with red piping; green cuff-flap piped yellow; red collar with yellow piping; horizontal pockets with yellow piping; white lining; white vest and breeches; cockade in Swiss colours (red, yellow and green); headwear and footwear as for French infantry.

A figure (No 629) labelled '*Suizzero della 2e ½ Brigata*' from the Rovatti Manuscript in Modena, Italy, differs from this description in that the uniform depicted has a yellow collar with red piping, yellow shoulder straps trimmed blue, blue cuffs and red cuff flaps trimmed with yellow. There is no trim visible on the yellow lapels. The figure also appears to have one button on the collar on either side of its opening. Modern illustrations of the blue uniforms of the Helvetian Demi-brigades can be found in Tanconville's 1930 article in *Le Passepoil*, Roger Forthoffer's *Fiche Documentaire* No 240 and in *Le Plumet*, Plate No 234 by Rigo, which covers in particular the uniform of a Sergeant-Major of the 3rd Demi-brigade wearing a black top hat *à la* William Tell with a silver hat band and a wide brim that is turned up on the left side.

In 1803 the Demi-brigades regained the traditional red coats worn by Swiss troops in French service—a clear sign that the Revolutionary spirit had waned after more than a decade of turmoil. New distinctive colours were assigned as follows by an order dated 10 Germinal Year XI (31 March 1803) (*Journal Militaire An XI*, pt II, pp. 3–4):

> Article 1er. The three Helvetian Demi-brigades in the pay of the French Republic will wear the following uniform, namely:
>
> The First Demi-brigade, coat and collar of *garance*, white lapels and cuffs, blue trim.
> The Second Demi-brigade, coat and collar of *garance*, blue lapels and cuffs, white trim.
> The Third Demi-brigade, coat and collar of *garance*, yellow lapels and cuffs, sky blue trim.

The Rovatti MS has one illustration (No 268) of an unidentified figure that conforms perfectly to the colour scheme for the 1st Demi-brigade and one (No 267) that conforms to that for the 3rd. *Le Plumet*, No 75, illustrates a Sergeant-Major of the 3rd Demi-brigade with silver buttons and silver fringed epaulettes on both shoulders.

Standard In 1799, each Demi-brigade was given a colourful white, yellow, red and green flag with the appropriate unit number. Each colour had a central white space decorated with elaborate paintings. The decoration on the obverse of each colour was a tableau of drums, flags, cannon and munitions at the base of an oak tree, with the legend 'Freyheit Einheit Gleicheit' (Liberty, Unity and Equality) over the tableau, and 'Freundschaft Zwischen Dem Französischen Und Helvetischen Volk' (Friendship between the French and Swiss People) under it. The French translations of these phrases appeared elsewhere on the colour. On the reverse was a painting of William Tell embracing his son with the apple, split by Tell's arrow, still on his head. Above the picture were the words 'Valeur et Liberté'; below were the same words in German: 'Muth Und Freyheit 1308'.

The arrangement of the constituent colours on each of these flags was very complicated and, based on surviving sketches of the colours of the 3rd and 6th Demi-brigades, different for each unit, as was the case for the tricolour standards of the French Revolutionary armies. In the case of the 3rd Demi-brigade, whose colour is illustrated in *Le Plumet*, Plate No 234, the central white space was octagonal in shape and surrounded by a larger, squarer yellow octagon touching the first one at four points. Both these were encompassed in turn in another white octagon which did not touch the yellow octagon at any point. The remaining space on the flag was divided equally between red and green corners, with the green in the upper staff corner. The unit number was painted in gold in the coloured corners.

The original standards of the Helvetian Demi-brigades were so elaborate that they were very prone to damage from ordinary wear and tear. In June 1803 an inspector noted that 'the flags [of the 1st Demi-brigade] are in the worst possible state' (Charrié, p. 167.) In March 1805, each Demi-brigade was given a single Eagle apiece along with a new colour in the same pattern used by French line troops from 1805 to 1812. (Charrié. p. 167.) The flag of this type of the 3rd Demi-brigade is illustrated in *Le Plumet*, No 75. These colours were returned to Minister of War when the Demi-brigades were transformed into the *1er Régiment Suisse* (see separate entry), and that of the 1st and 3rd Demi-brigades ended up in Berlin before the Second World War. That of the 3rd Demi-brigade is noteworthy for having, in effect, a typographical error–the word '*et*' is repeated twice in the legend on the reverse of the flag.

Demi-brigades Polonaises (Nos 1–3)

(Polish Demi-brigades [Nos 1-3])

In 1802 the 3rd Polish Demi-brigade became the 113th Line Demi-brigade of the French Army and the 2nd Polish Demi-brigade became the 114th of the Line.

Date of Creation An Organisational Order was approved on 19 Frimaire Year X (10 December 1801) and was carried out over several different days in that month. (Organisational Order quoted in Pigeard, *Troupes Polonaises*, p. 13.)
Circumstances of Creation These units resulted from a reorganisation of the *Légion Polonaise d'Italie* and the *Légion de Danube* into three separate infantry demi-brigades, with the cavalry and artillery of the Danube Legion being detached to form an independent cavalry regiment (see *Lanciers Polonais*). (Belhomme, Vol. 4, p. 246.)
Composition The 1st Polish Demi-brigade was formed from Battalions 1-3 of the *Légion Polonais d'Italie*; the 2nd from Battalions 4-6 of the *Légion Polonais d'Italie*; and the 3rd from Battalions 1-4 of the *Légion de Danube*. The strengths of the Demi-brigades

were equalised by the distribution of the men of the 7th Battalion and the artillery company of the Polish Legion of Italy among the first two units. Each battalion had nine companies—eight of Fusiliers and one of Grenadiers.

Commanders

1st Polish Demi-brigade *Creation to final transformation:* Colonel Joseph Grabinski (1771–?), a native of Poland about whom little is known despite the fact that he was to command the 1st Polish Demi-brigade and its successor formations for nearly six years. He was promoted to the rank of Brigade General on 25 March 1807.

2nd Polish Demi-brigade *Creation to final transformation:* Colonel Vincent Axamitowski (1760–1820), who had served exclusively in artillery units before his appointment to command of the 2nd Demi-Brigade. (His portrait can be found in Pigeard, *Troupes Polonaises*, p. 62.) His service record in Six states that he served in Haiti, but that is almost certainly not the case. He went on to become a Brigade General in the Army of the Duchy of Warsaw and then that of France. Colonel Tomasz Zagorski (?–May 1803) seems to have been appointed to act as Colonel Axamitowski's deputy in the field when the unit sailed for the Caribbean. (Pachonski, p. 151.)

3rd Polish Demi-brigade *24 July 1801–26 September 1802:* Ladislas François Constantin Jablonowski (1769–1802) (see entry for *Légion de Danube*). He went on extended sick leave shortly after taking command and never exercised active control. He went to Haiti independently from his unit and was killed before it could be reunited with him. For the expedition to Haiti, a French colonel named Fortunat Bernard (1768–1802), a veteran of the Egyptian campaign, was given field command. (Pachonski, p. 75.)

Operational History

1st Polish Demi-brigade The 1st Demi-brigade was organised at Modena as part of the French Army, but by order of 1 Germinal Year X (22 March 1802) it was passed back into the pay of the Italian Republic (the successor to the Cisalpine Republic). In autumn 1802 the 1st Demi-brigade received the unwelcome news that it was to be sent to Haiti as part of another wave of reinforcements for the effort to subdue the insurgent slaves. Enough information about the fate of the 3rd Demi-brigade had made its way back to Europe by this time for the officers and men of the unit to have significant fear for the future. Their commander, Colonel Grabinski, threw himself into a furious lobbying effort, knowing that his life might literally depend on the outcome. Since the unit was still part of the army of the Cisalpine Republic, he directed most of his energy towards convincing the leaders of the Republic's government that they could not afford to lose the best unit in their army. His appeal worked and, with Napoleon's approval, the 2nd Demi-brigade was chosen as a substitute. (Pachonski, pp. 138–9.) As a letter from Captain Paul Fadzielski of the 1st Demi-brigade reveals, the soldiers involved had no illusions about the significance of the change (quoted in Pachonski, p. 140):

> Our good luck is another's ill-fortune . . . [The 2nd Demi-brigade will] leave the Fatherland behind, perhaps forever, in order to travel to empty countries to fight Negroes for their own sugar.

As an ironic twist, the depot of the 2nd Demi-brigade and assorted other survivors of the Haitian expedition were incorporated into the 1st Demi-brigade by an order dated 4 Ventose Year XII (24 February 1804). (Nap O&A, No 5328, Vol. 4, pp. 27–8.)

The 1st Demi-brigade had a strength of 88 officers and 2,512 men according to official returns dated September 1802. (Returns from Carton A * IV 1390 of the French National Archives, quoted in Frasca, 'Returns'.) The Demi-brigade, which was eventually relabelled as a regiment, fought in the autumn 1805 campaign against the Austrians in Italy and served with distinction at the battle of Castel-Franco on 23 November. In 1806 it participated in the French conquest of the Bourbon Kingdom of the Two Sicilies. The Poles were consequently present at the Battle of Maida on 4 July 1806, where, at least according to British sources, they were routed and lost nearly 250 men as prisoners to the 81st Regiment. (Oman, *Studies*, p. 58.) The unit remained in the pay of the Republic (then Kingdom) of Italy until August 1806, when it was transferred to the Neapolitan army formed for the new monarch, King Joseph Bonaparte.

2nd Polish Demi-brigade The 2nd Demi-brigade also had only a short stint in the French Army, being transferred back to the Italian Army early in 1802 as an economy measure. By September 1802 it had a strength of 90 officers and 2,854 men. (Returns from Carton A * IV 1390 of the French National Archives, quoted in Frasca, 'Returns'.) As noted above, the 2nd Demi-brigade was selected for duty in Haiti only after the 1st Demi-brigade was able to change Napoleon's original choice. The news of the decision was delivered to the men at Reggio on 16 December and the French took great pains to sweeten the bitter pill with the announcement that the unit was being readmitted to the French Army as the 114th Demi-brigade of the line. (Pachonski, p. 142–3.) This meant that the men were entitled to wear the French cockade and could be accorded French citizenship through naturalisation—a very important benefit for stateless exiles. They also received a 50 per cent pay increase for colonial service.

Some 2,500 men of the Demi-brigade sailed from Genoa on 27 January 1803, but several hundred were left behind for lack of transports. (For 260 of these, the reprieve was only temporary: another contingent of 260 men sailed on 27 May.) (Pachonski, p. 154.) The convoy was scattered by a storm, so the Demi-brigade arrived in Haiti in bits and pieces throughout the month of March. Once they were assembled, one of the first things that happened was that the survivors of the 3rd Polish Demi-brigade/113th Line Demi-brigade were incorporated into the newly arrived 114th. (Decision of 11 March 1803 reported in Pachonski, p. 169.)

The situation in the colony of Saint-Domingue that greeted the new arrivals was much different, and much less optimistic, than the one that had greeted the 3rd Polish Demi-brigade. General Leclerc had died of yellow fever in November 1802 and his successor, General Donatien Marie Joseph Rochambeau (1755–1813), the son of the man who had helped the United States win its freedom at Yorktown, did not have a coherent plan for dealing with all the warring factions. He contented himself with setting an example in terms of spectacular cruelty and licentiousness that further sapped the abysmal morale of the European troops on the French half of the island. Ironically, the Spanish colony of Santo Domingo on the other half of the island had experienced little domestic turmoil during the same period.

Rochambeau attempted some ambitious expeditions with the Poles of the 2nd/114th and other reinforcements in the months just after they arrived, but these produced few results other than Polish casualties and a growing antagonism between the Poles and the French. The French had learned so little in terms of tactics that on one occasion a company of Polish Grenadiers was unsuccessful in an attack on an insurgent post because no one had thought to supply them with the machetes necessary for them to clear a path through the jungle to their objective. (Pachonski, p. 165.) On another occasion an attack faltered because of a language barrier between the French and Polish troops involved. (Pachonski, p. 173.) The Poles also came in for criticism for lacking personal initiative and stamina for expeditions in mountainous terrain and for insisting on wearing the heavy uniforms and czapskas they had brought from Europe. (Pachonski, pp. 166 and 174.) The view of the French commanders is summed up in a letter from General Pierre Thouvenet (1757–1815) to the Minister of War dated 10 May 1803 (quoted in Pachonski, p. 178):

> These sluggish and apathetic people, foreign to our ways and language, at such a distance from their own country, lose all their energy here. Unable to endure the rigours of marching, and frightened by the dangers of an unfamiliar style of warfare, they are suitable only for garrison duty, and even this is a risky proposition unless other troops are present to serve with them: desertions to the enemy are not uncommon with them.

As a result of such views, the Poles gradually came to be used almost exclusively in defensive posts, although they did initiate occasional local offensives to obtain some limited objective. The Poles consequently found themselves divided up among a myriad posts ranging from small blockhouses to redoubts to purpose-built forts. All the while the local diseases, especially yellow fever, took a constant toll. According to a French colonist (quoted in Pachonski, p. 170):

> Two regiments [companies?] of Polish troops, in the service of France, were landed at Cape Tiburon, from aboard a French fleet. . . . Ten days after the landing of these two beautiful regiments, more than half their number were carried off by yellow fever; they fell down as they walked, the blood rushing out through their nostrils, mouths, eyes; they died without any apparent suffering. . . .

In such difficult circumstances, a sense of hopelessness pervaded the whole French war effort. In one particular case involving the Poles, that feeling became so prominent that it led to the suicide of a senior officer. Battalion Chief Jasinski, the commander of the 114th's 2nd Battalion, was so discouraged about the prospects for any successful outcome for his defence of a small fortified post in late June that he chose to take his own life rather than fight on. He sent the following last message to his commander (quoted in Pachonski, p. 192):

> General! The First Consul has rewarded the valiant Polish Legions that have shed so much blood for France for the French cause and have received from her enemies the irrefutable proof of their bravery—by sending them to San Domingo [*sic*]; but here too, fighting a savage, barbarous nation, they have shown ungrateful France that they fulfil their obligations. Seeing myself surrounded by more than 3,000 Negroes, I see no prospect of holding out with such a small detachment, and rather than fall into the hands of this savage people fighting for its own freedom, I am taking my own life.

The situation was grim even in the larger posts, and it became grimmer still after the Peace of Amiens ended and the British fleet clamped a close blockade on the island and began sending supplies to Dessalines' forces. The French-held cities and towns began to fall one by one, starting in August. General Philibert Fressinet (1767–1821), the commander of Jeremie, added shame to defeat by fleeing on ship with most of his garrison without telling the 400 or so Poles and other soldiers manning the town citadel. (*Ibid.*, pp. 208–9.) He and most of the ships were captured by the British, while the men left behind had no choice but to surrender to Dessalines. Surprisingly, they seem to have been treated relatively well, since the enemy General Ferrou seems to have had sympathy for the plight of the Poles. Some were sent on to Cuba in neutral ships. (*Ibid.*, pp. 210–13.) Many were taken into the British Army.

Port-au-Prince was evacuated on 9 October, and on 12 October the town of Les Cayes surrendered to the British after a long siege and blockade. (*Ibid.*, p. 223–4.) There was still some fighting to come, as the French, holding out in Le Cap, were subjected to heavy assaults by Dessalines' main forces on 16–18 November 1803. (*Ibid.*, pp. 230–1.) The commander tried to negotiate terms with the British, but this effort was unsuccessful. He loaded all his forces and their dependants on ships and tried to escape on 30 November, but all were captured by the British and taken to Jamaica as prisoners of war. The last French post in the country, Mole Saint-Nicolas, was evacuated on 4 December by sea, and the escaping French were able to mingle with the captured ships from Le Cap in such a way that most of them made it safely to Cuba.

3rd Polish Demi-brigade After more than twelve months of peacetime garrison duty in the Kingdom of Etruria, the more professional fighting men of the 3rd Demi-brigade might actually have welcomed a proper combat assignment, but the bulk of the men were probably dismayed when they learned in the spring of 1802 that Napoleon had decided to send the unit to Haiti as part of the expeditionary force under General Victor Leclerc that was intended to restore French rule (and slavery) in the colony of Saint-Domingue.

The Poles were concerned both about the prospect of leaving Europe and that of fighting against other men seeking to defend their homeland against an invader, but, as a practical matter, they had little to say about the decision. The 3rd Demi-brigade consequently set sail from Livorno on 17 May 1802 with a strength of roughly 2,500 officers and men. (Pachonski, p. 75.) As a reward for undertaking this arduous service, the Poles were granted the 'honour' of having their unit taken formally into the French

Army as the 113th Demi-brigade of the Line, so that they were no longer foreign troops as a technical matter. The unit's new status was confirmed by a decree of 15 Fructidor Year X (1 September 1802), but it never had much practical effect. (Pigeard, *Troupes Polonaises*, p. 14.)

The voyage was hideously long, since it took nearly two months to reach Cadiz and then, after a two week layover, over another month to reach Haiti. When they landed in early September, the men had been on board ship for such a long time that they did not make a good first impression on General Leclerc (L. to Minister of Naval Affairs, 26 Fructidor Year IX (13 September 1802), Leclerc, *Lettres*, No CXXVII, p. 226): 'The Polish Legion is naked, badly armed and has not been paid for many months.' Leclerc was so low on manpower, however, that the Poles were nevertheless sent into action immediately after their arrival. (Pachonski, p. 81.) The three battalions of Poles were assigned to different commands and had different experiences, although, in the end, not different fates.

The 1st Battalion became part of the Left Northern Division. (Pachonski, p. 87.) Its companies were generally committed to action by ones and twos, and the men suffered severely as they became acquainted with the harsh conditions and nightmarish circumstances of the bitter fighting among whites, blacks and mulattos. They did not perform well in those conditions (L. to N., 29 Fructidor Year IX (16 September 1802), Leclerc, *Lettres*, No CXXIX, p. 229): 'The Poles are brave but very slow and let themselves be killed by the blacks.' The single worst event was the loss of the 5th, 7th and 8th companies in a single expedition at the end of October. Two colonial demi-brigades in the same force went over to the enemy, forcing the Poles to take refuge in an isolated building. The popular report that all the men perished when the building was burned to the ground seems incredible, but it does seem certain that no survivors re-joined the French Army. (Pachonski, p. 90.) That loss completed the destruction of the 1st Battalion. By 3 November 1802 only 150 men were left under arms out of the 984 who had disembarked. These survivors were incorporated into the 74th Line Demi-brigade in December. (Pachonski, p. 90.)

The 2nd Battalion lasted considerably longer than the 1st. It was assigned to Mole Saint-Nicolas, an established post, so it was less involved in jungle forays. It became involved in controversy surrounding a massacre of black troops by French forces. Some sources conclude that the Poles refused to participate in this ignoble act, but others say the Poles were definitely, if not enthusiastically, involved. (Pachonski, pp. 102–8.) The Battalion was subsequently transferred to Port-au-Prince and thereafter split up into numerous detachments serving in numerous locations. By February 1803, the 2nd Battalion still had 20–25 officers and some 400 men. (Pachonski, p. 128.)

The 800-man 3rd Battalion was destroyed by combat and disease with the same astonishing rapidity as the 1st Battalion. As part of the Right Northern Division, it was constantly in action and suffered constant casualties. On 21 September the best part of the 3rd Company was forced to surrender after having become lost in the jungle, in part because the Captain, Sangowski, who knew little French, may have misunderstood his orders. The Captain managed to escape into the jungle, but not before he saw most of the captives tortured in a fiendish manner that was typical of the unnatural behaviour of both sides in this vicious war: '. . . they cut off their [the Poles'] ears and noses, gouged out their eyes and then singed them with fire . . .' (Pachonski, pp. 94–5.) The 7th Company was captured by a ruse on 18 October. Their commander was killed, but the men may have been recruited into Dessalines' Honour Guard, which is reputed to have included many Poles. (Pachonski, pp. 98–9, 105 and 131.) By 9 November the 3rd Battalion had only 96 men in action, with 180 in hospital. On 1 December the survivors were amalgamated into the 31st Line Demi-brigade. (Pachonski, p. 100.)

Final Transformation

1st Polish Demi-brigade In early 1807 the 1st Demi-brigade/Regiment was transferred from the Neapolitan army back to the French Army, where it was combined with the Polish Lancer Regiment to form the *Légion Polacco-Italienne* (see separate entry).

2nd Polish Demi-brigade The 2nd/114th Demi-brigade disappeared when the last French forces surrendered (except for a few stray elements in Europe that were incorporated into the 1st Demi-brigade in 1804). Of the Poles who survived to the bitter end of the French effort, some remained in Haiti, but most of them ended up as prisoners of war in Jamaica. Many of these men (possibly 500 or more) were summarily incorporated into the polyglot 5th Battalion of the British 60th Regiment. (Pachonski, p. 259.) Some stalwarts escaped to Cuba, where there was even for a short time a successful privateering operation manned primarily by Poles. (Pachonski, pp. 282–7.) Very few—probably no more than one in ten—of the more than 5,200 Poles sent to the West Indies actually returned to France at one point or another. (Pachonski, pp. 305–6.)

3rd Polish Demi-brigade Although parts of its 3rd Battalion were still in existence in the spring of 1803, the 3rd Polish Demi-Brigade (officially at that point the 113th of the Line) effectively ceased to exist as an independent fighting force at the start of 1803. In the words of one officer: 'We who have been here seven months have lost as many as 2,000 people and almost all our officers; our brother Jan, killed by the blacks, and all my travelling companions are dead, so that I alone remain, having contrived to withstand the climate.' (quoted in Pachonski, p. 123.) The unit was formally incorporated into the *Légion du Cap* in May. (Belhomme, Vol. 4, p. 270; Pachonski, pp. 123 and 129.) There were nevertheless many Poles who remained in action, and some even survived long enough to join up with the 2nd Polish Demi-Brigade (114th of the Line) when it arrived on the island.

Uniforms

1st Polish Demi-brigade The 1st Demi-brigade wore the same uniform as the *Légion Polonaise d'Italie* (see separate entry), but the facings changed from crimson to yellow during the course of 1802.

2nd Polish Demi-brigade The 2nd Demi-brigade wore the same uniform as the *Légion Polonaise d'Italie* (see separate entry). The 2nd received new uniforms with yellow facings as the result of an order dated 26 June 1802. (Wielhorski, p. 116.) The unit was not re-uniformed for its assignment to the Caribbean (Letter of 2nd Lieutenant Wojcikiewicz quoted in Pachonski, p. 141):

> We shall continue to wear our new Polish uniforms until they tatter—since we are now French [a reference to the unit's transformation into the 114th Line Demi-brigade], we shall be changing uniforms again in a year's time, although in hot countries what need will there be for scarves, purls [sic], galoons . . . silver shoulder-belts . . . we shall surely go about in straw hats.

Charles Hamilton Smith, an English officer known for his prints of British military uniforms, painted a picture of a captured officer of the 2nd Demi-brigade in Jamaica in 1803 or 1804. (The picture can be found in Vol. 3, p. 88, of Smith's notebooks in the Victoria and Albert Museum in London.) The figure is wearing a blue czapka with a black leather base and visor, white cords, tall red plume and a brass, grenade-shaped ornament on the front. The Polish-style jacket is blue with yellow collar, cuffs, lapels and turnbacks, silver buttons and silver epaulettes. The figure is also wearing a wide silver sash and blue Hungarian breeches with silver Austrian knots on the thighs. The outfit is completed by black hussar boots with silver trim and tassels.

3rd Polish Demi-brigade The 3rd Demi-brigade inherited the blue uniforms with red facings of the *Légion de Danube* (see separate entry). The unit wore these uniforms to Haiti in 1802, although they wore straw hats instead of their normal leather czapskas. In January 1804 some companies received new uniforms consisting of 'loose white cloth jackets and trousers, with red facings'. (Quote from Polish language memoirs of Adam Skalkowski presented in Wielhorski, p. 116.)

Standard

1st Polish Demi-brigade Each battalion of this unit carried the colour it had received when it was part of the *Légion Polonaise d'Italie* (see separate entry).

2nd Polish Demi-brigade Each battalion of this unit carried the colour it had received when it was part of the *Légion Polonaise d'Italie* (see separate entry). No information has been found as to whether it received new standards when it was transformed into the 114th Demi-brigade. Some standards were carried to Saint-Domingue, because there is mention of the colour of the 2nd Battalion being at Mole Saint-Nicolas in December 1803. (Pachonski, p. 238.)

3rd Polish Demi-brigade Each battalion of this unit probably carried the colour it had received when it was part of the *Légion du Danube* (see separate entry). No information has been found as to whether it received new standards when it was transformed into the 113th Demi-brigade. Some standards were carried to Saint-Domingue, because there is mention of the colour of the 2nd and 3rd Battalions being at Mole Saint-Nicolas in December 1803. (Pachonski, p. 238.)

Éclaireurs de la Garde Impériale (No 3)

(3rd Scouts of the Imperial Guard;
also known as the *3ème Éclaireurs-Lancers* [3rd Scout-Lancers])

Date of Creation The unit was created by a decree dated 9 December 1813. (Brunon, *Éclaireurs*, p. 34.)

Circumstances of Creation Napoleon was so displeased with the performance of his cavalry against the clouds of Russian Cossacks that were such a prominent feature of the campaigning in 1812 and 1813 that he decided to raise an élite force of lightly equipped cavalry that would be able to contend more effectively with these adversaries. On 9 December he decreed the formation of three regiments of a new type of cavalry called 'Scouts'. The 1st Regiment was associated with the Mounted Grenadiers of the Guard and wore the same uniform as the Honour Guards. The 2nd Scouts were associated with the Guard Dragoons and wore a uniform similar to that for line chasseurs. The 3rd Scout Regiment was associated with the Polish Lancers of the Guard and wore a similar uniform. (Brunon, *Éclaireurs*, p. 15.)

Composition The 3rd Scouts were formed by a reorganisation of the fourteen companies (seven squadrons) of the Polish Light Horse in existence when the new regiment was decreed. The first eight companies were filled out to full strength and recognised as the Polish Light Horse Lancers of the Guard. The remaining men, including the weak company of Tatars, were designated as members of the new Regiment, which was intended to have a staff and four squadrons of 250 men each. Since there were not enough men available, the 3rd Scouts was authorised to draw recruits from the depots of the remaining Polish line formations. However, because even this expedient did not achieve the desired results, recruitment was opened to non-Poles, who ultimately accounted for nearly one-third of the total of 937 men enlisted in the Regiment from 1 January to 21 March 1814. (Brunon, *Éclaireurs*, pp. 34–5.)

Commanders Although the 3rd Scouts were an independent unit, they shared the same commander as the Polish Light Horse, General Krasinski (see separate entry on the *Chevau-légers Polonais*). The unit was commanded in the field by Squadron Chief Kozietulski of the Polish Lancers, now promoted to the rank of Major Commandant. (Brunon, *Éclaireurs*, p. 33.)

Operational History The first detachments of Scouts to join the main army in 1814 were jumbled together in a provisional unit of Guard cavalry. On 3 February the Scouts were redistributed to their parent units and two full squadrons of the 3rd Scouts arrived from the depot. From that time on, they and the Polish Lancers formed a single operational unit. The 3rd Scouts particularly distinguished themselves at Champaubert and Vauchamps. On 5 March, Squadron Chief Skarzynski of the Scouts was accorded the title Baron of the Empire by Napoleon himself for his courageous conduct in capturing a bridge at Berry-au-Bac. (Brunon, *Éclaireurs*, pp. 59–60.)

The numbers in action fluctuated greatly throughout the campaign as casualties were suffered and reinforcements arrived from the depot. According to a return dated 15 March, the 3rd Scouts had 200 men in the field, while the Polish Light Horse had 600. At Arcis-sur-Aube on 20–22 March, the 3rd Scouts provided one of the duty squadrons escorting Napoleon and also participated in some of the fierce fighting that took place as the French struggled to extricate themselves from the grasp of the main Allied army. (Brunon, *Éclaireurs*, p. 67.) The Regiment had twelve officers wounded. Elements of the 3rd were also heavily engaged in the Battle of Paris, where the unit suffered four officer casualties.

Final Transformation Like all other Polish troops, the 3rd Scouts ceased to be part of the French Army on 1 May 1814. The Polish members of the unit thereafter returned to Poland.

Uniforms The officers of the 3rd Scouts generally kept their uniforms from the Polish Light Horse, but almost all the men of the Regiment received new uniforms at the start of 1814. In principle, they were essentially the same as those of the Polish Light Horse of the Guard, but because of considerations of time and money they tended to be in fact of inferior quality. (Brunon, *Éclaireurs*, p. 37.) The kurtka had white counter-epaulettes on both shoulders rather than the fringed epaulette and aiguilette of the parent unit. The uniform of the trumpeters was a sky blue kurtka with crimson facings, which was the undress uniform of trumpeters of the Polish Light Horse. The weapons, equipment and horse furniture used by the Regiment were eclectic, having been gathered from any source possible to meet the needs of the unit.

Standard No information found, but it is unlikely that Napoleon found time to award them one during the last desperate months of his first reign.

Fusiliers Aragonais

(Fusiliers of Aragon)

Date of Creation Decree of 1 March 1811 (reproduced in Sorando Muzas, Document Appendix).

Circumstances of Creation This unit was created by order of Marshal Suchet because he felt that the Aragonese would make excellent soldiers and guides and could assist the French in pacifying the local population. (Sorando Muzas, Section I, quoting correspondence of Suchet.) The men of these units were enlisted for the service of the Empire and were not part of the armed forces of King Joseph.

Composition The unit initially consisted of four companies of Fusiliers, one at Calatayud, one at Daroca, one at Teruel and one at Alcaniz. An additional half company was formed on 24 July 1811 at Tarazona under the command of 2nd Lieutenant Miguel Martinez. After losses suffered during their first year of service, the Fusiliers were reorganised into two companies by a decree dated 1 July 1812, which also amalgamated the Fusiliers with two remaining companies of *Gendarmes Aragonais* (see separate entry) and two *Chasseurs à Cheval Aragonais* (see separate entry). (Decree reproduced in Sorando Muzas, Document Appendix.) The companies seem to have averaged 40–60 men in strength. (Sorando Muzas, Section II.2.)

Commanders The commanders specified in the Organisational Decree were as follows (Decree reproduced in Sorando Muzas, Document Appendix): 1st Company—Lieutenant Angel Wanluzel; 2nd Company—Lieutenant (later Captain) Magin Tondo; 3rd Company—Lieutenant Francisco Ballaster; 4th Company—Captain Joaquin Fernandez. When the unit was reorganised and combined with the Gendarmes and the Mounted Chasseurs in 1812, it was under the overall command of Colonel Pedro Garces de Marcilla, Baron de Andilla (1762–1816). The two post-reorganisation Fusilier company commanders were Captain Fernandez and Captain Polorell. (Sorando Muzas, Section II.2.)

Operational History The 1st Company was the first formed, but it was also the first to come to grief, since it was almost wiped out when a strong force of guerrillas surrounded and captured the French garrison of Calatayud on 4 October 1811 after a short siege. Lieutenant Angel Wanluzel and 24 Fusiliers were included amongst the prisoners. (Sorando Muzas, Section II.2.1.) The survivors were combined with the men of the 4th Company to form a new 1st Company under the command of Captain Fernandez, who was wounded on 16 June 1812 near Alcanitz. The Company was destroyed on 3 September 1812 when the men murdered their commander on the instigation of 2nd Lieutenant Mariano Layel and deserted *en masse* to the guerrillas. (Martin, pp. 384–5.)

Little is known of the 2nd Company except that Lieutenant Tondo was wounded near Daroca on 2 September 1811 and that on 1 October the strength of the Company was two officers and 36 men. (Sorando Muzas, Section II.2.2.) The unit was fortified in 1812 by the incorporation of a unit of *Volontaires Aragonais de pied* under the command of one Captain Antonio Mata. (SHA Carton X[l]42.)

Final Transformation All the remaining Gendarmes, Fusiliers and Mounted Chasseurs were disarmed and interned in France in October 1813. (Fieffé, Vol. 2, p. 151; Sorando Muzas, Section II.2.)

Uniforms No information found.

Standard No information found.

Gardes d'Honneur de Turin et de Florence

(Honour Guards of Turin and Florence)

Date of Creation Order of 1 April 1809.

Circumstances of Creation The Honour Guards were company-strength cavalry units that were formed, along with the *Vélites de Turin et Florence* (see separate entry), to increase the prestige and security of two of Napoleon's relatives in Italy. The Turin Honour Guards were created to serve Prince Camille Borghese, the second husband of Pauline Bonaparte, who served as the Governor-General for all the French departments beyond the Alps (i.e., the territory in northern Italy that was formerly part of the French state as opposed to being part of the Kingdom of Italy). The Honour Guards of Florence were created to serve Napoleon's sister, Elisa, the Grand Duchess of Tuscany. (Titeux, p. 778.)

Composition It was intended that the men of the Honour Guards would come from the best families of the relevant territories, as evidenced by a requirement that each Honour Guard had to have an allowance of 1,000 francs from his family. (Bucquoy, *Troupes Étrangères*, p. 120.) Each company had the following composition:

1	Captain Commandant
1	Lieutenant 1st Class
2	Lieutenants 2nd Class
1	Surgeon-Major
1	Veterinarian
1	Blacksmith
1	*Maréchal des Logis Chef*
2	*Maréchaux des Logis*
1	Brigadier Fourrier
8	Brigadiers
2	Trumpeters
50	Mounted Honour Guards
36	Foot Honour Guards

Each company also had a brigade of 22 '*palefreniers*' commanded by a chief *palefrenier*. These were working stable hands whose sole job was to relieve the wealthy Honour Guards from some of the more mundane tasks entailed in caring for their horses.

Commanders

Turin Honour Guards *Formation to May 1812*: Captain de la Hubaudière, who left the Company when he was promoted to the rank of Squadron Chief. (Most information in this section is from Fieffé, Vol. 2, pp. 116–117; the date of the Captain's promotion is from Decision of 5 May 1812, Nap. *P&T*, No 7214, Vol. 5, pp. 351–2 at 352.) *May 1812 to final transformation:* Captain Bodson de Noirfontaine.

Florence Honour Guards *Formation to 1813*: Captain Martelli. *1813 to final transformation:* Captain Doré de Brouville.

Operational History The Companies were not fully organised until 1810 and were engaged solely in ceremonial duties until 1812, when Napoleon had them completed to full strength and then moved to Berlin. (Note of 20 June 1812, Nap. *Inédits*, No 597, Vol. 1, p. 171; Decision of 19 July 1812, Nap. *O&A*, No 2249, Vol. 2, p. 358.) In

September 1812 they were ordered on to Warsaw. (Decision of 12 September 1812, Nap. O&A, No 2444, Vol. 2, pp. 420–2 at 421.) There is a widespread belief that the Companies were destroyed during the retreat from Russia, but that is certainly not the case since on 25 April 1813, they were serving as part of the cavalry force attached to General François Roguet's Old Guard Division, with the Turin Honour Guards mustering two officers and 65 men and the Florence Honour Guards three officers and 51 men. (Bowden, *1813*, p. 221.) On 1 May 1813 they were attached to the Mounted Grenadiers of the Guard. (N. to Berthier, 1 May 1813, Nap. *Corr.*, No 19935, Vol. 25, pp. 249–51 at 250.)

In the meanwhile, however, Napoleon had concluded that the Turin and Florence Honour Guards should be considered to be part of the four Regiments of Honour Guards he created at the beginning of April (Article 22 of Decree of 5 April 1813, reproduced in Saint-Hilaire, pp. 427–31 at 431):

> The honour guards from the departments of the 27th [Turin], 28th and 29th [Florence] Military Divisions that are already on active service with the army will count as part of the contingent those departments are required to furnish [for the Honour Guards] and consequently should be incorporated into the new regiments.

Bucquoy asserts, without supporting citations, that the two Honour Guards companies were in fact incorporated into the 4th Regiment of Honour Guards of the Imperial Guard by an order dated 19 May 1813. (Bucquoy, *Troupes Étrangères*, p. 123.)

Final Transformation The Honour Guards of Turin were formally disbanded on 16 July 1813. The Honour Guards of Florence remained in existence until 1 May 1814.

Uniforms The uniforms of the two companies were essentially identical (Titeux, p. 779):

> Red jacket with long tails, vertical pockets and blue collar, cuffs, lapels and turnbacks; silver buttons, epaulettes without fringe and an aiguilette [on the right shoulder];
> white vest and trousers;
> black boots with stiff tops; [and]
> black bicorne hat with silver lace.

This uniform is depicted on a sentry at the periphery of a contemporary painting by Benvenuti of a gala reception held by Elisa that was used by Bucquoy as the basis for a card in his series on the unit. (Bucquoy, *Troupes Étrangères*, p. 124.) The officers of the unit wore the same uniform except that all the facings were decorated with silver embroidery in the form of oak leaves. Titeux's article is illustrated by a portrait said to be that of an officer of one of the Honour Guard companies, but Bucquoy makes the persuasive case that the subject of the portrait is in fact an officer of the local Roman Honour Guards. (Bucquoy, *Troupes Étrangères*, p. 122.) NCOs had the same embroidery only on their cuffs, collars and pockets. The horse furniture was a red shabraque and holster covers with silver trim. The *palefreniers* wore jackets of the same livery colour worn by the servants of their respective commanders, Prince Camille and Grand Duchess Elisa. No information has been found, however, as to what those colours may have been.

On 22 August 1812 Napoleon turned down a request by Grand Duchess Elisa for permission for the members of the unit to wear fringed epaulettes after two years' service. (Decision of 22 August 1812, Nap. *P&T*, No 7529, Vol. 5, p. 533.)
Standard No information found.

Gardes d'Honneur Polonaises

(Polish Honour Guards)

Date of Creation 1813.
Circumstances of Creation The destruction of the rank-and-file of the Polish Army in the Russian campaign resulted in there being more officers available for service than there were troops for them to command. This excess manpower was formed into special units described by one officer who had been detached on staff duty during 1812 (memoirs of Alexander Fredro, quoted in Chelminski, p. 202):

> I sought to return to my regiment, but the effectives of the Polish Army was so reduced that there were way more officers than were needed. These excess officers were concentrated under the command of Generals N[iemojewski?] and Niesolowski and used to form a corps called, for some unknown reason, 'Honour Guards'. Our headquarters was in a little village next to Görlitz . . .

Composition A total of four companies of Honour Guards were raised, each one of which was composed exclusively of officers. To give an idea of the relative ranking of the officers, General Joseph Grabinski served in the 2nd Company as a mere lieutenant. (A. Martinien, p. 432.)
Commanders
1st Company General K. Niesolowski.
2nd Company *After Leipzig:* General Joseph Niemojewski, who had commanded a Duchy of Warsaw light cavalry brigade with distinction during the Russian campaign.
3rd Company *From 1 March 1814:* General Michel Sokolnicki (1760 or 1761–1816), a veteran of the Dombrowski's Legions who became a French Brigade General in 1812.
4th Company *From 1 March 1814:* General Jan Krukowiecki.
Operational History Chelminski states that Napoleon 'ignored' the existence of these companies during 1813, but they are mentioned in a letter dated 20 August 1813 in which Napoleon asks Berthier to assign the Polish Honour Guards that are armed and mounted to the defence of Görlitz. (Nap. *1813*, No 250, p. 100.) Chelminski also mentions, however, that the 3rd Honour Guard Company took part in the defence of Paris on 29–30 March 1814. (Chelminski, p. 202 n. 1.)
Final Transformation According to Fredro (memoirs of Alexander Fredro, quoted in Chelminski, p. 202):

> The campaigns of 1813 and 1814 did not involve much loss for the [Honour Guard companies]. Most of the officers made their way to Sedan and stayed there until the end

of the war. After Napoleon's abdication, they joined the debris of the Polish Army at Saint-Denis.

Uniforms No information found.
Standard No information found.

Gendarmerie de Prusse

(Prussian Gendarmes)

Date of Creation 2 November 1806.
Circumstances of Creation After Jena, Napoleon decided that the portions of Prussia he had conquered should be divided into ten departments for administrative purposes. (Nap. *Corr.*, No 11142, Vol. 13, pp. 454–6 at 455.) The commandants of the ten departments were each authorised to raise units of native Prussian Gendarmes to carry out peacekeeping functions.
Composition Each administrative department was supposed to have four 'brigades' of Gendarmes, each one consisting of six men (including the commanding 'brigadier' or corporal).
Commanders No information found.
Operational History No information found.
Final Transformation No information found.
Uniforms The uniform of the Prussian Gendarmes was set forth in an Order of the Day dated 9 December 1806 (Nap. *P&T*, No 833, Vol. 1, p. 415):

> The Prussian Gendarmery, which is being organised by virtue of the imperial decree of last November 3rd, will wear the following uniform:
>
> Iron grey coat, without pockets, fastened across the breast with nine buttons; red collar; white aiguilette on the left shoulder, with a trefoil of the same colour on the right shoulder; iron grey waistcoat and trousers; white buttons; cocked hat (*chapeau à cornes*); Prussian boots.
>
> They are to be armed and equipped as follows: cavalry sabre; pistols; cartridge box with black shoulder-belt; black belt.
>
> Corporals will be distinguished by a small strip of silver trim on the collar.
>
> These gendarmes will be protected in the exercise of their functions by all posts of French and allied troops.

Standard No information found, but it is unlikely that this ephemeral and small unit would have received any official flag.

Gendarmes Aragonais

(Gendarmes of Aragon)

Date of Creation 1810

Circumstances of Creation The first company of Gendarmes was formed in Jaca in January 1810, although there had been informal units of Aragonese guides assisting the French from August 1809. (Sorando Muzas, Section 2.) Another company was formed in Barbastro in February, followed by a third company in Zaragoza in March.
Composition Each company was expected to consist of 100 men between the ages of 18 and 40 who could read, write and speak Aragonese. On 1 March 1811, the number of Gendarme companies was reduced to two and at the end of June the unit was amalgamated for administrative purposes with the *Fusiliers Aragonais* (see separate entry). (Sorando Muzas, Document Annex 1.)
Commanders
1st Company *Formation to 1813:* Captain José Asenio was designated to command the Compnay, but he was replaced immediately by Captain Esteban de Robert. (Sorando Muzas, Section 2.1.) In April 1813, however, Captain Asenio seems to have been in command.
2nd Company *Formation to final transformation:* Captain Domingo Brun, a guerrilla officer who joined the French in 1809. (Sorando Muzas, Section 5, notes.)
Operational History The Gendarmes participated in many skirmishes against guerrillas fighting for the Bourbon monarchy. (Sorando Muzas, Sections 2.1.1 and 2.1.2.)
Final Transformation On 5 September 1812, the two remaining companies of Gendarmes mustered six officers and 141 men at Jaca and Zaragoza. (Sorando Muzas, Section 1.) They were dissolved at Dax on 26 December 1813. (Sorando Muzas, Section 2.1.1.)
Uniforms A letter dated 10 March 1811 specifies that the uniform of the Gendarmes was to consist of 'a blue jacket and trousers; white vest; red collar, cuffs and piping and gold buttons'. (Quoted in Sorando Muzas, Part 2.)
Standard No information found.

Gendarmes Catalans

(Catalonian Gendarmes)

Date of Creation December 1810 according to Dr Jean Sarramon, but in any event no later than April 1811. (Martin, *Gendarmerie*, p. 419.)
Circumstances of Creation This was a counter-guerrilla force formed by order of Marshal Louis Gabriel Suchet. (Morvan, Vol. 1, p. 178.)
Composition A footnote in the memoirs of an anonymous French cavalryman who served in Catalonia reports that this unit consisted initially of 'a company with a full strength of 100 men, all natives of Catalonia engaged voluntarily in French service, commanded by officers and NCOs of that nation. . . .' (Adjutant I., *Revue Retrospective*, Vol. 18, p. 108, fn.) The unit eventually expanded to three companies of gendarmes, at least one of which was not mounted.

Commanders
1st Company (Mounted) *Formation to December 1811:* Captain Loriol. *December 1811 to final transformation:* Captain Cosse.
2nd Company (Mounted) *Formation to final transformation:* Captain Clotte.
3rd Company (Dismounted) *Formation to final transformation:* Captain Noel.
(All the above information about the commanders of the unit is based on notes of Dr Jean Sarramon.)

Operational History According to one French observer, the Gendarmes were fierce and effective warriors for the French (Adjutant I, *Revue Retrospective*, Vol. 18, p. 108, fn):

> [The men] . . . were of an uncommon size and strength . . . and they were mounted on the best Andalusian horse and used blunderbusses instead of pistols. They were always with the advance guard or in the most perilous positions and they themselves used guerrilla tactics, attacking without order or obvious chain of command and exhibiting an intrepidness bordering on ferocity. The Spaniards feared them and referred to them as the 'Butchers' of the French Army.

Final Transformation The Gendarme companies were dissolved by an order of General Charles Decaen dated 16 December 1811, but the men were quickly re-cycled into three companies of *Guides Catalans* (see separate entry). (Decree reproduced in Alia Plana, pp. 73–4.)

Uniforms The Gendarmes were originally 'dressed in a uniform similar to that of the 10th Regiment of French Hussars which was worn with a fox fur busby with a red bag ornamented with a big yellow tassel with silver fringe which hung down to the left shoulder.' (Adjutant I., *Revue Retrospective*, Vol. 18, p. 108, fn.) According to some sources, the hussar uniform was soon replaced by a blue gendarme uniform with red facings, but the busby was retained. (Morvan, Vol. 1, p. 178; see illustration in Bueno, Pl. 41.)

Standard No information found.

Gendarmes Septinsulaires

(Septinsular Gendarmes)

This unit is noted in Fieffé (Vol. 2, p. 154) and Chartrand, Napoleon's Army (p. 128), but no other details of its existence have been found.

Guides Catalans

(Catalan Guides)

Date of Creation This unit was formed by orders dated 16 and 31 December 1811. (The 31 December Order reproduced in Alia Plana, pp. 73–4, contains recitals that explain the contents of the 16 December Order.)

Circumstances of Creation On 16 December 1811 General Charles Decaen dissolved three existing companies of *Gendarmes Catalans* (see separate entry). All the men of those companies who were bona fide natives of Catalonia were reorganised into two companies of Guides at Gerona formed by that same order. The men who were of French extraction were, although they spoke Catalan fluently, grouped into a separate company by an order of Decaen dated 31 December 1811. (*Ibid.*)

Composition Based on the details given for the last company formed, each company was to consist of the following components:

Mounted Men:	1	Captain
	1	Lieutenant
	1	2nd Lieutenant
	1	*Maréchal des Logis Chef*
	3	*Maréchaux des Logis*
	1	Brigadier-Fourrier
	6	Brigadiers
	38	Guides
	2	Trumpeters
Dismounted Men:	3	*Maréchaux des Logis*
	1	Brigadier-Fourrier
	6	Brigadiers
	88	Guides
	2	Drummers

An archival strength report for the Army of Catalonia for November 1813 records the existence of four officers and 108 NCOs and Guides at Gerona. (SHA Carton C[8]371.)

Commanders No information found except for an indication that one of the companies was commanded by Captain Jean Noel. (SHA Carton X[l]42.)

Operational History No information found except for the notation in Martinien that Captain Noel of the 1st Company of Guides was wounded on 3 June 1812 in a skirmish with smugglers on the road to Gerona.

Final Transformation The Guides were disbanded in France in May 1814. (Note of Dr Jean Sarramon.)

Uniforms The 31 December order specifies that the last company was to wear a single-breasted blue jacket with green collar, blue cuffs and turnbacks and yellow piping; silver hemispherical buttons; and buff vests and trousers. (See illustration in Bueno, Pl. 42.) Armament consisted of a short musket, a chasseur sabre for mounted Guides and an infantry sword for dismounted Guides.

Standard No information found.

Guides d'Omar

(Guides of Omar)

Date of Creation 2 September 1798.
Circumstances of Creation A Turkish officer who made himself useful to Napoleon in the early stages of the campaign in Egypt was rewarded with the command of a unit intended to help bridge the language and culture gap between the occupying French forces and the indigenous population. (Savant, *Les Mamelouks*, p. 42.)
Composition One company, composed primarily of ex-Turkish soldiers, that was attached to Napoleon's Guides. (Savant, *Les Mamelouks*, p. 42.) The force of the company was three officers and 114 men, including one French corporal. (Belhomme, Vol. 4, p. 170.)
Commanders Omar el Koladi, a Turkish Janissary officer. (This version of his name is given in Spillman, 'Corps Auxiliaires', p. 8.) Nothing is known of this officer before or after his association with the French Army.
Operational History The Guides were given a variety of assignments that called upon their cross-cultural skills as much as their military prowess. They were assigned to the French forces occupying Suez and then asked to survey the routes of march from Suez to Salehieh. (Savant, *Les Mamelouks*, p. 42.) They were then placed under the command of General Arrighi.
Final Transformation No information has been found about the Guides subsequent to the campaign in the Holy Land.
Uniforms All secondary sources are unanimous in reporting that the soldiers of the Guides wore a blue Egyptian shirt (caftan?) with green collar and cuffs and a turban. There is a Bucquoy card by P. Benigni that depicts a Guide wearing this uniform; it is reproduced in Bucquoy, *Dragons et Guides*, p. 99.
Standard No information found.

Hussards Croates

(Croatian Hussars)

Date of Creation 12 February 1813.
Circumstances of Creation Of all the losses suffered by the Grand Army during the disastrous Russian campaign, perhaps none had such an important impact on subsequent military events as the near total destruction of the mounted forces of the French and their allies. While it was possible to a great extent for Napoleon to create new infantrymen simply by handing muskets to untrained conscripts, his dearth of cavalry could not be similarly made good simply by mounting those same untrained conscripts on horses because cavalry must be properly trained and equipped before it

can make an effective contribution on the battlefield. This problem of replacing the mounted troops of the Grand Army thus required instead a more complex solution whose components ranged from the recall of veteran cavalry from Spain to the creation of entirely new mounted units. One of the first, and one of the most unusual, of these new forces was the short-lived regiment of Croatian Hussars.

General Henri Bertrand, the governor of the Illyrian provinces at the start of 1813, was an engineer rather than a cavalryman by profession, but he was quick to appreciate the Emperor's pressing need for mounted troops and, more importantly, he was equally quick to do something about it. As Governor, Bertrand had under his command the six regiments of Croatian territorial infantry which had been taken into French service when their homelands, the military regions bordering on the Turkish Empire, were ceded to France by Austria after the War of 1809. (See separate entry for *Chasseurs Illyriens*.) He knew they were experienced soldiers and, because of their frontier environment, he reckoned—correctly, as it turned out—that many of them were experienced riders and familiar with horses and horsemanship. He accordingly believed that by drawing on these units he could create a regiment of cavalry which could be organised and trained in a relatively short time and yet which nevertheless would have the attributes of a veteran unit.

Bertrand formally unveiled his plan in an order dated 12 February 1813 (SHA X[l]36) which called upon each Croatian regiment to provide the soldiers and horses for a troop of 100 'Hussars', exclusive of officers, NCOs and trumpeters, which would give him a regiment of six troops (i.e., three squadrons). (Boppe, *La Croatie Militaire*, p. 142.) The horses were to be delivered fully equipped with saddles and bridles, and each man was to be provided with basic stable dress and a full set of implements for caring for his mount (i.e. brushes, feed bag, etc.). The order also suggested quite pointedly that all the citizens of Illyria should strive to show their devotion to the Emperor by giving voluntary gifts of money, horses and equipment to complete the equipping of the new regiment, and to set an example Bertrand announced that he himself would be contributing 50 horses, fully outfitted. (*Ibid.*) On 15 February he wrote to Napoleon asking him to confirm his decision to raise the regiment of hussars and, not surprisingly, the Emperor responded with a formal decree, dated 23 February, authorising the regiment to be organised as part of the French Army with a total strength of 650 officers and men. (Boppe, *La Croatie Militaire*, p. 144.)

Composition The original three-squadron proposal of Bertrand called for a total regimental strength of 69 officers and 1,515 men. On 10 March Bertrand concluded that the project had such potential that a second regiment of hussars of the same size ought to be raised, and he actually started to put the formation of this second unit into effect. In the meantime, however, Napoleon had on 2 March amended his original decree to increase the strength of the original regiment to six squadrons. When Bertrand learned of the amendment, he immediately called off plans for the additional regiment, but in any event the point was mostly moot, because there were not enough recruits for anyone to think realistically about either the planned expansion or the second regiment. (L'Invalide, 'Les Hussards Croates', pp. 150–1.)

As contemplated by Bertrand's decree, all the men and most of the company officers of the Hussars came from the Illyrian Chasseur regiments. The staff officers for the regiment, however, came from a wide range of units, in many cases receiving promotions upon transfer, but they were primarily cavalrymen. The new Major, de Wimpffen, and one squadron chief, Henriquez, were both promoted from the 9th Light Horse Lancers. The two other squadron chiefs, Bretenet and Dubouzet, came with a step in grade from the 30th Dragoons and Regiment Isembourg, respectively. (Register of Officers, Boppe, *La Croatie Militaire*, Appendix V, pp. 255–7.) The officer who profited most dramatically from the formation of the hussars, however, was General Bertrand himself: having reminded Napoleon of his loyalty and initiative by the gesture of raising the Hussars, he was rewarded by being given command of the 4th Corps of the Grand Army. He was replaced in the governorship of Illyria by General Androche Junot.

Commanders *5 March 1813 to disbandment:* Bernard Pruès (1773–1852), General Bertrand's senior ADC, was 39 years old when he was promoted to the rank of Colonel and appointed to command of the Hussars but he had already seen 21 years of Army service.

Operational History The training and equipping of the Regiment proceeded at a fitful pace. On 5 March 1813 the headquarters of the unit was fixed at Karlstadt (now Karlovac). In April Napoleon ordered the Regiment to join General Bertrand's new corps in Germany, but even by the start of May the Hussars were still not properly ready to take the field. According to Colonel Pruès, this delay was in part due to the fact that Karlstadt was a poor location for the Regiment since the men were distracted by the close proximity of family and friends and in part due to the fact that many of his officers were slow in reporting for duty to the new regiment. (Pruès to Minister of War, 20 May 1813, quoted in Boppe, *La Croatie Militaire*, pp. 147–8.)

It was at this point that the Hussars received their baptism of fire in fighting against a very familiar enemy—Turkish brigands who had staged a raid into French territory. General Jeannin, the garrison commander at Karlstadt, responded to the incursion on 4 May by dispatching 1,000 men of the Sluin regiment and 220 hussars under Captain Giovanni Cattalinich to deal with the raiders. Being extremely short of equipment, the hussars were forced to arm themselves in a rather impromptu manner for the occasion, some with sabres, some with pistols, some with muskets and a very few with medieval halberds, and the general effect was to give the troop the appearance of a mercenary band from an earlier, more primitive era of warfare. The motley French force nevertheless surprised and decimated the raiders and retook a fortified village that the Turks had temporarily occupied after massacring its garrison. (Pisani, *La Dalmatie*, p. 402.)

This appearance and performance are consistent with the information provided in a letter written by the Hussars' commander about that time. In the letter, Colonel Pruès stated that he was generally pleased with the progress made by his men, and that they were well schooled in the care of their horses and could execute many basic manoeuvres on horseback. Nevertheless, he was forced to admit at the same time that the regiment still lacked shakos and weapons, that he needed more officers, riding instructors, veterinarians and trumpeters, and that 'one cannot pretend that they can manoeuvre in line.' (Prués to Minister of War, 20 May 1813, quoted in Boppe, *La Croatie Militaire*, pp. 147–8.) The Minister of War promulgated a decree on 13 June authorising all native Frenchmen enrolled in the Croatian infantry regiments to be transferred to the Hussar regiment, and this measure was so productive that it finally became possible to consider raising the additional three squadrons contemplated by the official establishment of the regiment, a process which was begun at Laybach in Illyria on 2 August. (Boppe, *La Croatie Militaire*, pp. 149–50.)

Even as the new squadrons started to take shape, however, the entry of Austria into the Sixth Coalition against France caused a significant dimming of the prospects for the continued existence of the regiment of Croatian Hussars in any form. As the Illyrian Chasseurs (see separate entry) began to desert in droves, Prince Eugene Beauharnais realised that it would be risky to put the Croatian Hussars in a position where they, too, would be facing former Austrian comrades in combat. The Regiment and its depot were therefore ordered away from the front, their ultimate destination being Lyon in France. (P. Boppe, *La Croatie Militaire*, p. 151.) Nevertheless, 500 of the most reliable men were collected into a provisional advance guard unit and allowed to remain with the Army of Italy for the autumn campaign. (D'Espinchal, p.388.) As a result, one officer of the regiment was wounded in the Tyrol on 15 August. In addition, 200 Hussars participated with 50 Chasseurs of the 19th Regiment in an extended reconnaissance mission near Garrets at the end of September which cost them some casualties and 20 men taken prisoner. (D'Espinchal, pp. 180–3.) On the night of 4 October, however, the worst fears of the French were realised when the remaining Croatian Hussars of the advance guard deserted *en masse* just before crossing the Isonzo River. (D'Espinchal, p. 388.) The Viceroy of Italy consequently decided to disband that portion of the Regiment still in Italy. D'Espinchal records that their mounts ('300 horse of small size, but excellent stock') were handed over the 31st Chasseurs, while the men 'were sent back to their own country in anticipation of the desertion that would have inevitably occurred.' (D'Espinchal, p. 185.) The few men left over were directed towards Lyon.

Martinien records that another officer of the Croatian Hussars was wounded in the combat of Alba on 10 November. Since the wounded officer had a French surname (de Chamby), however, he may have been serving in the field independently of his Regiment.

Final Transformation Reports of bad behaviour by the Regiment during its progress from Italy to Lyon hastened a conclusion by the Emperor that the Croats were using equipment and supplies which could be more profitably channeled to reliable French troops: 'If the horses and saddles of this regiment are in good condition, it would perhaps be most efficient to dismount the Croatians and give their horses and equipment to a French regiment, since it is probable that they will desert at the first opportunity.' (N. to Minister of War, 10 November 1813, Nap. *O&A*, No 6148, Vol. 4, p. 326.) Napoleon's thinking must have firmed up very quickly in this regard, because on 18 November he issued explicit orders for General Corbineau to travel immediately to Lyon to deal with the Regiment as soon as it arrived. (N. to Minister of War, Nap. *Inédits*, No 1189, Vol. 1, p. 316.) Corbineau discharged his duties well, for on 26 November the 1,276 men of the regiment of Croatian Hussars were disarmed and marched off under guard to Dijon. Of the 639 horses of the regiment, 431 were given to the 31st Chasseurs and 208 to the lst Hussars. The 1,232 carbines, 1,249 sabres and 469 bayonets of the hussars were placed in the arsenal of Lyon pending distribution to the forces being raised by Marshal Augereau for the defence of that city. (P. Boppe, *La Croatie Militaire*, pp. 157–9.)

At first there was some confusion as to how the men of the Croatian Hussars could best be reorganised in accordance with the Decree of 25 November 1813, but eventually it was decided to transform them into a battalion of *Pionniers Croates* composed of five companies under the command of Squadron Chief Pavlicza, a process which was completed at Nevers on 31 December 1813. (Pigeard, 'Pionniers', pp. 14–15.) Prior to that date, however, all French citizens serving in the Hussars were, regardless of rank, dispatched to join the 4th Dragoons, while a number of Croatian officers with particularly strong ties to France were permitted to petition the Minister of War for active employment with other cavalry regiments. (P. Boppe, *La Croatie Militaire*, pp. 157–9.) There may also have been other actions taken by regimental officers—witness the case of Colonel Pruès, who attached himself to the 3rd Hussars after the disbandment of his own regiment and served with the former unit throughout the 1814 campaign. With the abdication of Napoleon in April 1814, the pioneer battalion was repatriated and the remnants of the Croatian Hussars became Austrian citizens once again.

Uniforms The uniform of the Croatian hussars was set forth in Bertrand's original decree concerning the Regiment, and, except for one significant detail, it remained unchanged during the Regiment's brief life. Its elements, as set forth in Articles 8 and 9 of the 12 February decree (quoted in Boppe, *La Croatie Militaire*, p. 143) were as follows:

- (i) Shakos with a plate bearing the words '1er Régiment d'Hussards Croates';
- (ii) sky blue dolmans with chamois (light buff) collar and cuffs;
- (iii) pelisses;
- (iv) iron grey undress caps;
- (v) iron grey stable trousers with leather reinforcements;
- (vi) iron grey overcoats; and
- (vii) hussar boots with steel spurs.

There is no known depiction of this unit that is based on first-hand information, but it has been presumed that the uniform specified above was completed with white braid on the dolman, white metal buttons and a white and crimson barrel sash. Since the shako plates were not manufactured until after the Emperor indicated that he wanted only a single regiment, it is possible that they did not bear the prescribed regimental number, but there does exist a black leather sabretache in the Museum of Hussars at Tarbes that may have belonged to a member of the Regiment which has the number and letters '1 H.C.' (1er Hussards Croates?) in silver under a silver eagle. (P. Devaux, Response to Question IV, *Le Briquet*, 1983, No 3, p. 23.)

Bertrand's decree is silent on the subject of pelisse colour, and therein lies an interesting tale of military bureaucracy. (P. Boppe, *La Croatie Militaire*, p. 150, n. 2.) Noting that omission when he promulgated his own decree, Napoleon specified that the pelisses should be sky blue, like the dolmans. In fact, it appears that Bertrand had already had over 600 iron grey pelisses manufactured before he found out about Napoleon's decision. To resolve the awkward situation, Colonel Prués suggested that the original pelisses be turned into fur-lined stable jackets while the regiment could then be issued new pelisses in the imperial-sanctioned colour, but Napoleon baulked at the extravagance of that expedient. On 2 July 1813 Napoleon formally authorised the use of the grey pelisses rather than blue. (Nap. *Inédits*, No 1074, Vol. 1, p. 290.)

The equipment and horse furniture of the Croatian hussars were all of the standard pattern for French light cavalry, except that the sheepskin saddle cover was black, instead of the usual white, with chamois wolf-teeth edging and the valise was iron grey. (12 February Order, Article 7.) Because of a shortage of weapons, the Hussars were armed with sabres and cavalry carbines, but were not issued with pistols. (12 February 12 Order, Article 13.) Nothing is known for certain about the dress of regimental trumpeters, but it seems likely that they would have worn either the imperial livery or a uniform of reversed colours (i.e., chamois dolman with sky blue collar and cuffs).

Standard No information found.

Hussards Polonaises

(Polish Hussars)

Date of Creation 12 March 1807.

Circumstances of Creation This short-lived unit was one of several created by Polish aristocrats at their own expense after Napoleon defeated the Prussians and fostered expectations that he might restore the Polish state. The first official mention of this Regiment occurs in a letter dated 4 March 1807 (N. to Talleyrand, Nap. *Corr.*, No 11925, Vol. 14, p. 369):

> Please send to Neidenberg all the Polish volunteers who wish to serve in my armies. A Prince named Sulkowski has just arrived at my headquarters; he says he has raised a regiment of 600 men in Silesia. I told him that if he was able to bring them to me, I would pay for them. Let Prince Poniatowski know this has occurred. . .

Sulkowski apparently delivered his unit, because French records note that it was taken into French pay on 12 March 1807 (12 March 1807, Nap. *Inédits*, No 204, Vol. 1, pp. 60–1):

> The regiment of Polish light horse raised by Prince Jean Sulkowski will be taken into our pay. It will be transferred without delay to Warsaw with its horse, uniforms and equipment. . . . Our Minister of War will conduct a review of the unit which, immediately after the review is completed, will receive, from our treasury, the same pay as the regiments of cavalry which are now being formed for the new Polish forces.

(See also Decision of 27 October 1807, Nap. *P&T*, No 1399, Vol. 1, pp. 672–3.)

The Marquis of Bouillé, the officer appointed to inspect the new unit, was astonished to learn that the unit was essentially a sham when he caught up with it at Kozieglow in Silesia, 50 leagues from Breslau (Bouillé, Vol. 3, p. 127):

> . . . I learned that the Prince Sulkowski, after having committed a thousand offences against the civilians of Silesia and having been arrested by a Polish Major, who replaced him, had fled and that his corps really didn't exist at all since it consisted only of a hundred mounted men and as many on foot, badly armed and badly organised . . . .

Napoleon was so incensed by this revelation that he ordered the immediate arrest of the Prince (Order of the Day, 24 April 1807, Nap. *P&T*, No 1068, Vol. 1, p. 515; see also N. to Marshal Lefebvre, Nap. *Corr.*, No 11962, Vol. 14, pp. 397–8):

> All Commandants of Gendarmes and of posts of the French Army and its allies are hereby ordered to arrest on sight Prince Jean Sulkowski, who is the colonel of a regiment of Polish cavalry and who, after having committed many disorders in the Circle of Beuthen and on the frontiers of Upper Silesia, has abandoned his corps and disappeared.

No information has been found about the Prince's fate subsequent to his flight.

Composition Although the unit was raised as a regiment of light horse, Napoleon was explicit in changing it into one of hussars (12 March 1807, Nap. *Inédits*, No 204, Vol. 1, pp. 60–1): 'It will be organised with a strength of 1,043 men in conformity with the new establishment set for hussars by our decree of the 10th of this month.'

Commanders *Creation to final transformation:* Prince Jean Sulkowski. He should not be confused with Prince Antoine Sulkowski, the commander of 9th Regiment of the Duchy of Warsaw who ultimately reached the rank of division general, although the latter may have been a relation of the former.

Operational History The only reference to the unit (and it commander) in combat is a favourable one (6 March 1807, Nap. *Inédit*, No 202, Vol. 1, p. 60): 'Prince Sulkowski, the Colonel of a Polish regiment, is hereby named a member of the Legion of Honour because of his distinguished conduct at the combat of Dirschau.' No information has been found about the service of the Polish Hussars, if any, after that date.

Final Transformation The Regiment remained in existence, albeit in a very dilapidated state, until the autumn, when the remaining men were incorporated into the Lancers of the *Légion Polacco-Italienne* (see separate entry). (Decision of 27 October 1807, Nap. *P&T*, No 1399, Vol. 1, pp. 672–3.)

Uniforms No information found.
Standard No information found.

Janissaires

(Janissaries)

Date of Creation July–August 1798.
Circumstances of Creation These were independent formations of Turkish soldiers formed by Napoleon in most of the provinces and major cities of Egypt to play a peacekeeping role. (Belhomme, Vol. 4, pp. 169–70.) Additional Janissary units were formed from time to time when sufficient Turkish recruits (or prisoners) were available. Four more companies were formed in February 1799 from prisoners captured at El Arich—three of Maghrebins (inhabitants of North Africa) and one of Arnauts from Albania. (Savant, *Les Mamelouks*, p. 45.)
Composition Most of these units were companies that varied in size from 25 to 65 men, but the force assigned to Cairo was the size of a battalion and had five companies of 65 men each. (Belhomme, Vol. 4, pp. 169–70.)
Commanders The following names of Janissary commanders have come down through history: Ibrahim Aga, Hassan Tchorbadji, Eumer El Halkadji, Moustapha Aga and Abdel 'Al Aga.
Operational History The units raised in Egypt saw only local action, which was considerable in the case of the Cairo battalion because the city twice rose in rebellion against the French. The companies that accompanied Napoleon on the expedition to Syria received particular praise for their steady conduct during the subsequent French retreat. (Savant, *Les Mamelouks*, p. 45.)
Final Transformation The Janissary companies that had fought in Syria were organised in June into the *Légion Syrienne*. (See separate entry.) No information has been found about the fate of the other companies.
Uniforms The Janissaries wore native dress but were identified by wearing French cockades. (Savant, *Les Mamelouks*, p. 45.)
Standard Each of these units received a tricolour flag with an inscription from the Koran and an imprecation against the Mamelukes on each side (one in French, the other in Arabic). (Spillman, 'Corps Auxiliaires', p. 8.)

Janissaires Syriennes

(Syrian Janissaries)

Date of Creation 3 Vendémiaire Year VIII (25 September 1799).
Circumstances of Creation This unit consisted of two independent companies of Syrian

cavalrymen who took their name from the feared troops of the same name in the Army of the Ottoman Empire. The term 'Syrian' is somewhat misleading, because the unit encompassed men from a myriad nationalities and ethnic and religious groups in the Middle East, including Turks, Syrians, Druse and Egyptians. These companies fought with the French during Napoleon's invasion of the Holy Land, and were forced into exile when that expedition failed.

Composition The strength of the First Company when it was first organised was only 55 men. (Savant, *Les Mamelouks*, pp. 48–9.) The companies were reorganised by an order dated 18 Messidor Year VIII (20 July 1800), and thereafter each one consisted of 100 men divided as follows (Reorganisation Decree quoted in Savant, *Les Mamelouks*, p. 426):

1	Squadron Chief
1	Captain
1	Lieutenant
2	Sergeants
4	Corporals
91	Privates

Commanders

First Company Yakoub Habaibi (or Hubbub) (1767–?), a Syrian sheik with ancestral lands midway between Acre and Nazareth who allied himself with Napoleon. Surgeon Larrey said of him: 'It was during the campaign in Syria that Yakoub gave us irrefutable proof of his zeal, devotion and humanity.' He was given command of his company as a reward for his loyalty. He went into exile in France when the French were defeated, but did not thereafter serve in the military. (Savant, *Les Mamelouks*, pp. 207–10.)

Second Company Youssef Hamoui (or Haem) (1772–?), an adventurer who left a confusing tangle of stories of exactly how and when he came to be named as a Squadron Chief in the French Army. He, too, chose to leave Egypt with the French. (Savant, *Les Mamelouks*, pp. 149–51.)

Operational History The First Company fought at the Battle of Mount Thabor on 16 April 1799 and its commander was shot through the body. It also provided valuable service to the French by guarding the lines of communication back to Egypt from attack by marauding Arabs. (Savant, *Les Mamelouks*, pp. 208–9.)

Final Transformation Both companies of Syrian Janissaries were incorporated into the Regiment of Mamelukes when that unit was formed by an order dated 4 Brumaire Year IX (26 October 1800). (See separate entry for *Mameluks* [1st Formation].)

Uniforms The men of these companies wore their own native dress but were expected at least to have 'uniform headwear, adapted to their customs and usages, with some distinctive aspect which will enable them to be recognised as French auxiliary troops.' (Article 7 of the July 1800 decree quoted in Savant, *Les Mamelouks*, p. 426.) The

lithograph of a 'Syrian' that appears in Vernet and Lami depicts a horseman wearing a red hat encircled by a multi-coloured turban, a green jacket with short sleeves worn over a flowing, light-coloured shirt and baggy red trousers.
Standard No information found.

Krakus

(Regiment of Krakus [Polish Cossacks])

Date of Creation 18 December 1813.
Circumstances of Creation The Krakus were the continuation under French control of a regiment bearing the same name that had been formed in the Army of the Grand Duchy of Warsaw in early 1813. This first unit of Krakus was created by a decree of 29 December 1812. (Chelminski, p. 179, n. 1.) The unit was intended to be the Polish counter to the Cossacks that had plagued the Grand Army in 1812, namely a force of very light cavalry that excelled at skirmishing (Grabowski, pp. 50–1):

> It was at Cracow [in early 1813] that Poniatowski formed a new regiment of cavalry, composed solely of inhabitants of Cracow and surrounding areas, that was known as the 'Krakus'.
>
> These horsemen were mounted on small peasant horses and were of small stature themselves, but they were strong, adroit and full of spirit and courage .... This regiment had more than 1,000 horses ....

Napoleon was so impressed with the performance of the Krakus during the campaign that he specifically provided for the continuation of the Regiment when he reorganised the remaining Polish troops by his decree dated 18 December 1813. (SHA X[l]6 quoted in Pigeard, *Troupes Polonaises*, p. 50.)
Composition The original unit had four squadrons of 220 men each. The decree of 18 December 1813 called for an increase of the unit's size to six squadrons of 250 men each, but this was never achieved. (Chelminski, p. 201.) The Krakus did not have trumpeters—signals were transmitted by waving a horse tail on a pike known as a 'Bunczuk'. (Memoirs of Colonel Bialowski, quoted in Chelminski, p. 276.)
Commanders *Creation to October 1813(?):* Major Rzuchowski. (Chelminski, p. 179.) *January 1814 to disbandment:* Colonel Joseph Dwernicki (1779–1857), a veteran of Dombrowski's Legions who commanded some independent detachments of Polish cavalry in 1812. (Chelminski, p. 286).
Operational History The Krakus did not see any action until the autumn campaign of 1813, when they were combined with some 200 survivors of the 14th Regiment of Polish Cuirassiers to form an advance corps under Polish General Uminski. (Chelminski, pp. 179–80.) They were reviewed by the Emperor at Zittau early on in the campaign and he was impressed by what he saw (Grabowski, p. 106): 'I would like to have 10,000 men like these, mounted on "*konias*" [small peasant horses]. They are an excellent

troop.' Shortly thereafter, the Krakus were noticed escorting a flock of sheep through the streets of Dresden. The animals undoubtedly belonged to the subjects of Napoleon's ally, the King of Saxony, but the Poles argued that it was better to have them eaten by friends rather than by enemies. (Grabowski, p. 122.)

The first significant test of the Regiment came on 4 September 1813, when the Krakus encountered a strong force of Cossacks near the village of Eberbach. The unit easily defeated the enemy. On 9 September an NCO of the Krakus named Godlewski captured the horse-tail banner of Cossack Regiment Grekow, a feat that earned him both the Legion of Honour and the Polish Virtuti Militari decoration. (Wielecki, 'Krakus', p. 8.) Poniatowski was so pleased with the Regiment that he usually called upon it to provide his personal escort. (Chelminski, p. 188.) After the Battle of Leipzig, the Regiment mustered only 21 officers and 257 troopers. (Morawski, p. 159.)

Work on reorganising the Krakus was started in late 1813 but never achieved its goals. During the 1814 campaign the Krakus generally fought in one combined unit with the Polish Lancers (2nd formation) under General Pac. The Krakus were at the cavalry depot of Versailles when Paris came under attack at the end of March 1814. They were rushed to the scene and executed some successful charges against Prussian troops near the toll-gate of Clichy. (Chelminski, p. 211.) They lost seven officers in the fighting in and around Paris.

Final Transformation The Krakus were disbanded and repatriated to Poland after the abdication of Napoleon.

Uniforms In 1813 it seems that the Krakus looked very much like Cossacks because the rank-and-file wore simple blue overcoats and fur caps instead of fancy uniforms. The dress of the officers was more elaborate and included a crimson and fur confederatka headdress, a blue caftan with silver epaulettes and trim and crimson trousers. (See illustrations in Morawski, pp. 124–35.)

The uniform worn in 1814 was described by an officer of the Regiment (Memoirs of Colonel Bialowski, quoted in Chelminski, p. 276):

> The uniform [of the Krakus], which was different from any other in the Army, was the following:
>
> Melon-shaped crimson bonnet with vertical white stripes, trimmed at the bottom with black astrakhan fleece, and having a white boss at the top and a cockade and small white plume on the left side.
>
> Instead of a kurtka, the coat was in the form of a generously cut dark blue surtout [*sic*] reaching to the knees with crimson collar and cuffs and white piping Instead of a cartridge box, each soldier had two Circassian-style cartridge patches on the breast of his coat, each of which held five cartridges and was outlined with white braid (silver for officers). Dark blue overalls with a very thin crimson stripe and leather reinforcement on the inside of the legs.
>
> Instead of a cloak, a grey cape with a collar falling over the shoulders and a hood.
>
> Crimson waist sash
>
> Arms: lance without pennon, sabre, pistols.

There is a Kraku officer's tunic in the collections of the Russian State Historical Museum in Moscow.
Standard No information found.

Lanciers de la Légion de la Vistule

(Vistula Legion Lancers; see also *Légion de la Vistule*)

Date of Creation March 1808.
Circumstances of Creation The Lancers of the Vistula were the cavalry component of the *Légion de la Vistule* (see separate entry) created by Napoleon out of the old *Légion Polacco-Italienne* (see separate entry). Although the Polish-Italian Legion had only one administrative counsel for its constituent cavalry and infantry units, Napoleon changed that for the Vistula Legion and thereafter deployed the two components as separate units.
Composition The Organisational Decree for the Lancer Regiment specifies that it would have a staff, four active service squadrons, each of which had two companies, and a depot company, for a total force of 1,174 officers and men. (Cavalry Organisational Decree, Article I, Nap. *O&A*. No 5436, Vol. 4, p. 72.) The unit was organised exactly in the manner of a line regiment of French mounted chasseurs. (Cavalry Organisational Decree, Article III, *ibid.*)

On 7 February 1811 Napoleon decreed the formation of a second regiment of cavalry that was to have the same establishment as the original regiment. (Nap. *O&A*, No 5505, Vol. 4, p. 103.) On 18 June of that same year the two regiments were accorded the 'honour' of becoming regular troops of the French Army when Napoleon decided to create a corps of lancers in his army in order to be better prepared to deal with Cossacks in his next war against Russia. At the beginning of 1814 these two units were so reduced in strength that they were combined into a single weak regiment.
Commanders
1st Regiment of Lancers (7th Light Horse Lancers of the Line after 18 June 1811) *15 July 1807–6 August 1811*: Colonel Jan Konopka (1777-?), who fought for Polish freedom as a teenager, then went into exile as a soldier for the French. Konopka took command of the Regiment when it was still part of the *Légion Polacco-Italienne* (see separate entry). He left the Regiment when he was promoted to Brigade General.
22 October 1811–5 May 1812: Colonel Stanislas Klicki (1775–1841), who had been the Major and then Lieutenant-Colonel of the Regiment under Konopka. (Decision of 22 October 1811, Nap. *P&T*, No 6287, pp. 748–50 at 749.) He transferred out of the Regiment to join the staff of Prince Eugene's 4th Corps for the Russian campaign.
5(?) May 1812–9 June 1813: Colonel Ignace Ferdinand Stokowski (1776–?), a soldier who started his military career as a cadet in the Polish military academy in Warsaw, then fought in Dombrowski's legions and finally did a stint in the Polish Light Horse of the Guard. He was wounded and captured by Prussian partisans near Dresden in June

1813. *2 July 1813 to final transformation:* According to Chelminski, Stokowski was replaced by Casimir Tanski (1774–1853), an officer who had fought in the legions of Italy, the Vistula Legion infantry in Spain, the cavalry of the Grand Duchy of Warsaw and the 3rd Lancers of the Guard. He ended up besieged in Dresden and was made prisoner when that city surrendered to the Allies after the Battle of Leipzig.

2nd Regiment of Lancers (8th Light Horse Lancers of the Line after 18 June 1811) *8 February 1811 to final transformation:* Thomas Lubienski (1784-1869), who served in the Polish Light Horse of the Guard before being promoted to command this Regiment. (His portrait appears in Tranié, p. 45.) Colonel Lubienski was wounded in the foot at the Beresina on 28 November.

Combined Regiment *19 January 1814 to final transformation:* Colonel Lubienski of the 2nd/8th Light Horse Lancers. He was promoted to the rank of Brigade General on 15 March 1814.

Operational History The Lancers made a significantly favourable impression on the Emperor the first time he encountered them at Bayonne in June 1808. The story of the meeting is recounted by Désiré Chlapowski, a Pole serving as one of Napoleon's *Ordonnance* Officers (Chlapowski, pp. 82–3):

> One of the first regiments [to travel through Bayonne] was the regiment of Polish Lancers commanded by Colonel Konopka. It was an old regiment from the Legion of Dombrowski, organised in Italy by Rozniecki with Polish prisoners and Galician deserters from the Austrian Army. This superb and happy regiment was composed exclusively of experienced officers and men. Klicki was the Major.
>
> One morning before breakfast the Emperor held a review and ordered the regiment to conduct manoeuvres on a large esplanade behind the garden. All of the manoeuvres were executed with such speed and precision that all the French officers agreed that there was not a better regiment in the whole army, the Guard included. The Emperor invited the officers [of the Lancers] to a dinner which took place in the camp of the Polish Light Horse of the Guard and was a very brilliant affair.

According to another observer, Napoleon actually gave thought at this time to doing away with the unit's lances because they were inefficient (Petiet, p. 203):

> A regiment of Polish Lancers had just arrived at Bayonne. Napoleon said to their colonel: 'Since your lances cannot, in a charge, parry a sabre blow and since the red and white pennons are merely childish playthings, I am going to re-arm your regiment with carbines.'
>
> 'Sire,' responded the colonel, 'because of its length alone, the lance is a weapon that in the hands of a skilled user can create a powerful moral superiority over an enemy because the enemy can be killed or wounded without coming close enough to strike back with a sword. In addition, the pennons scare the horses of the enemy hussars and dragoons and give us a great advantage.'

When Napoleon heard that last assertion from Colonel Konopka, he was so sceptical the offended Colonel offered a demonstration on the spot. He thereupon led his men in a mock charge against the Emperor and his staff that caused Napoleon's own horse to bolt. The chastened Emperor had the last word, however: 'You can keep your lances, but I am going to give carbines to the men in your second rank.' (*Ibid.*)

The Lancers spent the next four years fighting in the Spanish Peninsula. Their first assignment was to join the covering forces for the first siege of Saragossa. On 13 June 1808 the Lancers played a significant role in dispersing a large enemy force and capturing 2,000 prisoners. Napoleon himself noted that '[t]he Polish Lancer Regiment swam across the Ebro River to pursue the Spaniards who escaped. Aside from a Captain of the Polish Lancers who drowned, we lost only four men killed and eight wounded.' (N. to Murat, June 16, 1808, Nap. *Corr.*, No 14103, Vol. 17, pp. 313–14 at 313.) They had numerous skirmishes with Spanish forces outside the beleaguered city. Martinien records that the Lancers had five officers, including Colonel Konopka, wounded on 4 August, the date of the grand assault by the French on the city, so they may have also taken part in the siege operations themselves on that day. The Lancers retired north of the Ebro with the rest of the French forces as a result of the defeat at Bailen and remained there from August to October while Napoleon built up his forces for the reconquest of the Spanish kingdom for his brother, Joseph.

The entire Regiment fought in its first formal battle at Tudela on 23 November, but thereafter the Regiment split into two operational components: Major Klicki and the first company of the first squadron stayed with the 3rd Corps while the rest of the unit marched south with the 4th Corps of the French Army. (Kirkor, pp. 612–13.) The squadron in Aragon went on to become the personal bodyguard of General (later Marshal) Gabriel Suchet. (Rigo, 'Lancers', p. 8.)

The main body of the Regiment was attached to General Antoine Lasalle's cavalry division, which also included the 5th and 10th Mounted Chasseurs of the Line and the 9th Dragoons. (Instructions for King Joseph, 17 January 1809, quoted in Balagny, Vol. 4, pp. 503–11 at 508.) After the recapture of Madrid, the Lancers were active in the territory between the Tagus and Guadiana Rivers that served as the buffer zone in 1809 between the French and Spanish spheres of influence. In March 1809 they were surprised by the arrival of a strong force of Spanish cavalry that was acting as part of a offensive intended to capture Toledo and, in the best of circumstances, threaten Madrid itself (Bouillé, Vol. 3, p. 216):

> A corps of 4,000 enemy horsemen marched on Yevenes and Manzaneque [south of Toledo] on 24 March, from where they were expected to advance on Mora and thus cover the approach of the main Spanish force against Toledo. At Yevenes they ran into the regiment of Polish Lancers, a brave unit, but one which, out of overconfidence and an unprofessional disdain for its enemies, committed the unpardonable military sin of letting itself be surprised. This incident is all the more inexplicable since the regiment should have been on the march executing orders it had received to rendezvous with the Polish infantry division [of the Grand Duchy of Warsaw]. The baggage of the regiment plus three officers and 57 lancers fell into the hands of the Spanish cavalry . . .

Even worse for the pride of the Regiment, that baggage apparently included all four of the unit's standards, one of which is still on display in the Cathedral of Seville. (Rigo, 'Lancers', p. 8; entry for Colonel Konopka in the Polish Biographical Dictionary, Vol. 15, p. 567.)

The Lancers had much better results in most of their other confrontations with Spanish armies. Always serving as part of General Horace Sébastiani's 4th Corps, the Regiment was victorious at Ciudad Real on 28 March and at least not unsuccessful at Talavera on 28 July. After the retreat of the British, the 4th Corps stopped another threat from the south at the Battle of Almonacid on 11 August. The Regiment played a particularly distinguished role in that action (Report of Sébastiani, 13 August 1809 in J. Bonaparte, Vol. 6, p. 342):

> Among the officers of cavalry, I must cite . . . M. [Adam] Hupet, the Captain commanding the Polish Lancers, and Messrs Konoptka [*sic*] and Janichevski [*sic*], officers of the same regiment. The latter officer, the commander of my personal guard, had his horse killed underneath him while charging an enemy post, which was captured to a man.

The Lancers were brigaded with the 10th Chasseurs under General Antoine Marie Paris d'Illins for the campaign leading to the Battle of Ocana. On 18 November 1809 the unit participated in the largest cavalry action of the entire Peninsular War as all the massed French cavalry accompanying the French 4th and 5th Corps drove off the cavalry screening the Spanish Army of La Mancha with relatively little loss, although General Paris d'Illins was killed in the fighting. The next day, the battle of Ocana itself was decided almost entirely by a bold flanking movement executed by the French cavalry that rolled up the enemy right wing and routed the Spanish army (Chlapowski, p. 223):

> The Regiment of Polish Lancers of the Vistula Legion, with Colonel Konopka, charged the flank of the retreating enemy infantry. I don't know if the Regiment captured all the prisoners themselves, or simply rounded up those captured by others, but in any event a detachment of this Regiment escorted to Madrid nearly 10,000 Spaniards taken at Ocana.

The Lancers and the 10th Chasseurs, now under General André Thomas Perreimond, spearheaded the French invasion of Andalusia in January 1810. They executed a number of successful charges in the passes of the Sierra Morena range and helped capture 4,000 prisoners. (Kirkor, p. 615.) For most of 1810 the Lancers were based at Baza in the eastern part of the province of Granada, facing off against guerrillas and Spanish regular forces in the province of Murcia. In November the Lancers helped to crush an invasion attempt by General Blake. In 1811 the Lancers were transferred to Seville to become part of Marshal Soult's strategic reserve for the whole of Andalusia. As a result, they became part of the force Soult pulled together in May 1811 to relieve the French garrison besieged at Badajoz. On 16 May Soult's army clashed with a combined Spanish, Portuguese and British force under Marshal William Beresford at a small Estremaduran village named Albuera.

Albuera was the finest hour of the Vistula Legion Lancers. They opened the action by spearheading a French feint against Albuera itself, then galloped across the front of the Allied army to join the real French attack, a sweep around Beresford's right flank. As the Allies shifted to meet this thrust, General John Colborne's Brigade, consisting of the 1st Battalion, 3rd Foot, the 2nd Battalion, 66th Foot, the 2nd Battalion of the 48th Foot and the 2nd of the 31st, was committed to an attack against a column of French infantry without proper flank support. The Lancers, supported by the 2nd Hussars, made the English pay dearly for that mistake. Aided by a rain squall and a temporary misidentification of the Lancers as Spanish cavalry, the French horsemen rode over the first three English battalions, inflicting heavy casualties and capturing four (possibly five) of six colours (the King's colour of the 3rd was saved by the incredible exertions of Lieutenant Matthew Latham) and five cannon. (Kirkor, p. 615.) One Polish Lancer attacked Marshal Beresford himself but the Marshal, a burly man, avoided the lancer's thrust and then dismounted his assailant by dragging him backwards off his horse by his collar. (G. Fitz-Clarence, *A Hussar's Life on Service in Four Letters* [London, n.d.], p. 49.)

By all rights, French victory should have been assured at this point, but the tenacious resistance of the remaining British infantry gradually stemmed the French advance. As the battle hung in the balance, English General Lowry Cole ordered his own 4th Division, which had been held in reserve, forward to attack the enemy. Marshal Soult called in turn upon the Poles to save the day, and they accordingly launched an attack on the advancing column. This time, however, the British flank was properly secured by the deployment of a brigade of Portuguese infantry, which repulsed the Lancers without much difficulty.

The Battle was a costly one for the Poles, since they lost 130 officers and men out of 591 present at the start, or just under 22 per cent. They were, however, well-rewarded for their performance. Colonel Konopka was shortly thereafter promoted to the rank of Brigade General and his brother, Vincent Konopka, was honoured for taking one of the British colours. Ten other officers and men were awarded crosses of the Legion of Honour. (Kirkor, p. 615.) Their performance may also have been the final decisive factor leading to Napoleon's decision to convert six of his dragoon regiments into Light Horse Lancers and to transform the 1st and 2nd Lancer Regiments of the Vistula Legion into the 7th and 8th Regiments of that arm in the French Army on 18 June.

The 2nd/8th Lancers did not see any action until the Russian campaign, for which they were brigaded with the 20th Mounted Chasseurs and attached to Marshal Oudinot's 2nd Corps. They suffered casualties in several actions (including the combat of Jakubowo on 30 July when one officer was killed and three wounded), but they survived the early stages of the campaign relatively unharmed because the actions of the 2nd Corps in and around Polotsk involved infantry more than cavalry. The Regiment, however, played a key role in the fighting at the Beresina, being the first unit to ford the river and scatter the Cossacks on the other side so that construction of the bridges could begin. (Chlapowski, pp. 294–5.) By the end of the last charges on 28 November the Regiment mustered only 16 officers and 77 mounted men. (Martinien, *Généraux*, pp. 428–9.)

Napoleon had apparently intended that both regiments of Lancers would take part in the Russian campaign but, despite direct orders to the contrary, Marshal Soult persisted in keeping the bulk of 1st/7th Lancers with him until the end of 1812. It seems, however, that at least one squadron of the 1st/7th made it to Russia. One piece of evidence in this regard is the fact that Lieutenant Konopka of the 1st/7th Lancers was wounded twice in Russia during 1812 (on 16 June and 2 December), but this evidence is not conclusive because his presence in that theatre may simply have been the result of some personal connection with General Konopka. Another piece of evidence—also inconclusive, since it is not confirmed by other sources—is the statement in Chelminski, p. 157, that Colonel Stokowski and 100 men of the Regiment were part of the escort for Napoleon when he left the Army on 6 December. According to Chelminski, Napoleon ordered the Lancers to kill him if he were ever in danger of being captured. The Lancers are said to have replied haughtily that his order could not be followed because if such a danger did arise, it could only mean that all the Lancers were already dead themselves.

Both Lancer Regiments were reconstituted for 1813 and took part in both the spring and autumn campaigns. The 1st/7th was defeated in a sharp action against Allied partisans on 9 June 1813 near Dresden, losing two officers killed and five wounded (including Colonel Stokowski, who was captured). At the start of the autumn campaign the 1st/7th mustered 45 officers and 670 men, while the 2nd/8th had 30 officers and 326 men. (S. Bowden, *Napoleon's Grande Armée of 1813* [Chicago 1990], pp. 277, 279.) Both Regiments enjoyed great success at the Battle of Dresden from 25 to 27 August but suffered heavy casualties. The 1st/7th thereafter remained in Dresden with the 14th Corps until it capitulated. A single squadron that escaped that fate ended up in Hamburg besieged with the 13th Corps. (Kirkor, p. 616.) The 2nd/8th Lancers fought at Leipzig and then retreated to France.

The remaining elements of both Regiments were combined on 19 January 1814 into a single unit referred to as the 7th Light Horse Lancers. It served under General Christophe Antoine Merlin as part of Marshal Marmont's 6th Corps, fighting at Champaubert, Vauchamps, Reims, Laon, Fère-Champenoise and Paris. When Marmont caused his Corps to defect to the Allies, the rearguard was formed by a squadron of Lancers under Captain Schultz. When the Captain realised what was happening, he led his men at the gallop back out of the enemy lines and was the first to bring news of the loss to Napoleon. (Kirkor, p. 617.)

Final Transformation The remaining Regiment was disbanded after Napoleon's abdication.

Uniforms The Lancers of the Vistula Legion started out using the same blue-faced yellow uniforms and same armament as they had as part of the Polish-Italian Legion.

(Cavalry Organisational Decree, Article IV, Nap. *O&A*, No 5436, Vol. 4, p. 72.) Based on an early print by Hoffman, many sources (including Rigo, *Le Plumet*, Plate No 52, 'Lanciers de la Vistule, 1er Régiment, Guidon 1800–1814') indicate that the regimental czapka had a yellow top but no cords or plate. Another controversial point is the shoulder ornaments for the uniform. Rigo says that the élite company had a white epaulette on the left shoulder and a fringed white epaulette on the right, but two fringed epaulettes are possible, as are plain blue shoulder straps trimmed yellow. It is impossible to resolve these points, however, because there are no verifiable first-hand sources that depict the dress of the Lancer Regiment in Spain.

When the Lancers were converted to French line cavalry in 1811, serious consideration was given to re-uniforming them in the same style as the first six Light Horse Lancer regiments. That plan was quickly rejected, but it took a ruling by the Emperor to prevent the Poles from being given French-style shakos in place of their czapkas. (Decision of 10 March 1811, Nap. *P&T*, No 5159, Vol. 4, pp. 116–18 at 118; see also Margerand, 'Lanciers', p. 237.) A surviving czapka of the 7th or 8th Lancers from the period in the collections of the French Army Museum at Emperi reveals an extremely elegant headdress with a blue top, trimmed yellow, yellow metal chinscales and lion's head bosses, and a sunburst czapka plate with an eagle over crossed lances design in the center. (See photographs in Blondieau, pp. 48 and 63.) Another example in the Sikorski Institute in London lacks the plate.

The dress of the two Regiments as Lione Lancers was specified in orders dated 24 July and 9 August 1811. The only difference between the uniforms of the two regiments was the colour of the collar (yellow for the 7th, blue for the 8th). (Margerand, 'Lanciers', p. 237.) The Martinet prints of these two units give the correct colour scheme, but must be used with caution with respect to other details because the same base print is also used for the Polish Light Horse of the Guard. Probably more accurate, but still subject to some reservations, are the watercolour drawings executed by Carle Vernet to illustrate the 1812 Uniform Regulations. (See reproductions in Pétard's two articles about the Lancers.) There are also some contemporary drawings from 1813 that add details such a grey trousers.

The memoirs of an anonymous 17-year-old who joined the Lancers as a trumpeter in 1810 add many interesting details concerning the dress of the 1st Regiment. (Anon., *Soldaten Leben*.) For instance, he reports that men of the Regiment always tilted their czapkas over one ear when they wanted to achieve an especially elegant appearance on parade. (*Ibid*., p. 22.) When he arrived at the Regiment in Spain, he noted that because of the coating of dust on everything it was almost impossible to distinguish the light [*sic*] blue colour of the jackets from the light yellow of the facings. (*Ibid*., p. 39.) (The reference to light blue may either be an indication that the dark blue jackets of the Regiment had faded in the Spanish sun or, less likely, that the trumpeters of the Regiment wore jackets of that shade.) He also noted that the men were wearing riding overalls made out of goatskin. (*Ibid*., p. 61.)

This same soldier had three interesting close calls in combat that illustrate points about his clothing. On one occasion, an English Dragoon cut his czapka in half with a sabre blow, but the soldier's life was saved because the shoes and brushes he was carrying wrapped up in a kerchief inside his headdress stopped the cut from penetrating his skull. (*Ibid.*, p. 62.) Another time, he was saved from harm by the fact that an enemy sabre cut could not penetrate his rolled-up cloak and his shoulder-belt. (*Ibid.*, p. 74.) In the last incident, a Spanish officer fired a pistol at him at point-blank range. His face was singed by the blast from the muzzle, but the bullet only ripped his epaulette. (*Ibid.*, p. 83.)

Standard According to Rigo, *Le Plumet*, Plate No 52, the 1st Lancers carried four tricolour republican standards that had been given to the Polish Lancers of the *Légion du Danube* in 1800 (see separate entry). As noted above, all four of these guidons fell into enemy hands in 1809. Despite the value that Napoleon placed on the Polish Lancers, it seems that neither the 1st nor the 2nd Regiment ever received any other standards, even after they had become integrated into the French Army in 1811.

Lanciers Polonais (1st Formation)

(Polish Lancers [1st Formation])

Date of Creation December 1801

Circumstances of Creation This cavalry regiment was created when the Polish *Légion du Danube* (see separate entry) was transformed into the 3rd Polish Demi-brigade. Since the latter was an infantry unit only, the cavalry that had been attached to the Legion was re-constituted as an independent unit.

Composition The Lancers were formed as a regiment of four squadrons. On 22 December 1801 the unit had a strength of 707 officers and men. (Nafziger, *Poles*, p. 74.)

Commanders *Creation to final transformation:* Colonel Alexander Rozniecki (1774–1849), who later became inspector-general of the cavalry of the Duchy of Warsaw. (Pigeard, *Troupes Polonaises*, pp. 68–9.)

Operational History The Lancers were transferred to the Army of the Republic of Italy on 31 December 1801 and thereafter saw only peacetime service until they served in the Army of Italy under Marshal Masséna during its campaign against the Austrians in the autumn of 1805. They participated in the French invasion of Naples in 1806 and were ultimately given by Napoleon, as King of Italy, to his brother, Joseph, then King of Naples, in order to provide him with at least one reliable cavalry regiment in his armed forces.

Final Transformation The Lancers were recalled to French service in early 1807 and became part of the *Légion Polacco-Italienne* (see separate entry) formed by an order dated 5 April 1807. The unit eventually became the Lancers of the Vistula Legion.

Uniforms Logic suggests that the Lancers initially wore the uniform of the cavalry of the

Légion du Danube (see separate entry) from which the unit was formed. Information as to what that uniform looked like is provided by a painting in the Rovatti Chronicle for 1801. (Boeri, Illustration No 69.) The horseman depicted has a blue czapka with a visor, yellow(?) cords and trim and a tall red plume tipped yellow. The uniform is otherwise entirely blue with silver buttons and red trim on the lapels, cuffs, collar and coat-tails. The figure has an aiguilette on his left shoulder and single white belt worn over the right shoulder (a detail that is probably wrong). He has blue breeches with double red stripes down the side and short black boots. His horse furniture is a sheepskin saddle cloth with scallop-edged red trim and no portmanteau. The figure is carrying a lance with a tricolour staff and stripes of red, white and blue (reading from top to bottom) on his lance pennon.

Standard Same as for the Lancers of the *Légion du Danube* (see separate entry).

Lanciers Polonais (2nd Formation)

(Polish Lancers [2nd Formation])

Date of Creation Decree of 18 December 1813 (SHA X[l]6 quoted in Pigeard, *Troupes Polonaises*, p. 50.)

Circumstances of Creation The remaining units of the Army of the Grand Duchy of Warsaw were so thoroughly destroyed during the autumn campaign of 1813 that Napoleon decided to place all the survivors into a few select new units designated collectively the 'Polish Army Corps'. All the remaining cavalrymen of the Duchy were consequently formed into two Regiments of Lancers and one of Krakus (see separate entry). All the officers and men were veterans of at least one campaign, and generally many more than that.

Composition Each Lancer Regiment was expected to have a staff and four companies of cavalrymen organised into two squadrons for a total of 25 officers and 505 NCOs and men, but neither Regiment ever achieved full strength. (Zaremba, 'Lancers', p. 54.)

Commanders

1st Polish Lancer Regiment *Formation to final transformation:* Colonel Sigismond Kurnatkowski, who had been commander of the 5th Cavalry Regiment (Mounted Chasseurs) of the Duchy of Warsaw when it was disbanded following the Russian campaign. He was promoted to the rank of Brigade General on 5 April 1814.

2nd Polish Lancer Regiment *Formation to final transformation:* Colonel T. Siemiatkowski.

Operational History The Regiments never served as independent units in the field, but instead each provided detachments of men for a so-called Polish Cavalry 'Brigade' under the command of General Louis Michel Pac that also included the Krakus (see separate entry). This brigade was attached to the 2nd Division of Guard cavalry under General Étienne Marie Antoine Champion Nansouty and therefore served at all the actions in the campaign at which the Imperial Guard was present. This was not so much

an honour for the Poles as a cynical ploy on the part of Napoleon to obtain maximum value from the relevant units (N. to Minister of War, 19 February 1814, Nap. *O&A*, No 6450, Vol. 4, p. 459): 'It is impossible to make the Poles perform well unless one includes them in the Guard, surrounds them with veteran troops and allows them to serve under my own eye.' The Poles of the Regiments responded by earning 25 decorations of the Legion of Honour during their short time of service.
Final Transformation The survivors of the Lancer Regiments were repatriated to Poland after Napoleon's abdication.
Uniforms The two Regiments were awarded 500 suits of new clothing each in early January, but it is probable that some of the men simply wore the uniforms of their original corps. (Decision of 5 January 1814, Nap. *O&A*, No 6357, Vol. 4, p. 402.) As can be seen by surviving examples in Museum collections in Poland attributable to specifc individuals known to have served in these units, the new uniforms were modelled on those of the 7th and 8th Light Horse Lancers of the Line (see separate entry on *Lanciers de la Légion de la Vistule*). Both Regiments wore czapkas with dark blue tops and dark blue kurtkas with minuscule tails. The 1st Regiment seems to have had red facings; based on an interpretation of a coloured 1814 engraving after Saint Fal, those of the 2nd Regiment might have been crimson instead. (Zaremba, 'Lancers', p. 55.) Officers also wore red trousers with a silver stripe down the side for full dress and had silver sashes with three red stripes.
Standard No information found.

Légion Copte

(Coptic Legion)

Date of Creation May 1800.
Circumstances of Creation During the campaign leading to the victory of the French Army of the Orient over Turkish invaders of Egypt at Battle of Heliopolis on 20 March 1800, part of the Turkish force reached Cairo and precipitated a revolt by the citizens of that city against the French and their collaborators. Part of the fury of the crowd was directed against the Christian Egyptians, or Copts, who were the principal tax collectors for the French (as they had been for the Mamelukes). Moallem Jacob, a Coptic leader who had already gained some fame by accompanying General Desaix on his conquest of Upper Egypt, was a resident of Cairo and his home became the heart of the resistance mustered by the Christian quarter to the ravages of their Moslem neighbours. (Fieffé, Vol. 2, p. 48, gives the name of this individual as 'Ma-Hallem-Yacoub'.) When the city surrendered to General Kléber on 15 April the French put Jacob in charge of levying a punitive contribution against the inhabitants who joined the revolt and authorised him to form a Coptic military force. (Homsy, pp. 97–100.)
Composition The Legion was composed of two battalions of five companies each, one

of which was Grenadiers. (Belhomme, Vol. 4, p. 207.) Belhomme says that the unit was formed on 25 August 1799, which is certainly wrong, although 25 August 1800 could have been the date when some official action with respect to creation of the Legion was taken. Fieffé, Vol. 2, p. 49, adds the information that the battalions had 300 men each and were commanded by Arragli and Abdallah-Mansourah, respectively.

Commanders *Creation to August 1801:* Moallem Jacob (?–1801), the Coptic leader described above. His biographer presents a detailed case for the conclusion that Jacob was named to the rank of Brigade Chief by an order of 22 Thermidor Year VIII (10 August 1800) and was promoted to Brigade General in 1801, but his name does not appear in either Quentin's dictionary of Napoleonic colonels nor Six's dictionary of generals. (Homsy, p. 103.) He died on board ship on the way back to France after the French surrender. *August 1801 to disbandment:* Colonel Gabriel Sidarious (1765–1851), a Greek resident of Egypt who rallied to the French after their invasion of his country. Sidarious was Jacob's nephew and served under him and Desaix in Upper Egypt. He was promoted to the rank of Colonel by Jacob and served as the second in command of the Legion until Jacob's death.

Operational History No information found other than statements in Fieffé that the Coptic Legion fought at the Battle of Canope (Alexandria) on 21 March 1801, where an entire battalion was forced to surrender to the British when it advanced rashly into the middle of the British lines. (Fieffé, Vol. 2, p. 105.)

Final Transformation The members of the Legion who chose exile in France after the surrender of the French were given an opportunity to join the *Chasseurs d'Orient* and the *Mamelukes* (2nd Formation) formed in 1801 (see separate entries for those units).

Uniforms The only potentially reliable depiction of the uniform of the Legion is that provided by a lithograph produced in 1821 that shows a wounded soldier of the Legion wearing a green uniform with yellow collar, cuffs and piping down the front, silver buttons, red epaulettes, buff trousers and short black boots. (Vernet & Lami.) The uniform is completed by a bicorne hat with a large, drooping red plume. (Lienhart & Humbert, Vol. 5, p. 572.) Whatever uniform was worn, it seems that the Legion was armed and uniformed at the expense of Moallem Jacob himself. After the unit arrived in France, his successor, Colonel Sidarious, claimed reimbursement for nearly 20,000 francs spent by his uncle to create the Legion. The inventory of items purchased that was submitted to the French authorities to support the claim mentions the following (Inventory of 7 Pluviose Year X [27 January 1802] quoted in Homsy, p. 101):

800	Shirts
850	Trousers
750	Jackets
750	*Bonnets*
750	Hats
800	Cartridge boxes

100	Bayonets
30	Kettles
180	*Nattes* (mats ?)

The *bonnets* mentioned seem to have been headwear made out of black sheepskin. (Homsy, p. 100.)

Standard The inventory noted above indicates that Jacob purchased two flags for the Legion, but no information has been found about their design.

Légion de la Vistule

(Vistula Legion)

Date of Creation March 1808.

Circumstances of Creation In March 1808 Napoleon recalled both the cavalry and infantry elements of the *Légion Polacco-Italienne* (see separate entry) from Westphalian service, brushing aside in the process his brother Jerome's request for monetary compensation or the *Régiment de Westphalie* as a replacement. (Decisions of 10 March 1807, Nap. *P&T*, Nos. 1695 and 1697, Vol. 2, p. 114.) To mark the change, he decided that the unit should be renamed the Legion of the Vistula. (N. to Minister of War, 29 March 1808, Nap. *O&A*, No 5434, Vol. 4, p. 71.)

Composition Although the Legion had traditionally been a combined unit of cavalry and infantry, Napoleon decided he would treat the two components as independent units and decreed that the cavalry and the infantry would even have separate administrative councils. (Infantry Organisational Decree of 24 June 1808, Nap. *O&A*, No 5441, Vol. 4, pp. 73–6.) This entry deals with the Legion infantry, while a separate entry on the *Lanciers de la Légion de la Vistule* deals with the cavalry.

The Infantry Organisational Decree divided the foot soldiers of the Legion into a staff and three regiments of line infantry, each of which had two battalions of six companies, plus a separate depot battalion. (Organisational Decree, Article II.) Since each company had a regulation strength of 140 men, the theoretical size of the Legion was 5,880 men. All the men were expected to be Polish except for one NCO per company and one adjutant per battalion who could be French to help with French language paperwork required by the military establishment. (Organisational Decree, Article XVIII.) The staff of the Legion included a band of eighteen musicians (Organisational Decree, Article IX) and each battalion had six sappers (Organisational Decree, Article VI).

In 1809 Napoleon tried to make use of the many Polish prisoners he captured from the Austrian Army by increasing the size of each Legion company from 160 to 200 men and by creating a second Vistula Legion. (Decisions of 8 July and 23 July 1809, Nap. *O&A*, Nos. 5461 and 5463, Vol. 4, pp. 83–4.) The new Legion was expected to have the same strength as the original and was commanded by General Nicholas Bronikowski (1772–?). As it turned out, however, after deducting the necessary numbers of men to bring the 1st Legion up to full strength, there were not enough men to create a full second Legion. The 2nd Legion was formally disbanded on 12 February 1810 and the two regiments that had been partially formed were combined to create a 4th Regiment of infantry for the 1st (and once again only) Legion. (Order of 12 February 1810, Nap. O&A, No 4014, Vol. 3, p. 252.)

At the start of 1812 Napoleon decided to expand the Legion by adding a third battalion and an artillery company to each regiment. (N. to Berthier, 24 March 1812, Nap. *P&T*, No 6992, Vol. 5, p. 245.) Each artillery company was equipped with two cannon, three caissons of artillery ammunition, two caissons of cartridges, two caissons for bread, a field forge and an ambulance. (Decision of 13 March 1812, Nap. O&A, No 5794, Vol. 4, p. 214.) The third battalions took some time to form, so they did not participate fully in the Russian campaign. While they were being raised, Napoleon had to caution the Legion's commanders to admit only Poles and to reject German and Russian recruits. (N. to Minister of War, 11 March 1812, Nap. O&A, No 5790, Vol. 4, p. 213.)

The strength of the four infantry regiments of the Legion was so reduced by the summer of 1813 that Napoleon decided to combine them into a single unit, to be known as the *Régiment de la Vistule*. The new regiment had only two battalions of six companies each, and the companies themselves had a strength of only 140 men. (Order of 18 June 1813, Nap. O&A, No 6001, Vol. 4, pp. 282–3.) An even weaker version of this Regiment served throughout the 1814 campaign.

Commanders The Polish-Italian Legion, and the 1st Polish Demi-brigade before that, had been commanded by General Joseph Grabinski, so it was expected that he would command the Vistula Legion as well. When the infantry and cavalry of the Legion were split up as a practical matter, however, his services were no longer required. Napoleon instead decided that the infantry would be commanded by the Colonel of the 1st Regiment acting as Colonel Commandant, while the other regiments were to commanded by Majors. (Organisational Decree, Article III.) This arrangement was not always observed, however.

1st Regiment *Formation to end of 1809*: Colonel Chlopicki, who had commanded the 1st Regiment of the Polish-Italian Legion from 1 July 1807. He was 'one of the bravest officers . . . [but] a severe and tyrannical disciplinarian'. (Brandt, p. 46.) He also habitually led his troops into action carrying a cane rather than some more threatening weapon. (Brandt, p. 126.) He was promoted to the rank of Brigade General on 13 July 1809, but he retained effective command of the 1st Regiment until 1810. He commanded a brigade formed from the 1st and 2nd Vistula Legion Regiments in Russia, but was wounded on 11 September 1812 and did not return to active duty thereafter. Chlopicki went on to be the commander of the Polish National Army during the Revolution of 1831. *March 1810–November 1812*: Colonel Kasinowski, who had previously been the commander of the 2nd Regiment (see entry below). He already held the position of Commandant of the Legion before he transferred to the 1st Regiment. He was wounded at the crossing of the Berezina and disappeared shortly thereafter.

2nd Regiment *1 July 1807– April 1808:* Colonel Simon Biatowieyski (?–1808), who was promoted from the rank of Major to command the Regiment. (Order of the Day of General Grabinski, 11 July 1807, in Chlopicki Archives, Warsaw; Nafziger, *Poles*, p. 79.) He died of unspecified causes while in command. *9 July 1808–March 1810:* Colonel Nicholas Alexander Kasinowski (1766–1812?), another veteran of the Italian campaigns. (Based on comparison with reports in the Chlopicki Archives, Warsaw, his name is mis-spelled 'Kosinowski' in Quentin.) Upon Chlopicki's promotion to the rank of General, Kasinowski became the Commandant of the whole Legion in addition to retaining command of the 2nd Regiment. (Return of the Vistula Legion, 1 January 1810, Chlopicki Archives, Warsaw.) He later transferred to command of the 1st Regiment. *March 1810–March 1812:* Colonel Michalowski (1770–?), the long-time Major of the Regiment. (Pigeard, *Polonais*, p. 41.) *22 March 1812–11 August 1812:* Colonel Joseph Chlusowicz (1776–post 1831), another veteran of Italy. He left the Regiment to become second-in-command of the 3rd Lancers of the Guard formed in Lithuania (see separate entry). He was captured along with his commanding officer and much of his new Regiment in October. *23 August 1812 to final transformation:* Colonel Stanislas Joseph Malezewski (1782–1813), who was serving in a staff position when he was selected to replace the departing Colonel Chlusowicz. (Brandt, p. 32.) He later became the second commander of the combined Regiment of the Vistula in 1813.

3rd Regiment *1 July 1807–31 May 1808:* Colonel Piotr Swiderski (1756–1826), who was promoted to command of the unit when it was still the 3rd Regiment of the Polish-Italian Legion. (Order of the Day of General Grabinski, 11 July 1807, in Chlopicki Archives, Warsaw.) He had previously been Major of the Lancers of the Legion and distinguished himself during the campaign in Silesia in early 1807. Unfortunately, he lost the use of his right eye during that campaign and ended up retiring from the Army a year later. *12 July 1808–March 1811:* Sixtus d'Estko (1776–1813), a nephew of General Kosciuszko. (Martinien, *Généraux*, pp. 425–6.) He fought in Italy in 1798–99, was captured at the Battle of the Trebbia and spent the next two years as a prisoner in Austria. Although he was appointed to command of the 4th Regiment on 23 May 1810, Marshal Suchet retained him in command of the 3rd until March 1811. *6 August 1811–5 February 1813:* Colonel Paul Fadzielski (1779–1813), who had fought in northern Italy, Naples and Spain as an officer of the 1st Regiment. (He is referred to as 'Fondzielcki' in Quentin.) He was wounded at the Battle of Krasnoi in Russia and died on 5 February 1813 without having fully recovered. After Krasnoi, the Regiment was commanded as a practical matter by Major Jan Szott.

4th Regiment *Formation to 23 May 1810:* Major Casimir Tanski (1774–1853), an officer who had fought in the legions of Italy. *23 May 1810 to final transformation:*

Colonel Sixtus d'Estko, formerly the commander of the 3rd Regiment. He did not actually join the Regiment until 12 March 1811. He became the first commander of the combined Regiment of the Vistula in 1813.

Combined Regiment *19 June 1813–11 July 1813*: Colonel d'Estko, formerly commander of the 4th Regiment of the Vistula. He left the Regiment upon his promotion to the rank of Brigade General. He distinguished himself in action thereafter and was mortally wounded on 18 October at Leipzig. (Martinien, *Généraux*, p. 426.) *11 July 1813–19 October 1813*: Colonel Malezewski, the former commander of the 2nd Regiment. He was killed at the end of the Battle of Leipzig. *4 January 1814–2 March 1814*: Colonel Michel Kosinski (1776–1835), the long-time Major of the 3rd Regiment. Kosinski was wounded at the capture of Soissons on 2 March 1814.

Operational History The Legion infantry became involved in the Iberian Peninsula when Napoleon called it to Bayonne in June of 1808 to assist with his overthrow of the Spanish Bourbon dynasty (Chlapowski, p. 84):

> Several days later, three regiments of Polish infantry arrived at Bayonne. These regiments were the descendants of the old Legions of Italy and formed the Legion of the Vistula.
>
> These very good-looking regiments were commanded by General Grabinski (afterwards replaced by General Chlopicki). They were also reviewed by the Emperor, who ordered his Foot Guards to make the Poles welcome and offer them dinner.

Another eye-witness has a very different story about an Imperial review of the Legion at Bayonne (Brandt, p. 178):

> On that particular day, Napoleon . . . was . . . in a foul temper. Some badly executed drill caused him to burst out and shout: 'The Prefect of Cassel [in Westphalia] is quite right when he writes that the officers of these regiments do nothing but gamble and the soldiers do nothing but guzzle food, but I will set you straight.'

The regiments of the Legion were almost immediately subjected to the horrors of the first siege of Saragossa from 15 June to 14 August 1808. The French forces committed to that task were over-confident and under-equipped to deal with the passionate resistance of the garrison and the citizenry. On 4 and 5 August elements of all three infantry regiments, as well as the Legion's regiment of lancers, took part in an assault on the monastery of Santa Engracia. The savage hand-to-hand fighting that ensued caused heavy casualties for the Poles (including a total of 30 officers wounded). (Officer casualties for the Vistula Legion reported in this entry have been taken from the listing by Jonathan North in Appendix C of Brandt that corrects and supplements the listings for the Legion found in Martinien.) At the height of this battle General Jean Antoine Verdier, the French commander, offered the defenders a chance for 'peace and capitulation.' The terse reply was 'War even to the knife!' (Rudorff, *War to the Death* [London 1974], p. 148.)

The unexpectedly stubborn resistance of Saragossa's defenders coupled with the defeat of General Dupont at Bailen led to the abandonment of the siege and the temporary retreat of the French. The units of the Legion then had to bide their time while Napoleon concentrated his Grand Army veterans for a decisive assault that began in November. After contributing to the route of a Spanish Army at Tudela on 23 November, the Legion infantry found itself back at Saragossa preparing for another, even more epic, siege that was to last from December 1808 until 20 February 1809.

The siege was not pressed vigorously at first because Marshal Lannes, the man charged with capturing the town, had been injured in a riding accident, but once he recovered the fighting started in earnest. On 27 January, one of the bloodiest days of the siege, the Poles, led by Chlopicki, found themselves once again fighting in and around the Santa Engracia monastery. The time the struggle would be immortalised via a vivid painting of the assault by Baron Lejeune. (See reproduction in Tulard, p. 205.) The memoirs of a young officer of the Legion, Heinrich von Brandt, give some idea of the gruelling nature of the house-to-house fighting (Brandt, p. 58):

> The more we advanced the more dogged resistance became. We knew that in order not to be killed, or to diminish that risk, we would have to take each and every one of these houses converted in redoubts and where death lurked in the cellars, behind doors and shutters—in fact, everywhere. When we broke into a house we had to make an immediate and thorough inspection from the cellar to the rooftop. . . . Often as we were securing one floor we would be shot at from point-blank range from the floor above through loopholes in the floor. All the nooks and crannies of these old-fashioned houses aided such deadly ambushes.

Both the attackers and the defenders made liberal use of mines, which added another hellish element to the scene (Brandt, p. 59):

> I was busy in the Coso with a detachment of some fifty men, setting up a barricade. . . . Suddenly our ears were shattered by the familiar whistling and roaring noise of an exploding mine. A neighbouring house collapsed and unmasked a Spanish battery which blasted us with grape at point-blank range. Miraculously, only three men were hit, but the rest ran for it as quick as they could.

During the course of the siege the Legion suffered casualties of at least eleven officers killed and twelve wounded and may have suffered 24 other officer casualties as well. (Fieffé, Vol. 2, pp. 241–2.) Despite the magnitude of the Legion's suffering, it received a disproportionately small share of the medals handed out after the siege was over. This circumstance caused Brandt to conclude that the French 'thought more of the Poles on the day of battle than they did afterward.' (Brandt, p. 84.)

After the siege had ended the regiments of the Legion were deployed as part of the 3rd Corps of the Army of Spain in a series of efforts to pacify the rest of Aragon and Navarre. Things started badly for the Poles when the 2nd Regiment lost all its grenadier and voltigeur companies in a bungled river crossing in May. (A sudden rise of the Cinca River caused an élite vanguard force of grenadiers and voltigeurs to be cut off from the main body of French troops in the presence of a superior Spanish force.) (Brandt, pp. 73–4.) Shortly thereafter, however, General Suchet assumed command of the Corps and, after one initial check, embarked on the string of successful campaigns that made him the only French officer whose reputation was enhanced by service in the Peninsula.

The part played by the 1st, 2nd and 3rd Regiments of the Legion in these campaigns from 1809 to 1812 was marked more by the grinding work of pacifying a hostile local population than by great victories on the battlefield. The struggle between the French occupiers and the Spanish populace mobilised by guerrilla leaders such as Mina and Villacampa was relentless (Brandt, p. 80):

> It was a real see-saw battle between the partisans and ourselves: they were everywhere we were not, they disappeared upon our approach, escaped our clutches and reappeared behind us. As most of the people of the region were on their side, they inevitably had all the advantages. We had to be vigilant at all hours of the day or night so as not to be taken by surprise and risk loss of either life or honour. Frequently, some unfortunate officer would be condemned to spend weeks, even whole months, with a detachment of thirty or forty men in some decrepit old building that had been transformed into a blockhouse. There he would be cut off from the rest of the world and had only himself to count on.

When the Poles went on the offensive, the feeling of having the initiative was exhilarating, but dangers still abounded. On one occasion Brandt and a small detachment were sent to rendezvous with another French force at Daroca, but when he arrived at that town he found it occupied by a large force of enemy troops. He had the presence of mind to charge through the enemy and throw his force into a solidly built chapel, from where he put up a stout resistance until relieved the next day. It turns out that a staff officer had mixed up the dates on the orders and had sent Brandt to Daroca one day before the other forces involved. (Brandt, pp. 85–6.) In March 1810 an entire company of Poles from the 1st Regiment was left without support at Aventosa and was captured *en masse* when it failed to find a refuge such as that occupied by Brandt and tried to flee cross-country back to a French base. (Brandt, p. 117; the regiment involved is specified in a document in the Chlopicki Archives.)

The wear and tear on the Legion was extraordinary (Brandt, p. 163):

> We marched incessantly, usually twenty or thirty miles a day along poor bridleways, climbed sheer rock faces, slid down precipices, endured time and again in quick succession the burning heat of the lowlands and the icy winds of the heights, and all to get at a slippery enemy, so as to foil their designs, or, at best, disperse them and force them to seek sanctuary some distance away—to which we would pursue them and start all over again.

It was perhaps inevitable that morale would crumble in such circumstances. Many of the Legionnaires responded to appeals from the Spaniards to desert. On at least one occasion the 2nd Regiment became mutinous and refused to follow orders on parade from an unpopular officer. The men came to their senses before any real harm had been done, but it was very fortunate that the regimental commander decided not to press for punishment. (Brandt, p. 161.) There were also strains among the officers, such as the one described below that was caused by a dispute over cards (Brandt, p. 160):

> The Captain was blamed for the quarrel by a majority of officers and they formed what one of their number chose to call a 'confederation'—meaning that the adversaries of the Captain collectively declared in writing that they would not serve under him and would thus oblige him to change regiments. He protested to the Colonel . . . .

The officers who signed the declaration but refused to retract their signatures after the Colonel became involved each received eight days arrest.

One or more of the three Polish regiments with the Army of Aragon was present at all the major victories of Marshal Suchet. The 2nd and 3rd Regiments were at the siege of Tortosa from December 1810 to January 1811. The 1st and the 3rd were at Tarragona in the summer, while the 1st alone fought in the important victory of Sagunto in October. All three regiments were represented at the siege of Valencia from November 1811 to January 1812.

Because it was created later than the other units, the 4th Regiment of the Vistula was the last to enter Spain. It arrived in 1810, but instead of joining the other Legion units in the 3rd Corps it was assigned to General Jean Mathieu Séras' division of the Army of the North which was charged with defence of Leon. The 4th was engaged in a typical mix of anti-guerrilla operations and static defence assignments and suffered a steady trickle of casualties. (Kirkor, pp. 613–14.) On 16 April 1812 it suffered a significant defeat at the hands of Spanish guerrilla forces at Peynaranda in Leon, when the Regiment's second Battalion was nearly destroyed. Ten officers were wounded in the fighting.

At the beginning of 1812 Napoleon decided to withdraw the whole Vistula Legion from Spain for rest and refitting prior to using against Russia. (Decision of 28 January 1812, Nap. O&A, No 1844, Vol. 2, p. 225.) Marshal Suchet was particularly saddened by the loss of the three reliable regiments that had served under his command for so long (Suchet, Vol. 2, p. 244):

> The Marshal regretted bitterly the loss of these brave troops and the distinguished officers and chief who commanded them. He honoured Colonel Klicki [of the Lancers] with the task of carrying to Paris the keys to the city of Valencia and the 22 Spanish standards captured there. The departure of General Chlopicki deprived the Army of an officer of merit destined for great things.

The men of the Legion may understandably have felt less regret at leaving Spain than their commander since, of the some 11,000 men of the Legion who had entered Spain, less than half were returning to France. (Kirkor, p. 613.) As the 2nd Regiment passed out of Spanish territory for the last time, one of the soldiers gave a unique salute to the country they were leaving (Brandt, p. 178):

> One of the [the soldiers], perched high on a rock . . . which served as a kind of pedestal, suddenly pulled down his trousers, stuck his posterior towards Spain and shouted out, 'There you are, cursed country which has devoured so many of my comrades!'

One of his officers, a Captain Smitt, added sagely (and somewhat treasonably), '. . . the soldier is mistaken. The country was not cursed, as it was the man she had to defend herself against who was the real guilty party.' (*Ibid.*)

As the Legion reorganised in its depot at Sedan, Napoleon decided to boost the morale of the Poles by combining all the infantry regiments of the Legion into a single division that would be classified as part of the Imperial Guard. The gesture did not have its full desired effect, however, because the Emperor ignored the obvious choice for command of the division, passing over General Chlopicki in favour of General Michel Marie Claparède (1770–1842). Chlopicki was given the 1st Brigade, consisting of the 1st and 2nd Regiments, while General Bronikowski took charge of the 2nd Brigade, which was to be composed of the 3rd and 4th Regiments. (Pigeard, *Polonais*, p. 41.) The 4th Regiment, however, was detained in Spain until June 1812, so it never took its intended place in the division and thus avoided participation in the Russian campaign. (Kirkor, p. 614.) Napoleon actually announced that the Legion would receive the new designation 'Légion du Grand Duché de Varsovie', but the name never caught on. (Note dated 14 March 1812, Nap. *O&A*, No 5797, Vol. 4, p. 218.)

The three regiments that did enter Russia crossed the Niemen River with a combined strength of nearly 4,000 men. (Pigeard, *Troupes Polonaises*, p. 41.) In the early weeks of the campaign the Vistula Legion infantry never fired a shot in anger, but by mid-July every company in the 2nd Regiment had already lost an average of 25 men to sickness, bad weather and lack of food, the same loss that might be expected from a major battle. (Brandt, p. 200.) The division got into action late in the day at Borodino, but the 257 killed and wounded from the 2nd Regiment shows that there was enough time for the fighting to be very fierce. (Brandt, p. 222.) The Legion units were marched straight through Moscow to join Murat's force in contact with Kutuzov's main army. They saw heavy fighting at Voronovo on 2–4 October (268 men killed or wounded in the 2nd Regiment alone) and at Vinkovo on the 18th. The 3rd Regiment was wrecked at Krasnoi (where it had five officers killed and 11 wounded).

The 1st and 2nd Regiments of the Vistula were, along with the Swiss, among the heroes of the Beresina River crossing. They were assigned to fend off Russian attacks to eliminate the bridgehead on the western bank of the river and they fought all day on 28 November in inconceivably bad conditions to achieve that result. The 1st Regiment had two officers killed and 24 wounded. The 2nd had two killed and fifteen wounded. All told, the 2nd Regiment had only 50 men left. (Brandt, p. 255.)

The survivors of the three regiments that served in Russia joined up with the 4th Regiment in Poznan in early 1813. They were not ready to take the field for the spring campaign, so they were assigned to various garrisons, with the bulk of the 4th Regiment taking post at Wittenberg. On 18 June 1813 Napoleon decided that it would make more sense to combine all the remaining men into a single Regiment of the Vistula, and this served with General Poniatowski's 8th Corps until it was virtually wiped out at the Battle of Leipzig. (Kirkor, p. 614.)

The ranks of the Regiment were re-filled for the campaign of France, but the unit was never much stronger than a single battalion. The Regiment, now under the command of Colonel Kosinski, was assigned along with a large number of National Guards to garrison the town of Soissons under the command of General Jean Claude Moreau. On 2–3 March the Regiment was involved in one of the most notorious episodes of the campaign. Unbeknownst to the garrison, Marshal Blücher was being harried by Napoleon's troops and needed to obtain the use of the Soissons bridge over the Aisne River in order to escape possible defeat. He tried to take the town by storm on 2 March but was driven off by the Poles, who suffered many casualties, including the Colonel. Blücher then proposed a capitulation that was rejected by Kosinski, but accepted by his superior. The French obtained the honours of war but Blücher got his bridge. Napoleon threatened to have Moreau shot but settled for putting Moreau and the other senior officers, including Kosinski, under arrest.

Final Transformation The final Regiment of the Vistula was disbanded after Napoleon's abdication and marched back to Poland.

Uniforms When the Polacco-Italian Legion re-joined the French Army from Westphalian service its clothing was in 'a very bad state' and it was estimated that it would cost a total of 471,300 francs to manufacture replacements and re-equip all 6,000 men of the infantry regiments. (Decision of 28 March 1808, Nap. *P&T*, No 1758, Vol. 2, p. 150.) The prescribed dress was a blue jacket with yellow lapels closed down to the waist and other yellow facings according the pattern for identifying each unit shown in Table 6 (*Le Plumet*, Plate No 77; Pigeard, *Troupes Polonaises*, p. 40).

The headwear seems to have been a French-style shako with a sunburst plate, but there are no first-hand depictions of the uniforms of the Legion that can confirm that fact. Blondieau has a photograph of a shako attributed to the Vistula Legion infantry, but the plate is diamond-shaped and bears a Polish-style eagle. (Blondieau, p. 27.) A relatively crude model of sunburst plate for the 'Pulk Nadwislanski' (Vistula Regiment) is illustrated in Pigeard, *Troupes Polonaises*, p. 40.

TABLE 6: VISTULA LEGION FACINGS

Regiment	Collar	Cuffs
1st	Yellow	Yellow
2nd	Yellow	Blue
3rd	Blue	Yellow
4th	Blue	Blue

The musicians and sappers of the Vistula Legion are covered by Rigo in two *Le Plumet* plates. Plate No 133 covers the drummers, musicians and Drum Major. The drummer has a red band around the top of his shako and red and white trim around the collar and lapels and arranged in six chevrons (point up) on each sleeve. The Drum Major is wearing a busby and has thick silver lace around his facings. Plate No 203 depicts a sapper with a tall bearskin with white cords, a brass sunburst plate and a long yellow bag, trimmed with white wolves-tooth trim. The figure is said to be based on information from the Carl Collection of paper soldiers, but the same details can be found in a print of the same subject in Vernet and Lami, which predates the Carl Collection. The sapper had two white fringed epaulettes plus an aiguilette on his right shoulder.

Brandt's memoirs demonstrate how the appearance of soldiers on campaign could vary widely from the regulation norms. For instance, he records that when he was chosen to parley with the enemy during the siege of Tortosa he was so proud to have been given that task that he put on his dress uniform and his epaulettes. To complement the impression he was trying to make, Brandt also got his 'bugler' to 'smarten himself up . . . and remain sober.' (Brandt, p. 127.) He also records a more gruesome story about how difficult it was to keep a uniform clean (Brandt, p. 222):

> He [a fellow officer] had just finished speaking when we were both splashed by the blood and brains of a Sergeant who had his head blown off by a cannonball . . . The horrible stains on my uniform proved impossible to remove and I had them in my sight for the remainder of the campaign as a *memento mori*.

The following description of Brandt's 2nd Regiment on the march from Smolensk in late August 1812 further demonstrates that the Vistula Legion was probably not known for its elegant appearance (Brandt, p. 268):

> To preserve at least their eyes from the oppressive dust, the men improvised spectacles from pieces of glass. Others marched with their shakos under their arms, the head enveloped in a kerchief with just a small opening left for the wearer to see and breathe.

There was even more improvisation in dress during the retreat (Chlapowski, p. 316):

> I had brought with me from Moscow a beautiful fur coat, but it was much to heavy for me to wear as a marching invalid so I exchanged it with profit for a Russian caftan. I adorned my crutches with lamb's wool and I bought from a soldier a big piece of heavy cloth to wrap around my throat and head.

Standard The Legion initially carried the same republican standards issued to the *Demi-Brigades Polonaises* (see separate entry). A decision of 26 January 1809 approved the distribution to the Legion of 'the same ensigns used by French troops that do not have Eagles.' (Nap. O&A, No 3845, Vol. 3, p. 209.) When, however, the Minister of War went back to the Emperor to obtain approval of a definitive design for the flags, communication lapsed and the Vistula Legion Regiments never received any new standards. (Regnault, pp. 123–4.)

Légion du Danube

(Danube Legion; also known as the *2e Légion Polonaise*)

Date of Creation 22 Fructidor Year VII (8 September 1799).

Circumstances of Creation With the massive reversal of fortune suffered by the French armies in Italy during the summer of 1799, it became a priority of the government to raise new forces (Organisational Decree, *Journal Militaire*, 1799, Pt. 2, p. 735):

> The Council of 500, considering that the Kings of the Coalition have deployed numerous armies against the freedom-loving people of Europe, has decided it is critical to admit into our ranks everyone who is driven by a sublime élan to fight for the sacred cause of liberty.

One of these was a new Polish Legion, to be paid for by France and to be formed from the mass of Polish exiles and former Russian and Austrian prisoners of war of Polish extraction gathered at Besançon. For a brief period of time after its formation, this unit was known as the 2nd Polish Legion, but it was quickly renamed the Legion of the Danube to distinguish it from the Polish Legion then serving in Italy (see separate entry on *Légion Polonaise*). (N.B. There was a '2nd Polish Legion' in the Army of the Cisalpine Republic at the start of 1799, but it was virtually wiped out as a result of heavy casualties in fighting that spring and the surrender of almost all of its remaining officers and men when the fortress of Mantua capitulated in July and so does not qualify for inclusion in this compendium. [Chelminski, pp. 10–11.])

Composition The Legion was intended to have four infantry battalions, four squadrons of light horse and an company of horse artillery. Each of the infantry battalions was composed of ten companies (one of grenadiers, one of chasseurs and eight of fusiliers), each of which had 123 officers and men. Each cavalry squadron was to have two companies of 116 soldiers each. (Organisational Decree, Articles 2, 3, 4 and 5, *Journal Militaire*, 1799, Pt. 2, p. 735.) The remnants of a cavalry unit under Colonel Karwowski that had been formed in January 1799 as part of the 1st Polish Legion of the Cisalpine Republic were incorporated into the Legion of Danube cavalry in December 1799. (Zaremba, p. 55; Chelminski, pp. 9 and 13.)

Some contemporary drawings by Albrecht Adam depict 'pontoniers' of the Danube Legion, but there is no mention of such specialist troops in the organisational charts for the unit. (Crusius, p. 15.) The only two possible explanations are that (a) the pictures were incorrectly labelled by the artist or (b) there was such an *ad hoc* specialist team in the Legion.

Commanders *Creation to 3 May 1801*: Charles Kniaziewicz (1762–1842), a general in the armies of Poland who went into exile after the last partition of his country. He was head of the 2nd Polish Legion raised by Dombrowski, but that unit was destroyed by the Russians and Austrians in the summer of 1799. In the autumn of that same year he was promoted to the rank of Brigade General in the French Army and assigned to organise the Danube Legion as its first commander. He resigned his command in protest over Napoleon's failure to promote Poland's interests in the peace talks of 1801. (See portrait in Zaremba, p. 55.) *24 July 1801–26 September 1802:* Ladislas François Constantin Jablonowski (1769–1802), a Pole who began his military service in the French Army in 1786 and only transferred to the Polish Army in 1791. He was back with the French Army of Italy in 1797–98 and joined Dombrowski's Legions as a General in 1799.

Operational History Organising all the components of the Legion took a number of months, so it was not ready for active service until March 1800, at which point it had a strength of 5,970 men. The infantry was attached to General Sainte-Suzanne's corps of the Army of the Rhine and fought in several combats prior to the summer armistice. Meanwhile, the light horse took longer to organise because they were being armed and trained as lancers, the lance being a traditional weapon of Polish cavalry. (Chelminski, p. 12.) All three elements of the Legion (2,312 infantry, 400 lancers and 64 artillery-men) were assigned to General Decaen's division for the autumn campaign and they played assorted important roles in the French victory of Hohenlinden on 12 Frimaire Year IX (3 December 1800). (Order of Battle in Picard, *Hohenlinden*, p. 388.) A simple lancer, Jan Pawlikowski, captured 57 Austrians single-handed. He was offered a battlefield promotion, but he declined because of his illiteracy and accepted a Sergeant's stripes and a carbine of honour instead. (Chelminski, p. 13.) In the pursuit after the battle, a grenadier private captured Austrian Prince Liechtenstein by pulling him off his horse. (*Ibid.*)

After the Peace of Lunéville was signed on 26 January 1801 the Danube Legion was transferred to Italy. On 21 March both Polish Legions then in existence were inspected by General Dombrowksi, the founding father of all the Legions in French service. (Chelminski, p. 17.) The Polish Legions were something of a political embarrassment for the Consulate, which was trying to play down its 'revolutionary' heritage, so a deal was arranged whereby the Danube Legion was stationed in the Kingdom of Etruria that had been formed out of the territory of the Grand Duke of Tuscany.

Final Transformation By an order dated 1 Nivose Year X (22 December 1801) the Danube Legion was transformed into the third of three *Demi-brigades Polonaises* (see separate entry). (Pigeard, *Troupes Polonaises*, p. 14.)

Uniforms Article 7 of the Organisational Decree provides the following details of the dress of the Legion:

> The uniform of the Legion will be a short blue jacket with red collar, cuffs, lapels and trim, blue vest and trousers trimmed with red, demi-gaiters for the infantry and short boots for the cavalry and the light artillery. The headwear will be a Polish bonnet with a plume.

Some naive colour drawings by 14-year-old artist Albrecht Adam in a sketchbook dated 25 June 1800–15 Apri 1801 prove that this order was not followed entirely. The picture of a Danube Legion infantryman found in that collection has the same basic look as that implied by the description above, but the jacket of the figure has blue lapels, shoulder straps, short turnbacks, cuffs and cuff flaps, all trimmed with red. (Crusius, pp. 22–3.) The infantryman also has a tall black leather czapka with white cords, a single black belt over his right shoulder and the hilt of an infantry sabre by his right side. Adam also executed two colour drawings of cavalrymen of the Danube Legion, both of whom are wearing the same basic colour and style of uniform as the infantryman, but their czapkas have yellow cords and tall red plumes and they both have yellow shoulder cords on the left shoulder. One is wearing blue trousers with red stripes and buttons on the outside seams and leather reinforcements and carrying a lance with a shaft decorated with narrow diagonal stripes of blue, white and red. The other is wearing light beige trousers.

Adam's sketchbook also contains black-and-white drawings of soldiers identified as pontoniers of the Legion. They are wearing jackets with indistinct lapels, short tails and thin black crossbelts. Their headgear is a top hat with the brim pulled up on both sides by two cords that stretch over the crown of the hat. (Crusius, p. 15.)

Other primary source evidence indicates that the red facings were adopted at some point. A print of a Danube Legion lancer by Hoffman depicts a mounted lancer wearing a czapka with a medium blue top over a black base and a red plume, a dark blue jacket with red collar, cuffs, lapels and turnbacks, all piped white, a single black shoulder-belt and blue trousers as before. The czapka has orange (!) cords, and an aiguilette of the same colour hangs from the left arm. The shaft of the lance is brown and the lance pennant has three horizontal stripes—blue over white over red. The horse has a white sheepskin saddle cloth with red, scallop-edged trim and a cylindrical blue portmanteau with orange trim and an orange '1' on the end. (This print is reproduced in Brosse, p. 83.) Hoffman also produced a print of a Legion officer that is consistent with the lancer print except that the officer has a blue cloth shabraque, a gold aiguillette on the right shoulder and a broad black waist-belt with gold buckle and wavy gold lace. (A copy of this latter print by B. Gembarzewski is reproduced in Pigeard, *Troupes Polonaises*, p. 12.)

No direct information has been found about the dress of the artillery companies of the Legion, but they may have had the same green uniform with black facings worn by the artillery company of the *Légion Polonais* of Italy (see separate entry).

Standard Since the infantry battalions of the Polish Legions in Italy are known to have received unit colours from the French Republic, it seems likely that those of the Danube Legion did as well. However, no concrete information has been found concerning this topic.

Rigo, who generally uses archival sources, asserts (without supporting citations) that the lancers of the Danube Legion received in 1800 four tricolour guidons (one per squadron) of heavily embroidered damask. (*Le Plumet*, Plate No 52—'Lanciers de la Vistule, 1er Régiment, Guidon 1800–14.) The flags were roughly rectangular in shape, except that the fly edge was rounded, and had vertical panels of blue, white and red (reading from the staff outward). On the white panel was a painting of wreaths, horns and a blue czapka with a red plume. The painting was surmounted on the top by a white ribbon with the words 'Republique Française' and on the bottom by one bearing the words 'Légion Polonais'. (This design was the same, but the words written in Polish, on the obverse.) The flag also had heavy gold fringe around the edge and elaborate gold embroidery around the perimeter of the flag itself. In each corner of the flag was a white circle, set off by gold and green wreaths, bearing the number of the relevant squadron in gold and the word 'swadron'.

Légion du Midi

(Legion of the South; also known as *1er Légion Piémontaise*)

Date of Creation This unit was the only one of four *Légions Piémontaises* (Piedmont Legions) contemplated by a decree of 28 Floreal Year XI (18 May 1803) that was actually formed. (*Journal Militaire* for Year XI, Pt 2, pp. 141–4.) After it became clear that the others would never be raised, the name of the first and only Legion that was created was changed to the Legion of the South on 30 June 1804. (Belhomme, Vol. 4, p. 291.) (The French word '*Midi*' can mean either 'south' or 'midday.' Surprisingly, there is a contemporary official notice in Italian about the Legion that refers to the unit as the '*Legione del mezzogiorno*' or 'Midday Legion'. Letter of the Prefect of the Department of the Po, 25 March 1806, Author's collection.)

Circumstances of Creation The mainland territory of Piedmont in Italy that was formerly part of the dual Kingdom of Piedmont-Sardinia was annexed by Napoleon in September 1802. Its inhabitants therefore became subject to conscription, but there were many inhabitants who were too old to be captured for army service by that mechanism. Napoleon accordingly decided to try to tap that pool of manpower by creating new units that would, he hoped, attract Piedmontese volunteers because they had a national identity. He also thought the Legions might provide an attractive alternative means of existence for the many Piedmontese men dislocated by the fighting in their country (N. to Berthier, 6 Thermidor Year XI [25 July 1803], Nap. *Corr.*, No 6939, Vol. 8, pp. 414–15 at 415):

> It is amazing to me that there are so many brigands in Piedmont. It seems possible that many of these men, who have so little means of existence, might want to join the Legions that are being formed in their country. You should accordingly move forward with organising these Legions as quickly as possible.

Initial optimistic estimates led him to believe that there were enough men available to fill four separate units, which were called Legions because they combined line and light infantry with artillery.

Composition Each of the four Piedmont Legions contemplated by the May 1803 decree was intended to have three line, or 'battle,' infantry battalions, two light infantry battalions, a staff of 32 persons and a single company of artillery. (May Decree, Articles II–IV.) Each of the battalions was to have five companies, four of fusiliers and one of grenadiers in the line battalions, and four of chasseurs and one of carabiniers in the light battalions. (Article V.) The total strength of each battalion was intended to be 765 men, with each Legion (including its artillery company and staff) consisting of 3,935 men. (Article V.) The officers were to be selected by Napoleon himself and were all supposed to be veterans of the French or Piedmont armies. (Articles VI–VII.) The men had to enlist for a ten-year term, be between the ages of 33 and 40 and be at least 5 feet 1 inch tall for infantrymen and 5 feet 4 inches for artillerymen. (Article X.)

Commanders *22 December 1803–26 September 1896*: Joseph Louis Victor Chevillard de Marlioz (1757–1836), who had begun his military career in 1773 as a volunteer in the Sardinian Navy. He was nominated to command of the *Tirailleurs of the Po* in 1805, but refused on the grounds of ill health. He proposed instead to stay on until the organisation of the Legion was complete, at which time he retired. *27 January 1807–8 November 1808*: Jean Pierre Maransin (1770–1828), a volunteer of '92 from the Revolutionary wars. He left the Legion when he was promoted to the rank of Brigade General and was never replaced, so thereafter the Legion was commanded by its senior field officer. Maransin served in Portugal and Spain during the whole of the Peninsular War and was grievously wounded at the Battle of Albuera.

Operational History Despite a vigorous recruiting effort, the volunteers necessary to fill the Legions were simply not forthcoming. In fact, the response of the populace was so poor that the first two line battalions of the 1st Legion were not completed until December 1803, while the first light battalion and the artillery company were not organised until early 1804. (Belhomme, Vol. 4, p. 273.) By June 1804 even Napoleon realised that his original idea would never come to fruition, and he therefore scrapped the four-legion plan and approved a name change for the sole legion formed.

The first active service of the Legion of the South was quite unusual. In September 1804, 2nd Lieutenant Victor Duplan, a Piedmont army veteran, and sixty men were sent to reinforce the French outpost of Senegal in West Africa. (Duplan, pp. 43–4.) The other noteworthy development in 1804 was the conversion of one of the centre companies in each battalion into a company of Voltigeurs. (Duplan, p. 42.)

In January 1805 the 1st and 2nd Battalions were embarked in their entirety for an expedition to aid the few remaining French forces in the Caribbean. (A second instalment of the Legion, consisting of the depot companies of the 1st and 2nd Battalions and two companies of the 3rd Battalion, was embarked in April. (N. to Minister of War, 16 Germinal Year XII [6 April 1805], Nap. *P&T*, No 83, Vol. 1, p. 36.) The small fleet bearing the Legion miraculously arrived at the town of San Domingo on the Spanish half of the island of Saint-Domingue on 27 March 1805, just as the small French garrison, composed of the few survivors from the earlier attempts to reconquer Haiti, was about to be overwhelmed by a force of Haitians under Toussaint l'Ouverture's successor, the brutal Dessalines. That occurrence was enough to cause the discouraged Haitians to break up their siege, but one battalion of the Legion was added to the garrison. (Pachonski, pp. 292–3.) The other battalion was disembarked at Martinique.

The newcomers quickly learned of the grim realities of life on the disease-ridden islands as yellow fever took a steady toll. According to returns dated 16 Thermidor Year XIII (5 August 1805), there were 226 men of the 1st Battalion at Martinique, of whom 183 were sick, and 569 men of the 2nd Battalion at San Domingo, with no record of the number ill. (The two companies of the 3rd Battalion embarked in April still seem to have been on board ships of Rear-Admiral Magon's fleet.) The morale of the Piedmontese plummeted and, according to one officer at Santo Domingo, they quarrelled frequently with the other French troops. When one of the Legionnaires killed another soldier in a knife fight, General Ferrand, the French commander at Santo Domingo, decided in May to disband the battalion there, send the cadres back to Europe and incorporate the men into the 5th Light and the 37th and 89th Line regiments. (Lemmonier-Delafosse, p. 154; Duplan, p. 44.) The battalion in Martinique was soon likewise incorporated into other units.

The 3rd Battalion that had been left in France under Battalion Chief Alexandre Giflenga, a former Piedmontese office who eventually rose to the rank of General, was eventually joined by a 4th Battalion formed with returning cadres, and when the fate of the two Battalions in the Caribbean became known, these were re-numbered as the new 1st and 2nd Battalions. (Duplan, p. 45.) These Battalions apparently had the standard nine-company establishment then typical of French units rather than the five company establishment originally decreed for the Piedmont Legions. (Note of 24 March 1808, Nap. *Inédits*, No 271, Vol. 1, p. 80.)

The Battalions of the Legion were stationed near the coast of Bay of Biscay, as was the Legion's artillery company, which was assigned to the Île d'Aix. (Order of 5 Thermidor Year XIII [24 July 1805], Nap. *P&T*, No 143, Vol. 1, p. 64.) Colonel Chevillard was sent to Turin to recruit, but progress towards filling out the ranks of the legion was barely perceptible. (N. to Minister of War, 6 February 1806, Nap. *Dernières Lettres*, No 349, p. 167, n. 1.) The volunteers that were enticed to join the Legion turned out to be poor specimens, who arrived at the regimental depot without coats or shoes. (N. to Minister of War, 6 February 1806, Nap. *Dernières Lettres*, No 430, pp. 203–4.) Napoleon finally decided that some drastic action was necessary if the Legion was ever to become a useful force. He accordingly ordered the replacement of all of the Legion's senior officers. (Decision of 10 August 1806, Nap. *P&T*, No 579, Vol. 1, p. 289.) On 3 September 1806 the force of the Legion stood at 42 officers and 1,636 NCOs and privates. (Duplan, p. 46.)

In early 1807 the 1st Battalion of the Legion was moved to Bayonne near the Spanish frontier, and in June it was ultimately included in the Observation Corps of the Gironde formed under General Junot. Napoleon had by now concluded that the Legion would never be a very effective force (Order of 18 October 1807, Nap. *O&A*,

No 3743, Vol. 3, p. 185): 'Give me a report on the organisation of this Legion. I want to reduce it size gradually . . . from year to year until it is eventually dissolved.' The Legion was nevertheless involved in the gruelling 1,100-kilometre forced march to Lisbon undertaken by Junot in November in a vain attempt to seize the Portuguese Royal family and the PortugueseNavy because they could be spirited away by the British Navy.

After the capture of Lisbon, the Legion was assigned to occupy the Algarve region, where Colonel Maransin often exercised command of the province due to the illness of his titular superior, General Maurin. (Foy, p. 104.) The 2nd Battalion of the Legion was included in a provisional regiment that left Angoulême for Portugal in October 1807 and ultimately reached Lisbon early in the following year. (Belhomme, Vol. 5, p. 384.) In March the establishment of the Battalions was reduced to the new six company format adopted for the French Army as a whole in February: 'The two Battalions of the Legion of the South, which are composed of eighteen companies, will be reorganised to have twelve companies, six for each Battalion.' (Note of 24 March 1808, Nap. *Inédits*, No 271, Vol. 1, p. 80.) There were also some Legion detachments sent to the Peninsula as part of various 'march' and other temporary battalions formed to convey small units efficiently to their parent formations. One of these was halted at Pampelona in July on its way to Portugal, and one of its officers was cited for valorous and distinguished conduct as a result of the part he played in the capture of the small town of Sos in Aragon in August. (Duplan, pp. 52–4.) Another may have been present at Madrid in May as evidenced by the odd case of Stanislas Cairasque, a 2nd Lieutenant in the '1st Legion of the South', who was court-martialled on the charge of having 'joined the ranks of the insurgents the day of 8 May [*sic*] at Madrid.' (Note of 8 October 1808, Nap. *Inédits*, No 294, Vol. 1, p. 86.)

The two Battalions of the Legion in Portugal were stationed at Alcoutim and Mertola until June 1808, when events in Spain began to upset the tranquillity of French rule. In that month, Portuguese loyalists took up arms against the French and trapped and captured in Olhao a small French force that included a detachment from the Legion. Junot thereupon decided to evacuate outlying areas in order to concentrate his forces in key areas. (Foy, p. 105.) During withdrawal from the Algarve, a small French force was assaulted by the inhabitants of the city of Beja and forced to retreat. The French retaliated on 26 June 1808, when the main French force, including the Legion, took the town by storm and then engaged in the type of uncontrolled, riotous behaviour that was to be all too frequent an adjunct to successful assaults on besieged cities in the Peninsula. (Foy, pp. 106–7.) Although resistance was negligible, the attack cost the Legion the lives of Battalion Chief Berthier-Crampigny and Captain Dabois.

When the British landed in Portugal to challenge Junot's rule, the Legion was left stationed at Saint Julian near Lisbon rather than deployed in the field. (Foy, p. 148.) It nevertheless seems likely that its élite companies would have been present at the Battle of Vimeiro on 21 August because one of the two regiments of massed grenadiers that constituted Junot's Reserve for that fight was commanded by Colonel Maransin. (Foy, p. 172.) No information has been found, however, that verifies that possibility. The Legion was repatriated back to France shortly thereafter by virtue of the Convention of Cintra. Napoleon sent it immediately back to active service in the Peninsula.

In November 1808 the two active service Battalions of the Legion lost Colonel Maransin through promotion and then underwent a noticeable reorganisation (Note of 24 November 1808, Nap. *Inédits*, No 303, Vol. 1, p. 89):

> In view of the weakness of the Legion of the South, it will be reduced to one battalion of five companies (of which one will be of carabiniers, one of voltigeurs, and three of chasseurs) with a total strength of 776 men, including 21 officers.

The Minister of War noted about this same time that the Legion was 'composed entirely of volunteers from the territory formerly known as Piedmont and therefore had need of being subjected to an exacting discipline.' (Duplan, p. 48.) The Legion was inspected by Napoleon himself at Valladolid in January, but there is no record of his thoughts about the unit. It then participated in the pursuit of General Moore's British army as part of General Heudelet's division, losing one officer wounded at the Battle of Corunna on 16 January 1809. (Duplan, p. 57.)

The Legion remained part of Marshal Soult's corps in early 1809, so it participated in the invasion of northern Portugal that led to the occupation of Oporto. During this campaign it was reunited with its old Colonel, Maransin, who now commanded the brigade in which the Legion was serving. Legion Captain Victor Duplan distinguished himself at the Bridge of Lima by leading two companies in a bold charge through artillery fire and *chevaux de frise* obstructions to capture the bridge intact. The action cost the Legion Duplan's lieutenant (not mentioned in Martinien), one Sergeant and several men. (Duplan, pp. 57–8.) The constant attrition the unit suffered while it was serving on this expedition prompted its commanders to ask for permission to recruit refractory conscripts because the number of voluntary enlistments had become negligible, but Napoleon refused that request. (Decision of 13 May 1809, Nap. *P&T*, No 3162, Vol. 4, p. 54.) The strength of the battalion in the Peninsula dropped to 444 officers and men. (Duplan, p. 49.)

After the French returned from Portugal, the unit was engaged in the type of unglamorous anti-guerrilla activity that made the war in Spain so hated by the soldiers of the French Army. One French officer mentions a particularly horrific incident involving the Legion that is said to have occurred in August 1809 (Illens, pp. 365–6):

> A company of Voltigeurs of the Legion of the South was sent on a foraging mission to the village of Torrejonaho [*sic*]. It was immediately attacked by a Spanish force of 1,000 men. Our Voltigeurs defended themselves for a long time with a courage and *sang-froid* that should have earned them a better fate. Crushed by superior numbers and out of ammunition, they refused to yield and instead launched themselves in a desperate charge against the enemy in which they all perished.

When a relief force arrived the next day, it found only one man still alive. He had been severely wounded in the fighting and, even worse, had then been mauled by wild pigs who had begun feeding on the dead Voltigeurs during the night. (Illens, p. 366.)

The one battalion of the Legion that had not participated in the campaigns in Portugal (which was now considered the 2nd Battalion) was included as part of a reserve division formed under the command of General Loison in October 1809 that consisted exclusively of battalions from regiments already serving in the Peninsula in General Heudelet's division. (Belhomme, Vol. 5, p. 459.) It entered Spain in November and was stationed in the Province of Biscay. (Belhomme, Vol. 5, p. 461.) The two divisions were eventually combined under the command of Loison and assigned to the 6th Corps in early 1810. (N. to Berthier, 11 January 1810, Nap. *Corr.*, No 16,131, Vol. 20, pp. 114–15; Bonnal, Vol. 3, pp. 288–9.) The two battalions seem to have been amalgamated so as to form a single surviving battalion organised into six companies (instead of five as was previously the case), with the extra company being designated as one of Chasseurs. In April 1810 the strength of the Legion stood at 21 officers and 689 NCOs and privates. (Duplan, pp. 49–50.)

The Legion started the 1810 campaigning season under the command of Battalion Chief Charles Spring. Several officers and men of the Legion were attached to the '*Chasseurs du siège*' formed from the best shots in the French Army to serve at the siege of Ciudad Rodrigo, but these were returned to their regular duties by the end of July. (Duplan, p. 59.) The rest of General Simon's brigade, including the Legion, was directly involved in siege operations. The Legion itself led a successful attack on the suburb of San Francisco on 1 July. (Horward, *Napoleon*, pp. 155–7.) The Legion was also designated for inclusion in the final assault on the breaches of Ciudad Rodrigo, but was spared that burden when the Spanish garrison surrendered at the last possible minute on 10 July. (Bonnal, Vol. 3, p. 353.)

The Legion's division next advanced against Almeida. The Legion itself was not engaged against the British in the Battle of the Coa on 24 July, but it did see action in repulsing a sortie by the 24th Portuguese Line Regiment on the 26th. (Horward, *Napoleon*, p. 258–9.) There followed several weeks of hard siege duty with shovels instead of muskets as the French siege lines moved ever closer to the fortifications of Almeida. Then, at dawn on 26 August, the French began their bombardment of the town. At dusk a French howitzer shell fell fortuitously into the open door of one of Almeida's main powder magazines and ignited most of the garrison's ammunition. (Duplan, pp. 60–1; Horward, *Napoleon*, pp. 300–1.) The resulting loss of supplies and general devastation to the town caused the British to surrender on 28 August and saved the Legion once again from having to participate in an assault on a heavily defended town. (Horward, *Napoleon*, p. 308.)

The Legion's good fortune in avoiding combat ran out at the Battle of Bussaco on 27 September 1810. Marshal Masséna's decision to launch a frontal assault straight up the side of Bussaco ridge was disastrous for the unit, which seems to have been the foremost unit in General Simon's brigade column when that formation advanced against the veteran British troops of the Light Division near the summit of the ridge just below Bussaco Convent. (Duplan, p. 63.) After a long hard climb up the ridge against skirmisher opposition, the Legion paused just short of the crest. The British responded by advancing the hitherto hidden 43rd and 52nd Regiments to the crest itself, from where they fired two, or possibly three, volleys that devastated the French column and then charged. (Chambers, pp. 97–9.) One French eyewitness reports that the Legion fled in panic before this attack, but that result is not surprising given the extent of the casualties it suffered. In the relatively short time it took to climb to the top of the ridge and then return to the base, the Legion lost 317 officers and men killed or wounded. (Koch, Vol. 7, p. 571; Chambers, p. 115.) Based on a 15 September strength of 563 men, the casualty rate was a stunning 55 per cent. (Koch, Vol. 7, p. 569.)

The remnants of the Legion advanced with the rest of the Army of Portugal towards Lisbon, where the French advance foundered on the impenetrable Lines of Torres Vedras. Captain Duplan, the acting Legion commandant, and his men apparently formed part of the force that escorted General Foy back to Spain in November to make a special report to the Emperor. (Duplan, p. 63.) They were sent right back to Portugal, however, and so suffered the privations that attended Masséna's attempt to last out the winter before the Portuguese capital. One of Masséna's aides-de-camp noted that the Legion was part of the extreme rearguard of the French Army when it began its withdrawal from Lisbon in March 1811. (Pelet, p. 425.)

After the French retreated back to Spain in the spring of 1811, the Legion played a prominent role in the Battle of Fuentes de Oñoro. The unit belonged to General Ferey's division, which was assigned to capture the eponymous village on 3 May and again on 5 May. (Koch, Vol. 7, pp. 528–9 and 539.) The French achieved a momentary success on the first day, when the impetuosity of their attacked briefly carried the town, but they were dislodged in turn by the British. By 5 May the ardour of Ferey's men had definitely cooled, and other French units bore the brunt of the fighting. Oman records that the Legion had more than 350 men when it went into action (Oman, Vol. 4, p. 626), but only 174 of them were left by the time the fighting ended. (Koch, Vol. 7, p. 597.)

Final Transformation Given the poor recruiting history of the Legion, it was unlikely that the losses from the campaign in Portugal could ever be made good. This prospect, plus Napoleon's growing disenchantment with the expense associated with his special foreign corps, led inexorably to an Imperial decision to disband the Legion (Decree of 11 August, Nap. *Inédits*, No 478, Vol. 1, p. 135):

> The Legion of the South is dissolved. The 1st Battalion, which is with the Army of Portugal, will be incorporated into the 31st Regiment of Light Infantry. The officers, NCOs and men who are in France or on recruiting duty at Turin will deliver make their way to Trèves to be incorporated into the 11th Regiment of Light Infantry [along with the men of the Po Tirailleurs and the Valais Battalion].

A follow-up note added the detail that former Legion prisoners of war returning from England would be assigned to the 11th Light. (Note of 11 August 1811, Nap. *Inédits*, No 479, Vol. 1, p. 135.)

Uniforms The May 1803 Organisational Decree of the four proposed Piedmontese Legions specified that the basic uniform was to be an iron grey jacket with scarlet facings. The jacket for the line infantry battalions was to be cut in line infantry style, lined with white cloth and worn with a white vest and breeches. The jacket for the light infantry was to be cut in light infantry style, have an iron grey lining and be worn with a white vest and iron grey trousers. (Organisational Decree, Section XII.) All jackets had scarlet lapels, but the rest of the details were intended to be varied in order to distinguish each Legion from the others, as shown in Table 7. The Organisational Decree also stated that both Grenadiers and Carabiniers would have the same bearskin caps as in French regiments and that the artillery company would have blue jackets, vests and trousers. The uniform buttons were to be marked with the Legion numbers.

A serious impediment to the implementation of this uniform scheme quickly surfaced: the officers and men did not like the colour grey because it was associated in Piedmont tradition with irregular units known as '*sbires*'. Since the Legion was founded on the principle of voluntary recruitment, the Minister of War pragmatically recommended that the colour would be changed. (Minister of War to N., 23 Messidor Year XI [12 July 1803], quoted in Bucquoy, *Troupes Étrangères*, p. 114.) The First Consul replied that he had no objection to the change so long as the colour chosen was something other than blue or red. (N. to Minister of War, 25 Messidor Year XI [14July 1803], quoted in Bucquoy, *Troupes Étrangères*, p. 114.) The result was the issuance of revised uniform specifications on 23 July that substituted dark brown ('*brun capucin*') and sky blue for the iron grey and scarlet of the original colour scheme. (Decree of 4 Thermidor Year 11 (23 July 1803), quoted in Bucquoy, *Troupes Étrangères*, pp. 114–15.)

Given the quick change in the original Legion uniform, it seems unlikely that the grey version was ever worn. The brown version worn would have initially been that of the 1st Legion, which would have had the sky blue facing colour only on the lapels, but once it became clear that there were not going to be any other Legions to distinguish, the facing colour might have been used in more places. Nothing conclusive has been

TABLE 7: PIEDMONT LEGION UNIFORM DISTINCTIONS

Legion	Collar	Cuffs	Shoulder strap	Buttons	Pockets
1st	Iron grey	Iron grey	Iron grey	White	Horizontal
2nd	Iron grey	Scarlet	Iron grey	White	Vertical
3rd	Scarlet	Scarlet	Iron grey	Yellow	Horizontal
4th	Scarlet	Scarlet	Scarlet	Yellow	Vertical

found on this point, however, although Print No 116 of the Marbot and Noirmont series from the 1840s depicts a uniform consistent with that decreed for the 4th Legion with the addition of turnbacks in the facing colour as well (which is shown as a very dark sky blue).

The only speculative element of the Legion uniform is the question of the headwear worn by the unit's centre companies. The Marbot print depicts a Carabinier wearing red epaulettes and a bearskin with brass plate and red cords and plume and a Voltigeur wearing green fringed epaulettes with a yellow crescent and a shako with a brass, diamond-shaped plate and a yellow pompom topped by a green plume with a yellow tip. The illustration of the Legion by Sorieul in Fieffé (opposite p. 92) depicts a soldier with epaulettes and an unusual black helmet with a metal foreplate and a crest that looks like that of a dragoon helmet without the horsehair mane. This helmet can be found on paper soldiers from the Wurtz Collection in the French Army Museum and is depicted in many other secondary sources, but there is no primary source evidence that verifies the use of such headwear. (Haussadis, Wurtz II, p. 46.) Some experts have plausibly theorized, however, that these helmets might have been recycled and modified Austrian infantry helmets.

There is one intriguing piece of primary source evidence that indicates that the uniform for at least some of the Legionnaires was changed to sky blue by the end of 1808. The source is a letter from a member of the Legion to his parents (quoted in Luraghi, p. 54):

> 1st Legion of the South, 2nd Battalion, 3rd Company
>
> . . . I have already received a new uniform which includes a shako with white cords and a plume and a yellow plate bearing an imperial eagle.
>
> My coat is sky blue with some red and some white elements, and I have also received a pair of white trousers and white and black gaiters.

Standard Charrié records that the Legion received three Eagles and 1804-model colours in 1805 (p. 183). No specific description of the colour has been found, but it seems reasonable to presume that it followed the general pattern of colours for units outside the line.

Légion du Nord

(Legion of the North)

Date of Creation 20 September 1806.

Circumstances of Creation The Legion of the North was created by Napoleon just as his campaign against Prussia was beginning because he was supremely confident that he would soon be receiving a large number of deserters of Polish extraction from the Prussian Army. To make service in the unit most attractive to its target audience, he gave the Legion a Polish commander and specified that at least two-thirds of its officers would be natives of Poland and that it would wear a Polish-style uniform. (N. to Minister of War, 20 September 1806, Nap. *Corr.*, No 10835, Vol. 13, p. 232.) He quickly decided that he liked the idea, and his prospects, so much that on 22 September he authorised the creation of additional legions if circumstances permitted. (N. to Minister of War, 22 September 1806, Nap. *Corr.*, No 10858, Vol. 13, p. 247.) He also decided to provoke the necessary desertions by distributing proclamations to the Prussian troops pointing out the advantages of service in the French Army, including the fact that deserting NCOs would be accepted into the new Legion with their old rank intact. Always the consummate politician, however, he cautioned that such proclamations should never promise the restoration of Poland. (*Ibid.*)

Composition The Legion had four battalions, each one of which had seven Chasseur, one Voltigeur and one Carabiner company. The establishment for each battalion was 1,224 men, giving a total strength (including the Legion staff) of 5,042 men. (Coqueugniot, p. 14.)

Commanders

1st Legion *Creation to disbandment:* General Joseph Zayonchek (1762–1826), a Polish officer who was admitted directly into French service as a Brigade General by Napoleon himself in 1797, was the titular commander of the Legion during the whole of its existence. A veteran of the Egyptian campaign, Zayonchek went on to become a Division General in the Army of the Duchy of Warsaw, with his active service ending when his leg was amputated and he was captured by the Russians at Vilna in December 1812. A twenty-one year old Polish nobleman, Prince Michael Radziwill, was named colonel of the 1st Legion midway through the siege of Danzig. (Coqueugniot, pp. 77–80.) This was his first military service of any sort, but Radziwill eventually rose to the rank of Division General in the Army of the Grand Duchy of Warsaw. The effective commander of the Legion during its service in the French Army was Major Lazare Claude Coqueugniot (1763–?), a Regular Army soldier under the Bourbons who fought in all of the wars of the French Revolution. His memoirs form the best primary source of information about the Legion.

2nd Legion *Creation to disbandment:* General Jean Henri de Wolodkowicz (?–1836), another veteran of Napoleon's First Italian Campaign. Although the 2nd Legion was never fully organised, Napoleon appointed a young Pole named Count Sobolewsky to be its commander in the spring of 1807. (Coqueugniot, pp. 77–8.)

Operational History Napoleon took in so many Polish deserters and captured so many potential Polish recruits at Saalfeld, Jena and Auerstadt and the pursuit thereafter that he had little difficulty in locating sufficient men for an initial legion, known as the 1st Legion of the North, which peaked at a strength of 5,314 men in December 1806. (Report to N., quoted in Coqueugniot, p. 179.) A 2nd Legion was decreed on 23 September 1806, but recruiting for that formation was never successful. (Decree of 23 September 1806, quoted in Coqueugniot, p. 167.) The 2nd Legion consisted of only 148 officers and men by the end of November, and recruiting became much difficult thereafter as a result of efforts to raise a national army in Poland itself, so very little came of that initiative. The few men raised for the 2nd Legion were eventually incorporated into the 1st Legion in March 1807. (Six, *Dictionnaire*, Vol. 2, p. 575.)

The speed with which Napoleon disposed of the Prussian armies in the autumn of 1806 and moved on to fight the Russian Army on formerly Polish soil caused a drastic change in the pace at which the Legion was organised. Napoleon had hoped to have time to organise it thoroughly on French soil, but he quickly changed his mind and began moving towards Poland even before it received officers and uniforms. It was in Mainz at the end of October, Leipzig in December and Stettin in January. As Major Coqueugniot complained in his memoirs, it was highly reckless of the French military authorities to assume that it would be possible to mould the prisoners and deserters who joined the Legion into a coherent force while marching them all over Germany. (Coqueugniot, pp. 15–40 *passim.*) That this objective was obtained even in part is a tribute to the talents of the Major, to the fact that the recruits all had some military experience and to the lack of initiative that characterised the Prussian Army of that era.

When the Legion reached Stettin, it was in such a tenuous state, due to exhaustion, desertion and lack of officers, that it fell prey to the efforts of Prussian agents who fomented a minor mutiny in which many of the men threw down their arms and refused to fight against their former sovereign, the King of Prussia. The mutineers were quickly cajoled into returning peacefully to their ranks, but a rash of desertions back to the Prussians followed. The famous Prussian partisan, Major Schill, assumed as a result that the Legion would provide little resistance to a surprise night attack he launched on 18 February 1810, when the unit was moved to quarters in a small village named Stargard. (Coqueugniot, pp. 53–7.) Both Schill and Major Coqueugniot were surprised, in different ways, when the unit put up a stout resistance and repulsed the attackers. Seventeen Prussians were captured single-handed by Assistant Surgeon Belhomme of the Legion, who was commanding a company because of the shortage of qualified officers. (Coqueugniot, p. 57.)

After this successful trial of arms, the Legion was quickly deployed as part of the French forces assigned to the siege of the fortress city of Danzig. The Legion had a dangerous post on the left bank of the Vistula River between the city proper and a large outlying entrenched camp called the Fort of Neufahrwasser. The work was more dull than deadly in March, as the French engineers responsible for the siege works concluded that the Poles were more adept with picks and shovels than their French comrades. (Coqueugniot, p.84.) The Legion was also called upon to provide a squad of men to work the siege guns because it had a number of ex-artillerymen in its ranks.

As the weather improved, the garrison became more active and the Legion found itself defending against a number of sorties. The Legion was successful in many of these actions, but on 1 April he 1st Battalion of the Legion was hit from two sides at once and suffered heavy casualties. Captain Miralowsky and his Grenadier company were captured almost to a man, while Captain Henry and thirteen other officers were killed

TABLE 8: LEGION OF THE NORTH OFFICER CASUALTIES

Date	Killed	Mortally wounded	Wounded
1 April	1	0	4
3 April	0	0	4
1 May	1	1	0
6 May	0	0	2
7 May	0	0	2
8 May	2	0	0
12 May	0	0	1
13 May	0	0	1
15 May	0	0	2
Totals	4	1	16

along with a proportionate number of soldiers. (Coqueugniot, p. 77.) Martinien's figures for the Legion of the North's casualties for that day are much lower, but there is no obvious reason to doubt Major Coqueugniot on this point or on his overall calculation that 34 officers of the Legion were killed or wounded during the siege. (Coqueugniot, p. 117.) Whether it is completely accurate or not, however, the information provided by Martinien gives a good indication of the ebb and flow of the actions of the Legion during the siege (see Table 8).

The most dramatic of these officer casualties occurred on 8 May during a night attack on a redoubt on the Isle of Holm held by a strong detachment of Russian troops. The French attackers were a mixed force of French, Saxon, Baden and Polish troops that included 300 men of the Legion, one of whom was a 19- or 20-year-old Lieutenant named Nowisky. Nowisky's platoon became separated from the rest in the dark and suddenly found itself in the middle of the enemy force. The young officer reacted boldly by calling out, in Polish: 'Friends! I am surrounded by Russians. Fire on me!'. His Polish colleagues did so and Nowisky was killed, but the attack succeeded. (Coqueugniot, pp. 101–2.)

There were many other triumphs by the Legion during the course of the siege. On 26 March, the 3rd and 4th Battalions earned a place in the 68th Bulletin of the Grand Army by comporting themselves well during a sortie by the Danzig garrison. (68th Bulletin, 29 March 1807, Nap. *Corr.*, No 12223, Vol. 14, pp. 571–2.) The men from the Legion combined with a squadron of the 19th Mounted Chasseurs and some Polish Lancers to capture a Prussian partisan leader named von Krockow and nearly the whole of his unit of 'Death Chasseurs' at the cost of only 30 casualties. (Coqueugniot, pp. 90–2.) (Von Krockow's men wore a unique helmet decorated with a white skull-and-crossed-bones badge that is illustrated on Plate 56 of Volume 13 of R. Knoetel's *Uniformenkunde*.) Lieutenant (later Captain) Tardivel of the Legion and his company of the 3rd Battalion made such a distinguished defence of a fortified house on the banks of the Vistula that it came to be identified as the 'Maison Tardivel' on maps of the siege. (Coqueugniot, pp. 86–7.) In a fight against a large Russian force towards the end of the siege, the Legion inflicted disproportionately heavy casualties on their foe because the Russians fought in a thick line 'packed like herrings' while his outnumbered men and those of the 2nd Light Regiment fought in skirmish order (*'en tirailleurs'*), accompanied by Madame Schramm, wife of the General commanding both corps, 'dressed as an Amazon'. (Coqueugniot, p. 95.) The Legion also took part in the capture of the British corvette *Dauntless* along with the Paris Guard on 19 May when that vessel ventured too far up the Vistula River and too close to shore. (Coqueugniot, pp. 97–100.)

Danzig surrendered on 26 May and Napoleon personally inspected the Legion shortly thereafter. He was appalled by the state of its uniforms and equipment but pleased enough with its combat performance to grant one Legion of Honour decoration for each of the Legion's 32 companies. (Coqueugniot, pp. 111–13.) Some of the men, however, preferred more concrete rewards for meritorious conduct. Grenadier Crasisky, a man of 'colossal size and extraordinary strength', distinguished himself by jumping into a Prussian redoubt through an embrasure and attacking the garrison with an axe. Major Coqueugniot responded by granting him double rations, an arrangement the good soldier declared to be preferable to any medal and, for that matter, any other recompense except for sufficient pocket money to buy a daily glass of schnapps. (Coqueugniot, pp. 103–5.)

Final Transformation After the siege of Danzig, a question arose as to whether the Legion should be assimilated into the Polish national army being formed for the new Grand Duchy of Warsaw. Surprisingly, Napoleon agreed to let the men of the unit decide for themselves, and in the subsequent vote the wishes of the overwhelmingly Polish rank-and-file prevailed. (N. To Rapp, 19 July 1807, Nap. *Corr.*, No 12948, Vol. 15, p. 449; Coqueugniot, pp. 119–22.) The Legion was consequently transferred to the service of the King of Saxony (who doubled as the Grand Duke of the Duchy) on 17 August 1807, although this development was a severe blow for the significant number of French officers and NCOs, many of whom were ex-emigrés. (Coqueugniot, p. 122.) The Frenchmen were, however, soon allowed to transfer back to French service. (Decision of 3 November 1807, Nap. *O&A*, Vol. 3, p. 187.) In March 1808 the Legion became the 5th Regiment of the Army of the Grand Duchy. (Coqueugniot, p. 138.)

Uniforms Article 2 of the Organisational Decree of the Legion stated that the Legion would be uniformed in a 'Polish-style costume', but gave no information beyond that. Following further correspondence on the subject, the Ministry of War was able to add the following details (Minister of War to Kellerman, 10 November 1806 quoted in Coqueugniot, pp. 176–7):

> Dark blue jacket with crimson lapels, cuffs and trim; crimson collar for the staff and the companies of carabiniers and chasseurs, but buff collars for the voltigeur companies; white vest, dark blue trousers; silver metal buttons stamped with the number '1'

> surrounded by the words 'Légion du Nord'; vertical pockets; half-gaiters and, for headwear, a shako in a style to be chosen by General Zayonchek. The officers will have a jacket with long tails and white or silver rank distinctions.

The uniform of the 2nd Legion was supposed to be the same except that the facing colour was pink and the buttons were marked with the number '2'.

The reality of the dress of the Legion was, for the most part, far from this theoretical ideal. The officers may have had the prescribed uniform, but the men were dressed in a very haphazard fashion using cast-off clothing supplies from Prussian stores that included (Coqueugniot, pp. 41–2):

> Overcoats made from bad cloth one could see through even though it was brown.
>
> White vests made from thin cloth that would not have lasted a year in the Prussian Army.
>
> Unlined trousers made from the same cloth as the vests, but cut very narrow.
>
> Heavy canvas gaiters with black leather buttons.
>
> Shoes from Prussian magazines that were of the worst imaginable quality . . .
>
> Blue wool socks that wore out almost immediately.
>
> Black neckstocks from Prussian supplies no one would have dared to give to French soldiers.
>
> Shakos made of bad felt that quickly faded to white, to which had been added visors cut in the shape of a shovel blade.

(A modern illustration depicting this version of the Legion's dress can be found in Courcelle, 'La Légion'.) By the time the siege of Danzig ended, this clothing, which had been bad enough to begin with, was filthy and in tatters. (Coqueugniot, p. 114.) Napoleon was so appalled by the appearance of the Legion when he inspected it on 2 June 1807 that he immediately ordered the replacement of all the Legion's clothing using stocks of cloth found in the captured city.

The resulting uniforms seem to have followed the original pattern prescribed for the Legion if some naive drawings that were found in the manuscript for Coqueugniot's memoirs can be believed. (These drawings were formerly in the Cottreau Collection but their whereabouts is now unknown [Coppens, *La Légion*]. Fortunately, they have been preserved through copies made by JOB that were reproduced in *Tenues de Troupes de France*, No 2, December 1901.) The salient features of the new uniform were a tall black leather czapka with a brass plate, cords and an even taller plume (red for Carabiniers, light blue for Chasseurs and chamois/yellow for Voltigeurs), red cuffs with red cuff flaps, vertical pockets in the coat-tails, and white grenade ornaments in the turnbacks. A picture of Coqueugniot himself includes a white plume, white trim at the top and mid-line of the czapka, a white plume and cords with rackets on the right side and white epaulettes with fringe on each shoulder. That same picture has the Major wearing white breeches and black heavy cavalry boots. He is also riding a horse with a

Above left: Captain de Brun of the Bataillon du Prince de Neufchatel, painted by Louis Boily. (Courtesy of René Chartrand)

Above right: A portrait of *Chef de Bataillon* Pierre Joseph Blanc of the Bataillon Valaisan, 1808.

Right: Chevau-léger Polonais de la Garde, 1810, after C. Vernet.

Above left: One of the Hussards Croates, 1813, by L. Malespina.

Above right: A Lancier de la Légion de la Vistule in Spain, 1809, after V. Huen.

Left: An 8th Light Horse Lancer (Lanciers de la Légion de la Vistule), 1813, after C. Vernet.

Above: A man of the Légion Copte, 1800, after C. Vernet.

Above: Infantrymen of the Légion de la Vistule in campaign dress, 1813, by Andrew Zaremba.

Left: A drum major of the Légion de la Vistule with a female admirer, 1808.

Left: A sapper of the Légion de la Vistule, 1812, after C. Vernet.

Left: A grenadier of the Légion du Midi, 1808, after Sorieul.

Above: Colonel Evers of the Mounted Chasseurs of the Légion Hanovrienne, 1806.

bove: A man of the Légion Grecque, 1799, fter C. Vernet.

ight: A mounted chasseur of the Légion anovrienne, 1810, after H. Knötel.

Left: An infantryman of the Légion Hanovrienne, 1804.

Right: A officer of the Légion Irlandaise, 1813, after C. Vernet.

Right: An infantryman of the Légion Italique, 1800, after C. Vernet.

Below: A grenadier of the Légion Maltaise, 1799.

Above: An officer of the Légion Polonaise, 1804, after a contemporary portrait.

Above: A lancer and a grenadier of the Légion Polonaise, 1800. (Courtesy of René Chartrand)

Left: An infantryman of the Légion Portugaise, 1812, after C. Vernet.

Left: A cavalryman of the Légion Portugaise, 1809, after C. Vernet.

Right: A Mamelouk of the Imperial Guard, 1805, after C. Vernet.

Left: An adjutant-major and fusilier of the Régiment de la Tour d'Auvergne in Naples, 1806.

Above: A flag of the Régiment de Prusse captured in 1812.

Right: An NCO, officer and musician of the Régiment de Prusse, 1806, after a contemporary recruiting poster.

Left: A voltigeur, fusilier, subaltern and field officer of the Régiment de Westphalie, 1808, after H. Knötel.

Right: A drummer of the Régiment de Prusse, 1807, after Neumann.

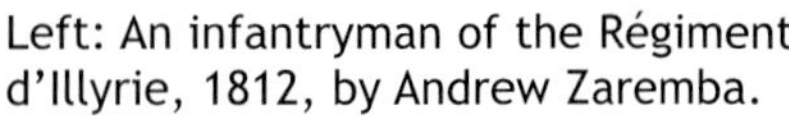

Left: An infantryman of the Régiment d'Illyrie, 1812, by Andrew Zaremba.

Above: A voltigeur of the Régiment d'Isembourg with a company fanion, 1809.

Left: A voltigeur of the Régiment d'Isembourg in Naples, 1806, after R. Knötel.

Left: A carabinier of the Ist Régiment Provisoire Croate, 1812, after H. Knötel.

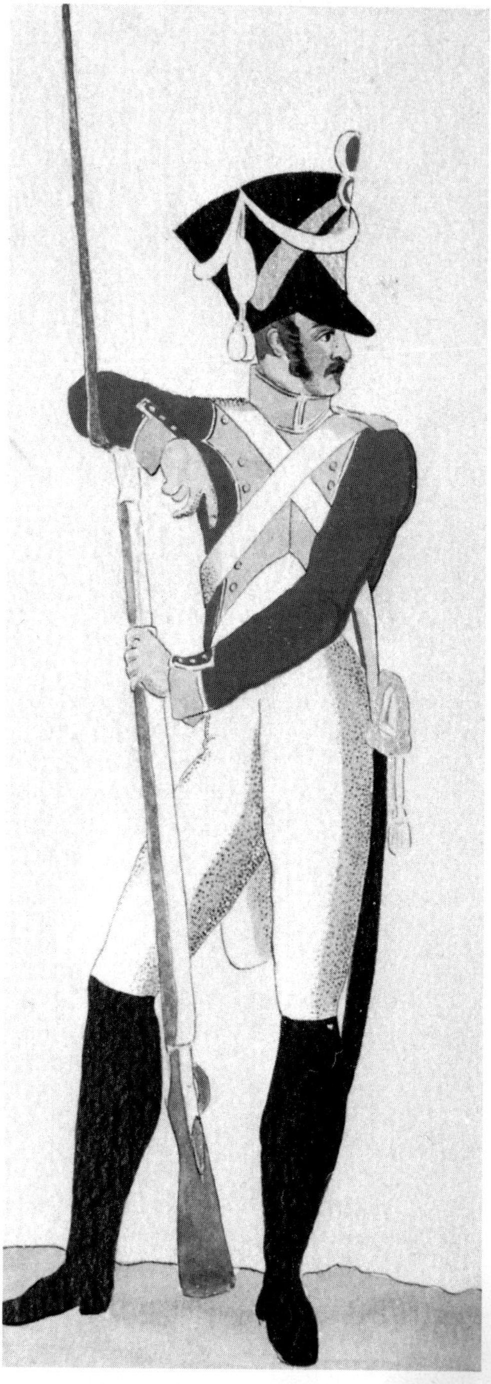

Right: A grenadier from the 1st Régiment Suisse, 1812, after Weiland.

Above: A watercolour of a sapper, musician and cantinière of the 3rd Régiment Suisse, 1808, by Henri Boisselier.

Right: A voltigeur officer of the 3rd Régiment Suisse, 1808. (Courtesy of René Chartrand)

Below: An NCO of the 3rd Régiment Suisse, 1813, from a contemporary drawing.

Below right: An officer of the 3rd Régiment Suisse, 1810. (Courtesy of René Chartrand)

Right: A Tatare Lithuanien, 1813, after C. Vernet.

Left: A Tirailleur du Po (with a foot hussar), 1800, after Marbot and Noirmont.

Below: A standard of the Vélites de Turin.

blue saddle cloth with a band of white trim along the outer edge and a smaller band of white within that.

Standard No information found, although it is known that a French general who had pretensions to take command of the Legion took action to purchase a separate coloured cloth flag for each of the Legion's 36 companies. (Coqueugniot, p. 43.)

Légion Franco-Hessoise

(Franco-Hessian Legion)

Date of Creation Formed by decree of 14 December 1806.

Circumstances of Creation The German Electorate of Hesse-Cassel, homeland of the Hessians, the archetypical mercenaries of history, was a loyal client state of the Prussian monarchy that mobilised against France in 1806. As a result the Electorate was occupied by French troops and its army technically disbanded. From Napoleon's perspective, this created an opportunity to make another addition to the ranks of his *troupes étrangères* (N. to Lagrange, 13 November 1806, Nap. *P&T*, No 799, Vol. 1, pp. 398–400 at 398):

> General, the intention of the Emperor is to enlist the troops of Hesse-Cassel into his service if they can be persuaded to accept. His Majesty consequently takes a great interest in this task that has been assigned to you . . . The first thing you need to do is to let all of the officers and men know that they will be permitted to wear their current uniforms, but that they will be organised into new regiments of light infantry, each with three battalions . . . The Emperor wishes to raise a total of five regiments of Hesse-Cassel troops: two in French service . . .; one in the service of Holland . . .; one in the service of the Kingdom of Italy . . .; and one in the service of Naples.

On 14 December 1806 Napoleon formally authorised the formation of the first two regiments (Organisational Decree reproduced in Fieffé, Vol. 2, pp. 168–9):

> . . . [C]onsidering the large number of soldiers of the army of Hesse-Cassel who have testified to their desire to continue to practice the noble profession of arms, we have resolved to give them the means to do so and, accordingly, have decreed,
>
> Article 1—Two regiments will be raised in the territory of Hesse-Cassel. Each will have three battalions and will be formed exclusively from the current soldiers of that state.

Composition Only the two regiments noted above were formed out of the five regiments contemplated and these, along with a force of Gendarmes, became the component parts of the Legion. As noted above, each regiment was supposed to have three battalions organised in the same manner as any other French light infantry battalion, but no more than a single battalion was raised in each case. (Pigeard, *L'Armée*, p. 438.)

One tantalising piece of correspondence indicates that the recruiting standards for the Regiments might not have been of the highest because it refers to a request from Lieutenant Colonel de Benneville, 'commanding the 1st Battalion of the 1st Hessian Line Regiment in French service', to incorporate into his unit 'the Hessian soldiers who were deported to France as a result of the insurrection that broke out in Hesse'. (Decision of 7 August 1807, Nap. *P&T*, No 1236, Vol. 1, p. 598.) Napoleon responded with his own request for more information about the men because he did not want to include *'mauvais sujets'* ('bad apples') in the unit.

Commanders

1st Franco-Hessian Regiment: Lieutenant Colonel de Benneville

2nd Franco-Hessian Regiment: Battalion Chief Gissot

Operational History The 1st Regiment was not organised until the end of June and the 2nd was not ready until the end of September, so neither unit took part in the campaigns of 1806 or 1807. (Pigeard, *L'Armée*, p. 438.)

Final Transformation On 11 December 1807 the two Regiments were transferred to the payroll of the new Kingdom of Westphalia and amalgamated to form the 1st Line Regiment of King Jerome Bonaparte. (Pigeard, *L'Armée*, p. 438.)

Uniforms The Regiments of the Legion were dressed in uniforms from Hessian regiments: 'These new regiments . . . should have the same uniforms, equipment and headwear that they have now, which will have the advantage minimising cost and maximising the use of existing materials.' (N. to Lagrange, 13 November 1806, Nap. *P&T*, No 799, Vol. 1, pp. 398–400 at 400.) According to one modern source, the 1st Regiment wore uniforms of the Hesse-Cassel grenadier Guard Regiment (Prussian-style blue jackets with red facings and white button-hole lace on the lapels), while the 2nd Regiment of the Legion wore uniforms from the Von Lossberg Regiment (Prussian-style blue jacket with yellow facings). (Pouvesle, pp. 5–6.) The men of both units wore bicorne hats. A gendarme of the Legion is depicted in the Hahlo Manuscript wearing a large bicorne hat with white lace edging, a French cockade and a white plume with a small red base, a blue Prussian-style jacket with braided white shoulder straps, red facings, a red vest, white trousers and black riding boots.

Standard Charrié (p. 171) reports that there were three Hessian regiments formed for the Legion and that each battalion of each regiment had a Model 1804 colour without an Eagle. He also states that the colour of the 3rd Battalion of the '2ème Régiment de Hesse-Cassel' can still be found in Cassel, although Regnault states only that the colour could be seen in the Neue Buhler Galerie in 1912, suggesting that it has since disappeared. (Regnault, p. 108.) Charrié also notes the existence of a collective standard bearing the legend 'L'Empereur/des Français/ Aux Trois Régiments/de Hesse-Cassel' which was used by the Westphalian Army.

Légion Grecque

(Greek Legion)

Date of Creation 15 September 1799. (Belhomme, Vol. 4, p. 207.)

Circumstances of Creation The nucleus of the Greek Legion was provided by three independent companies of Greeks based at Cairo, Damietta and Rosetta that had been formed in 1798 to provide security for French shipping on the Nile. (Spillman, 'Corps Auxiliaires', p. 9.) After Napoleon's flight from Egypt, General Kléber decided to use those existing units as a means to expand the military use of Egyptians of Greek origin.

Composition The Legion had two battalions, each with nine companies, with a total strength of some 1,500 men. Each battalion had one Grenadier company. (Belhomme, Vol. 4, p. 207.) The Legion also seems to have had an artillery company. (A. Boppe, 'Chasseurs', p. 17, n. 1.)

Commanders *Creation to disbandment:* Colonel Nicholas Papas-Oglou (1758–1819), a one-time admiral of the Mameluke Navy who switched allegiance soon after the French landed in Egypt and served Napoleon faithfully thereafter. He particularly distinguished himself in quelling a Mameluke revolt at Damietta on 17 September 1798 at the head of a company of Greek soldiers he formed at his own expense. (Savant, *Les Grecs*, pp. 290–1.)

Operational History Nothing is known of the Legion's combat service other than Fieffé's statement (Vol. 2, p. 105) that the Legion fought at the Battle of Canope (Alexandria) on 21 March 1801. That assertion is corroborated by two sources. First, a well-researched modern history of the British conquest of Egypt in that year cites General Reynier's memoir of the Egyptian campaign for the information that two companies of '*Grenadiers grecs*' from a 'native auxiliary unit' were included in a battalion of combined Grenadier companies that fought in the centre of the French line of battle. (Mackesy, p. 116.) Second, a short biography of Jean Stratis, a Cretan who was a lieutenant in one of the Grenadier companies, alludes to heroic conduct 'at the battle of 30 Ventose [21 March]'. (Savant, *Les Grecs*, p. 339.) The Legion Grenadiers may not have been that heavily engaged, however, because a modern French source states (albeit without supporting citations) that only seven men of the Legion were killed in action during its brief existence. (Anon., 'Légion Grecque.') Stratis' biography adds that he was wounded three times total in that campaign—once at Ghirgheh, once at Dlizeh and once at Salehieh.

Final Transformation The unit ceased to exist in September 1801 following massive desertion by its rank-and-file members, but some of the officers and men of the Legion were repatriated to France when Egypt was evacuated and the unit itself was not formally disbanded until it arrived at Marseilles. (Anon., 'Légion Grecque.') Many of these, including Colonel Papas-Oglou, went on to serve in the *Chasseurs d'Orient* (see separate entry) and the second formation of Mamelukes (see separate entry).

Uniforms No primary source information has been found about the dress of the Legion, but Vernet & Lami's work does contain a lithograph of a soldier of the unit in an exotic costume consisting of a red skull cap, a loose dark blue vest worn over a flowing lighter blue shirt, a red sash, blousy white trousers reaching only to the knee, red stockings and sandals. The legionnaires had Turkish-style equipment and armaments. (Fieffé, Vol. 2, p. 48.) The modern French source mentioned above says that the

Legion received a red-brown French-style uniform jacket and a leather helmet with red pompom on top in January 1800, but no supporting evidence for that statement has been found. (Anon., 'Légion Grecque'.)
Standard No information found.

Légion Hanovrienne

(Hanoverian Legion)

Date of Creation 12 August 1803, although the definitive Organisational Decree for the unit was not issued until 23 Germinal Year XII (13 April 1804). (The text of the decree, and other information about the Legion, can be found in SHA Carton X[h]20.)
Circumstances of Creation Napoleon's disbandment of the Hanoverian Army in July 1803 created a pool of experienced but unemployed soldiers which he hoped to tap for his growing military establishment. He therefore authorised General Mortier, the commander of the French forces occupying Hanover, to form a 'Legion' in French service from these troops. Mortier responded on 12 August 1803 by ordering Battalion Chief Louis Cyriac Striffler of the 94th Line to recruit such a force of some 750 infantry exclusively from Hanoverian natives. (Despreaux, Vol. 2, p. 393.) In November, Mortier instructed Squadron Chief Charles Joseph Evers of the 5th Hussars to form a companion cavalry unit subject to the same condition. (Despreaux, Vol. 2, p. 395.)
Composition According to the 1804 Organisational Decree for the Legion, its infantry component was organised as a unit of Light Infantry, except that there were only five (instead of eight) companies, four of which were composed of Chasseurs and one of which was an élite company of Carabiniers. The total strength of the original battalion, including the headquarters staff and a band, was rated at 801 officers and men. The cavalry component of the Legion was treated as Mounted Chasseurs and organised into six companies (three squadrons) plus a staff totalling 416 men. The official title of the cavalry force was the 'Regiment of Hanoverian Light Horse in French Service', but they were known more simply and more commonly as the cavalry of the Hanoverian Legion. (Despreaux, Vol. 2, p. 398.)

Enlistment in the Legion was intended to be limited to native Hanoverian volunteers engaged for four years' service. The voluntary enlistment feature was retained for the life of the Legion, but the geographic restriction quickly became impractical as the territory of Hanover was ceded first to Prussia and then to the new Kingdom of Westphalia. The unit also suffered from the recruiting competition posed by the German Legion raised contemporaneously by the British government. Nevertheless, by 3 February 1804 Mortier was able to report that 'the two corps of the Legion are composed of good-looking men, well-clothed and disciplined; the cavalry is comprised entirely of choice Hanoverian veterans. I have reason to believe that the Government will be satisfied with this Legion.' (Despreaux, Vol. 2, p. 398.)

The ethnic purity of the cavalry did not last long. By October 1806 there were 131 Frenchmen in the unit. (Nap. *O&A*, No 3744, Vol. 3, p. 185 and n. 2.) This state of affairs inspired Napoleon to complain: 'I never intended for this to be a French unit'.

Commanders

Infantry *1803–10*: Colonel Louis Cyriac Striffler (1772 –1834). Colonel Striffler was not replaced when he took sick leave at the end of 1810. Fieffé states that Colonel the Prince of Hohenzollern-Hechingen, who had briefly commanded the first battalion of the Westphalian Regiment, took command of the Legion after the amalgamation of those units, but those facts do not appear in the Prince's service records.

Cavalry *1803–11*: Colonel Charles Joseph Evers (1775–1818) (on sick leave from March 1810). Evers was 'an excellent, zealous officer who takes good care of his unit; his conduct is commendable and he shows a great deal of intelligence'. (Six, Vol. 1, p.433.) He was promoted to the rank of Brigade General in 1812.

Operational History

Infantry The first combat assignment of the Legion infantry was to participate in the invasion of Portugal in 1807 by the expeditionary force under the command of General Androche Junot. The Legion was engaged against Portuguese forces, but did not fight at either Roliça or Vimeiro. It was repatriated to France along with the rest of Junot's force in accordance with the terms of the Convention of Cintra.

At the end of 1808, the unit was assigned to the General Étienne Heudelet's 4th Division of Marshal Soult's 2nd Corps of the Army of Spain. It was present at, but played no role in, the Battle of Corunna. Later, in 1809, it participated in Soult's invasion of northern Portugal. No details of the Legion's service in that campaign have been found except for the information that the infantry had one captain killed and five other officers wounded at the capture of Braga, Portugal, on 20 March 1809. It was also, of course, a participant in the gruelling French retreat that ensued when they were chased out of Oporto by a British army led by Arthur Wellesley.

Napoleon approved the addition of both a 4th Squadron and a 2nd Battalion to the Legion on 7 September 1809. (Decision, Nap. *P&T*, No 3544, Vol. 3, p. 224.) There may have been an initial intention to assemble the new infantry battalion from elements in the Legion's depot, but its completion was assured by a decree of 30 September 1809 which announced that the first battalion of the *Régiment de Westphalie* would become part of the Legion. (See the separate entry for that regiment.) The Westphalians undoubtedly joined the Hanoverians in early 1810 when they were both assembled at Valladolid for the formation of General Louis Henri Loison's Division of Marshal Ney's 6th Corps. (N. to Berthier, 11 January 1810, Nap. *Corr.*, No 16131, Vol. 20, p. 114–17 at 115.) In practice, however, it apparently took a long time for the integration of the two units to be completed.

For the campaign of 1810 with the Army of Portugal, the Legion infantry was brigaded with the 26th Line and the *Légion du Midi* under the command of General Henri Simon in Loison's Division of Marshal Ney's 6th Corps. The Legion was at first part of the force screening Ciudad Rodrigo from British aid and tangled with the 95th Rifles of the British Army at Barba de Puerco on 19 March 19. (Horward, *Iberia*, p. 20.) By May, however, it had been re-assigned to the siege artillery train as both additional security and additional manpower. (Horward, *Iberia*, pp. 81, pp. 284–5.) The infantry suffered one officer killed and two wounded during the siege of Ciudad Rodrigo in June and July 1810, but was spared heavier casualties when the Spanish garrison surrendered as the French were on the verge of launching their final assault. The Legionnaires then played a similar role in the siege of Almeida.

The Legion, with a strength of 1,035 men, was back in a traditional combat role at the Battle of Bussaco on 27 September 1810. (Return of 15 September 1810, in Koch, Vol. 7, p. 569.) It was one of the units leading Loison's Division when it was launched on an assault against the portion of British position on Bussaco ridge held by the Light Division, and the reception it received was a rude one. The Legion was routed with a loss of 30 officers and men killed and 188 wounded. (Chambers, p. 115; Koch, Vol. 7, p. 573.) George Napier of the Light Division records an incident about Bussaco in his autobiography that may have involved a member of the Hanoverian Legion (quoted in Chambers, p. 108):

> One poor German officer in the French Army came to make enquiries about his brother who was in our service in the 60th Regiment, which was at that time composed principally of foreigners, and upon looking about found him dead, the poor fellow having been killed.

After a hard winter in front of the Lines of Torres Vedras and the difficult retreat back to Spain in the spring of 1811, the Legion mustered only 23 officers and 698 men. (Return of 15 March 1811, presented in Oman, Vol. 3, p. 541.) These men, consolidated into a single battalion, served in General Férey's division at the Battle of Fuentes de Oñoro on 3–5 May. On the first day of that action the Legion was part of a force engaged in a promising attack on the village of Fuentes de Oñoro when it became the victim of a dreadful misunderstanding described by Baron Marbot (Marbot, p. 463):

> Their uniform was red, like the English, but they had the usual grey overcoat of the French soldier, and accordingly their commander, who had several men killed by our people at Busaco [*sic*], asked leave for his men to wear their greatcoats instead of rolling them up, as the order was. But General Loison replied that he must follow the order given to the whole corps. The result was a cruel blunder. The 66th Regiment, having been sent to support the Hanoverians, who were fighting in line, mistook them in the smoke for an English battalion, and fired into them, while our artillery, equally misled by the red coats, played on them with grape. I must do the brave Hanoverians the justice to say that, placed as they were between two fires, they endured them for a long time without recoiling a step, but after losing 100 men killed and many wounded, the battalion was compelled to retire, passing along one side of the village.

The official French casualty returns for the battle are incomplete, but according to Martinien's invaluable compilation the Legion had six officers wounded that day.

Cavalry The cavalry of the Legion was transferred to the command of Prince Eugene Beauharnais, the Viceroy of Italy, in late 1805. In early 1806 it was detached to join the Army of Naples. On 16 April 1806 the Legion cavalry gained an unusual battle honour by participating in the capture by assault of the town of Civitella-del-Tronto. (Leconte, 'Evers', pp. 103–4.) Legion Captain Doldonel (or d'Oldenneel), who was wounded in the action, was even credited with forcing open the town gate with an axe. The Legion cavalry was recalled from Naples in early 1807 (N. to Minister of War, 21 April 1807, Nap. *P&T*, No 1055, Vol. 1, p. 510) and eventually returned to north Germany, where it occupied a number of different posts, including Potsdam. In 1808, King Jerome Bonaparte of Westphalia asked for the Legion cavalry to be transferred to his army in place of the Polish Lancers of the Vistula withdrawn to join the French Army, but that request was refused by his brother. (Decision of 10 March 1808, Nap. *P&T*, No 1697, Vol. 2, p. 114.) The squadrons were ultimately transferred to Spain, where they were attached initially to the light cavalry of the Marshal Victor's 1st Corps. (Decision of 9 June 1808, Nap. *P&T*, No 1987, Vol. 2, p. 262.) Before the autumn offensive, however, they were reassigned to light cavalry brigade of General Jean Baptiste Franceschi-Delonne along with the 5th and 22nd Chasseurs. (Journal of II Corps, 11 November 1808, reproduced in Balagny, Vol. 1, pp. 355–6.)

General Franceschi-Delonne's brigade and the Legion cavalry saw significant action in the pursuit of General Moore's army through north-western Spain in December 1808 and January 1809. The English 18th Hussars surprised and routed a small force of Legion cavalry and French infantry at Rueda on 13 December, but in revenge a detachment of Hanoverian chasseurs under Lieutenant de Fraye was one of the first units to provide Napoleon with important intelligence of the presence of English infantry near Valladolid on 19 December. (Balagny, Vol. 3, pp. 509–10; Tilly to Berthier, 19 December 1808, reproduced in Balagny, Vol. 3, pp. 432–3.) The constant action against English cavalry meant constant casualties. From 13 to 21 December the Legion cavalry lost thirteen rank-and-file killed and sixteen captured, then lost ten killed and thirteen captured near Cerbatos on 24 December. (Archival records cited in Balagny, Vol. 3, p. 587, n. 1.) The absence of any statistics as to wounded men suggests that the Hanoverians got the worst of these encounters and thus lost all their wounded as prisoners.

Franceschi-Delonne's brigade was then shifted to combat against the Spanish force of the Marquis de la Romana. On 29 December it combined with General Debelle's brigade of the 8th Dragoons and the 1st Provisional Chasseurs to route a superior Spanish force at Mansilla, capturing two standards and 1,500 prisoners. (Soult to Berthier, 30 December 1808, Balagny, Vol. 4, pp. 167–70.) The Spanish forces included the Regiments of Navarre, Leon and Naples. The French cavalry met up again with the Spaniards a few days later on the road from Astorga to Ponferrada and again achieved astonishing success: they captured five standards and took 2,900 prisoners (including General Rengel, four colonels and 105 officers) for a cost of one dragoon killed and one officer and two chasseurs wounded. The conduct of the Legion cavalry in the action was exemplary and caused General Fransceschi to recommend 2nd Lieutenant Mirbaut and Adjutant-Major Ébard of the Hanoverian Chasseurs for Legion of Honour decorations and Colonel Evers for an officer's cross. (Soult to Berthier, 5 January 1809, reproduced in Balagny, Vol. 4, pp. 307–10.) Berthier reported independently to King Joseph that the Legion cavalry itself had captured the general in question and the bulk of the rest of the prisoners. (Berthier to King Joseph, 3 January 1809, quoted in Balagny, Vol. 4, p. 189.) The Legion cavalry was apparently present at the Battle of Corunna on 16 January since it had one officer wounded in that action, but it did not play a significant role in the fighting.

Like the Legion infantry, the Legion cavalry was involved in Marshal Soult's invasion of Portugal early in 1809, suffering three officer casualties at the capture of Braga, Portugal, on 20 March and two more in a skirmish against the British at Coimbra on 10 May. Franceschi-Delonne's cavalry served with the rearguard during Marshal Soult's subsequent retreat from Oporto, during which Colonel Evers is said to have two horses killed under him. (Leconte, 'Evers', p. 104.) The campaign took a heavy toll on the Chasseurs and the other cavalry units. They mustered a combined 1,300 men on 19 February 1809 but only 87 officers and 739 men in June. (Le Noble, pp. 353–4.)

The Chasseurs spent the rest of 1809 and early 1810 engaged in pacification duties, but took the field again in the summer of that latter year as part of the Army of Portugal. Although it was by now a veteran unit, a detachment of 60 Hanoverian horsemen was surprised and captured on 22 August 1810 in an action against Portuguese cavalry at Ladoeiro because, according to the memoirs of General Foy, its commanding officer was inexperienced. (Girod de L'Ain, p. 97.) This individual may have been Captain Scharlook, who is reported to have been killed that day. The cavalry participated in the whole of the Masséna's invasion of Portugal in 1810–11, but no specific details of its service have been found.

Final Transformation After Hanover was annexed to the Kingdom of Westphalia, the ostensible national identity of the Legion was impossible to preserve. In such circumstances, there was little point in preserving the Legion as a special force organised on a basis different from the rest of the French cavalry and infantry forces. By 1810 Napoleon had already expressed a desire to disband the Legion, but it was inconvenient for him to do so while it was fighting in Portugal. Once that campaign was over, however, official action to dissolve the Legion was swiftly taken. In August 1811, the Legion cavalry was incorporated into the 30th Chasseurs, which had been formed from the Hamburg Dragoons and which would soon be transformed into the 9th Light Horse Lancers. The Legion infantry was transferred to a number of different units, including the Prussian Regiment, the Isembourg Regiment and, most prominently, the 127th, 128th and 129th Regiments of Line Infantry which had been formed in Napoleon's north German provinces.

An examination of the composition of one of the Legion's infantry battalions (possibly the one obtained from the Westphalian Regiment in 1809) at the moment of its disbandment reveals how little it had maintained its Hanoverian identity. Out of 503 soldiers, none was from former Hanoverian territories. Instead, they had the following nationalities (Fieffé, Vol. 2, p. 132):

226	Austrian	9	Swiss
129	Rhine Confederation states	7	Poles
53	Prussian	3	Spaniards
57	Dutch	3	Swedes
14	Russians	2	Neapolitans

On 2 September 1811 Marshal Davout requested that all former members of the Legion be removed from the 9th Lancers and transferred to a colonial battalion. The request is not specific as to its motivation, but it is likely that the reason for this initiative was that the Legionnaires became prone to desertion following the dissolution of their unit. Napoleon approved the concept of the request, but limited its application to only those soldiers who posed a real risk of flight. (Nap. *P&T*, No 6124, Vol. 4, p. 661.) More importantly in terms of the substantive problem of desertion, Napoleon also confirmed that involuntary transfer to a regular French Army unit did not affect the right of an ex-Legionnaire to obtain an unconditional discharge once his original term of voluntary enlistment expired. (Nap. *P&T*, No 6972, Vol. 5, p. 235.)

Uniforms

Infantry The Legion's formal Organisational Decree from 1804 contains the following information about the uniform of the Legion infantry:

> Red jacket [*habite veste*] with blue collar, cuffs and lapels, white piping, white tricot lining, white cloth vest and pantaloons *à la hongroise*, white metal button, black half-gaiters . . . Officers wear a long jacket with vertical pockets. Light infantry shako . . .

Additional details are provided by Mortier's correspondance. In a letter dated 9 April 1804 he specified that the Legion officers wore 'silver epaulettes and swords' while the non-commissioned officers were armed with 'small sabres found in Hanover'. (Despreaux, Vol. 2, p. 394.) He also ordered that all of the miscellaneous effects necessary to complete the uniforming of the Legion should be taken from those captured in the Hanoverian arsenals when the country was overrun. (*Ibid.*)

The chief controversy concerning the Legion uniform centres on the question of the shape of the lapels on the infantry jacket. Some experts have concluded that since the Legion was rated as a light infantry regiment, the lapels probably had same shape (i.e., pointed ends) as the lapels of the typical light infantry uniform. That conclusion is contradicted by the only contemporary depiction of a Legion infantryman. That picture, which occurs in the so-called Hahlo Manuscript of paintings by a German artilleryman of the Napoleonic era, depicts lapels (similar to those of the Prussian infantry coat of that time and of the French 1812 Model jacket) which are closed to the waist and thus hide the vest of the wearer.

Le Plumet, Plate No 171 (*Légion Hanovrienne, Drapeau 1808–1811*), shows an NCO wearing a red jacket with blue, line infantry-style lapels piped red, but this depiction is not supported by specific evidence. Rigo does provide two interesting pieces of information about the dress of the Legion. First, he states that the lining of the uniform jacket changed from white to blue in 1808 so that the troop could be better distinguished from the red-clad Swiss in French service. Second, he cites unit records in support of the contention that the Legion infantry received new uniforms, and new French shakos, arms and equipment, in 1808.

Blondieau gives the following description of the plate of the 1808 shako without specifying his source: 'White metal plate with regulation eagle bearing the legend 'Légion Hanovrienne'. (Blondieau, p. 26.) He also states that the Carabinier company wore a bearskin headdress without a plate.

Cavalry: The unit Organisational Decree also covers the uniforms of the mounted portion of the Legion:

> Green jacket [*habite-veste*] without lapels, yellow cuffs, collar and trim, yellow tricot lining, yellow cloth vest, and pantaloon *à la hongroise*, yellow metal buttons, Hungarian-style boots, shako *à la hussarde*, yellow belts with a plate . . . for the waist-belt, [and] the same horse equipment as for French Mounted Chasseurs.

A letter from Mortier provides the important additional detail that the cavalry force was armed with Hanoverian light dragoon sabres. (Despreaux, Vol. 2, p. 397.) According to Blondieau, the cavalry shako plate was brass stamped with an eagle and a hunting horn. (Blondieau, p. 26.)

Confirmation of all this information is provided by a naive, but detailed, painting of a Legion Chasseur *circa* 1806 which can be found in the Rovatti Manuscript. That source depicts a mounted trooper wearing a black shako with a green plume, tipped yellow, one strand of yellow cord across the front (with two long tassels hanging down from the right side), and a tricolour cockade in lieu of a shako plate. The saddlecloth is a white sheepskin with green trim. The Belgian Royal Army Museum owns an 1811 portrait of Colonel Evers by Jan de Landsheer which provides a close view of the pointed cuffs of the uniform jacket and of the two buttons located outside the cuff along the lower seam of the sleeve. The Colonel has a green cartridge box and shoulder-belt lavishly trimmed with gold, thick gold epaulettes, and a completely gold waist-belt with a gold belt plate bearing a crowned eagle. He also wears the Legion of Honour decoration. (This portrait is reproduced in Leconte, 'Evers', p. 99.)

There would be little left to say about these uniforms were it not for the existence of two other contemporary drawings in the Hamburg Manuscript which can be dated to 1807–08, both of which have captions identifying the figures as officers of the '*Franco-hannoverischen Legion*'. One of these depicts a dismounted figure wearing a uniform very similar to the green undress uniform of the Mounted Chasseurs of the Imperial Guard (including lapels, red facings, a busby and an aiguilette), while the other gives a rear/side view of a mounted figure wearing a bicorne hat, a green hussar dolman and green hussar breeches. If these captions are correct, then the only reasonable explanation is that the Hanoverian Chasseurs had a complete overhaul of their original uniform after they returned from Naples and adopted a more elaborate dress with hussar features instead. Although there are many unusual uniform points in the Hamburg MS that have been proved to be correct through corroboration by other sources, no corroborating evidence has been found in this case, so the question of whether the dress of the Legion cavalry changed in 1808 still awaits definitive resolution.

Standard According to a letter from Minister of War Dejean dated 19 Frimaire Year 13 (10 December 1804), the infantry battalion of the Hanoverian Legion received one Model 1804 infantry colour while each of the three squadrons received a Model 1804 cavalry colour, but in each case the flagstaff was surmounted by a spearhead finial instead of a Napoleonic eagle. (Charrié, p. 171.) The colours had the standard form of caption in the centre diamond, but the escutcheons in the corners were blank.

Légion Helvétique

(Helvetian [Swiss] Legion)

Date of Creation Late 1798.

Circumstances of Creation French military intervention in a fierce civil war in Switzerland during 1798 led to the establishment of a Helvetian Republic under French auspices. The new government showed its gratitude by agreeing to provide six *Demi-brigades Helvétiques* (see separate entry) for service with the French armies, but it also realised that it needed to form a national military force of its own to ensure its own continued existence. It did so by calling for the creation of eighteen battalions of territorial militia and by authorising the formation of a small corps of permanent troops of all arms to be known as the Helvetian Legion. (Bernegg, Pt 2, Book 8, p. 56.)

For the avoidance of doubt, it should be noted that this Helvetian Legion was distinct from the two legions of the same name that were formed in January 1799 out of the five Swiss regiments (commanded by Colonels Bellemont, Ernst, Peyerimhoff, Bachmann and Zimmermann) that had been in the service of the King of Piedmont-Sardinia until the mainland half of his realm was conquered by the French. The commanders of those two *Légions Helvétiques* were Colonels Bellemont and Andermatt. (Fieffé, Vol. 2, p. 36.) They were routed at the Battle of Magnano (erroneously called the Battle of Verona by Belhomme and Fiéffe) on 5 April 1799, surrendered in large part and were never re-formed. (Belhomme, Vol. 4, pp. 182, 186.) (The tricolour standard carried by the 1st Battalion of one of these Legions made its way as a trophy to the Austrian Army Historical Museum in Vienna and its photograph appears in John, p. 127.)

Composition The Helvetian Legion consisted of the following components (Bernegg, Pt 2, Book 8, p. 56.):

20	Staff Personnel
100	Artillerymen
600	Line Infantrymen
400	Light Infantry Chasseurs
400	Hussars

Commanders No information found.

Operational History No specific information found, but some orders of battle for General (later Marshal) Masséna's armies during 1799 show elements of the Helvetian Legion serving under General (later Marshal) Oudinot.

Final Transformation The elements of the Helvetian Legion were all ultimately incorporated into other units. The infantry was reorganised along the with Swiss Demi-brigades in 1800 (see separate entry for *Demi-brigades Suisses*). The artillery force eventually became the regimental artillery for the 1st Swiss Regiment, while the hussars became the Helvetian Chasseurs (see separate entry).

Uniforms No primary source information has been found about the uniforms of the Legion. In *Fiche Documentaire* No 240, Roger Forthoffer presents a reconstruction of the infantry uniform for the year 1799 with the following details: Bicorne hat with red/yellow/green cockade and short feathers; blue coat with red, rolled-down collar with yellow trim; yellow square lapels and cuffs with red trim; red cuff flaps, blue shoulder straps trimmed red; white vest trimmed red; white breeches and gaiters.

Standard No information found.

Légion Irlandaise

(Irish Legion; also known as
the *Régiment Irlandais* and the *3ème Régiment Étranger*)

Date of Creation 31 August 1803.

Circumstances of Creation The idea of raising a unit of Irish troops for the French Army way, like the idea of the invasion of Ireland itself, a recurring theme in the military planning of French revolutionary governments. The Revolution inherited a brigade of Irish regiments from the *Ancien Regime*, but its special identity was lost in successive reorganisations of the French armies. As early as 1796 the Directory contemplated recruiting Irishmen to participate in its planned invasion of Ireland, but the scheme never came to fruition. (See, generally, Van Brock.) The idea for an 'Irish Battalion' surfaced once more in 1800, but, despite the endorsement of the First Consul, it once again led nowhere. (Berthier to Thompson, 9 Pluviose An VIII [29 January 1800], Chuquet II, Vol. 1, No 141, p. 65.) In the end, however, the concept of a specifically Irish unit did not become viable until the rupture of the Peace of Amiens once again raised prospects for a French invasion of the British Isles. Finally, on 13 Fructidor Year 11 (31 August 1803) Napoleon issued a Consular decree which established a Legion to be recruited from Irishmen and Frenchmen of Irish descent. (Carles I, p. 28.)

Composition Although the unit was labelled a 'Legion', its original establishment called only for a single light infantry battalion with a staff and nine companies, including one of Carabiniers. (Carles I, p. 30.) Its establishment was eventually increased to four battalions and a depot, by which time it had been renamed the Irish Regiment and then the 3rd Foreign Regiment.

Commanders *1803–04*: Battalion Chief James Bartholomew Blackwell (1761–?) was officially the first commander of the Irish (Gallaher, p. 31), but real control was actually in the hands of Adjutant-Commandant Bernard MacSheehy (1774–1807), a native Irishman who had served with the Army of Egypt. *September 1804–1809*: Battalion Chief Antoine Petrezzoli (1764–?). *17 May 1809–12 November 1811*: Colonel Daniel Joseph O'Meara (1764–1837), a veteran of the Irish Brigade which had served France's Bourbon monarchy. *8 February 1812–27 October 1813*: Colonel William Lawless (1772–1824), who was a professor of anatomy at the Royal College of Surgeons in Dublin before he took part in the 1798 Rebellion and was forced to seek refuge in France. *4 December 1813–1814*: Colonel Jean François Mahony (1772–1842).

Operational History The organisation of the Irish Legion took place in Brittany in late 1803 and early 1804. There were officers aplenty, as exiles from Ireland competed with Frenchmen of Irish descent to obtain commissions in the new unit, but recruiting of the rank-and-file proceeded extremely slowly. As a result, even after more than a year of existence, the Legion contained only 22 NCOs and privates as against 66 officers. (Gallaher, p. 34.) These peculiar demographics were not necessarily problematic, however, because it is clear that Napoleon initially viewed the unit as being more of a psychological than a military threat to his British enemy. By providing employment to Irish exiles, he helped to keep alive the dream of rebellion and created a trained cadre of leaders which would have been very useful for mobilising local support in the event that a French invasion of Ireland had actually taken place. The First Consul reinforced the Legion's symbolic role in June of 1804 by granting it an unusual green standard decorated with Irish harps. (See the section on the Legion's standard below.)

Without the normal distractions of commanding real troops, the Irish Legion officers spent much of their time in factional strife and petty feuding about rank and privileges. This behaviour led to tragedy in the wake of the creation of the First Empire in May 1804. When the members of the Legion were required to swear a new oath of allegiance to the Emperor, some questioned whether that action was consistent with their position as Irish patriots and decided on a course of passive resistance. In particular, Captain John Sweeny apparently avoided taking the oath, but his dereliction was noticed and publicly proclaimed by Captain Thomas Corbet. (See, generally, Gallaher II.) Sweeny responded by initiating a fist-fight with his fellow officer on the parade ground which nearly became a full-scale brawl and led to both men being placed under arrest. (Gallaher, pp. 43–4.) When they were finally released in September, Captain Corbet demanded formal satisfaction. In the ensuing pistol duel (which involved an incredible five exchanges of shots at ranges as short as six paces), both men were wounded, Corbet mortally. (Gallaher, pp. 51–2.)

A forceful commander might have been able to restore discipline in the wake of such conflict. Adjutant Commandant MacSheehy, however, actually made things worse by taking sides in the various intramural disputes and by starting a feud of his own with his superior officer, General Arthur O'Connor (1767–1852), who had fled from Ireland and joined the French Army back in 1796. With his authority and credibility irretrievably compromised, MacSheehy was relieved of command in September 1804 and replaced by Battalion Chief Petrezzoli of the 16th Regiment of Light Infantry. (Gallaher, pp. 48–51.) The new commander was a veteran who had served under Napoleon in the Italian campaign, but he also had the equally important qualification of lacking any Irish heritage, so he was able to deal even-handedly with the factions which had sprung up in the Legion. Petrezzoli was not, however, any more successful than his predecessors in finding soldiers to serve in the ranks of the Legion, even though in December 1804 it became the first foreign unit to receive a Napoleonic Eagle. (Charrié, p. 170.) It remained a unit of officers throughout 1805, and so the Legion was left behind when the rest of Napoleon's 'Army of England' marched off to become the 'Grand Army' and to receive its baptism of victory at Ulm and Austerlitz.

By 1806, those of the original officers who had not resigned their commissions were both bored and frustrated with garrison life in the small provincial town of Quimper. Relations with the town citizens were good, as evidenced by the marriages of two Legion officers to local women, but the only professional diversions were provided by some assignments to escort conscripts from coastal districts to the inland frontiers of France. (Byrne, Vol. 2, pp. 23–5.) The closest the Legion came to combat was an unsuccessful attempt to come to grips with a British landing party of one midshipman and ten marines. According to Lieutenant Miles Byrne, this 'invasion' had been launched with the peculiar objective of temporarily kidnapping two French peasants to serve as live models for some would-be portrait artists among the officers of a blockading British naval vessel. (Byrne, Vol. 2, p. 31.)

To arrange for an escape from this dreary existence, the officers of the Legion took the extraordinary step of sending a formal communication to the Emperor in the summer of 1806 asking for more active duties. (Byrne, Vol. 2, p. 32.) Even if it did no more than remind Napoleon of the Legion's existence, this letter may have paved the way for Napoleon's decision after the Battle of Jena to complete the unit's organisation. (Byrne, Vol. 2, p. 37.) In December 1806 the Legion, then consisting of only some 80 men, was summoned to the city of Mayence, or Mainz, where it was finally completed to it full establishment (and beyond) by means of the enlistment of some 1,500 Prussian prisoners of war who had opted to enter French service. (Decision of 14 December 1806, Nap. *P&T*, No 841, Vol. 1, p. 419.) The bulk of these men were Poles, but a significant number were, of all things, Irishmen—the survivors of some political prisoners of the 1798 Rebellion who (it is alleged) were sold by the British government to the King of Prussia for service in his army. (Byrne, Vol. 2, p. 40.) With the aid of these German-speaking Irishmen, the other ex-prisoners (including a seven-foot-tall Drum Major) were swiftly incorporated into the unit. (Byrne, Vol. 2, p.44.)

This influx of new men precipitated a significant identity crisis for the Legion. As an Irish unit, the Legion's purpose had seemed closely intertwined with the prospects for an invasion of England or Ireland; as a Polish unit, that purpose no longer seemed relevant. A question therefore arose as to whether the unit should be given a new direction. Marshal Berthier, for one, proposed amalgamating it with a squadron of mounted Guide Interpreters then being raised at Mainz, thus giving it a true legion-like character, and dedicating the combined force to the task of guarding army headquarters. (Decision of 14 December 1806, Nap. *P&T*, Vol. 1, No 841, p. 440.) Others believed that, in view of its new ethnic composition, the Legion should become part of the predominantly Polish 2nd Legion of the North (see separate entry) being raised at that time. (Gallaher, pp. 80–1.) Napoleon never explained in detail how he viewed the situation, but on 20 February 1807, he resolved the unit's fate in the short run by ordering Marshal Kellerman to 'send the Irish battalion to the camp at Boulogne . . . '. (Decision of 20 February 1807, Nap. *P&T*, No 915, Vol. 1, p. 477.)

The Legion (now with a Voltigeur company, which had been organised in May 1807) was consequently sent back to the Channel coast to occupy various posts, first at Boulogne and then at Antwerp. (Carles I, p. 35.) This move to the West at first inspired hopes that Napoleon's British invasion projects were going to be resurrected. By September, however, the harsh reality that the Legion was destined for nothing more glamorous than coastal defence assignments had become obvious with the posting of the unit to Walcheren Island in the Scheldt estuary. Judging from an Inspection Report filed by General Monnet in December, morale and attention to duty suffered correspondingly:

> I am satisfied with the instruction of the soldiers. It was good and of a high quality. But the 'tenue', the company records and bookkeeping cause me to believe there is a great deal of laxity on the part of the officers towards their duties . . .

Monnet also noted that problems were exacerbated by the fact that the 'officers, noncommissioned officers and soldiers who make it [the Legion] up are foreigners and speak very little French.' (Quoted in Gallaher, pp. 88–9.) The detailed personnel assessments prepared by Petrezzoli in the same month concluded that, out of 39 active duty officers (the bulk of whom were still Irish), only four were 'excellent', while nine were incompetent and eight were of 'poor' quality. (Gallaher, pp. 89-90.)

Against this backdrop, it is ironic that Napoleon's increasing focus on the affairs of Spain and Portugal was just then leading him to give wider geographic scope to his employment of the Legion. The Legion's superabundance of privates (over 1,500 men according to an Inspection report dated 30 December 1807) was used to create a provisional battalion commanded by Captain Louis Lacy, which was then detached for service on the Spanish frontier, albeit still in an auxiliary role. (Carles I, p. 37; Byrne, Vol. 2, p. 60.) It was assigned to Marshal Moncey's observation corps, which entered Spain in January 1808.

The year 1808 was another relatively uneventful one for the Legion. The battalion on Walcheren Island was troubled by the local strain of malaria, but the sedentary nature of the unit's garrison service meant that most officers and men who fell ill could be given long periods of time to convalesce. There was also continued friction between and among the original Irish officers of the corps, their Italian commander and some Polish officers who joined the unit at the end of 1807. (Gallaher, pp. 94–6.) The detachment in Spain saw a lot of marching, but no combat, as it travelled to Madrid and then back to the Ebro River as the fortunes of the French waxed with the overthrow of the Spanish Bourbons in May and then waned after the defeat of General Dupont at Bailen in July. The detachment did, however, lose its commander along the way. It was thought at first that he had been kidnapped or killed by insurgents, but nearly a year later it was discovered that the Spanish-born Captain Lacy had defected to become a commander for the new central government of Spain. (Byrne, Vol. 2, pp. 60–1.) The detachment was reinforced in September by a 600-man contingent from the senior battalion under Captain Jerome Fitzhenry, who took command of the whole in the absence of Captain Lacy. (Gallaher, p. 93.) Fitzhenry, 'a very handsome man, six foot high, and about thirty six years of age' who was also a great horseman, was extremely popular and seemed to have the experience and other qualities to be a first-rate field officer. (Byrne, Vol. 3, p. 68.)

The Irish battalion in Spain was used only for garrison duty in the rear of the army even during the successful campaign led by Napoleon himself in the autumn of 1808. Nevertheless, the presence of the unit in Spain may have reminded Napoleon of the Legion's existence, for by imperial decree of 16 December 1808 the Legion was re-designated the Irish Regiment, with the detachment in Spain receiving official recognition as the unit's 2nd Battalion. (Historical Record of the Irish Legion, quoted in Clark, p. 168; Nap. *O&A*, No 5453, Vol. 4, p. 81.) The new 2nd Battalion soon thereafter had the honour of providing Napoleon's guard when he stopped at Burgos on 17 January 809 on his way back to France after abandoning the pursuit of Sir John Moore's British army. (Byrne, Vol. 2, pp. 76–7.) The Irish troops apparently made a favourable impression on the Emperor because on 13 April 1809 another decree authorised an increase in the strength of the Regiment to four field battalions and a depot unit. Napoleon also finally gave the unit a proper commander in the person of

Colonel Daniel O'Meara. O'Meara, however, was not a popular choice because he was viewed as a political appointee put forward by Henri Clarke, the Duke of Feltre, at the expense of more deserving officers. (Byrne, Vol. 2, p. 72.) The organisation of a new 3rd Battalion began at Landau on 1 June 1809, and work on a 4th was due to begin as soon as the third was completed. (Historical Record of the 3rd Battalion, quoted in Clark, p. 169.)

Just as the strength of the Irish Regiment was being increased in theory, however, it was being reduced in actuality. In a belated and forlorn effort to assist their Austrian allies, a British armada appeared off the coast of Holland in late July 1809 and on 1 August the garrison of the town of Flushing on Walcheren Island, including the 1st Battalion of the Irish Regiment, found itself besieged by immensely superior land and sea forces. The siege was at first conducted in a desultory fashion, although skirmishing cost the Irish their first recorded officer casualties. On 13 August, however, a British naval squadron moved up to the walls of the town and, together with land batteries, subjected Flushing to what was, by contemporary standards, a ferocious bombardment lasting for two full days and nights. (Gallaher, p. 104.) On 15 August, with the town in ruins and 600 civilians and an equal number of the small garrison dead, the Governor surrendered the town. The entire 1st Battalion was consequently taken prisoner, with the exception of a few officers.

Details have survived concerning the fate of two particular individual members of the captured unit. The most notable of these was the battalion's commander, Battalion Chief William Lawless. Severely wounded and, in fact, given up for dead, he convalesced incognito in Flushing and eventually made his way back to the mainland bearing the Eagle of the Regiment which he had been hiding. (Byrne, Vol. 2, pp. 86–7.) More amazing is the story of Matthew Norton. He was an Irishman who had been captured by the French while serving in the Royal Navy and who volunteered for the Legion from the prisoner-of-war depot at Arras. When he was identified by his British captors after the fall of Flushing, he was placed on trial for having deserted to the enemy. Miraculously, he was acquitted and even received the back pay which had been due to him when his ship, HMS *Pigmy*, was wrecked on the French coast in 1807. His adventures, however, did not end there. He joined the British Army only to be captured once again, this time while fighting in the Peninsula. He ended up in confinement at Verdun in 1813, where his story was recorded by a fellow prisoner. (Bussell, pp. 178–9.)

The 3rd Battalion, commanded by Battalion Chief Jean François Mahony (known in some records as 'O'Mahony'), a Frenchman of Irish descent who had emigrated during the Revolution and actually fought with the British Army in Egypt in 1801, had problems of its own during the last six months of the year. The 3rd, which had been raised in part by means of the recruitment of prisoners of war of Irish extraction, had only been rudimentarily organised, trained and equipped by the time the British attack on Flushing took place. It was nevertheless rushed to the coast to assist in the defence

TABLE 9: LOCATION OF IRISH REGIMENT, 1810

1st Battalion	Prisoners of war
2nd Battalion	15 officers and 700 men at Burgos, Spain
3rd Battalion	12 officers and 350 men at Burgos, Spain
4th Battalion	Recruiting at Landau
Depot	Landau

of Antwerp and then, after the British had departed, it was immediately sent to Spain, albeit by a very meandering route. The premature commitment to action accentuated the routine problems of organising such a polyglot unit, and so by the time the 3rd Battalion arrived in Spain sickness, straggling and heavy desertion had reduced it from an initial strength of over 1,300 men to less than half that number. (Gallaher, p. 125.) After a brief stint of independent service, it was reunited with the 2nd Battalion, which had spent almost the entire year on anti-guerrilla service in Old Castille and Leon, with a side trip into the Asturias. (Byrne, Vol. 2, pp. 70–1.)

Despite the loss of the 1st Battalion, work on the 4th still continued and it officially came into existence on 24 September 1809. (Historical Record of the 4th Battalion, quoted in Clark, p. 171.) Even with liberal recruiting from the prisoner-of-war camps, however, organisation of the unit proceeded at a slow pace. In January 1810 the status of the various components of the Irish Regiment was as shown in Table 9 (as per Carles I, p. 41). The majority of the privates recruited at this juncture were not Irish, but the Regimental records indicate nevertheless that 36 out of 51 officers had surnames of Irish origin. (Carles I, p. 43.)

The diary of a British prisoner at Verdun provides a grim anecdote that demonstrates the unusual dynamics of recruiting prisoners of war. (Bussell, pp. 114–15.) He describes the arrival in town in January of 1810 of a recruiting party that distributed cards with the following text in English:

> Any young man of spirit that has an inclination to serve in the first Irish regiment of foot, forming at Landau, has only to apply to the Recruiting Officer . . . [The Officer] will procure his release immediately. He shall be well fed, well paid, well cloathed [*sic*], receive rapid promotion, and will enjoy more advantages in this Regiment than in any other in France. The engagement is only for four years.

The diarist goes on to report the 'melancholy accident' that occurred when one prisoner who had succumbed to this sales pitch and signed on to the Irish Regiment changed his mind about turning his coat:

> [T]he Sergeants came for him, but the man refused to go. Being in liquor he became unruly, and still persisted he would not go, upon which, one of the Sergeants (a villain) drew his hanger [sword] and stabbed the poor fellow in the body. . . . He was taken to the Hospital, bleeding in a most dreadful manner.

Despite such setbacks, it is certain that recruiting for the 4th Battalion became more successful in the spring of 1810. In March the Regiment was able to send a detachment of reinforcements to the battalions in Spain, and in May the 1st Battalion was re-formed using excess rank-and-file from the 4th. (Carles I, p. 43.) Just as the Regiment was on its way back to a full establishment, however, it suffered a significant blow to its strength when Napoleon decided that all its recruits who had been British prisoners of war had to be disarmed and returned to confinement. (N. to Minister of War, 15 July 1810, Nap. *Corr.*, No 16654, Vol. 20, p. 476.) He later softened this order by clarifying that it did not apply to deserters or to Irishmen who had enlisted from prisoner camps prior to 1810, but according to one report it led to 932 NCOs and men ('mostly Scottish') being stricken from the Regimental rolls. (N. to Minister of War, 23 September 1810, Nap. *Corr.*, No 16943, Vol. 21, p. 141; Carles I, p. 45.) As a result, the 1st and 4th Battalions were amalgamated at the Regimental depot at Landau into a single battalion bearing the lower number. (Clark, p. 172.)

For the battalions of the Irish Regiment in Spain, 1810 began well with the 2nd Battalion Voltigeurs under Captain John Allen distinguishing themselves in a night attack on Spanish cavalry at Najara at the beginning of February. (Byrne, Vol. 2, pp. 116–17.) It then continued on an optimistic note as the two units were assigned to General Junot's 8th Corps of the Army of Portugal, thus giving rise to hopes that they would finally see service against the army of King George III. First, however, there were more Spaniards to fight since Junot was detailed to secure the flank of the Army of Portugal's intended advance by capturing the city of Astorga in the Province of Leon. When the walls were breached, the Spanish garrison refused to surrender, so Junot decided to take the town by storm. Captain Allen's Voltigeur company of the 2nd Battalion led the assault with distinction on 21 April, and although they could not advance more than a short distance through the breach they held on through the night in a house just inside the walls. The other companies of the 2nd took part in the preparations for a second attack to be made at dawn on the 22nd, but the garrison capitulated before that began. (Byrne, Vol. 2, pp. 119–21 and Vol. 3, pp. 74–5.) A drummer of the Voltigeur company was admitted to the Legion of Honour for having inspired his comrades in their attack by continuing to play his instrument even though he had received a disabling wound. (Byrne, Vol. 2, pp. 104-–5.)

The Irish battalions remained on active service with the Army of Portugal through the sieges of Ciudad Rodrigo and Almeida, the Battle of Bussaco and the full course of the advance to the Lines of Torres Vedras, but it never again played a prominent role in military events. However, Miles Byrne, the memoirist quoted many times in this entry, was the Captain commanding the Grenadier company of the 2nd Battalion for most of the campaign, and he reports that the Irish were often in action as part of the vanguard of General Jean Thomières' Brigade because they were great favourites of that officer. (Byrne, Vol. 2, p. 109.) The Irish did, however, figure in a noteworthy controversy when General Junot decided to remove both Colonel O'Meara, the

Regimental commander, and Battalion Chief Mahony, commander of the 3rd Battalion, from their respective duties and assign them to staff postings. His reasons for doing so with respect to Mahony are not recorded (although Byrne states that Mahony was 'on the worst terms with his officers'), but with respect to O'Meara they are: 'Colonel O'Meara is not capable of commanding a squad of ten men.' (Byrne, Vol. 2, p. 76; Junot to Masséna, 14 September 1810, quoted in Gallaher, p. 133.) Battalion Chief Fitzhenry reverted to command of the two battalions, but thereby incurred the enmity of Minister of War Clarke, who is said to have been angered by Junot's action against two of his protégés. (Byrne, Vol. 2, p. 76.)

Finally coming to grips with the hated English enemy may have given some personal satisfaction to the Irish officers of the battalions in Spain, but the campaign in Portugal was hard and unglamorous for their men. The units consequently suffered heavy attrition; in fact, the number of men present for duty fell from 861 to 439 from September to October. (Strength reports of the Army of Portugal for 15 September and 12 October, reprinted in Koch, *Mémoires de Masséna*, Vol. 7, pp. 569 and 575.) Orders were given in November 1810 for the combining of the two battalions into one, but this apparently did not take place until February, when the cadres of the 3rd Battalion were sent back to France to reorganise their unit. (Clark, p. 170; Byrne, Vol. 2, p. 77.) These official developments, however, had little effect on the soldiers of the Regiment surviving on short rations in Portugal as Masséna vainly hung on in front of the impregnable British fortifications outside Lisbon. According to Byrne: 'Scarcely a distribution of Indian corn could be made; as to meat, that was out of the question.' (Byrne, Vol. 2, p. 77.)

The re-formed 2nd Battalion saw hard service as part of the rearguard on the retreat from Lisbon, but no details of specific combats have survived. By the time it arrived back in Spain, the unit had nineteen officers and 254 men present with the colours, and another 128 men absent from sickness or other reasons. (Strength report of the Army of Portugal for 1 April 1811, reprinted in Koch, *Mémoires de Masséna*, Vol. 7, p. 581.) Around this same period the 2nd Battalion suffered two unusual blows to its morale. First, Captain Allen was wounded and captured by guerrillas while on detached service back in Spain on 26 March, and then Battalion Chief Fitzhenry, the unit's highly esteemed commander, suffered the same fate at the hands of Don Julian Sanchez' irregulars on 22 April. (Byrne, Vol. 2, pp. 111–12 and 114–15.) A somewhat strengthened unit was present at the Battle of Fuentes de Oñoro in early May, but it did not come under fire. It then spent the next months in familiar counter-insurgency and garrison tasks.

By a decree of 3 August 1811 the Irish Regiment was formally denationalised and was renamed the 3rd Foreign Regiment. (Gallaher, p. 168.) Napoleon then announced that he had earmarked the Regiment, along with the Prussian Regiment, for the defence of Holland and therefore that its establishment should be increased to five battalions, with new recruiting focusing particularly on Austrians. (N. to Minister of War, 11 August 1811, Nap. *Corr.*, No 18021, Vol. 22, pp. 395–7 at 396.) In another subsequent letter, Napoleon clarified the cynical purpose behind that assignment (N. to Minister of War, 19 October 1811, Nap. *P&T*, No 6271, Vol. 4, pp. 740–1):

> I attach a great importance to having these two regiments . . . guarding the islands of Zeeland and Holland, locations which are so unhealthy that the French troops I send there all perish; I wish to spare my regular line regiments such hard duty.

As a result, the 2nd Battalion in Spain was disbanded, the men were transferred to other units and its cadre brought back to France to be reorganised. In connection with that development, Minister of War Clarke made a special effort to keep together all officers and men of Irish descent. Surprisingly, Napoleon approved of this and other Irish-oriented initiatives (Decision of 12 November 1811, Nap. *Derniers Lettres*, No 1650, Vol. 2, p. 200):

> The Minister is authorised to allow the Regiment to use the name 'Irish' along with its Foreign Regiment numerical designation. I approve that all the native Irish soldiers [of the 2nd Battalion] . . . have been returned to France along with the Battalion cadre. I also approve that Irishmen by birth should be favoured for advancement in the officer corps and that, in general, the Minister should take all necessary measures to have a good Irish regiment.

Soon thereafter, however, the Emperor was once again using the Regiment as a repository for soldiers of all nationalities: 'The 3rd Foreign Regiment, also known as the Irish Regiment, should receive all the foreign soldiers who were serving in the regiments of the former Kingdom of Holland.' (N. to Minister of War, 16 January 1812, Nap. *P&T*, No 6647, Vol. 5, p. 46.)

When the remains of the 2nd Battalion did return to the regimental depot, one of its less pleasant tasks was to organise a court-martial for its missing Battalion Chief, Jerome Fitzhenry. He was accused of the crime of desertion because, in the interim since his capture, information had reached the Regiment that he had been allowed by the British government to live in Ireland as a free man. In addition, it was apparent that he was not making any attempt to re-join his unit. Fitzhenry was ultimately acquitted of all charges by a single vote, but his reputation was ruined amongst the Irish patriots in the officer corps. (Byrne, Vol. 3, pp. 80–1.)

Despite the availability of the entire Regiment for the Russian campaign, Napoleon persisted in his intention to use it for guard duty rather than combat. Early in 1812 the depot of the Regiment was shifted to s'Hertogenbosch (Bois-Le-Duc) in Holland and the three battalions were posted, respectively, to the coastal island of Goree and the towns of Bergen-op-Zoom and Willemstadt. (Clark, p. 169.) There they remained, resting and training, while the Grand Army perished in the snows of Russia. In December 1812, with the magnitude of the French disaster becoming apparent, the officers of the Regiment petitioned the Minister of War to be sent to the front. This time their petition was answered, and by February 1813 the first two battalions of the Regiment were on their way to join the new Grand Army. (Byrne, Vol. 2, p. 154.)

TABLE 10: COMPOSITION OF IRISH LEGION, 1813

Nationality	No of men	Nationality	No of men
French	57	German	77
Hungarian	99	Polish	40
Prussian	42	Silesian	29
Austrian	52	Irish	65
Westphalian	19	Saxon	21
Italian	4	South American	2
United States	5	Portuguese	2
Russian	15	Bavarian	17
Dutch	4	Swiss	4
Croat	3	Duchy of Berg	7
Bohemian	17	Moravian	18
Tyrolian	2	Spanish	2
Swedish	6		

The 1st and 2nd Battalions which marched off to war under the command of Colonel Lawless, the hero of Flushing, were to write the most important chapter in the history of the Regiment, and their composition reflects the way in which the unit had evolved since its creation as the Irish Legion. Although it was still the case that many of the officers were of Irish descent, a surviving muster roll of the 1st Battalion which gives a breakdown of its strength by nationalities reveals the extent to which the Regiment had become a foreign rather than Irish Legion, as shown in Table 10 (Carles II, pp. 64–5). The situation in the 2nd Battalion was even more extreme–it had only nine Irishmen as against 163 Poles, 124 Austrians and lesser numbers of other assorted nationalities. (Carles I, p. 50.)

When the war battalions arrived in Germany they were nominally assigned to the Vth Corps being formed under the command of General Lauriston, but because they represented a relatively experienced and well-trained force in an army of conscripts, or 'Marie Louises', they were almost immediately detached to help hold the line of the lower Elbe between Hamburg and Magdeburg. Under the command of Davout and, later, Sébastiani, the Regiment was engaged in near-constant skirmishing through March and April with the Allied Free Corps, Cossacks and regular troops roving over the Elbe. (Byrne, Vol. 2, pp. 158–63.) The Regiment thus missed the first major battle of the campaign at Lützen on 2 May, but it soon thereafter re-joined the main army and the Vth Corps as part of the 17th Division commanded by General Jacques Puthod. A forced march brought that formation to the battlefield of Bautzen at a strategic moment on the second day of that conflict (22 May 1813). General Jacques Alexander Bernard Law, Count Lauriston, the commander of the Vth Corps, 'was delighted to see the [R]egiment looking so well, after so much fatigue, and the fine band of music enchanted him, which contrary to custom (at their own request) preceded the [R]egiment until the battle began'. (Byrne, Vol. 2, p. 165.) The day ended with Colonel Lawless and Captain Byrne drinking captured Tokay wine in the former Allied headquarters with Marshal Ney and several other general officers. (Byrne, Vol. 2, p. 166.)

In the ensuing pursuit of the enemy, the Regiment was in action several times, with its Voltigeurs involved in the bulk of the fighting. (Byrne, Vol. 2, pp. 169–72 *et seq.*) On 25 May it helped stop a massive surprise Prussian cavalry attack against General Maison's division. On the 26th the Regiment was visited by the Emperor himself, and temporarily formed square to provide him with some battlefield protection for an impromptu planning session. That same day, Ney reprimanded an Irish sergeant named Costello for not responding promptly to a trumpet call. The feisty NCO replied 'that a Cossack had fired twice at him and that he wanted to kill the fellow before quitting the field. 'And did you kill him?' asked the Marshal. 'I hope so,' said Costello, 'for I saw him fall from his horse.' (Byrne, Vol. 2, p. 171.)

The Armistice of 4 June brought a welcome respite for the weary Regiment. Both officers and men were quite ragged, but when the baggage of the officers turned up the night before a review, the officers at least 'appeared to full advantage, in their uniform and accoutrements, which had not been used during the three months campaigning.' (Byrne, Vol. 2, p. 174.) The men had to be content with an issue of cloth for new 'pantaloons'. They also had to be content with hard work, for the interval 'was employed in exercising and manoeuvring the troops twice a day.' The Regiment took target practice, worked at digging field entrenchments and, most of all, perfected the manoeuvre of forming squares, since '[f]rom want of cavalry [in the French Army], this order of battle became more urgent.' (Byrne, Vol. 2, p. 175.) There were, however, some distractions, such as dancing and other amusements on Sundays, and significant festivities on the occasion of the Napoleon's birthday, when the '[t]en thousand soldiers and four hundred officers [of Puthod's division] dined at the same table and each man having his glass filled, drank to the health of the [E]mperor.' (Byrne, Vol. 2, p. 176.)

The final phase of the 1813 campaign was brief and tragic for the Regiment. The Armistice ended in mid-August with the Prussians under Blücher launching an offensive the opposing French forces, including the Vth Corps. Near the town of Löwenberg on 19 August the Regiment, now brigaded with the 134th and 143rd Line Regiments under General Martial Vachot, was attacked by a superior force of enemy infantry, nearly overrun by enemy cavalry and punished all the while by enemy artillery. (Nafziger II, pp. 30–2.) The butcher's bill of four officers killed and eight wounded and 300 other casualties tells only part of the harrowing story of the action (Byrne, Vol. 2, pp. 181–2):

> Commander Tennant was cut completely in two; the cannon ball striking a belt in which he carried his money served as a knife to separate the body. . . . Sergeant Costello who was remarked on 26 May by Marshal Ney . . . lost his arm in this affair. The officers who

> escaped being wounded in this action had their uniforms bespattered with the blood and brains of the men killed beside them . . .

Despite its losses, the Regiment spearheaded the counterattack of the French delivered under the eyes of Napoleon himself on 21 August. The Regiment crossed the Bober River under fire and pushed back the enemy with a brilliant charge. In the moment of triumph, however, the Regiment lost Colonel Lawless with a shattered leg. He was carried from the field on a door supported by six grenadiers of the Regiment. Napoleon witnessed the scene and sent Baron Larrey, the surgeon of the Imperial Guard, to perform the necessary amputation. (Byrne, Vol. 2, pp. 183–4.)

Now under the command of Major Hugh Ware (who had also been wounded, although less severely than the Colonel), the Regiment pressed forward and helped to carry the strategic Goldberg hill on 23 August in the face of tenacious Prussian and Russian resistance. At this juncture, Napoleon left the so-called Army of the Bober under the command of Marshal MacDonald and gave him orders to stand on the defensive. Unfortunately, the Marshal chose to continue his advance, detaching Puthod's division on a wide flanking march to envelop the Allied army under Blücher which he expected to dislodge from its position behind the Katzbach River. In the battle of that name on 26 August, however, the French were the ones to be routed, and Puthod's division suddenly found itself unsupported deep in enemy territory.

As soon as he received word of the French defeat, General Puthod began his own retreat, but by the time his 6,000 men reached the Bober River near Löwenberg the bridges had been destroyed and their escape route cut off by a rising river. Hemmed in against the river by the bulk of the Army of Silesia on 29 August, the division put up a ferocious resistance lasting over eight hours before the survivors were overrun (Byrne, Vol. 2, p. 190):

> . . . the enemy's army forming a complete half-moon round his division, each of their flanks joining the river, and no retreat possible, the general in the centre of his division fought until the last cartridge was fired, and even then, when the fire of his division ceased, the enemy hesitated before venturing to advance.

The only alternative to surrender was a plunge into the rain-swollen river, and so, during the confusion of the last of the fighting, Major Ware led the remnants of his men down to the river to swim for safety. Only Ware, nine officers and 30 men reached the other side, but they had brought the regimental Eagle with them. (Byrne, Vol. 2, p. 190.) The Regiment had been destroyed as a fighting force, but the small cadre which made its way slowly across Germany back to its depot in Holland, picking up wounded and stragglers along the way, had at least preserved some of the Regiment's honour. Back at the Regimental depot, the survivors of the German campaign were combined with men of the incomplete 3rd and 4th Battalions. The result was a very weak unit, but by 3 Novembe 1813 a reconstructed 1st Battalion was ready to go on active service to defend Holland. (Byrne, Vol. 2, p. 197.) Progress in filling out the unit was, however, hampered by execution of Napoleon's decree of 25 November, which purged the Regiment of many experienced officers and men because they were nationals of the powers allied against France. On the other hand, it received at the same time both an influx of new men from the disbandment of the 4th Foreign Regiment (or *Régiment de Prusse*) and the 1st Foreign Battalion and a new Colonel, Jean Mahony, to succeed Colonel Lawless. By 19 December 1813, the Regiment mustered 85 officers and 396 men, all of whom were assigned to the garrison of Antwerp. (Carles II, p. 52.)

The campaign in Belgium in early 1814 was obviously a sideshow compared to the last act of the Napoleonic drama being played out at the same time on the plains of France, but it was also a performance noteworthy in its own right. The primary objective of the Allies at the start of the campaign was the capture of Antwerp, and to oppose them the French could offer only a scratch garrison commanded by Lazare Carnot, the old Republican called to perform one last service for his country, and a small field corps commanded brilliantly by General Maison. The first attempt of the Allies to take Antwerp by storm was repulsed at the Battle of Merxem on the outskirts of the city on 13 and 14 January, during which the Regiment distinguished itself against the attacking Anglo-Allied corps commanded by General Graham. In the siege that followed, the Regiment was the strongest single unit in the city other than a battalion of veterans. (Strength Return of 1 January 1814, quoted in Calmon-Maison, p. 274.) Carnot employed four officers of the Regiment on his staff. (Byrne, Vol. 2, p. 203.) The only significant incident involving the Regiment that occurred during the siege was the imprisonment of Colonel Mahony for conducting treasonable correspondence with the enemy. (Byrne, Vol. 2, p. 209.) The garrison held out past the abdication of Napoleon and did not surrender until 4 May.

Final Transformation The end of the 1st Empire found the Regiment with a strength of only some 300 weary officers and men. No one had an inkling of what the Restoration government might have in store for the Regiment, and this suspense lingered through the late spring and summer. In the interim, the Regiment collected its returning prisoners of war plus those of the disbanded 4th Foreign Regiment, a situation which led to some significant friction as there were certainly not enough service positions for all those who wanted them. There was also friction in the officer corps following the reappointment of Colonel Mahony, which culminated in a duel between the Colonel and Major Ware, albeit one in which neither was hit. (Byrne, Vol. 2, p. 217–18.) By September the demographics of the unit had reverted to those of its early days—102 officers as against only 200 privates. (Carles II, p. 62.) Nevertheless, when the new French government decided it would keep three foreign units for its army, one of them was the Regiment, a development which was confirmed by a Royal decree dated 16 December 1814. (Carles II, p. 62.) The Regiment was thus still intact when Napoleon returned from Elba, and it immediately declared for the Emperor, replacing its royalist Colonel Mahony with the Bonapartist Major Ware and retrieving its Eagle standard from its hiding place among the Regimental stores. (Byrne, Vol. 2, p. 225.)

Despite its show of loyalty, however, its existence seemed somewhat problematical when Napoleon in April 1815 decreed the formation of six foreign regiments to be formed, respectively, of Piedmontese, Swiss, Poles, Germans, Belgians and Spaniards. (Carles II, p. 66.) These decrees made no mention of the three foreign units, including the Regiment, which remained from the previous army establishment. Napoleon rectified that oversight on 2 May when he ordered the dissolution of the 1st and 2nd Regiments. The 3rd Regiment, however, was spared (although it was now to be numbered the 7th Foreign Regiment) and it was once again intended to have a predominantly Irish character. (Carles II, p. 66.) Unfortunately, after all the non-Irish or English personnel had been distributed among the other units according to their various nationalities, the Regiment was not itself strong enough to take the field before it was blockaded in the town of Montreuil by Allied forces in the aftermath of Waterloo.

King Louis XVIII dissolved all of Napoleon's foreign regiments by a decree dated 9 September 1814. (Carles II, p. 71.) For the Irish, the actual end came on 29 September 1815. A lucky few of its officers and men were given the opportunity of enrolling in a 'Royal Foreign Legion', which was the forerunner of the more famous unit of that name founded in 1833. The rest, however, were left to return to civilian life in France or, if possible, in their native countries.

Uniforms Neither the Organisational Decree of the Irish Legion nor any other first-hand source gives information about the unit's initial uniform, but the two earliest reliable iconographic depictions (a rear view of an officer in Vernet & Lami and the profiles of an officer and a Grenadier in Marbot & Noirmont) suggest that it had the following features: (a) a black shako with brass plate and chinscales, (b) a dark green, light infantry-style jacket with brass buttons and yellow collar, pointed lapels, pointed cuffs, vertical pockets and turnbacks, (c) a white vest, (d) white breeches and (e) short (i.e. below-the-knee) black gaiters. The equipment and accoutrements of the soldiers, including musket, pack overcoat and overalls, were all standard French issue. Rigo's 1972 reconstruction of a Chasseur sergeant-major wearing this initial uniform differs from this information and instead features a bicorne hat, green breeches, green epaulettes and green hunting horn ornaments in the yellow turnbacks of the very abbreviated tails of the jacket. (Rigo, 'Drapeau'.)

There are two interesting uniform artefacts from the Legion in the National Museum of Ireland. (Drawings of these items can be found inside the back cover of *Irish Sword*, Vol. 1, No 3 [1951–52].) The first is a gilt cross-belt plate which is essentially octagonal in shape, albeit with two sides elongated to make it taller than it is wide. The plate is decorated with a silver harp in 'Maid of Erin' style (i.e., with the fore-pillar carved in the shape of the bust of a woman with wings) and bears the following inscription in an oval arrangement around the harp: '*LÉGION IRLANDAISE* EMPIRE FRANCAIS'. The second item is a brass gorget marked on the back with the name 'MacCann', which may have belonged to Captain Pat MacCann, who was mortally wounded at the siege of Flushing. The gorget is decorated with a silver bugle horn ornament which bears in its center a round device engraved with a harp (in this case with a plain fore-pillar) which rests on the words 'EMPIRE/FRANCAIS' (placed one on top of the other) and is surrounded on the top and sides by the words 'LÉGION IRLANDAISE'.

When the Legion received its first major influx of recruits at the end of 1806, it apparently took a fair amount of time to get them properly uniformed, since the diary of a British prisoner at Verdun notes for 26 April 1807 that the men of the Regiment then passing through that town 'were very much in want of clothing.' (Bussell, p. 48.) Nevertheless, Miles Byrne records that when Marshal Gouvion St-Cyr reviewed the Legion at Boulogne shortly thereafter (Byrne, Vol. 2, p. 49):

> . . . the brilliancy of its *'tenue'* [dress] pleased him much; indeed, it [the Legion] appeared to great advantage at the review, having got in time from Metz, the feathers and other ornaments for the soldiers; altogether their uniform was splendid.

According to the Marbot and Noirmont lithograph, these decorations included red plumes, epaulettes and shako cords for the Grenadiers and red plumes and gold epaulettes and cords for officers. There was also a strip of coloured trim around the top of the shako, red for Grenadiers and gold for officers.

Roger Forthoffer's prints concerning the Irish Legion present the uniforms of the Regimental Drum Major and a Regimental musician for the period 1811–12 based on a 'Dutch drawing of the period'. (*Fiches Documentaires*, No 222.) The former has the basic Regimental uniform heavily ornamented with silver lace trim around all the facings, the buttonholes on the lapels, the edges of the vest (which is green in this instance) and the seams of the breeches. The Drum Major is also wearing a large bicorne hat edged with silver lace and surmounted by a tall white plume with a yellow tip, silver trefoil epaulettes and black boots trimmed with silver lace. He carries a brass-hilted sabre on a red shoulder-belt trimmed with silver and ornamented with a gold grenade above a gold plaque bearing miniature drumsticks. His baton is wood with a silver tip and bulbous head and wound with silver chains. The musician has a shako, green lapels and a yellow vest, and displays silver trim only around the collar, cuffs and lapels.

The Legion's uniform apparently lost its yellow lapels when it was transformed into the 3rd Foreign Regiment. On 31 August 1811, the Minister of War informed the unit (quoted in Carles I, p. 49):

> The same decree [which specified the reorganisation of the Legion] having authorised me to determine the uniform to be worn by the Regiment, I have decided that the short jacket, vest, breeches and lapels will be made of green cloth, that the lining of the jacket will be green and that of the vest white, that the cuffs will be yellow, that the buttons will be white and carry the legend 'Régiment Étranger' around the number '3', and that the shako will continue to be the regulation headdress for the corps . . .

Plate No 268 of the Martinet *Troupes Françaises* series depicts a Chasseur of the 3rd Foreign Regiment in a uniform which is consistent with description except that the cuffs are green with yellow piping and yellow cuff flaps. The Martinet figure also has a shako with tall green plume and white cords, green piping around the yellow collar and green fringed epaulettes (which are roughly the same shade of green as the jacket) held by a red retaining strap.

The Wurtz Collection of paper soldiers in the French Army Museum in Paris contains a number of figures which seem to illustrate the uniform variations which existed among the different ranks and types of soldiers in the Regiment at the time of this changeover. (Photographs of these figures can be found in Haussadis, pp. 50–1.) Since little is known about the precise history of these artefacts, their reliability as a source of uniform information is not free from doubt, but they are accepted by enough experts to warrant a full description here. The different types of soldiers represented (all of which have dark green jackets, vests and breeches, yellow collars, green lapels with yellow piping and green cuffs, piped yellow, with yellow cuff flaps) are as follows:

Officer: Silver trim and cords for the shako, but gilt diamond-shaped plate and red pompom. The buttons and epaulettes on the jacket are silver, but the gorget is gold. Black hessian boots without trim.
Carabinier: Red cords, tall plume and upper rim for the shako, red fringed epaulettes on the jacket. In addition to the cartridge box worn from a belt over the left shoulder, carabiniers also carried a sabre and bayonet on a belt worn over the right shoulder. The sabre knot was red.
Chasseurs: Red pompom and white cords for the shako, medium green fringed epaulettes with red crescents. The sabre knot is white.
Voltigeur: Green plume, tipped yellow, and green cords and upper rim for the shako, yellow fringed epaulettes. Voltigeurs wore crossbelts and the sword knot for the sabre was yellow.
Sapper: Bearskin with red plume and cords. Red epaulettes with yellow/gold crescents. White insignia crossed axe insignia on each sleeve. The Sapper has a full beard.
Drummer: Same uniform as the Chasseurs except for chevrons of yellow and green lace worn point upwards on each arm.
Musicians: Shako with tall white plume (green base) and white cords. Silver trefoil epaulettes. Sword worn on waist-belt.
Fifer: Short figure dressed in the same uniform as the drummer.

It is uncertain whether the uniforms of the Irish Regiment were ever modified to reflect the changes which were made generally to French infantry uniforms in 1812 and 1813. Forthoffer believes that they were, but the only contemporary evidence runs counter to that conclusion. That evidence is a very small-scale figure drawing in the notebooks of C. Hamilton Smith in the Victoria and Albert Museum which has the caption 'Irish Regiment at Antwerp 1813' and clearly shows a soldier wearing a jacket with pointed lapels which leaves the vest visible.

Standard The first standard of the Irish Legion was an unusual flag designed to emphasise its national identity. The flag, which was ordered in January 1804, was green with a golden harp in each corner. (Carles I, pp. 30–1 and plate on p. 29, Charrié, p. 170, and Charrié II, p. 93; however, this standard is not mentioned in Gallaher.) The obverse had a central tricolour oval (blue, white and red, from top to bottom) outlined by a golden wreath which bore the following legend (painted in gold): 'LE PREMIER/CONSUL' in two lines on the blue, 'AUX IRLANDOIS [sic]' on the white, and 'UNIS' on the red. (This legend translates as 'The First Consul to the United Irishmen'.) The central medallion on the reverse of the flag was red outlined with a band of yellow decorated with a green wreath of intertwined laurel and oak leaves. This medallion had the following words painted in gold: 'LIBERTÉ/DES/CONSCIENCES/INDÉPENDENCE/DE L'IRLANDE'. (This legend translates as 'Freedom of Conscience; Independence of Ireland'.) The staff for this banner was surmounted by a simple spearhead finial.

The use of this first colour was extremely limited, however, because the Legion received both a new colour and an Imperial Eagle in December 1804. The colour had a design which was unique for the First Empire: a square (80cm by 80cm) green silk banner with gold fringe and the legend 'L'EMPEREUR/DES FRANCAIS/A LA LÉGION/IRLANDAISE' on the obverse, and a gold harp over the words 'L'INDÉPENDENCE DE L'IRLANDE' on the reverse. (Charrié, p. 170.) This description contradicts some details concerning the colour recorded in the memoirs of Miles Byrne, but a carefully reasoned article by a modern author suggests that Byrne's memory may have been faulty on some points. (Ede-Borett, p. 21.) The article also presents a persuasive case for the conclusion that the harp ornament on the colour would have taken the form of the 'Maid of Erin' harp used in the official seal of the United Irishmen which has the fore-pillar carved in the shape of the bust of a winged woman. (Ede-Borett, pp. 22–3.)

In addition to the colour displayed with the Eagle, which was carried by an officer of the 1st Battalion, at least two of the other battalions had their own standards (Byrne, Vol. 2, p. 238):

> Two beautiful standards were sent to Spain by the Emperor in 1810 for the 2nd and 3rd Battalions of the Irish Regiment, but they were left at Valladolid, as those battalions were then in Portugal. . . . They were green with a large harp in the centre. On one side in gold letters 'Napoleon Ier to the 2nd Irish Battalion' and on the other 'The Independence of Ireland'. The 3rd [had] the same.

Byrne also records that those standards were destroyed at Montreuil after the fall of the Empire in 1814.

There is strong evidence that the Regiment received a new tricolour standard some time in 1812. That evidence takes the form of a letter from General Clarke dated 20 May 1812 in which he makes the following point: 'The 1st Battalion of the 3rd Foreign Regiment should not have a fanion because it will carry the regimental Eagle. I have ordered a standard to be made for the Eagle without delay in accordance with the approved model . . .' (Charrié II, p. 93.) This colour would presumably have had the standard decorations and inscriptions, but no battle honours since the Regiment was not present at any of the battles recognised for such purposes. The 1st Eagle-bearer for the autumn campaign in 1813 was 2nd Lieutenant Malisieux, who was wounded in the fighting on 29 August. The 2nd Eagle-bearer was Sergeant Trebasch and the 3rd Eagle-bearer was Sergeant John Priest. (Charrié II, p. 93.)

There is recurring claim that a standard of the Irish Regiment fell into British hands at the Battle of Salamanca in 1812. This story is told in various forms, but it appears to arise from the capture of a green flag by the 11th Regiment of Foot. The most detailed history of that regiment states simply that the flag was taken from the 'colour party' of a foreign regiment in French pay. (Robinson, p. 430.) Since no part of the Irish Regiment was present at Salamanca, and since no other foreign regiment had a green flag, it seems more reasonable to believe that the green banner in question was one of the coloured battalion '*fanions*' adopted for use by French infantry battalions in 1811.

Légion Italique

(Italic Legion; later known as the *Légion Italienne*)

Date of Creation 22 Fructidor Year VII (8 September 1799).
Circumstances of Creation This Legion was one of the three units of foreign troops formed at the same time by the Directory for the purpose of replenishing the military forces of the Republic that had suffered so severely during the 1799 campaigns. (The other units were the *Légion de Danube* [see separate entry] and the *Légion des Francs du Nord* [see separate entry].) The manpower necessary to create the Legion was provided by the many soldiers from the various Italian units listed below who had been forced to take refuge in France because of the victories in Italy of the Austrians and Russians under Marshal Suvorov (archival list of constituent units listed in Perconte, Pt. 1, p. 9):

Cisalpine Troops
1st–3rd Line Demi-brigades
1st Light Demi-brigade
Depot troops
Detachment of Cisalpine Hussars
1st Regiment of Cisalpine Dragoons
Cisalpine Artillery

Piedmontese Troops
2nd Light Demi-brigade
Depot troops
Regiment of Brempt

Roman Republic Troops
1st and 2nd Roman Legions
1st Roman Dragoons
Roman Gendarmes
Roman Artillery

Parthenopean (Neapolitan) Republic Troops
Depot of the 1st Demi-brigade
Neapolitan Hussars
Neapolitan Artillery

Composition The Legion initially consisted of four battalions of infantry, four squadrons of mounted chasseurs and one company of light artillery. Each infantry battalion had ten companies, one of Grenadiers, one of Chasseurs and eight of Fusiliers. Each company had three officers and 123 men. (Organisational Decree, *Journal Militaire*, 1799, Pt. 2, p. 730.) An order of 11 Pluviose Year VIII (31 January 1800) reduced the strength of the cavalry to two squadrons but added another two battalions to the infantry. (Nap. O&A, No 144, Vol. 1, p. 67.) The commanders of the six battalions were Lechi, Girard, Fontanelli, Larat, Robillard and Rougier. (Perconte, Pt. 1, p. 10.)

In the spring of 1800 another large influx of refugees and soldiers returning from Austrian captivity added two unusual new units to the Legion's establishment. The first was a six-company Battalion made up exclusively of supernumerary officers which was added by an order dated 6 Floréal Year VIII (16 April 1800). The second was a pair of companies made up exclusively of supernumerary non-commissioned officers attached by an order dated 9 Floréal Year VIII (April 29, 1800). (Perconte, Pt. 1, p. 10.) By an order dated 28 March 1800, the unit became the *Légion Italienne* (Italian Legion) (Belhomme, Vol. 4, pp. 219–20). The Legion also continued to have a headquarters staff, a battalion of light infantry, two companies (one mounted, one not) of artillery, a regiment (squadron?) of mounted chasseurs, a regiment (squadron?) of hussars. The Legion was reinforced on 16 May by the incorporation of the *Bataillon de Patriotes Piémontais* (see separate entry). (Belhomme, Vol. 4, p. 227.)

Commanders *Creation to disbandment:* Joseph Lechi (1767–1836), a Brigade General in the army of the Cisalpine Republic who had begun his military service in the Austrian Army. He had a long military career after his service with the Legion, but it was marred by his arrest in 1810 on charges of corruption and abuse of power while he commanded the Italian troops in Catalonia during the Peninsular War. He was incarcerated for three years without a trial, then released at the request of Murat, who employed him as a General in the Neapolitan Army from 1813 to 1815.

Operational History The Legion (numbering some 4,000 men) was assigned to the Reserve Army for the 1800 campaign. Fieffé (Vol. 2, pp. 88–9) quotes the full text of a letter dated 10 Prairial Year VIII (30 May 1800) from then General Berthier to the

First Consul describing the participation of the Legion in the early stages of the fighting:

> I have the honour to inform you that the Italic Legion, under the orders of General Lechi, to which I gave orders to advance on Riva and follow the valley of Sesia, encountered the enemy at Sospello. The Legion threw back the enemy outpost and took 32 prisoners. The Legion then encountered the 600-man-strong Legion of Rohan [an emigré unit in Austrian service] at Varallo, where it occupied a position defended by field works and cannon. After having made his dispositions, General Lechi sounded the charge and, despite stubborn resistance, cleared the fieldworks and overthrew the enemy.
>
> General Lechi took 300 prisoners, including three officers, and one cannon and ammunition while leaving more than 100 enemy dead and wounded on the field of battle. The Legion had only a dozen men killed. Among this number were Citizens Ghiusepini and Gassaleni, both 2nd Lieutenants of Grenadiers.
>
> Brigade Chief Peyri, at the head of the Grenadiers, was the first to mount the enemy entrenchments. Squadron Chief Lechi, Captain Brunetti and 2nd Lieutenant Aumodeo particularly distinguished themselves.

Final Transformation Following Napoleon's victory at Marengo and the withdrawal of the Austrians from Lombardy, the Cisalpine Republic was re-formed and on 1 Messidor Year VIII (20 June 1800) the Legion once again became part of the Cisalpine Army rather than the French Army. (Perconte, Pt 1, p. 12.) By order of 17 Fructidor Year VIII (4 September 1800) the Legion was broken up and its constituent parts became separate units of the Cisapline Army. (Perconte, Pt. 1, p. 14.)

Uniforms The details of the uniform of the Legion are provided by the Organisational Decree:

> The uniform of the Legion will be a short green jacket with yellow collar, cuffs and trim, white demi-spherical buttons, green trousers and vest, half-gaiters for the infantry, short boots for the cavalry and artillery. The headwear will be a three-cornered hat with a plume and a felt shako with a plume for the foot and mounted chasseurs and the light artillery.

This uniform is depicted in a print in Vernet and Lami's work. According to that source, Legion Grenadiers had a tall, red-over-green plume for their hats and red epaulettes for their shoulders. Given the circumstances of its origins, it is likely to have taken some time before uniformity of dress was achieved, during which time the men of the Legion may have worn a wide variety of different uniforms from their prior units.

Standard No information found.

Légion Maltaise

(Maltese Legion)

Date of Creation July 1798.

Circumstances of Creation After having captured Malta on his way to Egypt, Napoleon was reluctant to leave behind any troops of the Order of Malta that might become a source of resistance to the new regime. He consequently incorporated into his expedition the following Maltese units (Belhomme Vol. 4, p. 169):

Grenadiers of the Grand Master (1 company)
The Regiment of Malta (500 men)
Maltese Marines (*Bataillon des Vaisseau*)
Maltese Chasseurs

When they arrived in Egypt, these units were assembled at Ramanieh at the end of July and reorganised as the Maltese Legion.

Composition The Legion consisted of two battalions, each of which had 750 men organised in nine companies, including one of grenadiers. Given the scarcity of Maltese replacements in Egypt, the Legion was authorised from the start to recruit Turks and Italians from the merchant ships trapped in the port of Alexandria by the British blockade of Egypt.

Commanders *29 August 1798–21 February 1800 (?)*: Bernard MacSheehy (1774–1807), a native-born Irishman whose family had moved to France before the Revolution. He began his military career in 1796 and was sent to Ireland on a secret mission by General Hoche. He met Napoleon when the latter briefly commanded the Army of England in 1798 and subsequently volunteered for the expedition to Egypt. His reward was promotion to the rank of Battalion Chief and command of the Legion. He was promoted by General Kléber to the rank of Adjutant Commandant on 21 February 1800 and probably had staff appointments thereafter. He was killed at the Battle of Eylau while serving as the Chief of Staff of the 1st Division of Marshal Augereau's 7th Corps.

Operational History The Legion was attached to General Reynier's division and fought at the Battle of the Pyramids. (Fieffé, Vol. 2, p. 47.) It was present at the capture of El Arish in 1799 but then returned to Cairo rather than continuing on into Syria. No trace of its services has been found thereafter, so it was probably much diminished in strength and restricted to garrison duty. It could not have been too heavily engaged, because its total loss for the three-year campaign is said to have been only 99 killed, of whom 36 died of the plague. (Anon., 'Légion Maltaise'.)

Final Transformation The remnants of the Legion were repatriated to France and incorporated into the *Légion Expéditionnaire* on 2 October 1801. (Belhomme, Vol. 4, p. 244.)

Uniforms The Maltese troops that were used to form the Legion arrived in Egypt wearing their own uniforms. In December 1799 they received new single-breasted cotton uniforms of the type distributed to all infantry troops of the Army of the Orient. According to a usually reliable nineteenth-century secondary source, the uniform was dark green with red collar, cuffs and turnbacks with white piping, red epaulettes, silver buttons, white vest and trousers, and a black bicorne hat with an orange cockade and

a drooping red plume. Citing unspecified material in the French War Archives, a modern secondary source states that the facings were *aurore* (golden yellow) and the centre companies wore a leather helmet of local manufacture with a *aurore* pompom or pouffe on top. (Anon., 'Légion Maltaise'.)
Standard No information found.

Légion Polacco-Italienne

(Polish-Italian Legion)

Date of Creation 5 April 1807.
Circumstances of Creation When war against Prussia in 1806 became a war against both Prussia and Russia in Poland in 1807, Napoleon sought to assemble all possible Polish troops under his direct command. He therefore recalled both the Polish infantry regiment and the Polish cavalry regiment that had been serving in the Army of the Kingdom of Naples to join the Grand Army in the main theatre of war and combined them into a new unit bearing this name.
Composition Napoleon's plans for the new Legion are detailed in a letter dated 6 April 1807 (N. to Daru, Nap. *Corr.*, No 12315, Vol. 15, pp. 37–8):

> The Major General has just sent you my decree for the formation of the Polish-Italian Legion of six battalions and a regiment of 1,200 Lancers. It is likely that the Legion [infantry] will arrive from Italy with a strength of 2,000 men. The cavalry regiment has 400 men; it will therefore need 800 more men . . . The horses must be purchased in Silesia, and the horse equipment and clothing for the men must be made there. . . . The horses of the cavalry unit are small . . . . As for clothing, . . . the uniform of the Polish Legion is known to everyone; the unit will wear both Polish and Italian cockades. Find out if there are enough cartridge boxes and belts in Silesia to arm a total of 6,000 men; if there are not, have the necessary material assembled there, but I am sure there will be sufficient from the disarmament of prisoners. Write to Prince Jerome [in Silesia] and tell him my intention is to give him a free hand to get this unit organised promptly.

It seems that the six infantry battalions were divided into three regiments of two battalions each.
Commanders The full Legion was commanded during its entire existence by Joseph Grabinski, who had been the commander of the 1st *Demi-Brigade Polonaise* (see separate entry) and who was promoted to the rank of General on 25 March 1807.
Cavalry *Formation to 13 July 1807*: Colonel Alexander Rozniecki, who had commanded the unit while it was still part of the Danube Legion. *13 July 1807 to final transformation:* Colonel Jan Konopka, who continued to command the Regiment after it was transformed into the Vistula Legion Lancers.
1st Infantry Regiment *Formation to final transformation:* Colonel Gregory Joseph Chlopicki de Necznia (1768–1854), a veteran of the legions of Italy. He continued to

command the unit after it was transformed into the 1st Regiment of the Vistula Legion.
2nd Infantry Regiment *Formation to final transformation:* Colonel Simon Biatowieyski (?–1808). He continued to command the unit after it was transformed into the 2nd Regiment of the Vistula Legion.
3rd Infantry Regiment *July 1807 to final transformation:* Colonel Piotr Swiderski, who was promoted after having distinguished himself in as Major of the Legion's Lancers. He continued to command the unit after it was transformed into the 3rd Regiment of the Vistula Legion.

Operational History The only unit of the Legion to see important combat action was the Lancer unit, which left Italy in January 1807 and arrived in Silesia in late May in time to be employed by Jerome Bonaparte, who was then commanding the IXth Corps of the Grand Army. On 15 May 1807, two squadrons of the Lancers under Major Piotr Swiderski were used by General Lefèbvre-Desnouëttes to rout a force of Prussian infantry and cavalry that included elements of the 6th Hussars (von Schimmelpfennig), the 3rd Dragoons (von Irving) and Bosniaks of von Prittwitz. During this combat at Struga, the Lancers captured two guns and over 800 Prussian rank-and-file, as well as freeing two battalions of Saxons fighting with the French who had been captured the day before. The Lancers themselves suffered only minor casualties. (Report of Jerome Bonaparte, SHA Carton C[3][1], cited in an Internet article about Struga found on 31 May 2001, at http://freeweb.pdq.net/jolsz/struga.html.) Swiderski was subsequently promoted to command of the 3rd Infantry Regiment of the Legion as a reward for his distinguished service.

Final Transformation After the Peace of Tilsit, the men of the Legion petitioned Napoleon for permission to be transferred to the Army of the Duchy of Warsaw, as the Legion of the North had been allowed to do. The Emperor responded by saying that was impossible because the Duchy lacked the financial resources to pay them. (Decision of 24 September 1807, Nap. *P&T*, No 1308, Vol. 1, p. 631.) The Legion was instead transferred to the service of King Jerome of Westphalia. (N. to Berthier, 22 October 1807, Nap. *P&T*, No 1374, Vol. 1, pp. 662–3.) The Legion was transferred back to French service and renamed the *Légion de la Vistule* in March 1808 (see separate entry).

Uniforms The uniforms of the Legion are depicted in two contemporary sources.

Infantry The Hahlo Manuscript of uniform paintings from 1807–08 includes one naive painting of an infantryman in classic Polish dress which presumably depicts the dress of the Legion infantry while it was in Westphalian service. (Copy in author's collection provided by M. Gärtner.) The figure is wearing a blue czapka with a black leather bottom and visor, a low brass plate in front surmounted by a small brass diamond-shaped plate bearing the number '1', yellow trim along the seams and edges and a tall red plume, tipped yellow, worn above a French cockade. The coat is blue with yellow collar, cuffs, lapels and turnbacks and has red fringed epaulettes on both shoulders. The long trousers are blue with a yellow stripe down the outer seam.

Cavalry The initial uniforms worn by the Legion lancers are probably the same ones captured in two drawings in the Rovatti Chronicle for 1805—No 473, 'Tromba [Trumpeter] di Cacciatori Polachi', and No 474, 'Cacciatore Polaco'. The rank-and-file horseman is a lancer in a blue uniform with a blue collar and blue lapels, yellow pointed cuffs and trim and silver buttons. The figure is wearing a blue czapka with a thin white base, no visor, white cords, yellow trim on the vertical edges and a short red plume atop a blue pompom. There is a white aiguilette on the figure's left shoulder and a white belt over his right shoulder, apparently holding a cartridge box, but the artist may have reversed this detail because Napoleonic cartridge boxes were almost invariably suspended from a belt over the left shoulder. The figure is wearing blue hussar trousers with yellow Hungarian knots and stripes and black hussar boots without trim and is carrying both a sabre suspended from straps descending from a waist-belt and a lance with green, red and white stripes on the staff (the Italian tricolour combination) and a tricolour arrangement of triangles of colour on the lance pennon (white next to the staff, red above and green below). The figure is mounted and the horse furniture consists of a white sheepskin saddle cover with red scallop-edge trim and a blue portmanteau with yellow trim.

The trumpeter is quite a surprise because he is wearing a similar style of uniform, but the base colour is red while the collar, lapels, cuffs and trousers are buff/yellow with white trim, as is the czapka (except for a short black fur base). The headwear also features white cords and a white plume, tipped red, over a red pompom. The trousers have red Hungarian knots and side stripes. The horse furniture is the same except for a yellow portmanteau with red trim.

The uniform of the lancers of the Legion during their time in Westphalian service is represented in a watercolour from the Hahlo Manuscript which depicts many of the early units of the Westphalian Army in 1807–08. (Copy in Author's collection provided by M. Gärtner.) The painting depicts two cavalrymen on foot, both of whom have essentially the same uniform described above except that the collar is yellow and the cuffs are blue with yellow trim. The lapels of the jackets of the figures are cut away over the stomach in the same way as those of French line infantry coats of the period, so that white vests with yellow trim are visible on both. (The right-hand figure has a more sophisticated czapka than the 1805 figure, with a better-defined black leather base with a visor and yellow metal chinscales.) The plume on the czapka is red tipped yellow worn over a yellow pompom. The figure is carrying a lance with a brown staff but with the same triangular arrangement of colours on the lance pennon, although this time there is a blue triangle on top and red below. The second figure is highly unusual because he is wearing a black busby with a tall red plume and a yellow bag. He appears to be an élite company soldier because he is wearing a white fringed epaulette on his right shoulder. It is interesting to note that the czapka illustrated in this painting is different from that illustrated in the Hahlo drawing of the Legion infantryman and that, unlike the infantryman, the figures in this painting have blue, and not yellow, lapels.

Standard
Infantry Same as for the *1er Demi-brigade Polonais* (see separate entry).
Cavalry Same as for the *Lanciers Polonais* (see separate entry).

Légion Polonaise d'Italie

(Polish Legion of Italy)

Date of Creation 21 Pluviose Year VIII (10 February 1800).
Circumstances of Creation This Legion, also known as the 1st Polish Legion, was formed through the reorganisation of the remnants of the two Polish legions that had been part of the Army of the Cisalpine Republic in Italy in 1799. (Pigeard, *Troupes Polonaises*, pp. 8–9.) The second of these legions had been effectively destroyed at the Battle of Magnano in April and the subsequent siege of Mantua, while the first had suffered debilitating casualties in later battles, including the loss of an entire battalion at the Battle of the Trebbia.
Composition The re-formed Legion was supposed to have the same composition as the *Légion du Danube* (see separate entry). By order of 3 March, General Dombrowksy cancelled the formation of the four cavalry squadrons called for by that establishment but increased the number of infantry battalions to seven (each one of which had nine companies, including one of Grenadiers) and the number of artillery companies to five. (Belhomme, Vol. 4, p. 216.) The 4th, 5th and 6th Battalions were organised at the end of April in Marseilles with recruits from the disbanded 2nd Legion. The 1st, 2nd and 3rd Battalions were organised at Nice in June with the surviving members of 1st Legion. The 7th (or depot) Battalion used the depots of the two units.

The composition of the Legion varied from time to time, but on 6 October 1801 the Legion establishment consisted of a staff, a foot artillery company and seven infantry battalions, giving a total strength of 6,600 men. (Pigeard, *Troupes Polonaises*, p. 9.)
Commanders *Creation to transformation:* Division General Jan Henryk Dombrowski (or Dabrowski) (1755–1818), the creator of the original Polish Legions in 1797. (A colour portrait of Dombrowski *circa* 1798 from the Polish Army Museum in Warsaw is reproduced in Zygulski, p. 51.)
Operational History The re-formed Legion seems to have been left on coastal guard duty in the rear of the French armies during the Marengo campaign. (Nafziger, p. 66.) When hostilities commenced again in the autumn of 1800, it was assigned to active duty with the Army of Italy and was part of the force besieging the fortress of Peschiera from December 1800 to January 1801. The Austrian garrison put up a tenacious defence that ended only with the news of the Armistice of Treviso. Brigade Chief Grabinski was wounded in the head during one of the garrison's many sorties. (Fieffé, Vol. 2, p. 100–1.) The Legion probably also provided men for the French force that besieged a Tuscan

garrison (aided sporadically by British troops and ships) in the fortress of Portoferraio on the island of Elba from May 1801 until June 1802.

Final Transformation The Legion was transformed into the 1st and 2nd *Demi-brigades Polonaises* (see separate entry) in December 1801.

Uniforms The Polish Legion of Italy certainly wore the same blue, Polish-style uniform that had been worn by the two predecessor legions. This means that the men of the Legion wore czapkas and jackets with short tails and lapels that closed across the stomach down to the waist. It is not entirely clear, however, what facing colour was worn with these uniforms, although one source (Nafziger, *Poles*, p. 66) states categorically that the facings of all the battalions were changed to crimson when the Legion was re-formed. That statement is consistent with the fact that the Rovatti Chronicle for 1801 depicts three Polish infantrymen, all of whom have blue uniforms with crimson lapels, collars, cuffs and turnbacks. (Boeri, Illustration 72 and others not reproduced in that work.)

The Rovatti figures provide extensive detail concerning the dress of the Legion: (a) the czapka is entirely dark blue except for white trim at the bottom and along each vertical edge of the headdress and it has a black visor; (b) the belts are white with a silver plate on the waist-belt; (c) the white vest has two rows of silver buttons; and (d) the buttons are silver and are visible around shoulder side of the cuff. One figure, identified as a Fusilier, has white cords on his czapka and a blue plume tipped red on the left side; another, identified as a Grenadier, has a red plume, red cords, red fringed epaulettes and a red sword knot, as well as a brass grenade (?) on the front of the czapka and a red stripe down the side seam of his trousers. (The red colour of these features is definitely different from the crimson of the facings.) The final figure is identified as a Chasseur, and he has a green plume, green cords, green fringed epaulettes and a green sword knot. He also has a brass bugle horn ornament on the front of his czapka and a green stripe on his trousers.

The Rovatti Chronicle for 1801 also has a picture of a 'Polish Artilleryman'. (Boeri, Illustration No 70.) This figure has the same style dress as the other Poles, but the uniform is green with black facings. The czapka is green with white trim, and has a black visor, mixed red and white cords and a red plume on the left. The figure also has red fringed epaulettes, a single white belt worn over the right shoulder, a red sword knot on his sabre and a black stripe down the side seam of his trousers.

Standard The Rovatti Manuscript and two surviving flags in the Army Museum of Warsaw make it relatively easy to reconstruct the colours carried by each battalion of the Legion. (Boeri, Illustration No 71; flag photograph in Pigeard, *Troupes Polonaises*, p. 10.) The basic design was similar to that of the French colours introduced by Napoleon in that there was a central white diamond surrounded by four blue triangles, but there was also a distinctive red arrowhead, outlined in white, running to each corner. The central space was decorated with a rooster (a traditional Gallic symbol) holding lightning bolts in one foot and a laurel wreath and oak leaves in the other.

There were two light blue ribbons, one over the bird bearing the words 'République Française', the name on the other under the rooster and giving the name of the Legion on the reverse and the number of the relevant battalion on the obverse. The staff of the colour was decorated with tricolour stripes and surmounted by a spear -head finial and white cords. A modern illustration of the colour of the 2nd Battalion of this Legion (referred to on the colour at the 'Première Légion Polonaise') can be found in Rigo, *Le Plumet*, Plate No 77 (*Légion de la Vistule, Infanterie, 2e Régiment, Drapeau 1800–1813*), since the Vistula Legion (see separate entry) inherited the colours of the Polish Legion of Italy.

The artillery force of the Legion of Italy also had a flag of its own. The pattern was generally the same, but the central field had the rooster resting on crossed cannon barrels. The inscription on the lower ribbon on the flag's obverse bore the words 'Bataillon d'Artillerie'. (See photograph of surviving standard in Pigeard, *Troupes Polonaises*, p. 10.)

Légion Portugaise

(Portuguese Legion)

Date of Creation 18 May 1808.
Circumstances of Creation When one of Napoleon's armies conquered the Kingdom of Portugal without resistance in November 1807, it found itself in the odd position of co-existing with the duly constituted army of that Kingdom, a 30,000-man force consisting of following components (Boppe, *Légion*, p. 14):

20	Regiments of Infantry
8	Regiments of Cavalry
7	Regiments of Dragoon
4	Regiments of Artillery
2	Regiments of Marine Infantry

Recognising the inherent danger in the situation, Napoleon instructed General Androche Junot, his commander on the scene, to take decisive action to reduce the risk. Junot responded on 22 December 1807 by discharging all Portuguese soldiers who had served for more than eight years (Boppe, *Légion*, pp. 17–18), and then, in a set of decrees dated 16 January and 15 February 1808, he followed up by reorganising the remaining men of the old regiments into six new infantry units, a new light infantry battalion and three new regiments of cavalry that did not have traditional ties to the Portuguese Royal family. (Boppe, *Légion*, pp. 18–22.)

Once those changes had been effected, Junot was ready for the final blow. On 21 March 1808 he ordered all of the units to leave Portugal for Valladolid in Spain, where they were to become part of the French Army. (Boppe, *Légion*, p. 17.) A lot of men deserted rather than leave their homeland, but many simply followed orders. When they arrived in Spain, they found themselves honoured with the dubious distinction of having been transformed by a decree of 18 May 1808 from the last remnant of the old Portuguese Army into a new force called the Portuguese Legion in French service. (Organisational decree reproduced in Boppe, *Légion*, pp. 37–41.) They were then sent on to various depots in France to be reorganised in accordance with the 18 May decree. At this juncture there were only 4,000 infantrymen and 680 cavalrymen still with their colours. (N. to Minister of War, 21 May 1808, Nap. *Corr.*, No 13947, Vol. 17, p. 173.)

Composition According to the Organisational Decree, the Portuguese Legion was to consist of six regiments of infantry (one of which was never formed), one depot battalion, two regiments of cavalry (with one depot squadron) and three artillery companies (which were never formed). (Article 1.) Each infantry regiment was to have a staff and two battalions, each of which was composed of six companies of 140 men each. Each cavalry regiment was to have a staff and four squadrons, each of which was composed of two companies of 100 men each. The total strength of the Legion was calculated to be 10,134 men. (Boppe, *Légion*, p. 39.) The decree also specified that the Legion would be divided for operational purposes into two brigades of three infantry regiments. (Boppe, *Légion*, p. 40.) Each brigade was expected to have a band of eighteen musicians. (*Ibid.*)

When Napoleon decided that he would like to use the Portuguese Legion in the campaign against Austria in 1809, he realised that no one of its regiments was sufficiently well organised to take to the field, so he instead assembled the élite companies of the Legion into a special temporary formation called the 13th Demi-brigade because there were twelve other composite Demi-brigades of élite companies in General Nicholas Oudinot's army corps. The precise organisation specified by a decree dated 10 March 1809 was as follows (Boppe, *Légion*, pp. 87–8):

> *Article 1*: There will be formed a 13th Demi-brigade for the corps of Grenadiers that will be composed of Grenadiers and Voltigeurs of the Portuguese Legion.
>
> *Article 2*: The Demi-brigade will be composed of three battalions, each of which will have four companies (two of Grenadiers and two of Voltigeurs) of 120 men . . .
>
> *Article 3*: The 1st Battalion will be formed from two Grenadier companies and two Voltigeur companies from the 1st Infantry Regiment of the Portuguese Legion.
>
> *Article 4*: The 2nd Battalion will be formed from one company of Grenadiers from each of the 2nd and 5th Regiments and two Voltigeur companies from the 2nd.
>
> *Article 5*: The 3rd Battalion will be formed one company of Grenadiers from each of the 3rd and 4th Regiments and two companies of Voltigeurs from the 4th Regiment.

Napoleon took a similar approach to mobilising the Portuguese cavalry for the 1809 campaign. On 31 March he organised a provisional Regiment of Portuguese Mounted Chasseurs by taking the best elements of the two existing regiments of

Portuguese cavalry. (Boppe, *Légion*, pp. 216–20.) He later supplemented this force with a special detachment from the 2nd Cavalry Regiment.

These temporary formations stayed in existence for over two years, at which point Napoleon opted for a complete reorganisation of the Legion. By a decree dated 2 May 1811 the Legion's establishment was reduced to three regiments of infantry and one of cavalry, plus a depot battalion. (Boppe, *Légion*, pp. 163–5.) Each regiment now had only two battalions, but each battalion had six companies. The 1st Regiment of infantry in the new establishment was an élite formation similar to the 13th Demi-brigade, and it continued to be recruited exclusively from Portuguese soldiers. All six companies of its 1st Battalion were of Grenadiers, while the six companies of the 2nd Battalion were all Voltigeurs. The other two infantry Regiments were initially composed exclusively of Fusiliers, but in 1812 Napoleon approved Marshal Ney's request for the creation of élite companies in the 2nd Regiment in 1812. (Boppe, *Légion*, p. 173; Decision of 26 May 1812, Nap. *P&T*, No 7270, Vol. 5, p. 384.) The ranks of the 2nd and 3rd Regiments were filled primarily with Spanish prisoners; there were only 84 Portuguese in the 2nd Regiment and 136 in the 3rd.

Commanders The Legion was commanded for most of its early existence by Dom Pedro d'Almeida, Marquis d'Alorna (1755–1813), a Portuguese general who rose to the rank of Division General in the French Army. He had served in the Portuguese auxiliary corps that fought with the Spanish Army against the French in 1793–95. He died at Königsberg in January 1813 after the retreat from Russia. D'Alorna was succeeded on 14 August 1810 by General Joseph de Carcome Lobo (1756–?), who had commanded the Portuguese forces in the field during the 1809 campaign. Carcome Lobo was succeeded in turn by General Gomez Freyre d'Andrade (1766–1817).

COMMANDERS OF THE ORIGINAL REGIMENTS

1st Infantry Regiment Colonel Joachim de Saldanha, Count of Albuquerque (1759–?).

2nd Infantry Regiment Colonel D. Thomas Teles da Silva, Marquis de Ponte de Lima (1779–1822).

3rd Infantry Regiment Colonel Fransisco Antonio Freire-Pego (1755–?).

4th Infantry Regiment Colonel Joseph de Botelho, Count of San Miguel (1771–1850).

5th Infantry Regiment Colonel Joseph de Vasconcellos (1772–1853).

1st Cavalry Regiment Colonel Roberto Ignacio d'Aguiar (?–?).

2nd Cavalry Regiment Colonel Agostinho de Mendonça, Marquis de Loulé (1780–1824).

REGIMENTAL COMMANDERS FOLLOWING THE 1811 REORGANISATION

1st Infantry Regiment Colonel Fransisco Antonio Freire-Pego, the commander of the original 3rd Regiment. He was promoted to the rank of Brigade General on 3 March 1813 and was replaced at the head of his Regiment by Colonel François Louis Trinité (1776–1820).

2nd Infantry Regiment Major Charles Ferdinand d'Haffrengues (1761–?), who was replaced for the Russian campaign on 17 April 1812 by Major Candide Joseph Xavier (1769–?).

3rd Infantry Regiment Major Antoine Joseph Baptiste de Sa Carneiro (1754–?), who was replaced for the Russian campaign on 17 April 1812 by Major Emmanuel de Castro (1779–?), who was wounded at the Beresina crossings and taken prisoner by the Russians a month later.

1st Cavalry Regiment The Marquis de Loulé, who had been the commander of the old 2nd Regiment.

Operational History The Legion and the Emperor first encountered each other at Bayonne on 1 June 1808 (Chlapowski, pp. 84–5):

> A short time later there appeared twelve [*sic*] Portuguese regiments that were being sent back to France by Junot, the Emperor's aide-de-camp, who did not have much confidence in them. These regiments were very weak and incomplete because they had suffered greatly from desertion while they were traversing Spanish territory. The soldiers that remained were in reasonably good condition; the Portuguese were small and thin, but very adroit.
>
> One after another, these regiments were reviewed by the Emperor and sent to garrisons in the south of France. They marched fast, much faster than the French. Their uniforms were white [?] with different contrasting colours on their collars and cuffs.
>
> Two squadrons of Portuguese chasseurs also arrived. They both had brown coats, one with green collars and the other with red collars. They had formed two complete regiments of cavalry when they left Portugal, but only several hundred reached Bayonne with their horses.

The Portuguese did their first fighting for Napoleon even before they were properly organised into their new Legion. As the various Portuguese units were making their way across Spain towards France, several of them were stopped and diverted to more pressing tasks as the French attempted to establish control over King Joseph Bonaparte's unruly new kingdom. In particular, the 5th Regiment and the battalion of chasseurs, a total of 800 men under General Gomez Freyre d'Andrade, were assigned to the siege of Saragossa in June 1808. (Foy, *Guerre de la Peninsule*, Vol. 3, p. 298.) By the time the French abandoned the siege in August, desertion and casualties had reduced the force by nearly half. (Boppe, *Légion*, p. 34.) The two units involved did not actually cross into France until 16 September 1808. (Boppe, *Légion*, p. 27.)

The organisation of the Legion was entrusted to two French inspectors, General Muller for the infantry and General Paris d'Illins for the cavalry. They thought the Portuguese had many good qualities as soldiers, but had great difficulty making progress with the Legion because of the lack of funds, equipment, clothing and recruits. The latter problem was particularly acute. By November 1808 the Legion mustered barely 2,500 men as against its theoretical strength of more than 10,000. (Boppe, *Légion*, p. 67.) Since Portugal itself was closed as a recruiting ground and since the French were never able to capture Portuguese prisoners in large numbers, it soon became apparent that it would be impossible to maintain the ethnic character of the unit. By December 1808 Napoleon had authorised the Legion to recruit Prussian prisoners of war, and he expanded this permission to include Spanish prisoners in February 1809. (Boppe, *Légion*, pp. 74–5.)

The Portuguese were represented in the 1809 campaign against Austria by an élite composite unit made up of Grenadier and Voltigeur companies from several different regiments of the Legion and by a small cavalry force. Both these units were attached to General Oudinot's 2nd Corps. On 18 June the 13th Demi-brigade had 54 officers and 1,417 NCOs and men present for action. At Baumersdorf on the evening of the first day of the Battle of Wagram, the Portuguese held steady even when some inexperienced units panicked and fled. All told, the 13th Demi-brigade lost three officers killed and five wounded, along with over 300 other casualties. The cavalry had one officer wounded at Wagram and contributed two noteworthy charges at Znaim on 11 July that were cited in the Bulletin for that action. (Kann, p. 373.)

The 13th Demi-brigade, supplemented by two other provisional battalions, spent the next several years in Germany. The rest of the Legion was based at Grenoble and led a placid existence. The records of the that city abound with routine correspondence and documents ranging from the Portuguese death and birth certificates to a request to the head of the Legion depot to permit his band to play at the ceremony marking the anniversary of Austerlitz on 2 December 1809. (Jalabert, p. 25.) During part of this time, General d'Alorna and many other officers of the Legion travelled back to Portugal on the staff of Marshal André Masséna as he led the French Army of Portugal to the gates of Lisbon in 1810 and 1811. When the French captured Almeida in 1810, d'Alorna tried to enlist most of the surrendering Portuguese garrison for the Legion. His efforts met with impressive initial success, but it soon became clear that the newest members of the Legion intended to desert as soon as possible, so very few of them actually reached France. (Oman, *Peninsular War*, Vol. 3, p. 276.)

All of the units of the reorganised Portuguese Legion were deployed for the Russian campaign. Even though there were Portuguese generals who might have been equal to the task, the Legion was not allowed to function as stand-alone corps. The élite 1st Regiment, with 51 officers and 500 men, was assigned to the 10th Division on Marshal Ney's 3rd Corps, while the 2nd Regiment, 49 officers and 1,432 men, was in the 11th Division. The 3rd Regiment was in the 6th Division in Marshal Oudinot's 2nd Corps with a strength of 37 officers and 1,264 men. (Pivka, pp. 112 and 117.) The Portuguese Mounted Chasseur Regiment was attached to the Guard for most of the campaign.

The 1st and 2nd Regiments were destroyed in three engagements that took place in a span of little more than three weeks. On 16–18 August he two units lost a combined total of two officers killed and ten wounded in fighting around Smolensk. A day later they were engaged in the bloody struggle of Valutina-Gora that cost seven dead officers and eleven wounded. At this stage, the size of the Regiments was so reduced that they were combined into a single unit. (Juhel, p. 14.) This combined force was present at Borodino on 7 September, where it lost a staggering thirteen officers dead and 22 wounded, plus over 500 other-rank casualties. They continued on to Moscow thereafter, but were never again a significant military force.

The 3rd Regiment never got as far as Moscow because the 2nd Corps ended up in Polotsk guarding the northern flank of the Grand Army. The 3rd survived the two major Battles of Polotsk in August and October relatively intact, but it was not as lucky at the Beresina. Between 24 and 28 November the Regiment had thirteen officers wounded and another 26 are listed simply as having 'disappeared'. The Cavalry Regiment also lasted a relatively long way into the retreat, losing six officers wounded, three mortally at Krasnoi on 18 November, five (three mortally) at the Beresina, seven (including one killed outright) at Smorgony on 5 December and four more at Vilna between 8 and 10 December.

Although there were some 800 men available at the Legion's depot in 1813, the Legion did not field any active service formations.

Final Transformation The Portuguese Legion was disbanded by Napoleon's decree of 25 November 1813 and was transformed into a Battalion of *Pionniers Portugais*. (Pigeard, 'Pionniers', p. 14; Boppe, *Légion*, pp. 275–7.) The Pioneers were dissolved by a Royal order dated 24 April 1814 and the last remaining Portuguese soldiers were placed at the disposition of the Portuguese government on 5 May 1814. (Pigeard, 'Pionniers', p. 15; Fieffé, Vol. 2, p. 142.)

Uniforms The Portuguese army wore dark blue uniforms when it was taken into French service, but that could not continue because of indigo shortages. Minister of War Clarke proposed sky blue as a replacement, but Marshal Berthier countered with grey brown (*gris de fer brun*), while Minister of War Administration Dejean preferred red-brown. Napoleon chose the last option. (Decision of 12 July 1808, Nap. *Corr.*, No 14186, p. 370.) The resulting dress of the Legion is very clearly prescribed in a letter from the Minister of War Administration dated 27 July 1808 (Boppe, *Légion*, pp. 47–8):

> *For the Infantry of the Legion:*
>
> Short jacket of Red Brown cloth with *garance* red square lapels closed to the belt and red collar, cuffs and vertical pockets and white turnbacks and white metal buttons bearing, for each regiment, the words 'Légion Portugaise' around the outside and the regimental number in the centre. White vest with silver buttons like those for the coat;
>
> Red Brown overalls with half-gaiters. . . .
>
> *For the Cavalry:*
>
> A Red Brown jacket in the style of a French mounted Chasseur of the line with *garance* red collar and cuffs, vertical pockets and white metal buttons.
>
> White vest with white metal buttons, Red Brown breeches with white trim.
>
> Red Brown cloak. . . .
>
> The rank distinctions will be white/silver.

The basic style of this uniform was different from that of other French units because the red lapels were closed but did not reach all the way to the waist, leaving one button and a small gap of brown jacket between the bottom of the lapels and the top of the trousers. The headwear of the Legion was also distinctive. The infantry wore the 'Barretina' shako adopted by the Portuguese Army in 1806 with a tall front and a brass metal band around the bottom. (Chartrand, *Portuguese Army*, Vol. 1, p. 41.) The cavalry wore Portuguese helmets with bearskin crests. (See photograph in Blondieau, p. 28.)

There are several primary iconographic sources that give further details of the Legion's dress. Martinet, Print No 227, reveals that the light infantry of the Legion had large yellow-over-red plumes and green cords for their shakos and green fringed epaulettes with red crescents. Plate 226 gives red plumes, shako cords and fringed epaulettes for Grenadiers. Both types of figures are wearing white overalls with double red (dark pink?) stripes down the outside seam. These figures match almost perfectly those from the Legion illustrated in Faber du Faur's prints of the Russian campaign. The cavalry of the Legion is depicted in Martinet, Print No 229. The figure is wearing the crested helmet and a single-breasted brown jacket with red collar, pointed cuffs and turnbacks. The jacket has brown shoulder straps trimmed with red. The outfit is completed by grey trousers with a broad red strip down the outside seam and black hussar boots. The saddlecloth is a white sheepskin with red wolf 's teeth edging and a brown portmanteau with a circle of red lace on each end.

The plate of Portuguese troops dressed in brown from the *Augsberger Bilder* series (c. 1810–12) is also instructive. (See photograph in Pivka, p. 70.) Three of the four infantry figures in the foreground are wearing short white gaiters with brown trousers while the fourth has tattered white overalls and sandals on his feet. One figure has red shako cords, a short red plume and red fringed epaulettes. Another has green cords, a short green plume and green fringed epaulettes with a yellow crescent. Another figure in the front, this one with no epaulettes, has white cords on his shako.

There are several interesting cavalry figures in the background of this print. One is a mounted officer of Chasseurs in a brown single-breasted jacket wearing a black busby with a red pompom and grey overalls. This figure also has silver epaulettes and a red shoulder-belt trimmed with two lines of silver lace. Standing next to the latter figure is another officer, this one with a large bicorne hat, a brown coat with brown pointed lapels cut to leave exposed a white vest, brown trousers and a wide red sash. The two other mounted cavalrymen depicted both have brown coats with brown pointed lapels and crested helmets, but one of the helmets does not have a visor. Both have visible white vests, but one has white overalls while the other has brown trousers with white Hungarian knots.

One contemporary observer was particularly impressed with the appearance of the Legion's cavalrymen when he encountered them in Russia at the end of October 1812. He noted that 'their clothes were entirely brown, like their faces.' (Roos, p. 147, quoted in Pigeard, *L'Armée*, p. 455.)

Standard Although the Legion did have two flag-bearer positions for each regiment, there is no indication that the unit ever received official colours from Napoleon.

Légion Syrienne

(Syrian Legion)

Date of Creation June 1799. (Belhomme, Vol. 4, p. 195.)
Circumstances of Creation The Syrian Legion was formed after the end of Napoleon's invasion of Palestine from a number of different units of Turkish infantry (see separate entry on *Janissaries*) that had fought for the French in that campaign. Interestingly, there is no mention of the Legion in Fieffé.
Composition The Legion consisted of a squadron of cavalry and one battalion of infantry composed of five companies of 40 men each. (Belhomme, Vol. 4, p. 195.)
Commanders No information found.
Operational History No information found.
Final Transformation No information found.
Uniforms No information found.
Standard No information found.

Légions des Francs du Nord

(Volunteer Legions of the North)

Date of Creation 22 Fructidor Year VII (8 September 1799).
Circumstances of Creation This was one of three foreign units decreed on the same day in 1799 to replace the losses suffered by the French armies in Italy during the summer campaign. The others were the *Légion Italique* and the *Légion de Danube* (see separate entries). The specifc group targeted for enlistment in this Legion were the inhabitants of the territory between the Rhine and s and between the Rhine and the Moselle. (Organisational Decree, *Journal Militaire*, 1799, Pt. 2, p. 726.)
Composition The Legion consisted of four battalions of infantry, four squadrons of mounted chasseurs and one company of light artillery. Each infantry battalion had ten companies–one of Grenadiers, one of Chasseurs and eight of Fusiliers. Each company had three officers and 123 men. Each squadron of cavalry consisted of two companies of 116 men each. (Organisational Decree, *Journal Militaire*, 1799, Pt. 2, p. 726.) An order of 11 Pluviose Year VII (31 January 1800) temporarily halted the organisation of the cavalry squadrons but added another four battalions to the infantry. That same order also changed the artillery force into a foot company instead of a mounted company. (Nap. O&A, No 144, Vol. 1, p. 67.) Those extra battalions were organised into a 2nd Volunteer Legion of the North by an order dated 15 March 1800, but since

neither unit was ever fully formed, the two Legions were consolidated back into a single unit by an order of 10 September 1800. (Belhomme, Vol. 4, pp. 218 and 234.)

Commanders *17 December 1799 to disbandment:* General Jean Marie Joseph Eickemeyer (1753–1825), a native of Mainz who saw significant action in and around that city during the Wars of the Revolution. He had retired in October 1799 but was called out of retirement to command the Legion.

Operational History The formation of the Legion attracted a mixed bag of Dutch, Belgian and Rhenish volunteers.

Final Transformation The Legion was disbanded by a decree dated 26 June 1801 and its men were incorporated into the 18th Light and 55th Line Regiments on 18 August. (Belhomme, Vol. 4, p. 244.)

Uniforms The Organisational Decree specifies the uniform of the Legion in great detail:

> The uniform of the Legion will be a short green jacket with red collar, cuffs and trim, white demi-spherical buttons, green trousers and vest, half-gaiters for the infantry, short boots for the cavalry and artillery.
>
> The headwear will be a three-cornered hat with a plume for the infantry and a felt shako with a plume for the foot and mounted chasseurs and the light artillery.

Standard No information found.

Légions Piémontaises

(Piedmontese Legions)

See *Légion du Midi*.

Mamelouks (1st Formation)

(Mamelukes)

Date of Creation 18 Messidor Year VIII (7 July 1800).

Circumstances of Creation After the assassination of his immediate predecessor, General Jean Baptiste Kléber (1753–1800), Jacques Abdallah Menou, the commander of the French forces in Egypt, tried to augment his diminished force of native Frenchmen by organising additional units of native auxiliaries. Accordingly, pursuant to an order dated 18 Messidor Year VIII (7 July 1800), he created two new companies of native cavalry, one of Mamelukes commanded by an officer named Barthélemy and the other of Syrian Janissaries commanded by Youssef Hamoui, and reorganised a third, also composed of Syrian Janissaries, that had been in existence since September 1799 under the command of Yakoub Habaibi (see separate entry for *Janissaires Syriennes*). (See decree reproduced in Savant, *Les Mamelouks*, p. 426.) Three and a half months later, on 4 Brumaire Year IX (26 October 1800), Menou authorised the amalgamation of the three existing companies into a new integrated force (see decree reproduced in Savant, *Les Mamelouks*, p. 427):

> The Commander in Chief orders that the *compagnie des mamlouks de Barthélemy* and the two companies of Syrian horsemen shall be combined into a single unit organised like a regiment of French cavalry.
>
> This corps, although organised as a French unit, will retain the typical weapons used by the mamelukes and will be used exclusively as light troops.
>
> . . . the new regiment . . . will carry the name of 'the *Régiment des Mamelouks* of the Republic'.

Composition Although the unit was designated a regiment, no information has been found to suggest that it ever consisted of more than the three constituent companies from which it was formed.

Commanders *Formation to final transformation:* Colonel Bartholomeos Serra (1759–?), better know as Barthélemy, a Greek from the island of Chios. He first came to Napoleon's attention for his services to the French during the first revolt of Cairo in October 1798. (Savant, *Les Mamelouks*, pp. 50–1.)

Operational History Some of the operations of the Mamelukes can be tracked via recollections of the services performed by Colonel Yakoub while he was part of that unit (quoted in Savant, *Les Mamelouks*, pp. 209–10). General Menou recalled, '[A]t the Battle of 30 Ventose Year IX near Alexandria, he fought with greatest intrepidness.' General Albert François Dériot recorded a favourable impression of both Yakoub and his unit: 'I have nothing but praise for the way he performed while serving under my orders during the blockade of Alexandria. Both his personal bravery and the discipline and polish of his unit were exemplary.'

Final Transformation After the French defeat in 1801, this polyglot unit was formally disbanded, but many of its members saw exile as the best of a limited set of options and chose to accompany the French Army back to France.

Uniforms No specific information found, but one can perhaps infer from the dress of the *Janissaires Syriennes* and the second formation of *Mamlouks* (see separate entries) that the Mameluke Regiment similarly wore native costume.

Standard No information found.

Mamelouks (2nd Formation)

(Mamelukes)

Date of Creation Order of 21 Vendémiaire Year X (13 October 1801), as modified by an Order of 17 Nivôse Year X (7 January 1802).

Circumstances of Creation When the French Army was repatriated from Egypt in 1801 many of the men from the indigenous units such as the *Mameluks* (1st Formation), the

Légion Grecque and the *Légion Copte* (see separate entries) that had served with the French chose to go into self-imposed exile in France rather than to face the consequences of their collaboration. From this raw material of Syrians, Egyptians, Greeks, Armenians, Circassians and many other peoples and nationalities, Napoleon created the most exotic of all his foreign units by decreeing the formation of a squadron of Mameluke cavalry. (Order of 21 Vendémiaire Year X [13 October 1801], Nap. *Corr.*, No 5802, Vol. 7, p. 288.) His stated intent was to provide some recompense for the men who had served the French faithfully in Egypt. (N. to Bessières, 4 May 1808, Nap. *Corr.*, No 13808, Vol. 17, p. 58.)

Composition The first detailed information about the Mamelukes is provided by an order dated 17 Nivôse Year X (7 January 1802) that amplified on the original decree forming the unit (Nap. *Corr.*, No 5914, Vol. 7, p. 359):

> *Article 1:* There will be formed one squadron of 150 Mamelukes.
>
> *Article 2:* This Squadron will be organised like a squadron of Hussars. It will be commanded by Colonel Rapp.
>
> *Article 3:* The officers and men will be drawn from the Mamelukes, Syrians and Copts who were repatriated with the Army of the Orient and who have previously served in the French Army.
>
> *Article 4:*The squadron will have two French officers, one for administration, dress and equipment and the other for discipline and training, one French quarter-master and two secretary-interpreters (one for each company), who will have the rank of Corporal-Fourier.

The Mamelukes became part of the Consular Guard pursuant to an order dated 9 Vendémiaire Year XI (1 October 1802), but there was no change in its composition—thirteen officers and 159 Mamelukes, with 40 horses for officers and 156 for the rest of the men. (Order reproduced in Savant, *Les Mamelouks*, pp. 433–4.) That order confirmed that the Mamelukes were an expensive luxury for Napoleon. The initial cost of the uniform and equipment for a single Mameluke was specified to be 1,000 francs, as compared to the comparative bargain of 689 francs for one of the Mounted Chasseurs of the Guard. (Savant, *Les Mamelouks*, p. 73.) By an order dated 30 Nivose Year XII (21 January 1804) (confirmed on 10 Thermidor Year XII), the squadron was reduced to a single company because of the difficulty of finding recruits who could meet Napoleon's strict criteria for admission to the unit. The composition of the company was reconfigured as shown in Table 11 (Savant, *Les Mamelouks*, pp. 435–6). This order also confirmed that the Mamelukes were to be administered as part of the corps of Mounted Chasseurs of the Guard.

The composition of the Mameluke company was modified slightly by a decree dated 15 April 1806 which raised the number of Mamelukes to 109 and added two more *brigadiers* and two more trumpeters. (Saint-Hilaire, p. 187.) The final official change to these arrangements came in 1813, by which time Napoleon had abandoned all

TABLE 11: MAMELUKES, 1810

Quantity	Rank	Nationality
1	Captain Commandant	French
1	Adjutant 2nd Lieutenant	French
1	Surgeon Major	French
1	Veterinarian	French
1	Master Saddler	French
1	Master Tailor	French
1	Master Bootmaker	French
1	Master Gunsmith	French
2	Captains	Mameluke
2	Lieutenants 1st Class	Mameluke
2	Lieutenants 2nd Class	Mameluke
2	2nd Lieutenants	Mameluke
1	*Maréchal des Logis Chef*	French
8	*Maréchal des Logis*	Mameluke (+ 2 French)
1	Fourrier	Mameluke
10	Brigadiers	Mameluke (+2 French)
2	Trumpeters	French
2	Blacksmiths	French
85	Mamelukes	Mameluke

pretence of enlisting only 'true' Mamelukes. (Order of 29 January 1813, reproduced in Savant, *Les Mamelouks*, p. 437.) He accordingly felt comfortable increasing the size of the unit back up to a squadron of 250 men, to be filled out using men from French departments from beyond the 'natural' borders of France. The original members of the unit were now to be called 'First Mamelukes', while those not qualifying for that group would be considered 'Second Mamelukes'.

The roster of all the Mamelukes that served during the period under study runs to no fewer than 577 names and gives some insight into the demographics of the unit. (The roster can be found in Savant, *Les Mamelouks*, pp. 439–79.) Only 263 of these soldiers enlisted before the Russian campaign, and most of these have exotic names like Mansour Abdallah (No 110) and Khalil Atoulis (No 39). The last 314 joined the unit between December 1812 and February 1814 when it was expanded to squadron strength and have names like Henry Wohlgemutz (No 357) and Dirk Kromdyk (No 401). The unit suffered only sixteen deaths in combat during the period, as compared to 25 deaths in hospital and 25 men who 'disappeared' during the retreat from Moscow. Thirty-two of the Mamelukes (5.5 per cent of the total roster) were taken prisoner during the entire period and 26 (3.9 per cent) deserted prior to April 1814, but the vast majority of these losses came in 1814 itself.

Commanders *13 October 1801–2 May 1803*: The Regiment of Mamelukes had been commanded in Egypt by Colonel Serra (also known as Barthélemy), but Napoleon decided not to use him in the new unit formed in France because the Emperor felt that a Frenchman would be better able to rise above the rivalries of the different nationalities and races represented within the corps of Mamelukes. (Savant, *Les Mamelouks*, p. 68.) He accordingly chose Colonel Jean Rapp, one of his own ADCs, to lead the unit. Rapp left the unit when he was promoted to command of the 7th Hussars. *2 May 1803 –29 August 1803*: Colonel Pierre Louis Dupas (1761–1823), who left the unit when he was promoted to the rank of Brigade General. *29 August 1803–7 April 1807*: Squadron Chief Antoine Charles Bernard Delaitre (1776–1838), a veteran of Egypt who had joined the Mamelukes in 1802. He commanded the unit at first as a mere captain, but he was promoted the rank of Squadron Chief on 18 December 1805. He left the Mamelukes to become 1st Major of the newly formed Polish Light Horse of the Guard (see separate entry). *7 April 1807–10 September 1808*: Commandant Jean Renno (1777–1848), the only member of the original Mamelukes to rise to command of the unit. He was promoted to the rank of Captain for his distinguished conduct at Eylau. He remained with the unit even after he was superseded by the arrival of Squadron Chief Kirmann. *10 September 1808 to final transformation*: Squadron Chief François Antoine Kirmann (1768–?), who stayed with the unit until it was disbanded. He rose to the rank of Major in 1813.

Operational History As members of the Imperial Guard, the Mamelukes were represented at every one of Napoleon's major actions although their level of active participation varied greatly. At Austerlitz, the unit was involved in the decisive charge against the cavalry of the Russian Imperial Guard immortalised in Gérard's famous painting of Rapp's presentation of captured standards to Napoleon. Marbot records that a Mameluke named Mustapha, 'well-known . . . for his courage and ferocity', appalled Napoleon by regretting that he had been unable to catch and decapitate Russian Grand Duke Constantine, but the truth of that tale is suspect. (Savant, *Les Mamelouks*, pp. 78–9 and 96–8.) The charge of the Mamelukes and all the Guard cavalry at Eylau was no less dramatic, but certainly less well-documented. At the other end of the spectrum, the Mamelukes were merely passive spectators at Jena, Wagram and Borodino.

The Mamelukes also had two long stints in Spain, the first of which involved them in two noteworthy actions. On 2 May 1808 the Mamelukes were at Madrid when the population rose in revolt against the French invaders. The exotic dress of the unit excited particular fury from the crowd because of Spain's long history of warfare against Islamic enemies—a situation evoked in Goya's painting of the crowd dragging a Mameluke from his horse. Five officers were wounded, but in fact only three men of the unit were killed in the fighting. The Mamelukes probably inflicted more casualties than they suffered, however, because one witness records the unit taking indiscriminately bloody vengeance on the inhabitants of a house from which they had been fired on. (Savant, *Les Mamelouks*, pp. 81–3.) The Mamelukes also fought against the British at Benavente on 29 December 1808 when General Lefèbvre-Desnouëttes rashly led a force of Guard cavalry across the swollen Esla River. An English counter-attack routed the French and cost the Mamelukes two dead and two wounded. (Savant, *Les Mamelouks*, p. 84.) They returned to Spain in 1810 and 1811, but were not involved in any significant actions.

The rigours of the Russian campaign eliminated most of the remaining original Mamelukes and paved the way for them to become a much more disciplined force in 1813. One cannot imagine the Mamelukes of Egypt executing the type of attack noted by one of Napoleon's Polish officers at Bautzen in May 1813 (Chlapowski, pp. 339–40):

> ... [T]he Mamelukes, who formed the first squadron of the Guard Mounted Chasseurs, arrived first, passed by our left and then advanced against the Russian cuirassiers. The commander of the latter could hardly have supposed a single squadron would attack a brigade with two lines of cuirassiers showing. The Mamelukes advanced slowly to within 50 paces, then fired a volley of carbines. The right wing of the cuirassiers fled and took the rest of the regiment with them.

The Old Guard Mamelukes stayed with the main army in 1813–14, while the Young Guard squadron fought in Belgium under General Maison. (Savant, *Les Mamelouks*, pp. 213–14.)

Final Transformation The Mamelukes were disbanded by the Bourbons in 1814 because they were viewed as being particularly loyal supporters of the deposed Emperor.

Uniforms The Mamelukes were the most distinctively and colourfully dressed unit in the French Army because of their exotic clothing derived from the traditional garb of the Mamelukes of Egypt. Article 3 of the 15 April 1802 Organisational Decree for the unit specifies that '[t]he clothing and equipment of the corps of Mamelukes will the same as they had in Egypt. The will be mounted like light troops and, as a mark of gratitude for their loyalty to the French Army, they will wear green *Kaouks* [brimless hats] and white turbans.' (Savant, *Les Mamelouks*, p. 430.) Another order gives more details of the incredible amount of equipment issued to each Mameluke (Order of 11 Germinal Year X (1 April 1802) in Savant, *Les Mamelouks*, p. 430):

1	Carbine
1	Blunderbuss
2	pairs of pistols (one worn in the waist sash)
1	Mameluke sabre
1	dagger
1	mace
1	lance
1	powder flask

The lances were never issued and the Mamelukes instead received special battle axes, but neither these nor the maces were used more than occasionally. (Brunon, *Les*

Mamelukes, p. 74.) The most important part of this equipment was the curved sabre, or scimitar, of damascus steel, which could inflict astonishing damage in the hands of an expert. (Teulière, p. 10.) The pistols of the Mamelukes were another special-issue item, and those of the officers differed from those of the enlisted men. (See illustrations in Ciejka.)

Over the course of the unit's existence, the basic components of the Mameluke uniform remained the same, but they changed noticeably in style. These components were (a) a *Kahouk*, or hat, with turban, (b) a *yalek*, or long sleeved shirt, (c) a *beniche*, or vest with short sleeves or no sleeves, and (d) baggy trousers. The style of these components evolved as the original Mamelukes, who generally wore their own clothing (as opposed to a true uniform), departed the scene to be replaced ultimately with Europeans who would accept a more standardised dress. (The most complete modern treatment of Mameluke uniforms can be found in Brunon, *Mamelukes*, pp. 70–3.)

There are a large number of primary source depictions of Mamelukes, but they all differ on details of the ensemble. For comparative purposes, the most significant of these are described in the Table 12.

One fascinating piece of information that must be consulted for any serious study of Mameluke uniforms is the black-and-white photograph of a Mameluke veteran that is reproduced in Plate 173 of H. Lachouque, *The Anatomy of Glory* (New York, 1962). The picture was taken no earlier than 1857 because the subject is wearing a St Helena Medal issued in that year. The subject is identified a 'Mameluk Ducel', and there is an individual by that name on the Mameluke register—No 311, François Ducel, born at Touches on 23 April 1789, enrolled as a volunteer in the Mamelukes on 7 March 1813, transferred to the Mounted Chasseurs of the Guard in 1814. (Savant, *Les Mamelouks*, p. 464.) Because of that provenance, the picture provides one of the most authentic pieces of evidence extant concerning Napoleonic uniforms (although there is no way to guarantee that the uniform was not altered in some respect between the time it was made and the time the photograph was taken).

TABLE 12: MAMELUKE UNIFORMS

Source	*Kahouk/* turban	*Yalek*	*Beniche*	Trousers	Saddle-cloth
Brunon MS (1802)	Red/white	Red	Red	White	Med. blue
Otto MS (1807)	Green/white	Red	Green	Crimson	Red
Martinet No 158	Red/white	Red	Yellow	Crimson	Green
Hendschel (1806)	Green/orange	Red	Lt purple	Crimson	n/a
Hoffman (1804)	Red/white	Orange	Green	Crimson	Lt blue
Zimmerman (1806)	Red/white	Orange	Green	Crimson	n/a
Breitenbach (1813)	Red/white	Blue	Yellow	Crimson	Green
Freyberg (1813)	Black/white	Red	Blue	Crimson	n/a

By 1804, the non-Mameluke officers had a recognised alternate uniform: 'The French officers of the company will wear a blue uniform with an aiguilette when they are not at the head of their unit. . . .' (Article 8, Order dated 21 January 1804, Savant, *Les Mamelouks*, p. 436.) Over the years this precedent was followed more widely, so that after 1812 even Mamelukes in the ranks may have had undress uniforms and stable outfits similar to those worn by other French Guard cavalry units. (See, generally, Bucquoy, *La Garde Impériale: Troupes à Cheval* [Paris, 1977], pp. 120–3.) As they lost their authentic character, the Mamelukes were also given a fanciful kettle drummer to enhance their appearance on parade. (Rigo, *Le Plumet*, Plate No 101 [*Garde Impériale: Mamelucks, Timbalier 1807–1808*].)

Standard Colonel Rapp had a guidon and four 'toug' standards (i.e., horsetails mounted on poles) made for the company in 1802, but there is no record of the design or of the colour. (Brunon, *Mamelukes*, p. 77.) Napoleon omitted the company from the distribution of Eagles in 1804, but the performance of the Mamelukes at Austerlitz changed his mind. The unit consequently received an Eagle and a Model 1804 cavalry guidon by virtue of an order dated 15 April 1806. The legend on the obverse was 'L'Empereur des Français/à la Compagnie de Mameluks/de la Garde Impériale'. The reverse side had the words 'Valeur et Discipline' underneath an embroidered crowned eagle. (Brunon, *Mamelukes*, p. 78.) This Eagle and colour are illustrated in *Le Plumet*, Plate No 32 (*Garde Impériale: Mamelucks, Guidon 1806–1813*).

In May 1813 the Mamelukes received a new 1812-model standard with the following legend on the obverse: 'Garde Impériale/L'Empereur Napoléon/A L'Escadron de Mameluks'. This was not, however, carried on active service. The Mamelukes used instead a fringed guidon of heavy crimson fabric. The battle honours of the unit were on one side and an embroidered eagle on the other. (Brunon, *Mamelukes*, p. 78.)

Miqueletes Catalans

(Catalonian Miquelets)

Date of Creation This unit was formed by an order of General Charles Decaen dated 13 January 1812. (Organisational Order reproduced in Aliana, pp. 70–3.)

Circumstances of Creation General Decaen's order was intended to provide a formal structure and composition for companies of irregular Catalonian soldiers, or 'Miquelets', formed to fight with the French occupying forces. The order mentions two specific companies already in existence at the moment the order was promulgated—the Miquelets of Santa Coloma and those of Besalu. (Aliana, p. 70.)

Composition Each company was to consist of 150 men commanded by a Captain, including 24 mounted men (a Lieutenant, a *Maréchal de Logis*, 2 Brigadiers, a trumpeter and 24 men). (Organisational Order, Articles 2 and 4.) The French intent was to recruit the Miquelets exclusively from native Catalonians, but foreigners who spoke Catalan could be admitted with special authorisation of the Chief of Staff of the Army of Catalonia. (Organisational Order, Article 3.)

Commanders No information found.

Operational History No information found except for officer casualties noted by Martinien. Lieutenant Escudier was wounded on 16 April 1812 during a reconnaissance near Santa Coloma. Captain Chacon was killed on 21 August 1813 during a skirmish on the road from Carascal to Pamplona.

Final Transformation The remnants of these companies accompanied the French back into France at the end of 1813 and were formed, along with the remaining men of the *Chasseurs du Lampourdan* (see separate entry) into a ephemeral company-sized unit called the *Chasseurs Étrangers*. (Fieffé, Vol. 2, p. 151.)

Uniforms Article 10 of the Organisational Order for these companies specifies that they were to be dressed in brown single-breasted jackets without tails but with red collars and cuffs; loose-fitting brown trousers with a red stripe along the outside seam; and top hats '*à la Henri IV*' with red plumes and tricolour cockades. The mounted men wore boots, but the foot soldiers wore espadrilles. Unit equipment consisted of musket with bayonet (for infantrymen) or a chasseur sabre and pistol (for cavalrymen); a waist-belt '*à la américaine*' that could hold three packages of cartridges; and a cloth sack for provisions. (See also Bueno, Plate 60.)

Standard No information found.

Pandours Albanais

(Albanian Pandours; also known as the *Bataillon Albanais* [Albanian Battalion] and the *Pandours de Cattaro* [Pandours of Cattaro])

Date of Creation 1 June 1810. (Lienhart & Humbert, Vol. 4, p. 344.)

Circumstances of Creation This unit was organised at Cattaro at the same time as the *Pandours de Dalmatie* (see separate entry), but it had a slightly different focus because it was intended for continual service against the Montenegrin inhabitants of the foreign lands surrounded the French-held city of Cattaro. (Belhomme, Vol. 4, p. 478.)

Composition According to Belhomme, the unit was initially battalion-size, composed of six companies of 50 men each. On 8 November 1811, its size was increased to eight companies and the name was changed to the *Bataillon Albanais*. (Belhomme, Vol. 4, pp. 478–527.)

Commanders No information found.

Operational History The Albanian Pandours participated in local actions against raiders from neighboring Balkan territories and states. Martinien lists three officer casualties for the *Régiment de Pandours Dalmates* (see separate entry), but since they all occurred after the date that unit was disbanded they are probably casualties of this unit instead. The casualties were as follows: Battalion Chief Bubich, wounded in an insurrection at Pastrovich (near Ragusa) on 15 February 1812; Captain Bassich, wounded near Clissa on 31 October 1813; and Captain Damarey, wounded at the capture of Knin on the same day.

Final Transformation Some companies participated in the unsuccessful defence of Dalmatia in 1813, but like most local units they were hard hit by desertion. At the fortress of Clissa, 141 out of 250 Pandours in the garrison deserted in one five-day period. (Pisani, p. 440.) As a result of such attrition, the unit simply disappeared. The Captain Quartermaster of the Pandours, a Dalmatian named Parodi, ended up serving in the Croatian Hussars. He subsequently petitioned the French Minister of War for a transfer to the regular French cavalry because he did not like serving with Croats. (P. Boppe, p. 260.)

Uniforms No primary information found, but Lienhart & Humbert describe the same uniform as that for the *Pandours de Dalmatie* (see separate entry). That source also states that the uniform was later modified to include French shakos, blue dolmans and red instead of white cloaks for the rank-and-file. (Lienhart & Humbert, Vol. 4, p. 344).

Standard No information found.

Pandours de Dalmatie

(Dalmatian Pandours; also known as the *Pandours de Raguse* [Pandours of Ragusa])

Date of Creation Formed by decree of 17 March 1810.

Circumstances of Creation A military unit of this name was first formed in 1748 by the Venetian authorities then ruling the region of Dalmatia abutting the eastern edge of the Adriatic Sea. The unit, which functioned as a sort of local police force, was inherited by the Austrians after the collapse of Venice and then was passed on to Italian control when the territory was ceded to the Kingdom of Italy in 1806. After the 1809 campaign, Dalmatia and the Pandours became part of the Illyrian provinces of the French Empire. Marshal Marmont, the governor of Illyria, decided in 1810 to give them an official role as keepers of the peace in Dalmatia. The recruits were taken exclusively from inland areas since the coastal regions were the recruiting grounds for the Regiment of Dalmatia in the Army of the Kingdom of Italy. This unit was organised at the same time as the similar *Pandours Albanais* (see separate entry) and taken into French service on 1 June 1810.

Composition The following are excerpts from the unit's Organisational Decree (P. Boppe, Appendix O, p. 233):

> *Article 17*: The corps of pandours will be divided into nine companies commanded by a Colonel, three Battalion Chiefs, five Adjutant-Majors (two having the rank of Captain and three the rank of Lieutenant), nine Captain-Commandants, one Captain Quarter-

> master, nine Lieutenants and nine Second Lieutenants, 27 *arambassas* [*sic*; presumably some local designation of military rank] and 54 Sergeants.
>
> *Article 19*: Each company will be composed of at least 36 and at most 48 pandours, including two drummers, depending on the size of the administrative district to which the company is assigned, and will be commanded by a Captain, a Lieutenant, a Second Lieutenant, three *arambassas* [?] and six Sergeants.
>
> *Article 24*: The officers, non-commissioned officers and pandours will be chosen from among the individuals serving in the existing provincial force, and among all other Dalmatians who have given proof of their fidelity to and zeal for the interests of His Majesty [Napoleon]; the pandours will be at least 20 and no more than 30 years old . . .

Each company was also assigned as auxiliary pandours 200 individuals from the local population who could be used to expand the size of the company in time of war.

Commanders Colonel Nachich, resident at Zara.

Operational History The Pandours were part-time soldiers, with each company being given three months' unpaid furlough on a rotating basis throughout the year. The main purpose of the Pandours was to escort couriers and convoys. (Belhomme, Vol. 4, p. 478.) Martinien lists three casualties for this Regiment, but since they all occurred after this Regiment was disbanded, it is likely that they were actually casualties suffered by the Albanian Pandours (see preceding entry).

Final Transformation The Dalmatian Pandours were dissolved on 1 January 1811. (Belhomme, Vol. 4, p. 493.)

Uniforms The Organisational Decree for the Pandours contains a wealth of information about their dress and equipment:

> *Article 28*: The uniform of the corps of pandours will be as follows:
>
> Red dolman trimmed with silver and having sheepskin edging;
> Red vest;
> Blue trousers;
> Red turban;
> Opanque
>
> When serving at the head of their troops, the officers will wear the same uniform with rank distinctions of the types used by light cavalry of the French Army [i.e. chevrons on their sleeves and trousers] and hussar style boots.
>
> On detached service, the officers are authorised to wear blue, French-style jackets with red lining, red trousersand silver epaulettes according to rank.
>
> *Article 29*: The pandours will furnish themselves at their own expense with capes or overcoats of white for simple pandours and red for non-commissioned officers.
>
> *Article 30*: The armament and equipment of the corps of pandours will remain as follows:
>
> Regulation musket;

Pistols;
Khangiar [a type of sword];
Cartridge box on a waistband.
For the officers: sabre and pistols.

Standard No information found.

Pionniers Blancs

(White Pioneers)

Date of Creation 15 February 1806.
Circumstances of Creation This unit was formed primarily from ex-Austrian prisoners of war who indicated a preference to remain in French service after the end of the War of the Fourth Coalition. (Index for SHA Carton X[h]4 in Ministry of War, *Inventaire*, p. 221.) One imagines it was called the White Pioneers in order to distinguish it from the existing unit of Black Pioneers (see separate entry for *Pionniers Noirs*).
Composition The unit took the form of a two-battalion Regiment plus a depot, each battalion being divided into four companies of Pioneers organised as shown in Table 13 (Pigeard, 'Pionniers', p. 12). All the enlisted men were foreigners, but all the officers and NCOs were French, and only the Frenchmen were armed. (Pigeard, 'Pionniers', p. 12.)
Commanders No information found other than the fact that the unit was commanded by a Major rather than a Colonel, but the Major is never named.
Operational History Traces of the White Pioneers are hard to find. Belhomme records that the three companies were armed with muskets in October 1808 and attached to the Engineer forces in Spain (Vol. 4, p. 429), and this information is borne out by the fact that the Regiment had three officers wounded at Bailen and two at the siege of

TABLE 13: WHITE PIONEER COMPANIES, 1806–1810

Company	Date of Formation	Location
1st	February 1806	Antwerp
2nd	February 1806	Strasbourg
3rd	February 1806	Alexandria, Italy
4th	24 May 1806	Poitiers
5th	February 1807	Strasbourg
6th	?	?
7th	?	Strasbourg
8th	11 March 1809	Juliers
9th	31 December 1809	Alexandria, Italy
10th	17 June 1810	Strasbourg

Gerona in June and August. The same source states that the 1st, 2nd, 4th and 6th Companies were armed by an order dated 7 March 1809 and attached the Engineer park of the Army of Germany formed for the campaign against Austria. (Belhomme, Vol. 4, p. 429.) Also in 1809, other companies apparently performed hard labour at Antwerp, Flushing and the island of Cadzand. (Fieffé, Vol. 2, p. 187.)

Final Transformation Napoleon decided in 1810 that he would keep the White Pioneers but scrap their regiment: 'It seems to me that the regiment of foreign pioneers, which is composed of deserters, does not have need of a headquarters staff.' (N. to Minister of War, 19 August 1810, Nap. *P&T*, No 4513, Vol. 3, p. 703.) The Regiment was consequently disbanded by a decree of 1 September 1810 and reconstituted as a Battalion of *Pionniers Volontaires Étrangers* (see separate entry) without a headquarters staff.

Uniforms The uniform of the White Pioneers was intended to consist of an shako and iron grey waistcoat, trousers, jacket without tails, overcoat and half-gaiters. (Pigeard, 'Le Pionniers', p. 16.) The buttons on the overcoat were of yellow metal; all others were covered in the same iron grey cloth as the rest of the uniform. (Fieffé, Vol. 2, p. 188.) Whatever the style of the uniform, the Minister of War was authorised to carry out the uniform decree of 12 March using more economical beige cloth because, in Napoleon's somewhat peculiar opinion, that shade 'is also an iron grey colour'. (Decision of 19 March 1806, Nap. *P&T*, No 326, Vol. 1, p. 197.) The rank-and-file soldiers carried pioneer tools only, but the NCOs were armed with dragoon muskets with bayonets. (Fieffé, Vol. 2, p. 188.)

A document dated 6 September 1806, mentions that officers and NCOs wore a long-tailed iron grey single-breasted jacket with vertical pockets and silver instead of cloth buttons and silver rank distinctions.

Standard No information found.

Pionniers Espagnols

(Spanish Pioneers)

Date of Creation There were several units bearing this designation, the first of which was formed in 1811.

Circumstances of Creation

1. The first formation to bear this name was a company-strength unit authorised by a decree of 27 June 1811 and organised at Maestricht on 27 July. (SHA Carton X[l]41.) According to related correspondence, the impetus for the formation of this unit was the presence at the depot of the Joseph Napoleon Regiment of 78 men who had been sent back from the active service battalions because of their 'bad conduct'. (Decision of 12 June 1811, Nap. *P&T*, No 5597, Vol. 4, p. 362.)

2. In early 1812, as part of a concerted effort to find more effective employment for

the vast number of Spanish prisoners of war then held in France, Napoleon authorised the creation of an additional battalion of Spanish pioneers to provide workmen for military engineering projects. This second unit was formed by Title III of an Imperial decree dated 10 March 1812 (reprinted in P. Boppe, *Les Espagnols*, Appendix E, pp. 199–202), but was not associated with the original company. The Spanish Pioneer Battalion was formed at Nimeguen in Holland on 22 May. (SHA Carton X[l]41.)

3. The designation of 'Spanish Pioneers' was also used for the Regiment of Pioneers formed with the men of the Joseph Napoleon Regiment who were disarmed on 24 December 1813. (See separate entry for *Régiment Joseph Napoléon*.)

Composition

1. The first unit was formed as a single company, and never exceeded that size.

2. The second unit of Spanish Pioneers was a battalion composed of four companies of 200 men each chosen from the best of the Spanish prisoners already engaged in supporting work of the Department of Roads and Bridges (Organisational Decree, Article 9). The men were required to volunteer for a six-year term of service, but they were promised their complete freedom in return for successful completion of the term (Article 4). As with most units formed from ex-prisoners, Napoleon made certain that all the officers and two-thirds of the NCOs were Frenchmen (Article 10) and that the men carried only infantry sabres in addition to engineering tools (Article 11).

Commanders

1. Pioneer Company: No information found.

2. Pioneer Battalion: Battalion Chief Saint-Jean de Pontis (Fieffé, Vol. 2, p. 150)

Operational History

1. No information has been found about the original Spanish Pioneer Company.

2. The Battalion (sometimes known as the '1st' Battalion of Spanish Pioneers) was part of the garrison of Danzig during the long siege of that fortress in 1813, but the only information that has been found concerning its role in the defence is that which can be gleaned from Martinien's listing of officer casualties. The Battalion had four officers wounded in fighting on 29 March 1813 and then a single officer casualty on 3 June. Captain Burnand was wounded 'in a sortie' on 29 August while 2nd Lieutenant Charles was wounded in an unspecified action on 16 October. Finally, Lieutenant Camet (who had also been wounded as a 2nd Lieutenant in the March action) was wounded again 'in a reconnaissance' on 19 October. Since all the officers were Frenchmen, they may have seen more active service than their Spanish subordinates.

Final Transformation

1. The Spanish Pioneer Company was disbanded at Perignon on August 2, 1814.

2. No information has been found about the fate of the Spanish Pioneer Battalion following the surrender of Danzig.

Uniforms

1. No information has been found about the uniforms of the original Pioneer Company.

2. There is no primary source information about the uniforms of the Battalion. The earliest secondary source is Lienhart & Humbert (Vol. 4, p. 345), which gives a description with no supporting citations. That work specifies that the Pioneers wore a type of jacket called a *'veste ronde'*, which may refer to a sleeved waistcoat without tails. The jacket was grey in colour, as were the vest and trousers, but the jacket also had sky blue collar, cuffs and, unusually, lapels, all piped yellow. The unit wore a grey fatigue cap (possible piped yellow) as its headwear.

Standard No information found, but it is highly unlikely that these units had colours.

Pionniers Étrangers

(Foreign Pioneers)

Date of Creation Formed by decree of 23 February 1811. (Fieffé, Vol. 2, p. 188.)

Circumstances of Creation This unit must not be confused with the *Pionniers Volontaires Étrangers* formed from the Pionniers Blancs (see separate entries). Unconstrained by any international standards for the treatment of prisoners of war, Napoleon felt perfectly comfortable in using captured enemy soldiers in his domestic public works projects. In this instance, he decreed the formation of 30 separate battalions of pioneers composed of prisoners of war from all nations, although the majority were Spaniards. Fifteen battalions were designated for work on fortresses and fifteen for civilian works such as the draining of marshes. He subsequently added to that total with decrees of 19 and 25 April creating eight additional battalions for marine projects. The workers received wages similar to those for local labourers, but deductions were made for shelter and substinence. (Pigeard, 'Pionniers', p. 16; Belhomme, Vol. 4, pp. 500–1.)

Composition Each Battalion had a staff of one Captain, one Lieutenant Adjutant-Major, one scribe, one Corporal drummer, one master tailor and one master shoemaker (all French), and four companies, each of which had one French Sergeant and one French *fourier*, eight Corporals, one drummer and 91 prisoners of war. (Belhomme, Vol. 4, p. 501.)

Commanders No information found.

Operational History No information found.

Final Transformation The remnants of these battalions were disbanded on 23 April 1814 and the survivors were repatriated to their homelands.

Uniforms The NCOs of these battalions had shakos without ornamentation other than a diamond-shaped plate and wore grey overcoats and trousers. They also carried infantry swords and muskets and had white belting. (Achard, p. 4.) The pioneers themselves did not have recognisable uniforms because the French government did not feel obligated to provide them.

Standard No information found, but it is highly unlikely that such units had colours.

Pionniers Noirs

(Black Pioneers)

Date of Creation 21 Floreal Year XI (11 May 1803).

Circumstances of Creation This unit was formed at Mantua under the name *'Bataillon de Pionniers'* through the amalgamation of five different independent companies of black soldiers. Some of these men were French citizens, but three of these companies had been formed in 1802 from blacks who had served in the French Army in Egypt and who had chosen to return to France when the French were defeated. (Auguste, *Déportés*, p. 77.) Others were made up of men of colour who had been deported from France's islands in the Caribbean, including one group that had been renamed the *Chasseurs Africains* and that was intended for service in India (assuming Napoleon ever figured out a way to get his armies there). (Auguste, *Déportés*, p. 77.)

Composition This 1,000-man Battalion had a staff and nine companies of 100 men each. The Battalion was supposed to be officered exclusively by whites, but this rule was never put into practice. (Article III.) The rank-and-file soldiers were designated 'Fusilier-Pioneers'. Napoleon apparently thought that there might be enough blacks in his army for the Black Pioneers to consist of two battalions, but that idea was never given practical effect. (N. to Berthier, 9 Thermidor Year XI [28 July 1803], Nap. *Corr.*, No 6953, Vol. 8, p. 423.)

Commanders *Creation to 28 October 1805*: Battalion Chief Joseph Damingue (or Domingue) (1759?–??), also called 'Hercules', a black from Cuba. He started his military career in the French infantry in 1784, transferring to the 22nd Chasseurs in 1793. (N. to Berthier, Nap. *O&A*, No 432, Vol. 1, p. 149, n. 1.) He became a Captain in Napoleon's Guides during the First Italian Campaign and won a sabre of honour for his conduct at the Battle of Arcola. (Carles, 'Régiment Noir', p. 344.) He retired in December 1805 and by 1809 was in sufficient financial distress to petition the Emperor for help. Napoleon granted him a one-time award of 3,000 francs. (Decision of 30 November 1809, Nap. *O&A*, No 838, Vol. 1, p. 276.) *28 October 1805 to transfer to Neapolitan service*: Jean Rémi Guiard (or Guyard) (1749–1817), a soldier who began his career as a private in the Auvergne infantry regiment in 1765. He was active during the wars of the French Revolution, but had actually retired in 1801. He was reactivated and given command of the Black Pioneers in response to Napoleon's request that the unit be given 'a very firm commander who can put it in shape to render the type of service one has a right to expect from it.' (Note dated 20 August 1805, Nap. *O&A*, No 652, Vol. 1, p. 218.)

Operational History The Organisational Order specified that 'the Battalion would armed with muskets, but it was to be especially employed in work on fortifications under the orders of Engineer officers'. (Article IV.) In practice, however, it was given more active employment, and, in fact, the unit first saw action at the very end of the campaign of 1805 in Italy when it participated in an attack on the Austrian-held city of Fiume on 19 December. In that fighting, the Black Pioneers had one officer killed and five wounded (one mortally), with Battalion Chief Damingue included among the latter. Damingue's wound was so severe that it caused him to retire from active service.

In February 1806 Napoleon decided to make better use of the unit's particular expertise by attaching it to the forces then besieging the Neapolitan fortress of Gaeta. At that stage it had a strength of 58 officers and 622 men. (Carles, *Régiment Noir*, p. 345.) While serving at Gaeta from May to July, the Pioneers suffered six officer casualties. They also attracted sufficient attention from the enemy that they became the target of a specific campaign of subversion by the forces of Naples and its allies which included the following communication (Chesney, p. 200):

> To the Soldiers of the Black Corps
>
> Salutations and fraternal greetings!
>
> The French have always treated you like dogs and they have led you here only to be massacred. Save yourselves, there is still time; escape from the French tyrants while you are still able. . . . Recall the fate of the brave General Toussaint-Louverture who was taken to France and allowed to die in prison for the crime of having served France well for many years. When peace comes, you will be free to return to your homes, to see once again your brothers and friends and to enjoy in the bosom of your family the benefits of the government of your Grand Emperor Dessalines. . . . [who] is a friend of the King of Naples and of the English and the sworn enemy of Bonaparte.

The Pioneers were noted by one observer for their reckless behaviour in disarming live shells fired from the fortress in order to sell them to the artillery corps to make good the French shortages of ammunition (Ségur, Vol. 1, p. 303):

> It is true that, for our part, habit, pride and boredom combined to render our men reckless. A battalion of Blacks particularly distinguished themselves in this regard, although they were driven by an entirely different motivation. One noticed these Blacks avidly observing the flight of the enemy shells (which would bring a price of 50 centimes if they were seized intact) and they would race to the spot where they landed and attempt to rip out the burning fuses before the bombs could explode and kill them. It was a very dangerous and not very lucrative game.

Final Transformation Joseph Bonaparte was so impressed by the appearance and discipline of the Pioneers that he asked his brother to permit them to become part of the Neapolitan army. This favour was granted on 14 August 1806 when all 868 remaining Pioneers passed into the service of Naples and were rechristened the Royal African Regiment. (Carles, 'Régiment Noir', p. 346; Belhomme, Vol. 4, p. 338.) They remained part of the Neapolitan Army until the overthrow of Murat.

Uniforms The Organisational Order (Article V) states that 'The uniform of the Battalion, except for the jacket (which will be brown with red lapels and cuffs), will be the same as that for any unit of line infantry.'

Standard Charrié reports that there is a letter of Berthier dated 30 November 1804, in which he informs the Pioneers that they are to receive a colour without an Eagle. (Charrié, p. 165.) This news seems to have inspired Hercule to trade upon his old acquaintance with Napoleon, and he consequently sent the Emperor a request for one of the new Imperial 'Cuckoos' for his men. Rigo, *Le Plumet*, Print No 109; Regnault, p. 31.) The request was granted early in 1806 and, according to official Neapolitan records, the Eagle was still being used by the Royal African Regiment in late 1811. (Carle, 'Régiment Noir', pp. 348–9.)

Pionniers Volontaires Étrangers

(Foreign Volunteer Pioneers)

Date of Creation 1 September 1810.

Circumstances of Creation This unit was a Battalion that was formed as a result of the disbandment of the *Régiment de Pionniers Blancs* (see separate entry). (Belhomme, Vol. 4, p. 482.)

Composition The Battalion initially had five companies of 200 men each that were formed from the existing companies and depot of the predecessor unit. The exact origins of the new companies were as shown in Table 14 (SHA Carton X[h]2 and N. to Minister of War, 19 August 1810, Nap. *P&T*, No 4513, Vol. 3, p. 703). There is no precise information of the fate of the 2nd and 3rd Companies of the White Pioneer Regiment, but they may have been destroyed at Bailen in 1808. There was also a 9th Company from the original White Pioneers serving on Corfu that was left undisturbed.

Napoleon specified that the Battalion should keep expanding whenever available manpower was found: 'I approve the creation of additional companies to be employed to work on fortifications.' (N. to Minister of War, 19 August 1810, Nap. *P&T*, Vol. 3, No 4513, p. 703.) A new 6th Company was formed on 16 February 1811, using the base of a group of 55 White Pioneers that had been on detached service in Spain. (Belhomme, Vol. 4, p. 501.) The concept of 'volunteer' was stretched to the limits of credulity in September 1811 when the new 7th and 8th Companies were formed from

TABLE 14: FOREIGN VOLUNTEER PIONEERS, 1810

New company	Origins
No 1	Same as No 1 of the White Pioneers
No 2	Formed from amalgamation of Companies No 5 and 7 of the White Pioneers
No 3	Formed from amalgamation of Companies No 6 and 8 of the White Pioneers
No 4	Same as No 4 of the White Pioneers
No 5	Formed from depot of the White Pioneers

531 former members of the bands of the Duke of Brunswick and Prussian Major Schill that had fought against the French in 1809, been captured and then spent the intervening two years in prison as galley slaves. (Decision of 12 September 1811, Nap. *O&A*, Vol. 4, No 5658, p. 170.) One can only imagine the elation felt by the survivors when they were summoned from prison and told that they were being pardoned by Napoleon and that it had been made an offence bearing three days' imprisonment in the guard house for any French soldier to insult them. August Böck, a trumpeter who had served with Schill, records that he was assigned to the 8th Company at Toulon and that all the men were told they would enjoy the same rank that they had in the Prussian Army. Since the White Pioneers did not have any musicians, Böck seems to have been given some type of NCO status since he records that he drilled daily with a musket. (Böck, *Leben*.)

A 10th Company was formed at Strasbourg on 17 June 17, and then a new 9th Company was formed at Alexandria on 7 August 1812 after the original 9th was incorporated into the *Sapeurs Ioniens* (see separate entry). (Index for Carton X[h]5 in Ministry of War, *Inventaire*, p. 221.)

Commanders No information has been found about the commanders of the individual companies.

Operational History The only evidence of the combat history of these Companies is the Martinien information on officer casualties which demonstrates that some of the Companies, including the 4th, saw duty in Spain. One Captain was wounded at the blockade of Figuieres in May of 1811, while two other officers were wounded in attacks on convoys. The 4th Company served in Spain until early 1812, when it was brought back to Orthez to recruit. (Decision of 25 February 1812, Nap. *P&T*, Vol. 5, No 6837, p. 173.) That effort was not successful, however, because the 4th Company was disbanded on 30 October due to a lack of soldiers. (Decision of 3 October 1812, Nap. *P&T*, Vol. 5, No 7580, p. 566.) Lieutenant Breugnot was wounded during the defence of Burgos in 1812, while Lieutenants Dardas and Wertvein were killed, and Captain Breugnot wounded, during the defence of San Sebastien in 1813.

Final Transformation The 4th Company was disbanded in 1812, but the others survived until 1814. The 8th Company, composed of Prussians, was completely disarmed on 26 February but was not disbanded until May. (Böck, *Leben*.) The debris of all these companies was incorporated into colonial battalions by a Royal order of 24 August 1814.

Uniforms Same as for *Pionniers Blancs* (see separate entry). (Article 7 of Organisational Decree of 1 September 1811.)

Standard No information found, but it is unlikely that these companies had colours.

Régiment Albanais

(Albanian Regiment)

Date of Creation 12 October 1807.

Circumstances of Creation The island of Corfu at the mouth of the Adriatic Sea was ruled by Russia from 1799 until 1807, when it and the other Ionian islands were transferred to French control in accordance with the terms of the Treaty of Tilsit. In a decision dated 12 October 1807 Napoleon gave his approval to a proposal to take into French service a unit of approximately 3,000 Albanians which had been organised on Corfu by the Russians. (Nap. *Inédits*, No 235, Vol. 1, p. 69.) The Albanians were primarily refugees from the harsh rule of Ali Pasha of Janina, the local Governor (theoretically on behalf of the Ottoman Empire) of much of what is now Albania. (A monograph history of the Regiment was published by Auguste Boppe in 1902 and then republished in its entirety in 1914 as an Appendix to his more expansive book *L'Albanie et Napoléon [1797–1814].*)

Composition The first French governor of Corfu, General César Berthier, specified on 25 December 1807 that the Albanian Regiment should consist of three battalions of nine companies each, but that arrangement was never achieved. The Regiment was subsequently given a definitive organisation on the French model by a decree dated 1 July 1809, which also incorporated a unit of *Chasseurs à Pied Grecs* (see separate entry) into the corps. That decree specified that the Regiment would have a staff and six battalions, giving it a strength of 160 officers and 2,934 men. (A. Boppe, *L'Albanie*, pp. 210–11.) On 6 November 1813, the size of the Regiment was reduced to a staff and two battalions, each consisting of one 'élite' company and five of fusiliers. The strength of each company was decreed to be three officers and 100 other ranks. Less officially, the regimental rolls at this juncture also included 1,036 women and children, 1,426 goats, 36 horse, a mule and a cow. (Baeyens, p. 95.)

Commanders *1807 and 1813–14*: Commandant (later Battalion Chief) Cristiachi. *15 November 1807–August 1813*: Colonel Jean Louis Toussaint Minot (1772–1837), who left the unit when he was promoted to the rank of Brigade General. Battalion Chief de Bruges of the Isembourg Regiment was apparently the first choice of local authorities for this command in 1807, but Napoleon countermanded that proposition because he believed that mercenary officers should not be promoted outside their corps when a Frenchman was available for the job. (Decision of 3 November 1807, Nap. O&A, No 3756, Vol. 3, p. 188.)

Operational History The Albanians had a impressive reputation as a race of warriors, but dissensions and rivalries among the refugees who made up the Regiment prevented it from ever becoming an effective military force. The unit was dispersed in garrisons throughout the Ionian Islands, and when the English attacked the outlying islands in October 1809 the Albanians there deserted almost to a man. In the most egregious case, all but thirteen of over 800 Albanians in the garrison of Santa Maura deserted at the first shot. (Baeyens, p. 93.) Many of these ultimately found themselves serving the Duke of York's Greek Light Infantry regiment raised by the British after that campaign.

Following that performance, Napoleon looked at several different plans to reduce the size of the Regiment in general and the proportion of its strength in Corfu in particular because he feared it could never be a trustworthy unit: 'The experience of the past has proven that one cannot count on the Albanians.' (Letter of 6 October 1810, Nap. *O&A*, No 4316, Vol. 3, p. 332.) One plan called for the excess soldiers to be deported to Naples for incorporation into the army of King Joachim Murat; another called for 500 Albanians to be added Napoleon's Imperial Guard. In the end, nothing was done and the Regiment retained its original establishment until the reorganisation in 1813. It remained based primarily on Corfu and it never again saw any combat.

The Regiment did subsequently contribute one interesting footnote to the Napoleonic saga when it decided in 1813 to offer Napoleon a contingent of three volunteer horsemen 'mounted, armed and equipped in the manner of their ancestors'. (Baeyens, p. 95) The trio of Yannis Phocas, Costa Yannis and Lolio Nacca actually made the journey to Paris, where they were inspected by the Minister of War, who noted that 'their arms and dress differ little from the weapons and uniforms of the Mamelukes.' (Report dated 20 October 1813, quoted in Baeyens, p. 95.) As a result of this similarity, the three soldiers were in fact incorporated into the squadron of Mamelukes and fought with them during the 1814 campaign. (The story of the three soldiers is told in more detail in Savant, *Les Mamelouks*, pp. 251–2.) Nacca was captured in action near Méry-sur-Seine that winter.

Final Transformation Following the surrender of Corfu in 1814, the Regiment passed under the control of the English governor appointed to rule the Ionian Islands, who allowed it to dissolve through attrition.

Uniforms The soldiers of the Regiment apparently wore Albanian-style dress, since an officer of the Isembourg Regiment stationed at Corfu noted in his memoirs that he was 'particularly impressed with the national costume worn by the soldiers of the Albanian Regiment'. (Friedrich, Vol. 2, p. 34.) The July 1809 decree states that the Albanian Regiment would retain its existing uniform, while a clothing inventory from 1812 (A. Boppe, *L'Albanie*, p. 270) specifies that each soldier would be issued the following items of clothing and equipment:

1	red wool beretta
1	overcoat
1	jacket (*surtout*)
1	vest
2	belts
2	shirts
2	pairs of drawers (*caleçons*)
1	pair of gaiters
2	pairs of wool socks
6	pairs of shoes
1	cartridge box
1	leather pistol belt with leather trim

1	musket
1	pistol
1	sabre (for fusilier NCOs and élite company NCOs and privates)

A letter from Colonel Minot to the Minister of War provides some additional details of this uniform (quoted in Baeyens, p. 99):

> Their dress is very luxurious, with a red wool beret with a gold tassel, sandals with thick soles, coloured gaiters, tunic with a short skirt [*tunique à fustanelle*], a short scarlet vest decorated with gold buttons with sleeves open to the elbow, a long red wool sash with gold tassels and a thick cloak of goatskin that is impermeable to rain and invaluable for bivouacking.

Bucquoy Series No 129 contains a card by H. Boisselier which presents a hypothetical rendering of the uniform based on a French description of Albanian soldiers in native dress at Corfou in the period 1797–99. Equally noteworthy about the appearance of these soldiers was their hairstyle: '. . . the head is shaved on the forehead, temples and neck, leaving nothing but a large disk of hair worn long and hanging down the back . . .'. (Memoirs of General Richemont, quoted in A. Boppe, *L'Albanie*, p. 229, n. 1.)
Standard No information found.

Régiment de Catalogne

(Regiment of Catalonia)

Date of Creation February 1812.
Circumstances of Creation In January 1812, Napoleon annexed all of the provinces of Spain north of the Ebro River and reorganised them as departments of the French Empire. Consistent with that development, Napoleon decided to raise an infantry regiment recruited from the residents of that territory. His decree of 7 February 1812 specified the following details (quoted in Fieffé, pp. 148–9):

> *Article 1*: There will be formed a Spanish regiment which will take the name of the 'Regiment of Catalonia.'
>
> *Article 3*: The Regiment will be recruited by voluntary enlistment from prisoners of war or other Spaniards from Catalonia, Biscay, Aragon, Valladolid and other territories on the left bank of the Ebro River. There should be one French non-commissioned officer in each company to handle administrative matters.

There is no mystery about the purpose of the Regiment of Catalonia (Letter of 12 February 1812, Nap. *Corr.*, No 18,487, Vol. 23, p. 212):

> [T]his Regiment is formed exclusively to promote the annexation [*réunion* in the euphemistic language of Napoleon]. The Regiment should have French uniforms,

> French cockades, and French administration, and we need to pick a good colonel who is in favour of the annexation.

Composition Article 2 of the Organisational Decree provided:

> This regiment will be one of line infantry and will be composed, like any French regiment, of a staff and three battalions. The strength of the corps will be 2,558 men, divided into 72 officers and 2,486 non-commissioned officers and men.

Commanders No information found.

Operational History The Regiment was never fully organised.

Final Transformation Napoleon began to have second thoughts about the creation of this Regiment almost immediately after the Organisational Decree was promulgated. By early March he concluded that the best thing to be done was to reverse the decree and use the recruits elsewhere (Note dated 11 March 1812, Nap. *O&A*, No 1905, Vol. 2, p. 245):

> His Majesty wishes the Minister of War to inform him about all that has been done to form the Regiment of Catalonia. His Majesty no longer wishes to raise this Regiment. He prefers instead to use the men assembled in his refractory regiments where they will be bolstered by French cadres . . .
>
> By this means, His Majesty will end up with four battalions [the 3rd and 4th Battalions of the Walcheren and Île de Ré Regiments] with French cadres and only a few Spanish non-commissioned officers; this will be much more useful than the planned Regiment of Catalonia.

The dissolution of the Regiment was made official on 17 March. (P. Boppe, *Les Espagnols*, p. 197.)

Uniforms Article 5 of the Organisational Decree provided:

> The uniform and effects of this corps will be the same as for French infantry regiments. The colour of the uniform coat will be white and the facing colour on the collar, cuffs and lapels will be sky blue.

Standard No information found.

Régiment de la Tour d'Auvergne

(La Tour d'Auvergne's Regiment)

Date of Creation 30 September 1805.

Circumstances of Creation In July 1803, Napoleon conceived the idea of creating a military formation which would be composed of officers and men who had fought for the Royalists in the civil war in the Vendée during the French Revolution. (N. to Berthier, 7 July 1803, Nap. *Corr.*, No 6889, Vol. 8, p. 390.) That idea did not lead to any immediate result, but it was resurrected in modified form by the Emperor in 1805: 'I think it would be useful to form a volunteer corps of two or three battalions which could give employment to all the partisan leaders on the Royalist side in the civil war and to other individuals who served in the Royalist Army of Condé.' (N. to Fouché, 20 August 1805, quoted in Belhomme, Vol. 4, p. 218.) Now, however, the ex-Royalists were expected to provide only the leadership element for the new corps; the rank-and-file of the unit would be recruited in Germany.

This time the follow-up was fast and definitive. By 30 September 1805, a draft Organisational Decree for a new Regiment, to be commanded by a member of the noble family of La Tour d'Auvergne, had been prepared. More importantly, Napoleon found time to approve it even though he was then engaged in the astonishing feat of transforming his Army of England into the Grand Army and embarking on the campaign against Austria which would end at Austerlitz. (Decree of 30 September 1805, Nap. *O&A*, No 5349, Vol. 4, p. 33.) The Organisational Decree also envisaged that the new Regiment would be the first corps in a new formation called the German Legion.

Composition The Organisational Decree of the Regiment gives very clear instructions about its composition:

> I. There will be raised a regiment of light infantry, composed of three battalions. It will carry the name of La Tour d'Auvergne.
>
> II. Godfrey de La Tour d'Auvergne is named Colonel-Commandant of this corps.
>
> III. The regiment will be organised in the same manner as a regular unit of light infantry. The base colour of the uniform will be green and will in all respects conform to the model approved by the Minister of War Administration.

As described below, the Regiment acquired a 4th Battalion in 1809. Its establishment was ultimately increased to six battalions in 1810.

Commanders *30 September 1805–13 February 1809*: Colonel Godefroy Maurice Marie Joseph de La Tour d'Auvergne (1770–1837). The Prince's service record states that, as a practical matter, he actually stopped functioning as the Regiment's commander in May 1808. *13 February 1809–31 March 1812 and 8 April 1813–1814*: Colonel Louis Pierre Milcolombe Drummond de Melfort (1760–1833), an émigré whose last military service prior to joining the Regiment had been in 1791. He was removed from command in 1812 amid allegations of fraud involving regimental funds, but he was restored to command after being exonerated by a commission of inquiry. *31 March 1812–8 April 1813*: Colonel Jean Baptiste Danlion (1770–1853), who had been Lieutenant-Colonel (*Colonel en second*) under Colonel Drummond de Melfort. When his predecessor returned to the unit, Danlion was transferred to command of the 18th Light.

Operational History La Tour d'Auvergne's Regiment was organised at Strasbourg and then Wissembourg in the late months of 1805 and the early ones of 1806 under the auspices of Marshal Kellerman. (Report of 21 December 1805, Nap. *P&T*, No 243, Vol. 1, pp. 163–4.) Within the Regiment itself, many details of its organisation are reputed to have been handled by ex-emigré Battalion Chief (later General) Charles-Marie-Robert Escorches de Sainte-Croix (1782–1810) rather than by the Colonel. (Dard, p.

211.) The exclusive recruiting of German volunteers turned out to be an ambitious objective, so the Colonel requested, and received, permission in February of 1806 to recruit prisoners of Russian as well as German origin, both of which were in plentiful supply. (Order of 12 February 1806, Nap. *O&A*, No 3344, Vol. 3, p. 96.) The Colonel also had a run-in with Napoleon when he tried to introduce the rank of 'cadet' for his unit and make some other slight modifications in its make-up. The message from the Emperor was very clear: 'Monsieur de La Tour d'Auvergne is not permitted either to establish a corps of cadets or to deviate in any fashion from the organisation specified for a French [Light Infantry] unit.' (Order of 26 February 1806, Nap. *O&A*, No 3345, Vol. 3, p. 96.)

The 1st Battalion was fully staffed by late February and was immediately dispatched to join the French forces in the Italian Peninsula. (N. to Dejean, 11 March 1806, Nap. *P&T*, No 321, Vol. 1, p. 203.) The earliest recruits for the nascent 3rd Battalion were then reassigned to the 2nd in order to speed its completion so that it, too, could set out for Italy, albeit by way of the South of France. Along the way, these units were ordered to incorporate some German soldiers who had been removed from the Vistula Legion in an attempt to enhance the homogeneity of that latter corps. (Decision of 30 April 1806, Nap. *P&T*, No 412, Vol. 1, p. 247.) By May the 1st Battalion was in Ancona, where it attracted some Imperial wrath: '[E]xpress my displeasure to the Colonel of the Regiment of La Tour d'Auvergne on account of the bad discipline of the battalion of this regiment which is at Ancona.' (N. to Dejean, 30 May 1806, Nap. *P&T*, No 466, Vol. 1, p. 248.)

This indiscipline extended to the ranks of the Regiment's officers as well. In the spring of 1806 rumours abounded that the Colonel and his second-in-command, Lieutenant-Colonel Sicaud de Mariole, a distant cousin of the Empress, were supplementing their incomes by selling commissions in the Regiment. These accusations were so prevalent that they were apparently common knowledge; one cadet at Fontainebleau military school wrote home on 28 May 1806 that 'the officers of . . . La Tour d'Auvergne's regiment owe their nominations to their money.' (Malhet, p. 69.) When the Lieutenant-Colonel claimed Sainte-Croix (who had been promoted to Major) was guilty of the same conduct, the latter challenged his superior to a duel and shot him dead. (Dard, pp. 213–15.) As Baron Marbot tells the story, misbehaviour by the dead man's supporters caused the Paris police authorities to believe at first that Sainte-Croix had fired a second shot after his opponent had fallen and so was guilty of murder. Police Minister Fouché was, however, a friend of Sainte-Croix's family, and his influence led to a more thorough investigation which cleared the officer of wrongdoing and permitted him to return to active service. (Marbot, pp. 362–3.) This outcome may also have been desirable from an official point of view because it allowed the regime to play down the underlying administrative scandal.

By the end of September 1806 all three battalions of the Regiment (having a combined strength of over 2,300 officers and men) were present and ready for duty in the Kingdom of Naples, having been hurried there to reinforce the French army of occupation after its setback at the Battle of Maida. (N. to Dejean, 3 September 1806, Nap. *P&T*, No 617, Vol. 1, p. 323.) A biography of Sainte-Croix states that the unit was involved in a number of combats against Neapolitan insurgents during the summer and autumn, but these did not leave any trace in terms of officer casualties. (Dard, p. 215.) Despite the Emperor's orders prohibiting officers of the Regiment from receiving staff positions, Sainte-Croix accompanied Marshal Masséna to Poland in 1807 as one of his ADCs, but the Regiment remained in Naples. The three battalions were often dispersed in different locations and were frequently involved in deadly (and unglamorous) actions against the Neapolitan loyalists, who refused to accept the new regime imposed by Napoleon and waged a bloody guerrilla war against its supporting French troops. This hard service left the Regiment in administrative disarray, lacking pay, supplies and clothing, while its erstwhile leader, Colonel La Tour d'Auvergne, enjoyed the comforts of the City of Naples.

When King Joseph Napoleon finally found time to take note of this situation, he found it intolerable and arranged for Major Sainte-Croix to be sent back to the Regiment in February of 1808 to take effective command. (Dard, p. 215.) Sainte-Croix was generally successful in reimposing order and discipline on the unit even though he faced the unique difficulty that the vast majority of his men did not understand the French language. He solved his linguistic problems to a great extent by using a few native Frenchmen in key administrative positions, but that expedient ran foul of the military bureaucrats who pointed out that, aside from its officers, the Regiment was supposed to be recruited exclusively from foreigners. Napoleon himself finally had to grant specific permission for the unit to retain two French-speaking NCOs to assist the Regimental Quartermaster. (Decision of 3 September 1808, Nap. *P&T*, No 2252, Vol. 2, p. 421.)

Unfortunately, the nature of the warfare in which the unit was engaged made it impossible for Sainte-Croix to solve all its behavioural problems. When some men from the Regiment were murdered near Lagonegro in November 1808, King Joachim ordered an investigation, but he also offered the comment that 'the Regiment of La Tour d'Auvergne has conducted itself so badly that I would not be surprised to find that the motive for the attack was vengeance on the part of the inhabitants of this commune.' (Murat to Saliceti, 29 November 1808, Murat *Lettres*, No 3629, Vol. 8, p. 430.) Nevertheless, the Neapolitan Minister of War noted less than a month later that the Regiment was impressive and showed 'excellent' spirit. (Quoted in Rambaud, p. 270.) As a result, the élite companies of the Regiment were chosen to serve as a temporary Royal Guard for King Joachim while his own units were being organised. (Rigo, *Le Plumet*, Plate U35.)

Major Sainte-Croix was never promoted for his efforts, so when Colonel Drummond de Melfort joined the Regiment in early 1809 he took final leave and joined the staff of Marshal Masséna with the Grand Army. (Sainte-Croix' superb performance in the

1809 campaign against Austria brought him swift promotion to the rank of General, but he was killed in action in Portugal in 1810, still serving under Masséna.) The duties of the Regiment remained unchanged, except that some of its individual actions were becoming more noteworthy, such as an ambush near San-Marco-de-la-Catola in Calabria which cost the 1st Battalion a large number of casualties (including two wounded officers) on 4 June 1809. The attrition suffered through this constant combat and through a significant amount of desertion led to a peculiar decision by Napoleon to allow the Regiment to recruit from Spanish prisoners of war, although in practice the Regiment seems to have focused on the enlistment of non-Spanish POWs only. (Decision of 7 January 1809, Nap. *P&T*, No 2628, Vol. 2, p. 604.)

Ironically, the Regiment also underwent its first official increase in size in 1809. Realising that his victories over the Hapsburg armies had resulted in an inordinate number of Austrian prisoners, the ever-calculating Emperor decided to recruit a 4th Battalion for the Regiment from this manpower pool. The new Battalion was raised at Belfort, but instead of being sent to join the Regiment in Naples it was detached for service in Spain. (Belhomme, Vol. 4, p. 459.) It initially formed part of General Georges Joseph Dufour's division of General Junot's new 8th Corps, but it was eventually assigned to the 7th Corps serving in Catalonia. The Battalion was not recalled to Naples until June 1811, when it was caught up in the general reorganisation of the French armies which Napoleon undertook in anticipation of war with Russia.

The Regimental highlight of 1810 was the concentration of all six élite companies of the Battalions in Naples as part of the force designated by King Joachim to invade Sicily. Elements of the Franco-Neapolitan invasion force actually managed to get ashore in Sicily briefly on 17 September 1810, but they were defeated by a British counterattack and forced to re-embark, albeit with significant losses, including the colour of the Royal Corsican Regiment. (*Le Plumet*, Plate U35.) By a decree dated 6 October 1810 the establishment of the Regiment was reorganised to include six battalions of six companies each. (N. to Minister of War, 17 October 1810, Nap. *P&T*, No 4723, Vol. 3, p. 832.) When the first five battalions were assembled at Montelevra in March 1811, they had an aggregate strength of 52 officers and 3,368 men. The newly raised 6th Battalion was at the same time at Salerno with eight officers and 827 men. (*Le Plumet*, Plate U35.)

This was an impressive force, in terms of both size and quality, especially as compared to the average unit of the Neapolitan Army. That circumstance led King Joachim to make another of his several unsuccessful requests to have the Regiment transferred to his service. (Decision of 8 June 1811, Nap. *P&T*, No 4521, Vol. 4, p. 349.) Instead, Napoleon withdrew the Regiment from Naples and used all six of its battalions to form the second brigade of the Observation Corps of Central Italy. (Order of 24 June 1811, Nap. *Inédits*, No 466, Vol. 1, pp. 131–2.) It was also renamed as the 1st Foreign Regiment in August of 1811. Since it was intended to be used primarily for the defence of Tuscany and the Kingdom of Italy, Napoleon decided that the unit should no longer accept Austrian recruits, since that nation was likely to figure prominently in any attack on Italy. (N. to Minister of War, 11 August 1811, Nap. *Corr.*, No 18021, Vol. 22, p. 396.)

The unit was thereafter moved north in the Italian peninsula and spent much of 1812 in Florence. Because of Napoleon's views about the Regiment, it escaped inclusion in the Russian campaign and was left free to be preoccupied with a scandal involving Colonel Drummond de Melfort, who was alleged to have embezzled some 60,000 Francs from Regimental funds. (Minutes of a Meeting of the Council of Ministers, 26 February 1812, Nap. *P&T*, No 6840, Vol. 5, p. 174–5.) On a more mundane level, the Regimental establishment was increased by the addition of an artillery company armed with two 6-pound cannon. (N. to Minister of War, 23 March 1812, Nap. *P&T*, No 7259, Vol. 5, p. 379.) The guns were commanded by Lieutenant Schwerghaust and manned by three sergeants, three corporals and 56 cannoneers. (*Le Plumet*, Plate U35.)

Despite the magnitude of his Russian disaster, Napoleon apparently never seriously considered employing the Regiment as part of his reconstructed Grand Army in 1813. It remained instead in effective exile through the spring and summer until the impending defection of Austria made it imperative for the Emperor to make some use of the unit. The surprising twist was that he did so by detaching the Regiment's twelve Grenadier and Voltigeur companies and organising them into two independent élite battalions which were assigned to the Reserve Division of the Army of Italy. (Vignolles, p. 20.) They first saw action against the Austrian forces attacking from the Tyrol, but this start was not auspicious: a company of Voltigeurs of the Regiment assigned to the fort of Muhlbach surrendered on 11 September after presenting only minimal resistance. (Cayron, 'Ramaeckers,' p. 259.) The two battalions did, however, fight well at Brixau on 3 October, where they had three officers wounded, and at Muhlbach again on 7 October. They had eleven officer casualties at Alba on 10 November. As the military situation deteriorated, even the battalions which had been initially left behind found themselves in combat defending against the combined Austrian and Neapolitan advance from the south. The centre companies of the 5th Battalion were surrounded and destroyed or dispersed at Forli on Christmas Day. (Vignolles, p. 106.)

Final Transformation Despite the fact that they were then engaged in active service against the enemy, the men of the Regiment were not exempted from Napoleon's decree of 25 November 1813 calling for the disarmament of most foreign troops. On 1 January 1814 General Jean Montfalcun assembled the third to sixth battalions of the Regiment at Legnano and used them (along with the nationals of enemy countries in the first two battalions) to form a single battalion of pioneers which was marched off to Alexandria on the way to France. (Carles II, p. 59.) The two remaining Battalions of the Regiment, supplemented by incorporation of the surviving members of the élite company battalions and of the soldiers from the élite companies of the 2nd Foreign Regiment, were spared the indignity of being disarmed and remained with Prince

Eugene's main army. They fought on until Napoleon's abdication, seeing noteworthy action (and suffering five officer casualties) in the French victory at the Battle of the Mincio on 8 February 1814. (Vignolles, p. 191.)

When it was repatriated to France in May 1814, the Regiment still had 24 officers and 446 men (Carles II, p. 60), but that number swiftly diminished through voluntary discharges and desertion. The new government spent some time considering whether it should keep some foreign regiments on the military establishment and ultimately decided in December 1814 to maintain three of them, numbered 1, 2 and 3, so the Regimental number lived on. (Carles II, p. 62.) There is, however, no evidence that the new 1st Foreign Regiment had anything substantive in common with the Regiment of La Tour d'Auvergne.

Uniforms As noted above, the decree forming the Regiment specified that it was to wear a green uniform. The Bucquoy Card Series covering the Regiment fills in the details with lavish specificity, citing information obtained from a portrait (and accompanying papers) of Baron Chrétien Léopold de Dettlingen, who joined the Regiment as a lieutenant in 1805 and eventually rose to command of the 6th Battalion in 1813. (This series is reproduced in Bucquoy, *L'Infanterie*, pp. 124-129.) Unfortunately, the whereabouts of these materials is currently unknown, so it is impossible to verify precisely how much of the information in Buquoy's prints comes directly from the Dettlingen primary source and how much was added by Buquoy for the sake of completeness. However, Bucquoy does state that his print of the Regiment's 'Adjutant-Major en petite tenue' is an exact copy of the portrait of Baron de Dettlingen. The Bucquoy cards give the following uniform information:

Adjutant-Major Dettlingen in Undress Uniform Black bicorne hat worn perpendicular to shoulders with tall green plume and cockade on front left secured by a strip of silver lace held by a silver button; green jacket with green pointed cutaway lapels, red closed collar and round cuffs, green cuff flaps and long tails with green turnbacks, all with white piping; white vest; buff breeches; black hussar-style boots with silver trim and tassel; silver gorget; silver fringed epaulette on right shoulder and epaulette without fringe on left; sabre worn from wide white belt worn over right shoulder.

Carabinier, 1805 Bearskin cap without plate, red cords and raquette on right side, red plume on left; jacket as for Dettlingen except red fringed epaulettes on both shoulders, green round cuff and red cuff flap; green breeches; short black gaiters with red trim and tassel; white crossbelts. The Dettlingen source also shows another Carabinier, this time with an 1806 Model shako with red plume and cords and brass shako plate and chinscales. This figure is wearing a white waistcoat with sleeves and a red collar and red epaulettes. He is also wearing white overalls over white gaiters.

Voltigeur, 1805 Early-model shako with green cords and green-tipped yellow plume on left side over cockade held in place by a strip of green lace; jacket as for the Carabinier but green epaulettes with yellow fringe; otherwise same as the Carabinier except green trim and yellow tassel on gaiters and yellow sword knot on sabre.

Fusilier (Chasseur), 1805 Black bicorne hat worn parallel to shoulders with green plume; jacket as for the Voltigeur except white epaulettes; otherwise same as the Voltigeur except white overalls and white sword knot on sabre.

Colonel Bucquoy, Rigo (*Le Plumet*, Plate U35), Richard Knötel (*Uniformenkunde*, Vol. XII, Plate 33) and Roger Forthoffer (*Fiches Documentaires*, Nos. 210–14: Le 1er Régiment Étranger [Regt. de la Tour d'Auvergne]) all depict a number of other uniform variants attributed to the Regiment, but, with a few partial exceptions, none of these is supported by citations to primary sources. Most are based on the paper soldiers depicting the Regiment which were painted by Theodore Carl at the end of the nineteenth century. Although Carl was probably acquainted with the artist, Henri Ganier-Tanconville, who is reported by Bucquoy to have been the owner of the Dettlingen materials, there is no indication that Carl thereby knew of any primary information which was not used by Bucquoy.

Rigo states that Regiment received the 1812 Model Light Infantry uniform (in green rather than blue, with a plain green pointed cuff) during the course of 1813, but does not cite any specific source for that proposition. He also mentions at the top of his plate a contemporary Austrian engraving in the Heeresgeschichtliches Museum in Vienna, but never indicates which figures in his print are based on that source.

Standard Charrié states unequivocally that the Regiment received three Eagles and accompanying colours near the end of 1806, of which one Eagle was still in use in 1812. (Charrié p. 170.) He also says the Regiment ultimately received one 1812 Model standard (without battle honours) with the legend 'L'EMPEREUR NAPOLÉON/AU 1ER RÉGIMENT ÉTRANGER'.

Régiment de Prusse

(Prussian Regiment)

Date of Creation November 1806.

Circumstances of Creation By means of a letter from Marshal Berthier dated 13 November 1806, the Prince of Isenburg, the Colonel of the Regiment in French service bearing his name (see separate entry), was notified that Napoleon wanted him to form another mercenary regiment, this one to be composed of citizens of Prussia. (The letter is quoted in Pigeard, 'Régiment de Prusse', p. 17.) Napoleon's instructions specified that the officers were to be selected from among the Prussian prisoners of war, but that the recruits for the other ranks should be chosen exclusively from those Prussian soldiers who had deserted before they were included in a capitulation or surrender. The Prince was given full discretion to name the unit's colonel and all of its officers. The letter also authorised the Prince to create a second regiment on the same basis if the establishment of the first was successful.

Composition The unit was intended to have four battalions, but only three were raised at first. There is no clear evidence as to whether the Prussian Regiment was organised as a light or a line infantry formation.

Commanders *13 November 1806–January 1808:* Colonel (later Brigade General) the Prince of Isenburg (see biographical details under the separate entry for his own Regiment). *29 January 1808–August 1813:* Colonel Fortuné Antoine Rodolphe de Hartmanis (1765–1825), a Swiss native who had served in the French Army under the Bourbon monarchy. On 1 July 1813 Napoleon wrote to his Minister of War that he had been informed that the Colonel of the 4th Foreign Regiment (whose name was tactfully omitted from the official edition of Napoleon's letters) had never been under fire, did not project a professional image and had a wife who meddled in the affairs of the Regiment. (N. to Minister of War, Nap. *Corr.*, No 20213, Vol. 25, p. 449.) These accusations may not all have been strictly true (since, for instance, Hartmanis had been in action in 1799–1800), but they sealed his fate from the point of view of the military hierarchy. Napoleon went on to recommend that the unit should be given a French Colonel: 'It is a good unit and should have a good commander.' *6 August 1813 to disbandment:* Colonel Jean Falba (1766–1848), who had served over fifteen years in the Marine Artillery.

Operational History Formation of the unit took place in Leipzig in November and December of 1806. The Prince of Isenburg himself composed a recruiting poster which ended which the exhortation to all 'valiant warriors' to 'rally to the standards of Napoleon the Great and follow his steps which will guide you to victory and immortal renown.' (Pigeard, 'Régiment de Prusse', p. 18.) The Prince's recruiting efforts, aided by a bounty of 12 francs per man, were so successful that the unit was quickly organised. As a reward, the Prince of Isenburg was promoted to the rank of Brigade General on 16 December.

A member of the Leipzig municipal council recorded, however, that this success was owed in no small part to subversion of Napoleon's intention to recruit only former members of the Prussian Army. Instead, the Prince's recruiters enlisted all volunteers without regard to nationality, even though some were 'suspect individuals and vagabonds'. (Gross, p. 11.) Counsellor Gross also reported that the presence of the Regiment created substantial economic hardship for many of Leipzig's inhabitants because the soldiers were billeted in private homes and the municipal government had to subsidise the cost of feeding the Prince and his '72 officers, 274 non-commissioned officers and more than 2,000 men, without counting women and children, since many of these soldiers were married'. (Gross, p. 12.)

Thanks to the direct complaints of Leipzig's own sovereign, the King of Saxony, Napoleon agreed to transfer the Regiment to a garrison post. Once that decision was made, Napoleon expected instantaneous compliance; when it was not forthcoming he fired off a scathing note to his Minister of War: 'I cannot understand why this unit is still at Leipzig. Who is this Prince of Isenburg that he thinks he can disobey my orders?' (N. to Minister of War, 28 March 1807, Nap. *Corr.*, No 12211, Vol. 14, p. 565.) Not everyone welcomed the unit's departure, however, because (Gross, pp. 12–13):

> Isenburg's soldiers, with their handsome green uniforms, had made many amorous conquests, particularly from among the ranks of the town's cooks. . . . Many of these women, sobbing torrents of tears, accompanied the Regiment right up to the gate of Ranstadt.

As the different battalions of the Regiment made their way into French territory, the unit again found itself a target of Imperial ire. As Napoleon himself explained matters in a letter to Dejean dated 3 May 1807, rumours had started that the Emperor was taking a particular interest in the new Prussian formation (Nap. *Corr.*,No 12519, Vol. 15, p. 181):

> I see that in all the newspapers the 1st Prussian Regiment in French Service is being referred to as the 'Régiment Napoléon'. Find out immediately for me who has been so abusing my name.'

He was right to be concerned about the connection.

The unit lost literally hundreds of men through desertion on the march out of Germany, which was marked by all sorts of irregularities on the part of the officers and men. This behaviour can be blamed in part on the lack of proper administration for the Regiment. In an inspection report dated 6 June 1807 General Gouvion St-Cyr recorded that the men of the Regiment were for the most part badly clothed, including some who were 'nearly naked', while in the absence of the Colonel there existed 'not a trace' of good organisation or normal administration. (Pigeard, 'Le Régiment de Prusse', p. 18.) In the circumstances, one might speculate that Napoleon had ulterior motives when he assigned the Prussians to the unhealthy garrison post of Flushing on Walcheren Island in the Scheldt estuary in October 1807. The Regiment nevertheless had an impressive paper strength of over 2,700 officers and men when it was reviewed on 19 November 1807. (Pigeard, 'Le Régiment de Prusse', p. 18.)

The New Year of 1808 produced some positive developments for the Regiment: Colonel Hartmanis took command in January and the 1st Battalion was assigned to active duty with the French forces heading for Spain. It was attached to the 3rd Division of Marshal Moncey's Coast Observation Corps and consequently took part in both the suppression of the 2 May revolt in Madrid (during which two officers were wounded) and in Moncey's unsuccessful offensive against Valencia in June (in which it suffered no officer casualties). When the French were pushed back to the line of the Ebro River following the French defeat at Bailen, the Prussians were detached for garrison duty at Vitoria and therefore missed participating in Napoleon's whirlwind reconquest of northern and central Spain in November. In January 1809 the battalion was reassigned to Burgos, where it remained for the rest of the year. The unit was severely disorganised when it arrived, apparently as a result of the incompetence of Battalion Chief Lagerstrom, but it recovered quickly following his removal. By 17 July 1809 the battalion was 'fully uniformed, armed, equipped and trained'. (Inspection Report quoted in Pigeard, 'Le Régiment de Prusse', p. 19.)

The 2nd and 3rd Battalions, which had remained behind in Flushing, mustered collectively over 1,700 effectives when the British attacked in the summer of 1809. (Bond, p. 208.) The Prussians participated actively in the town's defence and suffered a total of ten officer casualties (all wounded). The surviving members of the Prussian contingent became British prisoners of war (and potential recruits for some of England's foreign military units such as the King's German Legion) when Flushing surrendered on 15 August.

The two battalions which had been destroyed were reconstructed by means of men from the Regimental depot and some liberal recruiting which further diminished the percentage of Prussian natives in the unit. In early 1810 the new 2nd Battalion was posted to Spain and achieved some distinction along the way by virtue of the quantity and infamous nature of the depredations it committed while *en route* through France. When asked to approve the exemplary punishments imposed on the worst offenders, Napoleon added the editorial comment: 'In general, it seems that such troops will make things worse rather than better in Spain.' (Decision of 15 May 1810, Nap. *P&T*, No 4223, Vol. 3, p. 558.) The new 2nd Battalion was coincidentally brigaded with the 4th Battalion of the Isembourg Regiment for service against the guerrillas in Navarre. Both units became renowned for the number of deserters they lost, many of whom ended up fighting for the very guerrillas who were target of the French forces. (Martin, *Gendarmerie*, p. 222.) The 2nd Battalion nevertheless had five officers wounded in separate small skirmishes during that summer.

The 1st Battalion, on the other hand, was proving its worth in Leon and Castille at the same time that the 2nd Battalion was failing so miserably in Navarre. At the start of 1810 it was assigned to active duty with General Junot's 8th Corps of the Army of Portugal. That force was given the task of capturing the town of Astorga as a preliminary to the main campaign of the year. Spanish resistance was determined, but on 21 April the élite companies of the Battalion helped spearhead a successful assault on the town. The Prussians lost one officer killed and two wounded in the action.

On 5 August the Emperor ordered the amalgamation of the two battalions in Spain so that the Prussian Regiment 'will have only two battalions, one in Spain and the other in Walcheren Island'. (N. To Minister of War, Nap. *Corr.*, No 16763, Vol. 21, pp. 20–2 at 22.) This statement reveals that even Napoleon could not keep track of all the individual sub-units of his army because there was, in fact, another battalion of the Prussian Regiment (intended to be No 4) then being formed at Lille. When he discovered this information a month later, Napoleon's response was rigorously consistent with his prior views: 'I have no need of a fourth Prussian battalion. All the men should be sent to "Dutch" regiments.' (Decision of 13 September 1810, Nap. *P&T*, No 4579, Vol. 3, p. 755.)

The combined Prussian Battalion in Spain apparently participated actively in the whole of Masséna's unsuccessful invasion of Portugal in 1810–11. Early in the campaign the Prussians saved the artillery and baggage of the 8th Corps from a surprise attack by Portuguese militia. (Gallaher, p. 135.) It was present at Bussaco with a strength of 29 officers and 957 men (according to returns in the French National Archives cited in Oman, Vol. 3, p. 542), but Junot's corp was played only a reserve role in that action. Nevertheless, the course of the campaign in general was so gruelling that by 1 January 1811 the same source reports that the unit had seven fewer officers and just over 600 fewer men. When the Army of Portugal returned to Spain in the spring of 1811, the Prussians were added to the garrison of Ciudad Rodrigo, so they missed the Battle of Fuentes de Oñoro. They did, however, fight a sharp action of their own on 18 June near Ciudad Rodrigo which cost them one officer killed and four wounded, one mortally.

From the summer of 1811 onwards both Battalions of the Regiment remained relegated to garrison duty. This continued to be true even after Napoleon included the unit in the French military establishment on a permanent basis in August as the 4th Foreign Regiment. The Battalion in Spain continued to waste away, but there were gains in strength elsewhere as Napoleon reversed his earlier views and ordered his Minister of War to bring the unit up to the five-battalion establishment norm for French infantry regiments. (Letter of 11 August 1811, Nap. *Corr.*, No 18021, Vol. 22, pp. 395–7 at 396.) He stated that it was particularly important for the Prussian Regiment to retain its German-speaking character because he intended to use it—and, incidentally, the 3rd Foreign Regiment (former Irish Legion)—primarily to guard the coast of Holland.

In 1812, the Prussians saw combat only in Spain, and the results were shameful. The 4th Battalion was assigned to some defensive works guarding an important bridge crossing over the Tagus River at Almaraz that had become the target of a British strike force under General Sir Rowland Hill. The British stormed a fort south of the river and then began to bombard the one on the northern shore garrisoned by the Prussians. (See, generally, Oman, Vol. 5, pp. 327–9.) The French commander, who was the Captain of the Prussian Carabinier company (possibly named Bracen), panicked and abandoned his post, losing in the process the regimental cash-box and accounts. (Inspection Report dated 22 September 1812, quoted in Pigeard, 'Le Régiment Prusse', p. 19.) More importantly, the Battalion's standard was captured by the 71st Regiment of Foot (although it is unclear whether this trophy was actually captured by the British or merely recovered by the victors from the Tagus River, where it had been thrown by the Russians). (Report of General Hill, 21 May 1812, reproduced at www.ifbt.co.uk/wpe76830.gif.) According to one source, the officer in question was tried for cowardice and shot. (Sarramon, *La Bataille des Arapiles*, p. 25.) In any event the Battalion, completely demoralised and plagued by desertion, was finished as a fighting force. The few survivors were sent packing back to the regimental depot at Lille.

Given this development, it is perhaps surprising to find the re-formed 1st Battalion, along with the existing 5th, receiving a favourable inspection report in November of 1812. Noting that these units were recruited in large part from deserters from foreign armies and prisoners of war, the presiding Inspector of Reviews concluded that the men were generally experienced and well-disciplined and would probably be a reliable force as long as they were watched carefully. (Pigeard, 'Le Régiment de Prusse', p. 19.) Nevertheless, the Inspector did conclude that there were 'a certain number of officers from Prussia and from countries at war with France who could not be counted on completely.'

On the basis of such information, Napoleon apparently gave serious consideration to employing the Prussians with the Grand Army to help make up the disastrous losses of the Russian campaign. (N. to Minister of War, 24 December 1812, Nap. *O&A*, No 5872, Vol. 3, p. 333.) After further enquiry, however, the Emperor decided against using the unit in Germany: 'If the men are mostly Prussian, they will not be worth anything and they should be left in Holland.' (Decision of 12 January 1813, Nap. *Inédits*, No 704, Vol. 1, p. 204.) The last time the unit is known to have seen action was in the defence of Woerden in Holland on 24 November 1813.

Final Transformation By a decree dated 25 November 1813 Napoleon ordered the disarming of all soldiers in his army who were subjects of one of the countries then in coalition against him. As a result, the Prussian Regiment was officially disbanded, the loyal men being assigned to the 3rd Foreign Regiment and those that were suspect being posted to a new Foreign Pioneer Regiment formed at Arras on 19 December. (Fieffé, Vol. 2, p. 186.) The decree had no effect, however, on the two understrength battalions besieged in Holland with Colonel Falba, which survived intact until the coming of peace. (Carles I, p. 60.)

Uniforms The uniform of the Prussian Regiment is remarkably well-documented given the sometimes obscure history of the unit. The key source of information is a detailed print issued *circa* 1807 in Leipzig by a publisher named Geissler. This print—which is reproduced in colour in Pigeard, 'Le Régiment de Prusse', p. 19—bears the title (in German) 'First Prussian Regiment in French Service, organised in Leipzig by the Prince of Isenburg'. It depicts an officer, four soldiers and two musicians of the Regiment and presents the following details concerning the unit's uniforms:

Officer (left profile) Large, black bicorne hat worn 'fore-and-aft' (and only shown from the back) with a tall green plume and two gold stripes in the middle of the brim (presumably representing visible portions of the cords used to hold it in shape); green jacket with red collar, square cuffs, long turnbacks and straight, closed lapels having seven yellow buttons on each side; green breeches; and black boots with gold trim and a small tassel. The officer is also wearing a large gold gorget with a crowned and wreathed 'N' decoration; a black sabre belt with a square gold plate (bearing the same decoration) and a sabre with a silver scabbard; and a gold aiguilette worn from the right shoulder with three strands looping across his breast to buttons on the left side of the lapel. There is no ornamentation at all on the officer's left shoulder.

Non-Commissioned Officer (full face) Same uniform as for the officer except for a tall black cylindrical (Prussian model) shako with tall green plume, blue, red and white (from inside out) cockade at top of front, gold trimmed visor, three strips of gold lace

around the top (the middle one bigger than the other two), two strips around the bottom, gold trim on visor, gold diamond-shaped plate and a single strand of gold and green mixed cord hanging across the front, with two gold and green raquettes (one long and one short) on the right side and one short raquette on the left; green shoulder straps fastened with a button near the collar; two straight gold chevrons with red trim placed on a diagonal above the right cuff; white shoulder-belt worn over the right shoulder holding an infantry sabre. This figure is holding a wood cane.
Grenadier (full face) Same as for NCO except no lace on shako, red cords and plume and the shako plate appears to be a somewhat different, but indistinct, shape (a grenade device?); white crossbelts; short gaiters with red trim and a musket.
Voltigeur (rear view) Same as for Grenadier except yellow cords and plume for shako (plate not shown); one long (elbow length) loop of yellow cord hanging from right shoulder; black cartridge box; short jacket tails which do not descend below the cartridge box, red turnbacks; yellow trim on short gaiters; brown scabbard for infantry sabre. This figure is distinctly shorter than the other infantrymen.
Fusilier(?) (partial figure) Same as for Grenadier except white plume and cords and same shako plate as NCO.
Drummer (full face) Same as for Fusilier except no shako cords; two contiguous bands of lace around shako below cockade, the upper one white with red edging (Type 1 lace) and the lower one white with repeating vertical red stripes (Type 2 lace); white coat with red collar, cuffs and lapels, all trimmed with Type 1 lace, which is also used for edging along the turnbacks and for five decorative bands on each sleeve; red 'swallow's-nest' on each shoulder trimmed on bottom edge with Type 2 lace over Type 1 lace; three buttons along cuff opening; single shoulder-belt with short sabre in brown scabbard; wide white drum belt with brown drumsticks; brass drum (carried on back) with red, white and blue triangles around upper rim. This figure is even shorter than the Voltigeur, suggesting that the artist was attempting to depict a drummer boy. Rigo purports to reproduce this drummer in *Le Plumet*, Plate No 4, but, based on a comparison of sources, it seems that he used Richard Knötel's plate of the Regiment (*Uniformenkunde*, Vol. 4, No 25) as the basis for his illustration. That is unfortunate because Knötel's version of the drummer, from the Geissler print, includes so many inexplicable variations from the original that it is wholly unreliable.
Musician (right profile) Bicorne hat as for officer; red single-breasted coat with green cuffs, turnbacks and turned-over collar with gold trim; white breeches; black boots with gold trim and tassels; single shoulder-belt over right shoulder.

The style and details of the uniforms in the Geissler print are corroborated by a set of line drawings in the Museum of the Battle of Nations in Leipzig. Two of these are reproduced in Pigeard, 'Le Régiment de Prusse', p. 18, and others are presented in facsimile in Fosten, pp. 18–20. The Fosten article reproduces in black-and-white some figures said to be illustrated in a contemporary watercolour painting of soldiers of the Regiment at Madrid in 1808. The shape and style of the uniform coats are the same as in the Geissler print, but the shakos, equipment and rank distinctions all have a strong French flavour.

Le Plumet, Plate No 4, by Rigo reproduces two Drum Major uniforms, one based on a drawing by Benjamin Zix dated late 1806 and the other based on a picture by Geissler from early 1807. Both uniforms feature a bicorne hat; white coat with red lapels, collar and cuffs, all outlined with thick gold braid; a gold aiguilette on the right shoulder and a gold trefoil shoulder strap on the left; green breeches; and hussar boots. The main difference between the two is that the coat in the Zix drawing is cut in traditional French line infantry style so that a green vest is visible, while the lapels of the Geissler coat are closed down to the waist. Neither original source could be traced by the author of this work, however, so the uniforms must remain in question until the sources can be found.

Several sources also show the uniform of a Sapper of the Prussian Regiment. While there is no reason to think that the Prussians did not have such specialists on the Regimental rolls, the only source given for this costume is a painted paper soldier in the Carl Collection in Strasbourg which is not contemporary to the Napoleonic Era.

The information from the Geissler print has been supplemented in recent times by the publication of photographs of a garment from a private collection which is identified as the jacket of a soldier of the Prussian Regiment. (Pigeard, 'Le Régiment de Prusse', p. 19.) The photographs show the coat from a number of different perspectives. Assuming that this identification is accurate, and that such jacket has not been materially altered over times, this artefact confirms the basic information about uniform style and colour which is presented by the Geissler print provide the following additional or conflicting points of detail:

(a) All the facings are outlined with thin white piping.
(b) The shape of the upper edges of the lapels is different from that in all other French uniforms.
(c) The yellow metal buttons are all plain and all one size.
(d) The cuff does not have a flap, but it does have a line of piping down the edge and two buttons.
(e) There are no devices in the turnbacks, but each pair is joined with a single button.
(f) There are two types of pockets in each coat-tail, each of which is outlined with white piping—a normal horizontal pocket and a vertical pocket '*à la soubise*'.
(g) There are no visible indications of the type of shoulder ornament which might have been worn with this jacket.

Various pieces of documentary evidence provide further details of the Regiment's dress. A letter dated 9 August 1807 from Dejean reports that out of a total of 1,712 men present, only 623 have the 'new uniforms' purchased by the Prince of Isenburg. The others are wearing 'old Prussian uniforms' of different types and colours. (French National Archives Carton AF IV 1117, as quoted in the manuscript notes in the sketchbooks of the French artist, E. Fort, which are currently in the Print Room of the French National Library.) That same source provides a letter from Clarke to Napoleon dated 28 December 1808 which suggests that the Regiment probably changed over to a French Light Infantry-style uniform in 1809:

> The Colonel of the Prussian Regiment has informed me that the cut of the jackets of this corps is bad and more expensive than that prescribed for light infantry since the lapels are straight and the same length as the vest. Since the rest of the uniform follows the French model, the Colonel has asked me to authorise the adoption of a French pattern for the jacket as well in the next distribution of clothing. The shakos that the corps received from Prussian stores are very bad and will not last the prescribed amount of time.

The Prussian Regiment may have lost its red lapels in the course of the changeover because a 2 June 1810 report specifies that the unit had green forage caps, beige overcoats and collars, cuffs, turnbacks and trim which were *rouge garance* in colour, but does not say anything about the lapels. (French National Archives Carton AF IV 1178.) Blondieau reports that when the unit changed to a French-style shako it had a diamond-shaped brass plate decorated with an eagle on top of the words 'Régiment de Prusse'. (Blondieau, p. 26.)

There is no reliable evidence which bears on the question of whether the 4th Foreign Regiment ever adopted the style of dress prescribed by the Bardin Regulations of 1812.

Standard The 1st Battalion received a large (162cm by 162cm) Model 1804 standard on 21 October 1807. (Charrié, p. 170.) On the face of the colour was the legend 'L'EMPEREUR/DES FRANÇAIS/AU RÉGIMENT/PRUSSIEN [sic]', while the wreaths in the corners were empty. The pole for the standard was, however, surmounted by a simple spear finial rather than an Eagle. The 2nd and 3rd Battalions had similar standards that were captured along with those units at Flushing in 1809. They were triumphantly displayed by the British in morale-building public ceremony in London on 18 May 1811. (Regnault, pp. 108 and 229–30.) The 4th Battalion lost its standard in 1812 at Almaraz. (All the details of design and decoration referred to above—except those relating to the finial—are confirmed by a small watercolour of one of the colours of the Regiment painted by Charles Hamilton Smith, the British military artist, who probably observed the display in London.)

On 12 April 1813 Napoleon authorised the granting of an Eagle to the 4th Foreign Regiment and the creation of the position of Eagle-bearer in its command structure. (Decision of 12 April 1813, Nap. *Inédits*, No 873, Vol. 1, p. 243.) There is, however, no evidence to indicate whether these instructions were ever carried out before the unit was disbanded.

Régiment de Westphalie

(Westphalian Regiment)

Date of Creation 11 December 1806.

Circumstances of Creation The Organisational Decree for this unit (Nap. *O&A*, No 5396, Vol. 4, pp. 54–5) records that the purpose for which it was created was to give employment to the numerous disbanded Prussian soldiers to be found in the territories west of the Elbe following the triumphant French pursuit of the Prussian Army after the Battles of Jena and Auerstadt.

Composition Napoleon's plans called for the creation of a light infantry regiment of four battalions, with each battalion composed of six companies and each company staffed by one captain, one lieutenant, one sub-lieutenant, one sergeant-major, one corporal-quartermaster (*caporal-fourier*), four sergeants, eight corporals, two drummers and 120 privates. Both the regimental and battalion staffs were same as for a French light infantry unit.

It has been suggested that the reason the battalions were formed with only six instead of nine companies (when the latter was the then normal complement of companies for a French infantry unit) was that Napoleon intended that the Regiment would not have any élite companies. In reality, archival materials indicate that each battalion had a carabinier company early in its existence and that voltigeur companies were created in June 1807. (SHA Carton X[I]31.)

Commanders *1806–10:* Colonel Charles Antoine Frederick Meinrad Fidele, the Prince of Hohenzollern-Sigmaringen (1785–1853). This crown prince of a small German state married a niece of Marshal Murat in February 1808 and thereafter served as an ADC to his uncle-in-law and spent little time with his regiment. *1808–09:* On 13 October 1808, Frederick Hermann Othon, the Prince of Hohenzollern-Hechingen (1776–1838), was named as Colonel of the 1st Battalion of the Regiment despite the fact that the Regiment as a whole already had a Colonel, albeit one who was serving as a General in Murat's Neapolitan army. The Prince barely had time to join that unit in Spain before the Regiment was reduced to a single-battalion establishment, which development made his position redundant. *1807–10:* Originally the commander of the 4th Battalion raised in Erfurt and Fulda, Battalion Chief William Schenck served as the actual field commander of the whole unit during much of its existence.

Operational History Each of the four battalions was organised in a different location (i.e., the First Battalion at Münster, the Second at Minden, the Third at Brunswick and the Fourth split between Fulda [three companies] and Erfurt [three companies]). Recruiting for the Regiment proceeded very slowly in the winter of 1806/07, but it had reached a strength of over 3,000 when it was assembled in a single location for the first time near Aachen in May. (Woringer, p. 395.) That was to be Regiment's largest size ever, because desertion began to take a significant toll as soon as it was led off to new posts in France and Belgium. By 31 October 1807, its strength was so reduced that the

3rd and 4th Battalions had to be incorporated into the first two in order to produce two battalions of close to regulation size. (SHA Carton X[l]31.)

In November 1807 the 1st Battalion under Schenck was assigned to Marshal Adrien Moncey's Ocean Coast Observation Corps, which was one of the many peculiarly named formations Napoleon used in his build-up of forces aimed against Portugal and then, later, against his erstwhile Spanish allies. This corps moved into Spain in 1808 and on 17 March it was inspected by General Georges Mouton at the town of Aranda. Mouton wrote a favourable report about the Westphalians (which was copied by the artist, E. Fort, and can now be found in Fort's notebooks in the Print Division of the French Bibliothèque Nationale in Paris):

> [The unit has] 690 non-commissioned officers and men present under arms. The men are very handsome [*très beaux*] and the uniforms are reasonably good. This is the battalion in [Moncey's corps] which makes the best impression [*à le plus d'éclat]*. It is the only one that has a band.

General Mouton's judgments may have been somewhat relative, however, since all the other units in the Westphalians' division were provisional regiments created from scratch. The Regiment also had a drum major for its band, but he deserted (with his mace) in 1809. (Maempfel, p. 121.)

Following the replacement of the Spanish Bourbon dynasty in May by that of the Bonapartes, Marshal Moncey's corps was given the difficult job of pacifying the province of Valencia. Although he was heavily outnumbered, Moncey actually attempted to take the city of Valencia by storm on 28 June. The 1st Battalion was involved in some of the most severe fighting and lost a total of one officer killed and six wounded (three of whom subsequently died). Moncey's force was able to escape back to Madrid only through a combination of good luck and Spanish mistakes.

Meanwhile, back in Germany, Napoleon decided to use the 2nd Battalion to bolster the forces of his brother Jerome's new Kingdom of Westphalia. On 29 January 29 it was converted into the 2nd Line Regiment of the Westphalian Army, which gave good service until it was annihilated in the Battle of Leipzig in 1813. (Woringer, p. 395.)

The 1st Battalion participated in the French retreat from Madrid to the Ebro River after the disaster of Bailen, but when Napoleon took his reinforced army back on the offensive in the autumn of 1808 the Westphalians had only a supporting role. They were assigned to garrison duty in Vitoria, switching to Valladolid in January 1809. (N. to Berthier, Nap. *P&T*, No 2666, Vol. 2, p. 625–6 at 625.)

Colonel Hohenzollern-Sigmaringen made an effort to reinvigorate his command in March 1809 when he petitioned the Emperor for permission to recruit his unit back up to a strength of four battalions by voluntary enlistments. Napoleon astutely specified, however, that no recruiting could begin for a new battalion until all existing battalions were up to strength. (Decision of 10 March 1809, Nap. *P&T*, No 2913, Vol. 2, pp. 761–3 at 763.) The Colonel countered by obtaining permission on 29 March

1809 to recruit from soldiers of German origin who were captured while serving in the Spanish Army. (Nap. *P&T*, No 3037, Vol. 2, pp. 829–31 at 830.)

Final Transformation There is some fragmentary evidence that Prince Hohenzollern-Sigmaringen actually commenced the formation of a second battalion in the course of his initiative, but, ultimately, his efforts were not successful. On 30 September 1809 the Westphalian Battalion lost its independent existence and was incorporated into the Hanoverian Legion. (Despreaux, p. 398, n. 2.) This development may have had more theoretical than practical effect, however, because the units were serving in Spain, far from the watchful eye of Army administration. The memoir of a soldier serving in the Battalion (J. C. Maempfel) does not make any mention of the Hanoverian Legion during the period 1809–11, although it otherwise gives a multitude of details about the Westphalians' service in General Loison's division of the 6th Corps of the Army of Portugal, including the fact that the Regiment lost 48 men killed and wounded at Bussaco. (Maempfel, p. 193.)

Uniforms The Organisational Decree of the Westphalian Regiment was quite specific about the details of the uniform to be worn by the unit:

> XIII. The uniform will be white with red collar and cuffs; the jacket, headwear, armament and equipment will conform to the models used by Prussian infantry and the Regiment can therefore make use of captured material.

The peculiar circumstance of the unit being organised in five different locations by five different commanders could have been a recipe for confusion insofar as the actual uniforming of the Regiment was concerned. General Thiébault in Fulda, however, took the initiative of preparing uniform sketches and specifications which he then shared with the other commanders so that some co-ordination was achieved. (Thiébault, Vol. 4, p. 22.) His battalion was the first one completed (in February 1807), and, in his humble opinion, he found that its appearance was 'superb,' in terms of both its clothing and the quality of its rank-and-file soldiers.

Despite Thiébault's efforts, there was controversy over two particular elements of the unit's uniforms. (See, generally, SHA Carton X[l]31.) Some of the battalions had silver buttons and officer epaulettes, while others had gold, and at least three companies ended up with black belting, while the rest wore white. The Colonel requested a fashion ruling from the Minister of War and, on 8 June 1807, he received confirmation that yellow metal distinctions and white belts should prevail. A document in the archives dated 28 November 1807 notes that, true to the Organisational Decree, the jackets of the Westphalians were cut 'German-style', so that 'the lapels came together over the wearer's stomach all the way down to the waist'. The inspection report of General Mouton mentioned above provides the additional details that (a) 'the cartridge boxes were taken for the most part from Prussian magazines and are quite bad, particularly in terms of their shape', and (b) the men of the unit were wearing overalls and overcoats.

The uniforms of this unit are illustrated in *Le Plumet*, Plate No 65 (*Infanterie Légère: Régiment de Westphalie, Drapeau 1807–1815*). It is clear that the reality of campaigning wreaked havoc with such pristine clothing. The uniforms of the unit were in such bad condition in Spain that, after inspecting the unit at Valladolid, Napoleon ordered that the Regiment (by then reduced to a single battalion) be given enough cloth for 400 coats, vests, trousers and overcoats so that it would be completely re-uniformed within a month. (N. to Berthier, 13 January 1809, Nap. *P&T*, No 2666, Vol. 2, pp. 625–6.)

Standard Prince Hohenzollern-Sigmaringen tried his best to obtain an Eagle for his Regiment, but on 20 June 1807 Napoleon ruled that it could have a standard but not an Eagle. On 26 August, when the Minister of War Administration asked another question to clarify Napoleon's preference as to the dimensions of the standard, the Emperor responded that the 'old form' of standard should be used, a statement which Dejean interpreted as referring to the massive 5 foot by 5 foot flags used during the Revolution. Each battalion of the Regiment consequently received a colour of those dimensions, carried on a staff surmounted by a golden spearhead and decorated in the same manner as the 1804 Model French infantry standard. (Charrié, p. 171.) 'The colours were consecrated with the greatest pomp at Villefranche. The Regiment appeared in full dress and formed a square, with the colours in the centre and the officers standing around.' (Maempfel, p. 43.)

Régiment d'Illyrie

(Illyrian Regiment)

Date of Creation Decree of 16 November 1810.

Circumstances of Creation It is symptomatic of the treatment accorded to prisoners of war during the Napoleonic era that in January 1810, nearly six months after the end of active hostilities, Napoleon still held in France many thousands of captured Austrian soldiers. By an order dated 1 January Napoleon organised three battalions of prisoners who were natives of Illyria and sent them on their way home. At the same time, however, it seems that there were other Illyrian prisoners who were requesting the opportunity to serve with the French Army. To accommodate these men, Napoleon formed an additional two battalions (one at Dôle and the other at Besançon) of six companies each, which were designated the 1st and 2nd Illyrian Battalions. As soon as they were organised they were transferred to former Piedmontese fortress of Alexandria in Italy. (Belhomme, Vol. 4, p. 464.)

The two Illyrian Battalions languished there until the end of 1810, when Napoleon decided that he needed to do something more to turn them into a useful addition to his army. His solution was to use the two existing battalions as the foundation for a new Illyrian Regiment that would have four battalions and a depot. The Emperor intended that the Regiment would be populated exclusively of men from the non-frontier provinces of Illyria (i.e., the provinces that were not already supporting the Illyrian Chasseurs–see separate entry) as well as the territories of Istria and Fiume. (N. to Minister of War, 15 November 1810, Nap. *O&A*, No 4362, Vol. 2, p. 344.)

Composition The organisational minutes for the Illyrian Regiment, dated 22 January 1811, confirm that it was organised in the same manner as any other regiment of French light infantry. Each battalion had six companies, including one of carabiniers and one of voltigeurs. (A.G. Carton X[h]30.) One unusual feature of the Regiment was the composition of its officer corps. As Napoleon put it: 'My intention is that one-third of the officers will be French and the rest will be Belgian and French officers who have been in Austrian service . . .'. (N. to Minister of War, Nap. *O&A*, No 4566, Vol. 3, p. 401.)

Commanders *2 March 1811–16 June 1813*: Colonel Nicolas Schmitz (1768–1851), who started his military career as a private in the Bourbonnais Regiment of Infantry. A veteran of Austerlitz, Auerstadt and Eylau as a member of the 108th Line, he was promoted Colonel after a stint in Spain. He served actively with the regiment until he was wounded in the right leg at Krasnoi on 19 November 1812. He oversaw a minimal reconstitution of the Regiment in 1813 until he was promoted to the rank of Brigade General. *1 August 1813 to disbandment*: Colonel Jean Muller (1771–1835), who had been the Major of the Regiment since 1811. He was another veteran of the Revolutionary Wars who had soldiered with the 102nd Demi-brigade (later the 102nd Line) from 1796 until 1811.

Operational History The organisation of the Illyrian Regiment was so painfully slow that in April 1811 Napoleon appointed General Louis Baillet de Latour, a former Austrian general, to take special charge of the task. A little later Napoleon changed his mind and assigned the job to the former Prussian and Dutch General Erhard Gustave Wedel. By the end of July a total of five battalions had been organised, and they were assembled at Turin. (N. to Minister of War, Nap. *O&A*, No 4680, Vol. 3, p. 444.) They were short of officers, however, which led to an Imperial order permitting Illyrians who had been officers in the Austrian Army to serve in the Illyrian Regiment (but not, it was emphasised, in the Illyrian Chasseurs). (Decision of 2 August 1811, Nap. *P&T*, No 5898, Vol. 4, p. 533.)

Forward progress in organisation was matched with backward regression. Bored with garrison duty in a foreign land, the Regiment had a significant desertion problem. (Decision of 10 September 1811, Nap. *P&T*, No 6145, Vol. 4, p. 673.) There were also an amazing number of problems with the clothing for the unit: the jackets were too small and had not been properly lined, buttonholes had simply been cut out and not bound, shirts were too short, the shoes did not fit, the haversacks were of bad quality and less than half the required number of shakos had been delivered. (N. To Minister of War Administration, 10 September 1811, Nap. *O&A*, No 4741, Vol 3, pp. 463–4.) Amidst all the work there must have been some play, however, because one finds Colonel Schmitz requesting leave at the end of 1811 to travel to Paris to get married. (Decision of 16 January 1811, Nap. *P&T*, No 6656, Vol. 5, p. 54.)

After another six months of effort, four battalions were finally ready for active service, and they were assigned to Marshal Ney's Corps for the war against Russia. On 1 August 1812 the four war battalions had a combined strength of 65 officers and 2,505 men. (Nafziger, *Invasion of Russia*, p. 469.) The Illyrian Regiment missed much of the fighting in the first half of the campaign because it was assigned to garrison duty at Kovno and then at Minsk. It suffered enough attrition, however, to cause Napoleon to authorise the Regiment on 24 August to incorporate up to 500 Lithuanian recruits. (Order of the Day, Nap. *P&T*, No 7537, Vol. 5, p. 542.)

At least part of the Regiment re-joined Marshal Ney's Corps in time for the bloody Battle of Valutina-Gora (Lubino) on 19 August. A Württemberg officer on the scene recalled later that his own unit was spared a difficult task when the Illyrians rallied after an initial repulse to capture an important Russian position by moonlight in some of the last fighting of the day. (Suckow, pp. 171–2.) The Illyrians continued on to Moscow and suffered two officer casualties in combat near there on 16 October. The Regiment was committed to a full-scale action at Krasnoi on 16 November. The fighting was desperate, and so were the casualties suffered by the Illyrians. On that one day, no fewer than nine officers were killed and 23 wounded (nine of which subsequently died from their injuries).

The portion of the Regiment that stayed in the rear of the Grand Army survived longer than the portion that went forward, but the final result was the same. This force was sufficiently organised to put up cohesive resistance to the Russians during the stage of the retreat from Smorgony to Vilna from 3 to 11 December, but it suffered 23 officer casualties (thirteen of whom never recovered). The four battalions that had entered Russia had effectively ceased to exist.

The surviving battalion was attached to Marshal Oudinot's Corps for the 1813 campaign, which accounts for the fact that it did not see much action during the spring campaigning. The fighting after the end of the Armistice in August was, however, a different story. The battalion was attached to General Brun de Villeret's division, and it was present at both the Battle of Gross-Beeren and that of Dennewitz. General Brun recorded in his memoirs that Battalion Chief Louis Mattutinovich, the commander of the Illyrians, was galloping about in such a panicky fashion at one point during the latter action that Brun had to restore order by threatening to run the unfortunate officer through with a sabre if he did not dismount and take a proper station at the head of his men. (Brun de Villeret, *Cahiers*, pp. 158–9.) Eight officers were wounded in the battle, including Mattutinovich, who had begun his military career in the Venetian Navy, fought for the Austrians in 1800 and 1805 and only joined the French Army after the transfer of his Dalmatian homeland to France in 1806. He became a General in the Austrian Army after the fall of Napoleon, but this did not save him from being reminded of his cowardice and threatened with ejection from a nearby window when he met up again with Brun, still a Colonel, at the French Ministry of War and spoke to the Frenchman in a haughty tone.

The Illyrians had suffered heavily in the campaign, both from desertion and enemy fire, but it was still organised enough to be present at the Battle of Leipzig in October as part of a brigade of General Reynier's 7th Corps commanded by General Lejeune, the famous soldier, painter and memoirist. His memoirs are silent on the performance of the Illyrians during the Battle (in which five officers, including Battalion Chief Aubert, were wounded), but they do contain the unusual statement that the Illyrians were commanded by Colonel de Tromelin, the commander of 2nd Banat Regiment of Illyrian Chasseurs (see separate entry). (Lejeune, *Memoirs*, Vol. 2, p. 290.) There is no mention of this appointment in de Tromelin's service records.

Final Transformation Completely wasted from hard campaigning, the Illyrian Regiment was formally disbanded by the decree of 25 November 1813 and the remaining soldiers were ordered to Corsica to join the 2nd Colonial Battalion serving on that island. Some arrived at that destination; most did not make the trip, however, because they lacked proper clothing and shoes for the journey. (Fieffé, Vol. 2, p. 161.)

Uniforms The choice of uniform for the Regiment was a reflection of the stereotypical attitudes then prevailing about the relative merits of French versus foreign troops. Marshal Marmont proposed that they should have exactly the same dress as a regular French light infantry unit, because that would be 'an efficacious way to honour the Illyrians as well as to assimilate them with the rest of the Grand Army'. Napoleon, however, wanted to ensure that there was never any possibility of confusion between his French and foreign units, so he insisted that the uniform have a 'sufficient distinction to let people know at first glance that this was in fact a foreign regiment'. (Fieffé, Vol. 2, p. 161.) That distinction was a semi-circular patch of cloth worn rounded side up at the top of each sleeve. Some sources (such as Lienhart & Humbert) say this 'swallow's-nest' was red; others (Fieffé and Chartrand) say it was blue. All agree, however, that there was a line of white trim along the straight edge of the patch. The white metal regimental buttons had 'Régiment d'Illyrie' in the middle and 'Empire Français' around the edge. One contemporary noted that the Regiment had a particularly strong contingent of fifers that accompanied it into battle along with its drummers. (Suckow, p. 171.)

Standard Charrié (p. 172) reports that the Illyrians did not receive either a regimental colour or an Eagle.

Régiment d'Isembourg

(Isembourg's Regiment)

Date of Creation The Regiment was formed pursuant to an Imperial order dated 10 Brumaire Year XIV (1 November 1805) (Nap. *O&A*, No 5355, Vol. 4, p. 36).

Circumstances of Creation The formation of this Regiment was a task given to Prince Charles Frederic Louis Maurice of Isenburg to enable him to demonstrate his loyalty (and usefulness) as the head of a small member state of the Confederation of the Rhine. (Birstein, p. 45.) (The name of the Regiment differs from the name of the principality because of chronic mis-spelling by the bureaucrats in the French Ministry of War.) From the coincidence of timing, its seems likely that an important part of the impetus for this initiative was Napoleon's perception that he would soon have large number of Austrian prisoners of war to draw on for recruits. Much of the information we have about the Regiment comes from the memoirs of C. F. Friedrich (1789 –?), who joined the Regiment as a cadet in 1805 and served with it on and off until 1814. His memoirs dwell at length on his many exploits with the opposite sex, but they seem reliable in their military details and include many official documents as appendices.

The Regiment was organised at Mayence predominantly from Austrian and Russian soldiers captured during the 1805 campaign. As a commentary on the recruiting methods used to identify 'volunteers' for the Regiment among the Allied prisoners, Friedrich noted that the Austrians responded to bribes but the Russians had to be starved into co-operation. (Friedrich, Vol. 1, p. 9.) The 'bribes' took the form of a sign-on bonus paid in two instalments, one-half paid upon signature of a four-year enlistment contract and one-half paid six months later. (Friedrich, Vol. 1, p. 337.) Since the second instalments were generally not paid, it is not surprising that the depot eventually had to be moved to Toul in France in order to make it harder for the non-French soldiers to desert. (Friedrich, Vol. 1, pp. 9–10.)

The Prince also seems to have cut some corners in his efforts to recruit officers. For instance, the Adjutant-Major, one Jean Baptiste Wable, had been cashiered from the Customs Service for theft. (Friedrich, Vol. 1, p. 10.) Friedrich himself, a self-confessed rogue, would have been made an officer immediately at the age of 16 if he had not chosen to start as a cadet NCO in order to learn something about soldiering before he was placed in a command situation. The Prince took the trouble to travel to Paris to defend his choices, but he was unsuccessful and Napoleon ultimately decided that he would approve all future appointments himself. (Order of 12 March 1806, Nap. *O&A*, No 3359, Vol. 3, p. 99; Decision of 18 September 1807, Nap. *P&T*, No 1300, Vol. 1, p. 628.) Napoleon's initial unfavourable impression of the Regiment's leadership proved to be enduring. When he was forming the *Régiment d'Illyrie* in 1810 (see separate entry), Napoleon cautioned his subordinates to chose only officers from good families so that the officer corps of the new regiment 'would not be composed of adventurers like those of the Tour d'Auvergne and Isembourg Regiments.' (N. to Minister of War, 15 November 1810, Nap. *O&A*, No 4362, Vol. 3, pp. 344–5.)

Composition The Imperial order creating the Regiment specified that it was to be organised in the same manner as a French regiment of light infantry (i.e., with seven companies of Chasseurs, one of Voltigeurs and one of Carabiniers). (Article II.) The order also prohibited the recruiting of any French 'soldier or subject' so that the Regiment would be formed entirely from German, Poles, Russians and other foreigners. (Article IV.) The Regiment at first stayed with the nine-company establishment when French regiments changed to a six-company establishment in 1808, but it eventually conformed to the later standard in 1810. (Decision of 24 October 1808, Nap. *P&T*, No 2403, Vol. 2, p. 508; Order of 17 October 1810, Nap. *P&T*, No 4721, Vol. 3, pp. 813–14.)

Commanders *1 November 1805–6 January 1807*: Colonel the Prince Charles Frederick Louis Maurice of Isenburg (1766–1820), who served as a general in the Prussian Army before joining the French Army in 1804. He left the Regiment as a result of his promotion to the rank of Brigade General. *6 January 1807–12 January 1808*: Colonel William O'Meara (1764–1828). A Frenchman of Irish extraction, O'Meara had been the Major of the Regiment for nearly a year before he was promoted to command. He left the Regiment to become an ADC to Marshal Lannes. *12 October 1808–7 September 1811*: Colonel Philippe Jacques Stieler de Lanoville (1772–1847), who had begun his military career as a private in a French infantry regiment in 1788. He left the Regiment to take command of the 14th Light Regiment. *28 January 1813 to disbandment*: Colonel Adrien François Meijer (1769–1845), a native of Holland, who had been Lieutenant-Colonel of the unit since February 1812.

Operational History By 10 March 1806 two battalions of the Regiment had been formed and were ready for inspection. Despite the strict prohibition of the Organisational Order, many of the officers had French names. These included Battalion Chief Jean Baptiste de Duret of the 1st Battalion, who had commanded the small indigenous military force of the Principality of Isenburg, and the commanders of his Carabinier and Voltigeur companies, Captains de Bruges (aged 48) and de Granet (aged 26), respectively. (A complete listing of the officers of the Regiment is given in Friedrich, Vol. 1, p. 340.) The appearance of the men was impressive: 'It is certain that the Prince accepts only men with agreeable physiques into his Regiment.' (Friedrich, Vol. 1, p. 19.) Their quality was less so (Friedrich, Vol. 1, p. 15):

> Our regiment, which now had its full complement of 3,000 men, counted in its ranks representatives of every European nationality. It was a collection of the worst possible specimens of humanity . . . [E]ach day was marked by some sensational development such as a murder or a theft or a desertion carried out in extraordinary circumstances.

Although Friedrich records in his memoirs that he was present at the siege of Gaeta in the summer of 1806 and at Naples shortly thereafter (Friedrich, Vol. 1, p. 49), there is no evidence to suggest that any portion of the Regiment was there with him. (For example, the name of the Regiment does not appear in the list of troops employed at Gaeta that appears in Appendix G of Gachot, p. 353.) What can be confirmed is that the first two battalions were ordered to Avignon in May of that year. (N. to Minister of War, 4 May 1806, Nap. *P&T*, No 425, Vol. 1, p. 231.) By April 1807 the 1st and 3rd Battalions were at Toulon while the 2nd was at Genoa. Napoleon then moved the 3rd Battalion to Genoa and the other two to Civita Vecchia near Rome. (N. to Minister of War, 21 April 1807, Nap. *P&T*, No 1055, Vol. 1, p. 510.) They apparently did not get closer to Naples until October 1807, however, when Napoleon wrote to his brother to announce that all three battalions of the Regiment had been dispatched to Naples (as Napoleon had promised to Joseph in September). (N. to Joseph, 16 October 1807, Nap. *Corr.*, No 13262, Vol. 16, p. 94; see also N. to Joseph, 25 September 1807, Nap. *Corr.*, No 13183, Vol. 16, p. 49.) Napoleon's interest in the Regiment's movements apparently led to speedy progress because the Regiment recorded its first officer casualty in Calabria that same month.

While the Regiment was shifting from post to post through France and Italy, controversy was building concerning the handling of the unit's finances. The Prince was apparently somewhat careless in distinguishing between personal and private expenditures, a habit that had already cost him money when Napoleon refused to reimburse him for the cost of manufacture of 1,800 overcoats for the Regiment. (Order of 14 May 1806, Nap. *O&A*, No 3429, Vol. 3, p. 114.) The Regimental accounting records were also sloppy, which led the War Ministry to launch a formal inquiry to determine whether all the reported expenses of formation of the Regiment were legitimate. A report was prepared for the Emperor in September, and he delegated the matter to his Council of State in November. (Decision of 6 November 1807, Nap. *P&T*, No 1430, Vol. 1, p. 686.) After six months of deliberation, the Council found no criminal wrongdoing on the part of the Prince, but it did rule that he had to pay some 93,000 francs for debts incurred by the Regiment in violation of regulations because of the undue influence exercised by the Prince over the other members of the unit's administrative council. (Report of 11 May 1808, Nap. *P&T*, No 6861, Vol. 2, pp. 198–200 at 199.)

Despite this scrutiny, the financial affairs of the Regiment continued in turmoil. In January 1809 Murat (now King of Naples) reported to Napoleon that the regimental accounts were in complete disorder, showing 427 more men on the rolls than were actually enlisted. Murat surmised that this problem had not been tackled vigorously by the War Ministry itself because Colonel O'Meara was the brother-in-law of General Clarke. Apparently Murat was unaware that Colonel Stieler had been appointed to head the Regiment in October of 1808, for he concluded that it was 'indispensable' to give this 'unfortunate' regiment a new commander. (Murat to N., 25 January 1809, Murat *Lettres*, No 3759, Vol. 6, pp. 509–10.)

The Voltigeur company of the Regiment participated in the daring capture of Capri in October 1808, losing three officers killed and one wounded. 2nd Lieutenant Lecaux, who took command of the company after all the more senior officers were disabled, and four of his men were cited distinguished conduct in General Lamarque's report. (Report of 18 October 1808, quoted in Perrot, p. 337.) Nevertheless, the Regiment continued to be known more for its exploits off, rather than on, the field of battle. It was plagued by desertions, while the men who remained in the ranks were constantly causing trouble (Murat to Huard, 12 January 1809, Murat *Lettres*, No 3734, Vol. 6, pp. 494–5):

> I am receiving complaints from all sides about the indiscipline of this corps and, above all, the terrible way that the men treat my subjects . . . I am particularly offended that this behaviour takes place despite the fact that the unit is commanded by French officers who ought to know better . . . But that is not the worst—according to some reports I have received, this unit's attachment to the Emperor is at best equivocal. Make sure it is kept under close surveillance and let the officers know that, if they continue to conduct themselves in this fashion, I will be forced to ask the Emperor to recall them from my territory.

Murat himself contributed in some degree to the problems by stealing the best men from the Regiment to serve in his Guard. (See September 1809 complaint of Colonel Stieler reproduced in Friedrich, Vol. 2, pp. 371–2.)

Despite these problems, Napoleon agreed to increase the size of the Regiment by another battalion in order to make use of the prisoners he acquired in his 1809 campaign against Austria. The only restriction he imposed was that the Regiment was forbidden to enlist Poles. (Decision of 17 July 1809, Nap. *P&T*, No 3319, Vol. 3, p. 126.) A fourth battalion of nine companies and nearly 1,100 men was duly formed, but it was dispatched to Spain instead of to the Kingdom of Naples. There it was brigaded with the 2nd Battalion of the *Régiment de Prusse*, the other unit formed by the Prince of Isenburg. (Report of 9 March 1810, Nap. *P&T*, No 4086, Vol. 3, p. 481.)

From the beginning, however, the effectiveness of these units was undermined by constant desertion on the part of the German soldiers, who were dismayed at the prospect of fighting for an unpopular cause in difficult circumstances. This weakness was effectively exploited by the guerrillas through initiatives such as that described in the following proclamation distributed over the signature of one 'Charles, baron Hohenstein, commanding the German volunteers' of Mina (quoted in Martin, *Gendarmerie*, p. 228):

> German soldiers and comrades!
>
> If you want to live better, join the Spanish forces; Many of your comrades have already done so and are now part of my company. You will find a better life and you will receive 10 sous a day plus bread, wine and meat in abundance. Germans are viewed favourably by my commanders and by the whole Spanish nation. Come, my brothers, leave the French . . . Anyone who receives this letter is urged to communicate its contents in secret to his comrades.

Desertion became so widespread that 29 former members of the Regiment were captured in a single skirmish with guerrillas on 29 April and summarily executed in order to intimidate would-be deserters still in the ranks. (Notes of Dr J. Sarramon in text to Hourtoulle Plates No 49 and 50, 'Régiment d'Isembourg'.) This tactic backfired, however, as German deserters became some of the most tenacious fighters in the guerrilla bands since they knew they would receive no quarter if they surrendered. The 17th Squadon of the French Gendarmes of Spain was severely mauled in a combat at Peralta on 26 May against an enemy that included two companies of German deserters from the Prussian and Isembourg Regiments. (Martin, *Gendarmerie*, p. 222.) On 18 June 1810, Lieutenant Torrelli and 103 men of the 4th Battalion surrendered to a guerrilla band under Mina without firing a shot. (Notes of Dr J. Sarramon.) The unit performed more appropriately in a fight at near the woods of Carascal on 27 July in which Battalion Chief Debons was mortally wounded, Lieutenant Delonlay was killed and Lieutenants Crova and Rivarol were wounded, but the remaining men were subsequently assigned primarily to garrison duty. (*Ibid.*; Decision of 27 July 1810, Nap. *P&T*, No 4440, Vol. 3, p. 658.) The only officer casualties the 4th Battalion suffered thereafter were two officers 'assassinated' in an ambush of a French column carried out by Mina on Christmas Eve 1810. The 4th Battalion was ordered back to France in early 1811. (Decision of 8 February 1811, Nap. *P&T*, No 5049, Vol. 4, p. 59.)

The other three battalions of the Regiment suffered eight officer casualties during the course of 1810 in combat against 'brigands' in the Kingdom of Naples. Their performance was so improved that Murat decided to ask for transfer of the Regiment to the Neapolitan army, but Napoleon refused the request. (Order of 3 October 1810, Nap. *P&T*, No 4649, Vol. 3, p. 776.) Instead, the Emperor transferred the 2nd Battalion to Corfu and one of the other two to Rome. The regulation establishment of the Regiment was reduced from nine to six companies, the excess companies being used to create two extra battalions for a total of six distributed one in Spain, three in Naples and two on Corfu. (N. to Minister of War, 17 October 1810, Nap. *P&T*, No 4721, Vol. 3, pp. 813–14.)

The year 1811 opened with an unusual combat between a contingent of the Regiment and a small British warship on the coasts of Calabria on 6 January that left one officer wounded, but the focus of the year was reorganisation rather than fighting. Murat once again asked to have the Regiment (as well as the 1st Swiss and the Tour D'Auvergne Regiment) transferred to his army and was once again denied, this time because the Napoleon had other plans in mind. (Decision of 8 June 1811, Nap. *P&T*, No 5571, Vol. 4, p. 349.) On 24 June, the Emperor disbanded the French Army of Naples and reassigned his men, including the Isembourg unit, to a new force called the Observation Corps of Central Italy that was stationed near Rome in the Papal States. The 3rd Brigade of that force was composed of the four Isembourg battalions not on Corfu. (Nap. *Inédits*, No 466, Vol. 1, pp. 131–2.) At the same time, the two battalions on Corfu were called upon to furnish men to complete an artillery company, a sapper company and a company of pioneers. (N. to Minister of War, Nap. *P&T*, No 5908, Vol. 4, pp. 538–9.) Finally, the Regiment lost its distinctive name and gained a new designation as the *2ème Régiment Étranger* by a decree of 11 August that relabelled all the foreign regiments. (Belhomme, Vol. 4, 523.) It also gained an artillery company stocked with two 6-pound cannons. (N. to Minister of War, Nap. *P&T*, No 7259, Vol. 5, p. 379.)

Recruiting for the Regiment remained extremely eclectic. When the regiments of the Dutch Army were converted into French line units, miscellaneous 'foreigners' such as Austrians and Hungarians were dispatched to join the unit. (Decision of 27 December 1810, Nap. *P&T*, No 4936, Vol. 3, pp. 936–40 at 938.) One decision added 26 discharged Swedish soldiers to the unit (Nap. *P&T*, No 7048, Vol. 5, p. 271), while another ordered Marshal Suchet to send to the Regiment all German deserters who surrendered to him (Decision of 22 December 1812). The uneven quality that resulted from such recruiting is suggested by an Imperial decision dated 22 August 1811, in which Napoleon approves General Donzelot's plan to form a hard-labour detachment using '51 incorrigibly bad characters of the Isembourg Regiment'. (Nap. *P&T*, No 6046, Vol. 4, p. 619.)

As Napoleon sought to rebuild his shattered armies in 1813, the six battalions of the Regiment should have been an important asset, but concerns about the Regiment's quality made the Emperor reluctant to draw on this resource. He did, however, use the Carabinier and Voltigeur companies of the Regiment to form an élite battalion to serve with the main force of the Army of Italy. This unit fought well at Mülbach on 7 October 1813, when it suffered four officer casualties. (Cayron, 'Ramaeckers', p. 260.) Its performance deteriorated from that point and it does not appear in any French order of battle after 9 November. (Cayron, 'Isembourg', p. 260.)

Final Transformation The Regiment was included to a limited extent in the 25 November Decree about foreign troops. General Miollis in Rome assembled the two battalions of the Regiment and the 2nd Foreign Battalion found there, disarmed all the men who were natives of states then at war with France and formed them into yet another pioneer battalion. The men left over were used to create a new 1st Battalion for the Regiment plus two depot companies. (Carles II, p. 58.) The two battalions on Corfu remained undisturbed until the abdication of Napoleon. All three battalions were retained in French service after the return of the Bourbons.

Uniforms The basic information about the uniforms of the Regiment is provided by the Organisational Order:

> *Article VI*: The uniforms of the Isembourg [*sic*] Regiment will have the same cut as those of the French [regiments of light infantry]. The colour will be sky blue with a yellow collar, white piping and buttons and sky blue lining.

This information is confirmed and enhanced by a set of three paintings (Nos 119–121) from the volume in the Rovatti Manuscript in Modena, Italy, that covers the year 1806. The Rovatti pictures depict a Carabinier, a Voltigeur and a Chasseur. All three have the same basic uniform, which is dark sky blue with a yellow collar and sky blue cuffs with a rectangular yellow cuff flap bearing four silver buttons. None of the figures is wearing a shoulder strap or aiguillette. The Carabinier has a shako with a red grenade ornament instead of a shako plate and also has a red plume and red cords. The Voltigeur is wearing a shako with a brass shako plate of indeterminate design and a yellow plume and cords, while the plume and cords of the Chasseur are green. Martinet, Plate No 148, depicts a Chasseur in roughly the same dress, but the shako has a diamond-shaped plate and a yellow plume with a green base, and the figure has epaulettes with green fringe and yellow shoulderpieces.

The rest of the details we have about the dress of the Regiment come from Friedrich's memoirs. The specific points mentioned by Friedrich are as follows:

Cadets Each cadet wore a counter-epaulette on each shoulder in addition to the badges and rank markings appropriate for the rank to which the cadet had been appointed. (Friedrich, Vol. 1, p. 16.)

Drum Major 'The dress uniform of the Drum Major which he [the Prince] had manufactured in Paris, was made of yellow cloth with light blue facings, but it was so richly decorated with gold and silver lace that one could hardly see the underlying colour. The hat of the Drum Major was also richly decorated and was surmounted by an enormous plume made up of ostrich feathers of all colours held in place by a golden plume holder. The boots were also decorated with silver. The Drum Major himself was a huge devil of a Bohemian, not less than 6 foot 3 inches tall, who handled adroitly a baton with an enormous silver bulb on one end.' (Friedrich, Vol. 1.)

Musicians 'The parade uniform of the musicians was the same style and colours as that of the Drum Major.'

Carabiniers 'At a quarter hour's march before Avignon, the Regiment halted to put on full dress uniforms. The Carabiniers put on their bearskins with red plumes and their red epaulettes. . . .'

Voltigeurs and Chasseurs '. . . the Voltigeurs and Chasseurs put on their respective yellow and green plumes and epaulettes.'

Miscellaneous Men of the Regiment wore goatskin sandals in Calabria.

Forthoffer devotes five plates to the Isembourg Regiment, but his source references, as usual, leave much to be desired so his depictions cannot be relied upon with confidence. (Forthoffer, *Fiches Documentaires*, Nos 215–219.

The gap between theory and reality in terms of the dress of a military unit is vividly illustrated in the following correspondence about the Battalion of the Regiment on Corfu in 1808 (Murat to Saliceti, 1 December 1808, Murat *Lettres*, No 3630, Vol. 6, p. 430):

> Dear Minister,
>
> Monsieur Donzelet, the Governor-General of the Ionian Islands, has been complaining for a long time about the terrible state of the clothing of the 2nd Battalion of the Isembourg Regiment. Most of its soldiers are without jackets and no one in the battalion has an overcoat. Given the approach of winter, you will no doubt judge it expedient to give immediate orders to the administrative council of this Regiment to take corrective measures.

One intriguing footnote to the uniform history of the Regiment is provided by the memoirs of a German named Karl Meltzer, who served in Lutzow's Free Corps. He was captured by the French in 1813 and persuaded to serve in the Regiment. He states unequivocally that the depot battalion of the Regiment had just been issued new green

uniforms with [light?] blue facings that were intended for distribution to the entire unit. (Meltzer, quoted in R. Knötel, *Uniformenkunde*, Vol. 11 [1902], pp. 43–4.) This may have represented a belated attempt to reduce the expense of the foreign units by dressing the 2nd Foreign in the same colour as the others three regiments.
Standard Friedrich mentions a solemn consecration of the colours of the Regiment in 1806, but he specifically says the unit did not receive any Eagles. (Friedrich, Vol. 1.) He must have been mistaken in some regard, however, because Napoleon approved the distribution of Eagles to the Regiment on 7 May 1806 (Nap. *P&T*, No 430, Vol. 1, p. 232) and later correspondence confirms that colours with Eagles were in fact delivered (Nap. *P&T*, No 1267, Vol. 1, p. 612). Friedrich specifies that the colours also had richly embroidered 'cravats' that had been presented to the Regiment as a gift from the Empress Josephine and bore an inscription to that effect.

Régiment Joseph Napoléon

(Joseph Napoleon's Regiment)

Date of Creation The Regiment was formed pursuant to a decree dated 13 February 1809 (P. Boppe, *Les Espagnols*, p. 91–5), but was not actually organised until a year later.
Circumstances of Creation The origins of this unit are unique in that it was formed almost exclusively with soldiers from an expeditionary force of the regular army of the Bourbon monarchs of Spain that had been sent to Northern Europe in 1807 to serve with Napoleon's Grand Army. This large contingent, which was commanded by the Marquis de la Romana, consisted of four regiments of line infantry, five regiments of cavalry, two battalions of light infantry and supporting artillery and engineer formations. (See, generally, Godechot.) La Romana's corps performed well as part of the force besieging the Swedish fortress of Stralsund in the late summer of 1807, but it was subsequently split up and stationed in different parts of Denmark in anticipation of further Scandinavian campaigning. It was still there in the spring of 1808 when news began to arrive of the astonishing political developments taking place back in Spain.

The abdication of the Bourbons in favour of Napoleon and his bestowal of the kingdom of Spain on his brother, Joseph Bonaparte, may have been distasteful to many of the men in La Romana's force, but they were initially too far from home (and too close to other French forces) to do anything about it, so most of the units had to submit when called upon to swear allegiance to the new dynasty. The situation changed dramatically, however, when the British contacted the Marquis in secret with an offer of transportation back to Spain in British ships. The Marquis accepted, and, in one of the most audacious episodes of the whole of the Napoleonic wars, seized the Danish port of Nyborg in August and managed the safe embarkation of the bulk of his men. Unfortunately from a Spanish perspective, he was unable to co-ordinate the flight of all his troops from their different island locations so that they could all be brought off safely. The Asturias and Guadalaxara infantry regiments mutinied against their French commanders, but were surrounded and disarmed by overwhelming French and Danish forces before they could effect their escape. The Algarve Regiment of cavalry was the farthest from headquarters at the critical moment, and, whether because of that circumstance or because of an actual reluctance to break faith with the French, it did not put up any resistance and two of its officers even revealed La Romana's plot to the French. (P. Boppe, *Les Espagnols*, p. 53.) All the Spanish prisoners (totalling over 3,500 men) were then dispersed to a number of different camps in France. (P. Boppe, *Les Espagnols*, p. 81–2.)

In the meanwhile, Napoleon successfully re-established his brother on the throne of Spain in the autumn of 1808 and began to have thoughts about assisting his sibling by forming some Spanish regiments in French service that might eventually be sent back to the Peninsula to become part of Joseph's army. His thinking along these lines was encouraged by the suggestions of General Jean Kindelan (1759–1822), La Romana's second-in-command, who remained faithful to his oath of allegiance to King Joseph during the insurrection. (P. Boppe, *Les Espagnols*, p. 51, n. 3.) Kindelan became a consultant to the French and he championed the idea that within the population of prisoners there were a sufficient number of Spaniards who accepted the change of dynasty to provide the nucleus for a new military unit destined for service in the Peninsula. Napoleon agreed, and passed Kindelan on to the Ministry of War, which thereupon formulated a proposal for the creation of two Joseph Napoleon Regiments, one of infantry and one of cavalry. The plans for the cavalry unit were rejected by Napoleon on the grounds of cost, but those for the infantry came to fruition.

Composition The 13 February Decree specifies that the Joseph Napoleon Regiment was to consist of four service battalions and a depot, all organised in the same manner as for a French line infantry regiment so that each battalion had four Fusilier, one Grenadier and one Voltigeur companies, and the total theoretical strength of the unit was 107 officers and 3,220 men. (Article 2.) All aspects of regimental life were to be governed by French regulations, but Napoleon did allow the unit the extraordinary concession of conducting all its drills and manoeuvres in Spanish. (Article 4.) In 1812 Marshal Davout started to form an artillery company for the portion of the Regiment serving under his command, but Napoleon forbade him to do so as soon as he became aware of the initiative. (Decision dated 28 March 1812, Nap. *P&T*, No 7027, Vol. 5, p. 259.) It seems likely, however, that the unit was not disbanded before the start of the Russian campaign.

Commanders *13 February 1809–19 January 1812*: General Jean Kindelan (1759–1822), a Spaniard of Irish extraction who had been a career soldier in the Spanish Bourbon army and who had served against the French in the Revolutionary Wars. (He also had the unique experience among Napoleonic generals of having been twice wounded in action against the armies of the Emperor of Morocco at Ceuta in Africa during the period from 1790 to 1793.) He was instrumental in the formation of the Joseph

Napoleon Regiment, and retained command of the unit for many years despite his rank as a general. *19 January 1812 to disbandment:* Colonel Jean Baptiste Marie Joseph de Tschudy (1774–1834), a French emigré who served successively in the Army of the Prince of Condé, the British Army (in Egypt with the Queen's German Regiment in 1800) and the Portuguese Army before entering French service again in 1808 as a Battalion Chief in the Portuguese Legion. He promoted to the rank of Major in the Joseph Napoleon Regiment on 2 May 1809 and then to Colonel in January 1812. His brother served in the 2nd Swiss Regiment in Napoleon's service and was wounded and captured in fighting at the crossing of the Berezina. (P. Boppe, *Les Espagnols*, p. 242.)

Operational History Recruiting for the Joseph Napoleon Regiment went very slowly because the pool of eligible recruits consisted solely of Spanish prisoners of war who could be persuaded to serve King Joseph, known colloquially in Spain as '*El Rey Intruso*' ('The Intruder King'). General Kindelan therefore needed to take great care to distinguish between potential recruits who were genuinely willing to serve the new Bonaparte dynasty and those who might be feigning allegiance in order to have a chance to be sent back to Spain and, ultimately, desert to the forces of the old regime. It is interesting in this regard to examine the type of certificate that had to be signed by a Spanish prisoner in order to join the Regiment (P. Boppe, *Les Espagnols*, p. 229):

> I swear to be faithful to the French imperial dynasty and to conduct myself as a loyal and brave soldier, in return for the promise that has been made to me that after I have served for four years, I will receive an absolute discharge that will permit me to return to my homeland.

By the spring of 1810 the unit was fully organised (although not at full strength), and King Joseph asked for it to be sent to serve with his armies precisely in order to help prove that the Emperor was not opposed to letting former prisoners of war serve in the Peninsula. By this time, however, it had become clear to all concerned that the loyalty of the unit could never be assured if it were sent to Spain, so Napoleon bluntly refused the request: 'The Regiment is animated by such a bad spirit that its own officers have asked for it to be removed further from the frontiers of Spain.' (N. to Minister of War, 29 May 1810, Nap. *Corr.*, No 16513, Vol. 20, pp. 382–3.) The four service battalions were thereupon dispersed to separate bases in Italy, the Netherlands and Germany, although the Regiment's depot remained at Avignon in France.

It was not until the spring of 1811 that Napoleon began to make serious use of the Regiment. In April, the 2nd and 3rd Battalions were reunited and placed under the command of Marshal Davout pursuant to orders from Napoleon that made it clear that he still had doubts about the unit's loyalty (N. to Davout, 16 April 1811, Nap. *Corr.*, No 17611, Vol. 22, p. 67):

> I am sending you two good Spanish battalions amounting to 2,000 men commanded by a general [Kindelan]. The soldiers are good; they enlisted voluntarily and have been under arms for two years. I think they will fight as well as the Portuguese and will not

> have many deserters, but take care not to use them for outpost duty or as garrison troops in any first-line fortress. It is probable that they will be surrounded by *embaucheurs* [enemy agents enticing soldiers to desert], so it would be a good idea to keep these battalions under secret surveillance.

A month later the 1st and 4th Battalions were combined and attached to the Army of Italy. This provisional unit was commanded by 2nd Major Jean Baptiste Doreille, an officer who was transferred from the 13th Line for that purpose. (P. Boppe, *Les Espagnols*, p. 131.) The division of the Joseph Napoleon Regiment into two operational halves remained in effect up to and through the Russian campaign.

When the French Army crossed the Niemen River in June 1812, the Regiment was deployed in the following manner: (a) the 2nd Battalion (Battalion Chief Ramon Ducer) and the 3rd Battalion (Battalion Chief Rodrigo Medrano) were assigned to General Friant's Division of Marshal Davout's 1st Corps, and (b) the 1st Battalion (Battalion Chief Joseph Marie Kindelan, replaced by Sansot in August) and the 4th Battalion (Battalion Chief Alexandre O'Donnell) were with General Broussier's Division of the Prince Eugene's 4th Corps. The units were at full strength, but ill-health on the part of General Kindelan had caused him to cede command of the Regiment to Tschudy, now promoted to the rank of Colonel. Tschudy had personal command of the 2nd and 3rd Battalions during the ensuing campaign, while Major Doreille commanded the 3rd and 4th Battalions

The first verifiable mention of the performance of the Spaniards on campaign is not a flattering one. It is well known that the forced marches and bad weather that characterised the first stages of the advance of the French into Russia led to much straggling by the men of the Grand Army, and the Joseph Napoleon Regiment was apparently no exception in this regard. In late July Jean Coignet, the famous memoirist, was promoted to the rank of Lieutenant and given the job of returning 700 stragglers to the 1st Corps. One day *en route* he noticed that a large detachment, consisting of '133 Spaniards from the Joseph Napoleon Regiment', was heading in the wrong direction and he rode up to order them back to the main track. The response he received was decidedly unexpected:

> You can imagine my terror in seeing these bandits turn about-face and fire on me . . . They had plotted this bold desertion, but happily they were unable to persuade any of the French stragglers to join them.

Coignet was unable to stop the deserters at that moment, but when he reached the next French garrison the commander, a cavalry colonel, sent out a pursuing force of fifty cavalrymen who surprised the Spaniards in bivouac and captured all of them. When they returned to base the unnamed commander exacted a terrible penalty for their crime. After identifying two sergeants and three corporals as the ring-leaders, he forced the rest of the men to divide themselves into two equal groups by lot. Those who drew black tickets were then assembled with the guilty NCOs to hear the Colonel's verdict:

> You have pillaged, stolen and burned down villages and you fired on your commanding officer. The law condemns you all to the punishment of death and I could have you all shot. Instead, I have decided to spare half of you, but the rest must pay the penalty. I hope this will serve as an example for all.

The chosen 69 Spaniards were thereupon executed by firing squad without further ceremony or due process. The grotesque conclusion to this episode occurred when Coignet handed over the survivors to Colonel Tschudy:

> When I asked the colonel of the Joseph Napoleon Regiment to sign a receipt for the full 133 men, this officer, who was a Frenchman, remarked that I had only delivered half that number. 'The rest are dead,' said I. 'How did they die?' 'They were shot.' 'And why was that?' 'Because they fired on me, they deserted and they committed a multitude of other crimes.' 'If that is the case, I will shoot the rest myself.'

Coignet reports that he was able, with some difficulty, to persuade Tschudy to spare the survivors. (The source for this story is pp. 141–3 of the original edition of Coignet's memoirs cited in the Bibliography of this work. It differs in many details from the version in the better-known English translations of his Memoirs, which, for instance, state that only 62 men were executed.) No explicit corroboration has been found for Coignet's tale. In support of its veracity, however, are the facts that (a) Tschudy's command was reduced from nearly 2,000 to 400 men between the start of the campaign and the beginning of September, and (b) the Russians were able to form a full infantry unit (commanded by defecting Battalion Chief Alexandre O'Donnell and named the Imperial Alexander Regiment) from the large number of Spanish prisoners and deserters that fell into their hands during the campaign. (Gomez Ruiz, p. 85.)

The 2nd and 3rd Battalions finally saw more positive action on 5 September during the fighting at the Shevardino redoubt before the Battle of Borodino. When the 111th Line Regiment was roughed up by a cavalry charge, Tschudy formed his two battalions into a square under the cover of a burning village and then deployed his Voltigeur company to decoy the Russians away from the disordered French unit. The Russian cavalry took the bait and suffered heavy casualties when the Voltigeurs retired into the square, leaving their colleagues free to blaze away at the enemy horsemen. Tschudy claims that his men suffered no casualties in this affair. (Tschudy narrative quoted in P. Boppe, *Les Espagnols*, p. 147, n. 1.)

Both contingents of the Regiment were present at the Battle of Borodino itself, but this time the two battalions under Major Doreille had the more active role since Broussier's division was engaged in fighting around the Great Redoubt. Tschudy's contingent had two men killed and 34 wounded (including two officers), while Doreille's force lost one officer killed and two wounded, plus an unspecified number of other casualties. (P. Boppe, *Les Espagnols*, p. 147–8.) Ironically, the Spaniards suffered a much greater loss three days later when Tschudy was placed in the French vanguard with his own two battalions and one from the 33rd Line. Advancing rashly without cavalry or artillery support, he was assailed by a superior Russian force of all arms and barely held out until help arrived. Tschudy was wounded and had two horses shot from under him. More importantly, the two battalions had two officers and seventeen men killed, plus ten officers and an astonishing 246 out of 300 other combatants wounded. (Tschudy narrative quoted in P. Boppe, *Les Espagnols*, p. 149, n. 2; Martinien in fact records two additional wounded officers on the day.) These losses nearly wiped out the battalions on a temporary basis but, miraculously, after two days' repose in Moscow, Tschudy found that the return of stragglers and lightly wounded men had brought total strength with the colours back up to 300 men. (Tschudy narrative quoted in P. Boppe, *Les Espagnols*, p. 150, n. 1.)

While Tschudy's men rested in Moscow, Major Doreille's contingent was assigned a garrison on the main road from Moscow to Mojaisk along with two regiments of Bavarian Light Horse. There they encountered staff officer Boniface de Castellane, who was trying to organise an effort to rescue some foragers threatened by Cossacks. The Bavarian commander refused to assist on the grounds that his horses were too worn out to gallop, but the Spaniards provided 50 Grenadiers who accomplished the task with ease. Castellane came away with a favourable impression of both the contingent and its commander: 'Major Doreille . . . is a good soldier with great energy; his regiment, composed of veteran Spanish soldiers, is excellent.' (Castellane, Vol. 1, p. 178.) Castellane also added the curious note that Doreille, a native of Provence, 'did not know French'. Whatever regional dialect the Major spoke, however, the two men were nonetheless able to communicate well enough for Doreille to explain that he had already had six brothers killed in the wars of the Revolution and Empire. (Castellane, Vol. 1, p. 187.)

The supreme test for both contingents of the Regiment came at Krasnoi in mid-November, when the Russians made a bold move to cut the retreating French army in two. On the 16th Doreille's contingent was destroyed as a fighting force along with the rest of Broussier's division of the 4th Corps, and the Major himself was killed in a vain effort to hold an escape route open for the French units to come. Among these were Tschudy's battalions, now in the vanguard of Marshal Ney's 3rd Corps. On 18 November their division (commanded by General Ricard in place of the wounded Friant) blundered into a superior Russian force in heavy fog and was cut to pieces. The total loss to the Regiment in officers for both days was five killed and eighteen wounded (three mortally). Tschudy and his few remaining men thereupon became participants in Ney's epic escape from encirclement that remains one of the most heroic feats in all military history. When Ney's force miraculously re-joined the main force at Orsha on 21 November, the two contingents of the Joseph Napoleon Regiment were finally, albeit briefly, united. They had a combined force of little more than 100 men. (P. Boppe, *Les Espagnols*, p. 155–6.)

That was the end of the Russian campaign for both contingents of the Regiment as organised fighting forces. In January 1813 an optimistic Colonel Tschudy called for the complete re-stocking of the Regiment from 'reliable' prisoners of war, but, given the deteriorating military and political situation in Spain, Napoleon categorically rejected that possibility: 'Cease immediately the recruitment of Spaniards; I have absolutely no desire for these regiments.' (N. to Minister of War, 8 February 1813, Nap. *Corr.*, No 19549, Vol. 24, p. 492.) The Emperor was, however, willing to find an active use for the 1,200 men already assembled at the Regiment's depot. In February he used some of those men to recreate the 1st Battalion of the Regiment, but he added a veteran component to the unit by forming its élite companies exclusively from the survivors, stragglers and returning wounded and sick men who had fought in Russia. (P. Boppe, *Les Espagnols*, p. 158–9.) The new battalion was placed under the command of Battalion Chief Nicolas Romain Isidore Dimpre of the 5th Light, a Frenchman who was married to a Spanish woman he had saved from harm after the French capture of Lerida in 1810. (P. Boppe, *Les Espagnols*, p. 160, n. 1.)

Since there were still a large number of trained soldiers at the Regimental depot, the Emperor authorised the formation of a second battalion in April, but he simultaneously forbade the military authorities from recruiting any more new men for the Regiment. The 2nd Battalion was supposed to have a voltigeur company formed from veterans of the old 1st and 4th Battalions who had regrouped in the fortress of Glogau during the spring of 1813, but the company ended up besieged in that city during the autumn and winter as well. The company was one of several foreign units that were expelled from the garrison in January 1814 because they had ceased to be reliable. (Brun, pp. 146 and 194–6.)

The reconstituted 1st Battalion was assigned to the second division of Marshal Marmont's 6th Corps along with the 27th Line, the 37th Light and the 4th Regiment of Marine Artillery, and when Marshal Kellerman reviewed the unit on 7 April he found it to be 'superb and in perfect condition.' (P. Boppe, *Les Espagnols*, p. 159, n. 2.) Napoleon nevertheless remembered the embarrassing experience of La Romana's defection and he cautioned his subordinates not to take the loyalty of the Battalion for granted (N. to Marmont, 17 April 1813, Nap. *Corr.*, No 19868, Vol. 25, p. 201):

> Give orders so that the Spanish battalion is never broken up into detachments and is always kept close at hand and protected from contact with enemy agents seeking to subvert its allegiance. It should never be used on outpost duty and it should instead always be kept close at hand, surrounded by French battalions . . . .

These orders were followed with care, so the operational history of the Battalion in the spring and summer of 1813 was identical to that of the 6th Corps as a whole. The unit took casualties at both Lützen and Bautzen, and Napoleon was sufficiently pleased with its performance that in June he named eight of its officers, including Colonel Tschudy, as chevaliers of the Legion of Honour. (P. Boppe, *Les Espagnols*, p. 162, n. 1.) In the meanwhile a new 2nd Battalion was formed and another batch of prisoner-of-war recruits was assembled with a view to adding a third battalion as well. This last initiative earned the Minister of War a stinging rebuke from the Emperor because it contradicted his explicit instructions (Decision of 8 August 1813, Nap. *Dernier Lettres*, No 2120, Vol. 2, p. 440):

> Words cannot express my dissatisfaction with the actions of the Minister. The more I forbid the recruitment of Spaniards, the more they are recruited. These Spaniards are nothing but deserters who will fill up the rank of the legions the enemy is organising. I authorised this last battalion . . . but I do not wish any others.

Colonel Tschudy briefly entertained hopes of taking command of the combined battalions for the autumn campaign. These hopes went unrealised as the 2nd Battalion under Adjutant-Major Villaba was assigned in September to the garrison of Magdeburg, where it remained for the duration of the siege of that fortress. The 1st Battalion marched on to Leipzig, where it was heavily engaged on 16 and 18 October. One of the officers who survived the latter day had a grim recollection of the fighting (Gallardo de Mendoza, 'Mémoires', published in Lumbroso, *Miscellanea Napoleonica*, Series III–IV (1898), quoted in P. Boppe, *Les Espagnols*, p. 161, n. 1):

> On the morning of the 18th we saw Bernadotte reviewing his Swedish troops and then the cannonade recommenced along the whole front; we were surrounded by a storm of fire. We had a small wood on our right flank where we were deployed company by company in skirmish formation ['*en tirailleurs*'] to halt the enemy. We fought all day and our brigade was destroyed in detail by the enemy who was constantly reinforced and by the continuing bombardment on our flanks. . . . Of the 500 men we had at the start of the day, we were able to assemble only 150 at 4 p.m., and almost all of these were wounded.

Final Transformation The remains of 1st Battalion retreated to France along with the 6th Corps, but was shortly thereafter earmarked for disarmament by the 25 November Decree. At Sedan on 24 December 1813 the 1st Battalion and all the men from the depot (totalling 28 officers and 2,038 NCOs and privates) were forced to surrender their weapons and were converted on the spot into a two-battalion 'regiment' of pioneers under the orders of Major Joseph Kindelan. (P. Boppe, *Les Espagnols*, p. 165, n.1.; Fieffé, Vol. 2, p. 150.) This pioneer regiment was disbanded on 17 April 1814.

Uniforms Article 5 of the Organisational Decree for the Regiment specifies:

> The uniform of the unit will be the same, in terms of cut and style, as that of our regiments of infantry. The principal colour of this uniform will be white and the distinctive colour of the collar, cuffs and lapels will be bright green [*vert clair*].

The Minister of War subsequently legislated the following additional details of the Regiment's dress: white lining, vest and trousers, bright green piping and yellow metal buttons with the words 'Infanterie Espagnole' around the perimeter and 'Joseph Napoleon' in the centre. (P. Boppe, *Les Espagnols*, p. 93, n. 1.) One officer described his ensemble in 1811 in the following words: '. . . our uniform is most attractive, being white with green lapels, and we also wore gold epaulettes and shakos festooned with heavy cords of the same metal that add at least a quintal to the weight on the head—but that was the fashion during the Empire.' (Gallardo de Mendoza, 'Mémoires', published in Lumbroso, *Miscellanea Napoleonica*, Series III–IV (1898) and quoted in Rigo, 'Le Régiment Joseph Napoléon', p. 25.)

Based on the evidence of an artefact now found in the Historical Museum of Vilnius (Vilna) in Lithuania, the shakos referred to above were apparently adorned with a unique form of shako plate. The artefact is a yellow metal, trapezoid-shaped plate with the crowned initials 'JN' sitting on a sprig of laurel and the words 'Infanteria' on the left and 'Espanola' on the right. (A photograph of this plate is reproduced in Rigo, 'Le Régiment Joseph Napoleon', p. 25.) It also seems likely that the Regiment wore red Spanish cockades on their shakos until at least 1811. (Letter from Major Doreille to the Minister of War, 20 September 1811, cited in Rigo, 'Le Régiment Joseph Napoléon', p. 24.) On 11 June 1809 Napoleon gave permission for the Grenadiers of the Regiment to wear bearskin hats, and on 21 November he agreed that all Spanish soldiers who had served for ten years or more would be entitled to the same pay and long-service chevrons as their French colleagues. (Decisions, Nap. *P&T*, No 3233, Vol. 3, p. 85 and No 3760, p. 332.)

The only three known contemporary pictures of soldiers of the Regiment date to the end of the Napoleonic era: two are in the so-called Danzig Manuscript of 1813 and one is in the Berne Manuscript (also known as the Gaudard Album) from 1813–14. The modern whereabouts of these manuscripts is unknown, but the descriptions and/or reproductions of the pictures that can be found in secondary sources provide the additional details of the Regiment's dress. The Danzig MS depicts an officer and a Grenadier. Both figures are wearing standard French line infantry-style uniforms in the colours prescribed for the Regiment (including green cuff flaps), but the officer has overalls and a shako with a tall plume, an 1810-model shako plate and double inverted 'V' chevrons on the side. The shako of the Grenadier has cords and a short tufted pompom and a semi-circular shako plate. The Fusilier figure in the Berne MS has white shoulder straps with green piping, green cuff flaps and green turnbacks piped white and a red cockade and round orange pompom on his shako.

Standard Correspondence of the Minister of War from 1809 confirms that the Joseph Napoleon Regiment did not receive an Eagle standard when it was formed: 'Since this Regiment has received flags, but not an Eagle, it does not need to have an Eagle Standard Bearer [*porte-Aigle*] . . . ' (Minister of War letter dated 10 May 1809, quoted in Rigo, 'Le Régiment Joseph-Napoléon', p. 28.) The question of entitlement to an Eagle was raised again in 1812, and this time the response of the Minister included a description of the Regiment's unique colours (Minister of War letter [date not specified] quoted in Rigo, 'Le Régiment Joseph-Napoléon', p. 28.):

> The decree of 25 December 25 1811 specifies that Eagles should be given to every corps that has an establishment larger than 1,200 men. On that basis, the Joseph Napoleon Regiment would be entitled to an Eagle, but since the Regiment is composed of subjects

> of His Catholic Majesty of Spain and since it has possessed since the date of its formation four tricolour flags on which are imprinted the coat of arms of that sovereign, I think that it should not be given an Eagle and instead should retain its current colours.

No information has been found about the exact pattern of these colours.

Régiments Provisoires Croates

(Croatian Provisional Regiments; see also *Chasseurs Illyriens*)

Date of Creation 1811–13.
Circumstances of Creation Given the reputation of Austrian soldiers from the *Grenz*, or frontier region between the Austrian and Turkish Empires, as superb light infantrymen, it is not surprising that Napoleon would seek ways to make active use of the *Grenzer* in the six Croatian territorial defence regiments (renamed '*Chasseurs Illyriens*') that he acquired pursuant to the Treaty of Vienna in 1809. (See separate entry.) Since these units had strong territorial ties, it was not feasible to assign any single one of them in its entirety to service with the Grand Army. Napoleon dealt with this issue by combining battalions from different Regiments of Illyrian Chasseurs to form so-called Croatian Provisional Regiments to fight in Russia and Germany. Three such units ultimately served with the Grand Army (the third in number being the first to be formed). A fourth and final Provisional Regiment had a brief existence in the late summer and autumn of 1813 but was never fully organised. (P. Boppe, *La Croatie Militaire*, p. 140.)

For the sake of convenience, information about the Commanders, Operational History and Final Transformation of each of the Provisional Regiments has been broken out separately below, although the sections on Composition, Uniforms and Standards apply to all units.
Composition These Regiments had the same basic organisation as the Regiments of Illyrian Chasseurs from which they were formed, except that they probably all had élite companies of Voltigeurs and Grenadiers.

1st Croatian Provisional Regiment

The 1st Provisional Regiment was formed on 26 October 1811, by combining the 1st Battalions of the Lika and Ottochatz Regiments. (P. Boppe, *La Croatie Militaire*, p. 119.) It was brigaded with the 8th Light Infantry and the 84th Line Infantry in General Huard's brigade of General Alexis Joseph Delzons' division of the 4th Corps of the Grand Army commanded by Prince Eugene. On 15 February 1812 it had a strength of 48 officers and 1,610 NCOs and soldiers.
Commanders *26 October 1811–5 February 1813*: Marc Slivarich von Heldenbourg (1762–1838), former commander of the Lika Regiment of Illyrian Chasseurs, served with the 1st Provisional until he was promoted to the rank of Brigade General. He was

present at the Battles of Ostrowno (where he was wounded), Borodino, Malojaroslawetz, Viasma and the Beresina. His commanding officer said of his performance during the Russian campaign (P. Boppe, *La Croatie Militaire*, p. 130.):

> Colonel Slivarich has conducted himself very well; constantly sick, weakened by extreme hardship and privations, he has always remained at the head of his regiment and commanded it well; by his example, his good counsel, and his commanding presence he has contributed powerfully to the good conduct of his soldiers.

5 February 1813 to final transformation: Major Jean Joseph Coste (1774–?), a veteran of the Revolutionary Wars who had served as a lieutenant in the 5th Line Infantry from 1798 to 1810. He was a Battalion Chief from the 1st Regiment of Illyrian Chasseurs. A fitness report from 1813 notes that he was ripe for promotion because he was 'neither a drunk nor a gambler' and that 'he stayed out of quarrels and out of debt.' (Brun, p. 57, n. 7.)

Operational History The 1st Provisional Regiment had its baptism of fire against the Russians at Ostrowno on 25 July 1812, when it was nearly overwhelmed by a cavalry charge but instead earned a favourable mention in Napoleon's 10th Bulletin of the campaign at the cost of one officer killed and nine wounded. The Emperor also singled out the unit for praise at a subsequent review and generously allotted it six crosses of the Legion of Honour. (P. Boppe, *La Croatie Militaire*, pp. 124–5.) By this time, however, its strength had already fallen below 1,000 men.

The Regiment saw some action, but took few casualties, at Borodino and went on to reach Moscow. On 24 October Delzons' division led the entire 4th Corps into action at the ferocious Battle of Malo-Jaroslavetz. As the village of that name changed hands at least five times, Delzons himself was killed and the Croats suffered thirteen officer casualties. The valour of Prince Eugene's men almost changed the outcome of the entire campaign because it forced the battered Russian Army to contemplate a retreat that would open a new escape route towards the south for the French. Before this occurred, however, the 'fog of war' factor intervened and Napoleon began to retreat first instead.

The Croats lost more officers at Krasnoi on 17 November and again on the 19th, but apparently still retained enough unit cohesion to participate in heavy fighting at the Beresina crossing, which cost the Regiment seven wounded officers. The 1st Provisional Regiment thus fairly earned the praise it won from General Delzons ('The [1st] Croatian Regiment has performed marvellously…'), but the cost was high. On 27 December 1812 the total force of the Regiment was only 22 officers and 31 other ranks. (P. Boppe, *La Croatie Militaire*, p. 129.)

Slivarich, the ex-Colonel of the Regiment, was promoted to the rank of General and sent back to Croatia early in 1813 while the cadre of his Regiment was assigned to the fortress of Glogau. A mixed detachment of reinforcements totalling over 1,000 Croats from the 1st, 2nd, 5th and 6th Illyrian Chasseurs arrived there on 19 February and was immediately combined with the cadre to reconstitute the 1st Battalion of the 1st Provisional Regiment. (Brun, pp. 118–19.) The unit served with distinction during the first blockade of Glogau from 1 March to 31 May. The 2nd Battalion was likewise reorganised in July with the remnants of the 3rd Provisional Regiment and some reinforcements from Croatia, and it was assigned to be part of the garrison of Magdebourg.

Final Transformation The performances of the two battalions of the 1st Regiment during 1813 were very different. The Battalion in Magdebourg, commanded by Colonel Joly of the 3rd Provisional Regiment, was one of the few units to perform effectively at the Battle of Hagelsburg on 27 August, when a corps under General Girard that had been sent out from the city was routed by the Prussians. As part of the garrison in Magdebourg thereafter, it served honourably during the course of the siege sustained by General Le Marois, who surrendered only after the abdication of Napoleon. (Gillot, *Le Marois*, pp. 221–37.) The 2nd Battalion had a strength of 618 men on 1 May 1814, but they disappeared from French records following the surrender. (P. Boppe, *La Croatie Militaire*, p. 133.)

The saga of 1st Battalion at Glogau, on the other hand, is shameful. During the summer, an understrength battalion from the 2nd Provisional Croatian Regiment (see below) joined the garrison and was combined with the 1st Battalion of the 1st Regiment to form a so-called 'brigade' of Croatians under the command of newly promoted Major Coste. When Glogau was blockaded again starting on 17 August, the Croats took their place on the walls, but as the blockade turned into a formal siege in November and as the isolation of the garrison persisted, the morale of the Croats plummeted, as did that of the Frankfurt and Spanish units in the garrison. Desertion became rife and the men still with the colours became so sullen and mutinous that, ultimately, the garrison commander decided that it made more sense to let them all leave so that they would not turn their arms on the loyal French troops. The departure was arranged for 23 January, but at the last minute a stunning development occurred. The Croats abandoned their posts and went on strike, refusing to leave until they had been paid the back wages owed to them. Miraculously, the besieging force failed to take advantage of the situation and General Laplane, the military governor of the fortress, hammered out a compromise based on paying out two months of arrears. The Croats finally left on 26 January, and the governor was able to confide to his journal that 'the city has now been purged of all of its most dangerous enemies'. (Brun, pp. 194–6.) Major Coste chose to remain with the garrison. No information has been found about the fate of the Croats thereafter.

2nd Croatian Provisional Regiment

The 2nd Provisional Regiment was not formed until 1813, when the manpower-desperate Napoleon called upon the only two units of Illyrian Chasseurs that had not previously been forced to send men to the northern theatre of war. The 2nd Provisional was formed at Trieste in February 1813 from the 1st Battalion of the Sluin (4th) Regiment and the 2nd Battalion of the Ogulin (3rd) Regiment. (P. Boppe, *La Croatie Militaire*, p. 135.)

Commanders *25 February 1813–16 May 1813*: Colonel Robert de Gordon (1781–1815), the former commander of the Ottochatz Regiment (see separate entry). He left the 2nd Provisional on the occasion of his promotion to a staff post as an Adjutant-Commandant serving under General Betrand with the 4th Corps of the Grand Army. In 1815 he was the Chief of Staff for the 4th Division of the 4th Corps of Napoleon's Army of the North, but he deserted on the very morning of the Battle of Ligny and rejoined Louis XVIII the next day. On 8 July he was sent by King Louis to persuade Jean-Gerard Bonnaire (1769–1816), the Bonapartist commander of the fortress of Condé, to surrender, but he was shot down on the glacis of the fortress. General Bonnaire was arrested for this crime and died in prison. *16 May 1813–June 1813*: Colonel Joseph Mamulla von Türkenfeld (1779–1826), a former Austrian officer who had been a Battalion Chief in the Sluin Regiment of Illyrian Chasseurs before joining the 2nd Provisional. He is reputed to have been 'the best officer of his Regiment', and he had the additional advantage of being able to speak a little French. (Brun, p. 146.) *June 1813 to final transformation*: Battalion Chief Simeon Winisch (1778–?), who had begun his military career as a private in the Sluin Regiment in 1793.

Operational History The unit was 1,800 men strong as it mustered at Trieste, but attrition began almost immediately as it moved to Germany take up its place alongside four battalions of the 23rd Line in the 12th Division attached to General Bertrand's IV Corps. The Croats missed the Battle of Lützen, but they suffered six officer casualties on 13 May while guarding a convoy against an attack by Prussian partisans at Radebourg. On the second day of the Battle of Bautzen (21 May 1813), Bertrand's entire Corps was launched in an assault on the centre of the Allied line; this was ultimately successful but it cost the 2nd Regiment two officers killed and nine wounded, while its overall force fell to under 650 men. (P. Boppe, *La Croatie Militaire*, p. 139; Brun, p. 146.) The performance of the Croats in these actions also earned them five Legion of Honour decorations.

Final Transformation The coming of the summer armistice gave the Regiment time to take stock of the events of the spring. On4 July there were only 31 officers and 410 men with the colours. The rest were accounted for as follows: 75 killed, 250 wounded, 304 sick in hospital, 145 taken prisoner and 585 deserters or stragglers. (Brun, p. 146, quoting SHA X[l]34.) Colonel Mamulla and the cadre of the second battalion returned to Croatia to organise a recruiting effort. The much-reduced remaining battalion under Winisch was posted to Glogau, where it shared the inglorious fate of the 1st Battalion of the 1st Regiment (see entry above).

3rd Croatian Provisional Regiment

The 3rd Croatian Provisional Regiment, organised pursuant to a decree of 21 September 1811, was in fact the first of the Provisional Regiments to be formed as a chronological matter. It incorporated the first battalions of, respectively, the 1st and 2nd Banat (5th and 6th) Regiments of Illyrian Chasseurs. (P. Boppe, *La Croatie Militaire*, p. 97.)

Commanders *1 October 1811 to final transformation:* Étienne Joly (1771–1850), the Colonel of the 1st Banat (5th) Regiment of Illyrian Chasseurs (see separate entry).

Operational History The 3rd Provisional Regiment was quickly organised to a strength of 1,860 men (including a company of artillery) and then had the unusual experience of being called to Paris at the end of the year where it was fêted by the Imperial Guard and reviewed by the Emperor himself. (P. Boppe, *La Croatie Militaire*, pp. 101 and 102, n. 2.) They received new uniforms (see 'Uniforms' section below), but they lacked much with respect to training and equipment. In a letter to his Minister of War dated 12 January 1812 relating to the 3rd Provisional Croatian Regiment, Napoleon wrote the following (Nap. *Corr.*, No 18428, Vol. 23, p. 165):

> Before they [the Croats] leave [Paris] they need to have their caissons, their artillery company, their packs filled, [and] two pairs of shoes in their packs and one on their feet; they need to learn to manoeuvre a bit and to have their clothing adjusted and finished. I will see them at the first parade I conduct in February and will give them marching orders then.

For the next year the Croatian Regiment experienced garrison life at Aix-la-Chapelle and Magdebourg, all the while creating an identity for itself separate from those of its two constituent battalions and improving the level of its training and efficiency.

As war with Russia began to loom on the horizon, the Croats found themselves brigaded with the 1st and 4th Swiss in Marshal Oudinot's II Corps and the units had a long time to become accustomed to each other. One Swiss officer described the Croats as 'excellent soldiers', but he also added that they were 'the worst marauders in the whole army. Even with that, however, they were very good fellows and we never had any difficulties with them.' (Begos, p. 177.) Oudinot's corps saw very little action during the earliest stages of the Russian campaign, but that changed at the Battle of Polotsk on 18 August. The Croats were cited in General Merle's action report as having been distinguished in repulsing a charge by the Russians. (P. Boppe, *La Croatie Militaire*, p. 110.) This action earned crosses of the Legion of Honour for Battalion Chiefs Vacanovich and Cottenet, Captain Rebracha, Lieutenant André, Sergeant-Major Stanoevich and Private Malcovich.

The Croats remained in the vicinity of Polotsk through the end of the summer and beginning of the autumn and consequently also saw action in the second battle of that name on 18 and 19 October. The French were on the defensive this time, but at one point both the Croats and the Swiss joined in a notable counterattack that drove back a dangerous Russians threat. (See separate entry for *Régiments Suisses*.) Unfortunately, however, the charge was carried a little to far, and the Croats in particular suffered heavily when Russian supports came into action. According to one eyewitness, the

Croats also had one or more companies captured when Russian cavalry disguised as Bavarians and using French trumpet calls slipped in amongst them. (Begos, p. 184.) The French won the battle, but still needed to withdraw, and the Swiss and Croats provided the rearguard that disputed possession of the town until the last French troops had passed to the other side of the Dvina River. The intensity of the fighting can be judged from the fact that the unit had one officer killed and nine wounded.

The 3rd Regiment was still an organised fighting force at this point, however, and would remain so until the crossing of the Beresina. On 28 November 1812 the Croats and the other foreign troops of the IInd Corps wrote one of the most glorious and forlorn pages in the saga of the Grand Army by sacrificing themselves to hold off possible Russian encirclement of the Grand Army. The loss of eighteen officers wounded (two mortally) put an effective end to the 3rd Regiment; on 30 December Colonel Joly was able to muster just 157 men.

Final Transformation During the spring of 1813 a small component of the Regiment under Battalion Chief Jean Cottenet (1774–1823; originally of the 2nd Banat, or 6th, Regiment of Illyrian Chasseurs) was blockaded in the fortress of Custrin and remained there until the town surrendered on 20 March 1814. Another cadre was assembled by Colonel Joly at Ingolstadt, but when he had trouble obtaining enough officers for his own unit he took the radical step of using the available recruits to re-form instead the 2nd Battalion of the 1st Provisional Croatian Regiment. On 1 July he wrote a letter to the Minister of War explaining that the 3rd Provisional Regiment 'no longer exists'. He subsequently commanded the re-formed unit during the siege of Magdebourg, and even argued that this development qualified him to claim that he was Colonel of the 1st Provisional Croatian Regiment rather Colonel of the 3rd.

4th Croatian Provisional Regiment

The 4th Croatian Provisional Regiment was organised in August of 1813 by combining the second battalions of the 1st and 2nd Banat (5th and 6th) Regiments of Illyrian Chasseurs at Montechiaro in Italy. (P. Boppe, *La Croatie Militaire*, p. 157.)

Commanders The commander would have been the senior of the Battalion Chiefs of the two constituent battalions.

Operational History Since French confidence in the loyalty of the Illyrian Chasseurs dropped precipitously during the autumn of 1813, the 4th Provisional Regiment was never deployed for active service. It ended up stationed in the Grand Duchy of Tuscany.

Final Transformation When his sister, Elisa Bonaparte, complained that the 4th Provisional Regiment was behaving badly in her territory, Napoleon immediately authorised her to transfer the unit to Corsica. (N. to Elisa Bonaparte, 18 November 1813, Nap. *Corr.*, No 20910, Vol. 26, p. 441.) One wonders how this was accomplished in the face of British command of the Mediterranean Sea, but, in any event, shortly thereafter General César Berthier, the local French commander (and the brother of Marshal Berthier), was complaining that he had over 2,000 Croats and Illyrians on the island. (C. Berthier to Minister of War, quoted in P. Boppe, *La Croatie Militaire*, p. 156.) The two battalions of the 4th Provisional Regiment were formally disbanded and disarmed at Ajaccio on 23 January 1814 and the officers and men were then incorporated into the 2nd Colonial Battalion already stationed on Corsica. Battalion Chief Augier of the 1st Banat was made the commander of the 2nd Colonial Battalion on 18 February. (P. Boppe, *La Croatie Militaire*, p. 157.)

Uniforms The units of Illyrian Chasseurs from which the Provisional Croatian Regiments were formed generally wore brown, black or blue uniforms (see separate entry). When the 3rd Provisional Regiment reached Paris and was reviewed by Napoleon, however, the Emperor was apparently displeased with its appearance. On 9 December 1811 he set his Minister of War the task of studying the matter and coming up with a new uniform for the Provisional units. The military bureaucracy must have been running very efficiently because the following formal report came back with astonishing speed on 13 December (Arch. Nat. Carton AF [IV]1118, quoted in L'Invalide, 'Régiments Croates', pp. 133–4):

> . . . I believe I have fulfilled your intentions by deciding on the following uniform for the two battalions:
>
> Green jacket.
> Crimson facings [the same as for the Ottochatz Regiment].
> White buttons.
> Light infantry style.
> White vest.
> Green trousers.

Unfortunately, the report does not indicate whether the uniforms were designed in the normal style for 1811 or in the style that was introduced the following year for the entire Army.

To make sure that the new specifications were implemented quickly, production of the new uniforms was turned over to the tailors of the Imperial Guard, and Napoleon's ADC, General Mouton, the Count of Lobau, was assigned to inspect the rest of the unit's equipment and supplies. He reported back on 19 January as follows (Arch. Nat. Carton AF [IV]1179, quoted in L'Invalide, 'Régiments Croates', p. 134):

> . . . it seems to me an opportune time for Your Majesty to prescribe the placement of grenade and hunting horn ornaments in the turnbacks of the Carabiniers and the Chasseurs; those [the turnbacks] of the sappers should be decorated with axe ornaments and the sappers themselves should receive axes, axe cases, aprons, cartridge boxes, shoulder-belts and musket straps; The unit also needs a heavy leather belt for the Eagle-bearer to use to carry the Eagle and lace for chevrons for the 2nd and 3rd Eagle-bearers.

Much of this new material did not catch up with the Croats until after they had moved on into Germany.

It is thus clear that the 3rd Regiment wore green. The evidence to support the conclusion that the 1st, 2nd and 4th Provisional Croatian Regiments also had green uniforms is reasonably strong but circumstantial. First, it seems likely that such a specific Imperial decision would have been carried through the next time a similar unit was formed. Second, Herbert Knoetel, the son of the famous German military artist Richard Knoetel, reports that a number of primary sources in private collections depict Croatian soldiers in green uniform with *yellow* facings (emphasis added). (Drawings of Croatian figures by Herbert Knoetel in such uniforms are reproduced in Forthoffer's *Fiches Documentaires*, Nos. 49 and 96–106.) Unless the facings of the 3rd Regiment changed at some point from crimson to yellow, those sources must have been depicting at least one other Croatian unit that was also dressed in green. Finally, there is a June 1813 report from the Minister of War that implies that all the Provisional Regiments were then wearing green because it recommends that such uniforms should be scrapped and that all the Croats should be dressed instead in blue uniforms (Arch. Nat. Carton AF [IV] 1119, quoted in L'Invalide, 'Régiments Croates', pp. 137–8):

> Your Majesty decided in December 1811 . . . that the uniform of the Provisional Croatian Regiments would be green; those of the six sedentary regiments from which the provisional units were drawn were assigned blue uniforms by order . . . of the Duke of Ragusa [Marmont]. I have received a number of complaints about this difference in uniforms, both about the disagreeable lack of uniformity that results when soldiers from the sedentary regiments join the Provisional Regiments . . . and when men are discharged back to Croatia and find themselves dressed differently from their original regiment.

The Minister argued that the blue uniform should prevail because of the scarcity of green cloth in Croatia and because 'that colour flatters the Croats because it is the one worn by French infantry', but it is unclear whether this initiative had any definitive outcome.

It is certain, however, that brown uniforms were worn by some of the Croatian reinforcements sent to the Grand Army in 1813 to make good the losses from the Russian campaign. (See Pegau MS, 14 February 1813 in R. Knotel, *Mitteilungen*, Vol. 15, No 4 (1908), p. 1 (brown uniforms with red 'cuffs'); Forthoffer, *Fiches Documentaires*, No 50 (brown uniforms with yellow facings); and Freiberg MS, Plate 44, in R. Knotel, *Mitteilungen*, Vol. 17, No 8 (1912), p. 29 (brown uniform with red facings).) Perhaps this means that the old Austrian uniforms were given to men destined for the Grand Army as a means of saving on blue uniforms.

Standard The inspection report Count Lobau referred to above listing equipment for the Eagle bearers seems to confirm that the 3rd Provisional Regiment did receive an Imperial Eagle, but there is no evidence as to whether the accompanying colour would have been an 1812 Model tricolour. On the basis of that information, Charrié (p. 19) concludes that it is 'very likely' that the 1st and 2nd Regiments would also have received Eagles, but the fact that one was raised before, and one after, the Russian campaign suggests equally persuasively that they might not have been treated the same. In any event, it is unlikely that the 4th Provisional Croatian Regiment received either a standard or a colour. It and the other units raised or reorganised in 1813 may have carried *fanions*, or little flags, from their parent units of Illyrian Chasseurs (see separate entry).

Régiments Suisses (Nos 1–4)

(1st–4th Swiss Regiments)

Date of Creation 1805–07.

Circumstances of Creation The four Swiss Regiments that served in Napoleon's army were organised pursuant to a military convention signed by the French and the Swiss on 27 September 1803. (Schaller, p. 17.)

Composition The convention specified that the Swiss Confederation would provide a total of 16,000 soldiers for the French Army, divided among four regiments of equal size. The numbered articles of the 1803 convention set forth detailed specifications for the organisation of the four Regiments (reproduced in Schaller, pp. 18–20):

> *Article 3*:Each of these Regiments will be composed of a staff and four battalions. Each battalion will have nine companies (one of grenadiers and eight of fusiliers). Each Regiment will be organised as follows:
>
> **Regimental Staff Officers**
>
> 1 Colonel
> 1 Lt. Colonel (**Colonel en second**)
> 1 Major
> 4 Battalion Chiefs
> 4 Adjutant-Majors
> 4 Quarter-Masters
> 4 Flag-bearers
> 1 Chaplain
> 1 Minister
> 1 Judge
> 4 Surgeons
>
> **Regimental Staff Non-Officers**
>
> [56 men, including four drummers and thirteen musicians]
>
> The grenadier company will have four officers, fifteen NCOs, 72 soldiers, two drummers for a total of 92 men; fusilier companies will have four officers, fourteen NCOs, 92 soldiers and two drummers, for a total of 112 men.
>
> *Article 4*: There will be four companies of foot artillery, organised like those of the French Republic, each with four officers and 64 men. . .
>
> *Article 7*: The Swiss selected for these regiments must be between the ages of 18 and 40, be at least 5 feet 2 inches (1.678 metres) tall and have no physical infirmity. They must agree to serve the French Republic faithfully for four years, at the end of which term they can enlist again for a period of two, four, six or eight years.

Among the other points addressed in the convention were the appointment of officers by the First Consul rather than by the Swiss authorities, a prohibition against service out of Europe and the specification that the Regiments would have the same rank and privileges as French troops. There was also an emergency clause (Article 24) that permitted the Swiss Diet to recall the Regiments on ten days' notice if Switzerland were to become menaced with invasion.

Although the convention was signed in 1803, it was not fully implemented for several years. The 1st Regiment was not formed until 1805, while the other three did not come into existence until 1806–07. Part of the delay can be explained by the difficulty of finding enough native Swiss volunteers to fill out the units, because Napoleon would accept no substitutes (N. to Minister of War, 20 February 1807, Nap. *Corr.*, No 11838, Vol. 14, p. 316):

> . . . I am extremely unhappy that the Swiss Regiments have been recruiting among the Prussian prisoners, including those of the Prussian Royal Guard. In truth, this is idiotic; it is putting weapons into the hands of my enemies. Order a strict inspection of all four Regiments and dismiss on the spot anyone who is Prussian or, more generally, anyone who is not Swiss.

To make certain that his wishes were carried out, he wrote another letter on the same subject to his Imperial Arch Chancellor: '. . . make certain that no foreigners are admitted to these regiments. I want my Swiss units to be composed of Swiss, who are known for their loyalty, and not of my enemies. This result is very important to me.' (N. to Cambacérès, 25 February 1807, Nap. *Corr.*, No 11872, Vol. 14, p. 330.)

For the sake of convenience, information about the 'Circumstances of Formation', 'Commanders', 'Operational History (pre-1812)' and 'Uniforms' has been broken out separately below for each individual regiment, but the sections on 'Composition', 'Operational History (1812 and later)' and 'Standards' apply to all units.

1st Swiss Regiment

The formation of the 1st Swiss Regiment was not decreed until 15 March 1805, but the work went very quickly because the unit was not formed from scratch. Instead, Napoleon created the new 1st Swiss from the last surviving elements of the *Demi-brigades Helvétiques* (see separate entry) that had been brought into the French Army back in 1798. The exact incorporation of units was as follows (see Rosselet, p. 90., for more details of the process):

1st Swiss	Prior Unit
1st Battalion	3rd Helvetian Demi-brigade
2nd Battalion	3rd Helvetian Demi-brigade
3rd Battalion	1st Helvetian Demi-brigade
4th Battalion	2nd Helvetian Demi-brigade

A Swiss artillery company that had been formed for French service on 19 April 1803 was attached to the 1st Swiss from 1 April 1806. (See separate entry for *Artillerie Suisse*.)

Commanders *18 July 1805–9 December 1812*: Colonel André Raguettly, the former commander of the 3rd Helvetian Demi-brigade (see separate entry). He was captured by the Russians in Vilna in 1812 and died one day later. *December 1812 to disbandment:* Colonel Rodolphe Louis Emmanuel Réal de Chapelle (1754–1837), who had been Lieutenant-Colonel under Colonel Raguettly and who was another veteran who had served in the Swiss regiments of the Bourbon monarchy.

Operational History (Pre-1812) Of the four battalions of the 1st Regiment, the 1st was organised on Corsica, the 2nd on Elba, the 3rd near Modena and the 4th at Genoa. The 4th Battalion under Louis Clavel was attached to the division of the Army of Italy commanded by fellow-Swiss General Jean Louis Ebénézer Reynier (1771–1814) and performed well in action on 24 November 1805 in the combat of Castel-Franco, when 7,000 Hapsburg soldiers under the Prince de Rohan attempting to reach the safety of the Austrian-held fortress of Venice were surrounded and captured in sight of their objective. (Schaller, p. 36.)

Only the 4th Battalion, still serving under Reynier, was included in the French invasion of the Kingdom of Naples in December 1805. (Schaller, p. 37.) This led eventually to its most famous combat experience, namely participation in the Battle of Maida on 4 July 1806. The story of that British victory is well known, but the role played by the Swiss is not. They were brigaded with two battalions of the 1st Polish Demi-brigade (see separate entry) in the centre of Reynier's advance against the British and, after the rout of the French right wing, they very nearly saved the day for the French because of the confusion caused by their red coats (Fortescue, Vol. 5, p. 348):

> The Swiss . . . almost succeeded in turning the whole tide of the action. They wore a scarlet uniform; and it is said that the 78th, mistaking them for Watteville's Swiss, allowed them to approach unharmed within very close range and received from them a very sharp volley. Certain it is that for a few minutes there was some confusion in both battalions of Acland's brigade, that the two commanding officers misapprehended orders and lost their heads, and that the 78th actually began to retreat. The retrograde movement was fortunately checked in the nick of time by the Major, David Stewart [footnote omitted]; the 78th recovered itself at once; and after a short struggle the Swiss retired in good order towards their right, where they rallied and re-formed upon Digonet's brigade.

General Reynier's report is less flattering to the Swiss (Reynier to Joseph, 5 July 1806, Nap. *Confidential*, No 205, Vol. 1, pp. 161–8 at 165–6):

> The Swiss Battalion, carried away by the example of the other troops [that had fled] hesitated; however, I made several of its companies advance, which checked a little the enemy's pursuit of the 1st and the 82nd.

The Swiss then teamed up with the 23rd Light, the 9th Mounted Chasseurs and four cannon to cover the retreat of the rest of the French Army. Schaller records that, of the 600 Swiss engaged in the battle, 82 men were killed or wounded and 55 taken prisoner (Schaller, p. 39), but that number may be low because the official British returns show 102 Swiss prisoners of war. (Oman, *Studies*, pp. 71–2.) One officer was killed and five wounded, with Battalion Chief Clavel included amongst the latter. He was rescued from the battlefield by the Swiss of the de Watteville Regiment serving in the British Army, who also organised his exchange for French prisoners. His wounds were very severe, however, and he ultimately died from their effects on 23 July 1808, over two years after they were inflicted. (Schaller, pp. 39, 48.)

The red uniforms of the Swiss also helped them another time during the French withdrawal from Calabria after Maida. They were in the vanguard of the Reynier's army when it approached the village of Marcellanara on 5 July, desperate for food and water. To the amazement of all the French, they were welcomed enthusiastically by the populace shouting 'Long live the British!' and 'Death to the French!' because the Swiss had been mistaken for English soldiers. This comical situation had a tragic ending, however, when the Swiss opened fire on the populace and the village was sacked. (Finley, p. 51.)

The 3rd Battalion had originally also been scheduled for inclusion in the Army of Naples, but it was diverted to assist in the suppression of a significant uprising by Italian peasants in Parma, Plaisance and the Trebbia valley in January 1806. This incident, involving upwards of 20,000 inhabitants driven to insurrection by the abuses of the occupying French forces, gave the Swiss a taste of the type of action they would encounter again in Calabria. The 3rd Battalion finally made it to Naples in September 1806, followed shortly thereafter by the 1st and 2nd Battalions. The 4th Battalion was held back at Naples because it still had not made good the losses it suffered at Maida, but the other three battalions found themselves plunged into fighting in 1807 as the French attempted to pacify Calabria once and for all.

There were few highlights to this type of campaigning, only hard marching, significant privation in terms of pay and provisions and a steady stream of casualties. The Swiss carried out their duties diligently, however, and the 1st Battalion even managed to distinguish itself at the crucial siege of Cotrone at the end of June, when two of its officers earned the Legion of Honour medal. (Schaller, p. 44.) Because of its reliability in the field, King Joseph conceived the plan of transferring the 1st Swiss Regiment into his own nascent Neapolitan Army and even persuaded Napoleon to permit that to happen. (N. to Joseph, 27 October 1807, Nap. *Confidential*, No 337, Vol. 1, p. 276.) He negotiated a convention to that effect in December 1807, but it was not ratified by all the cantonal governments in Switzerland until June of the following year, by which time Joseph had already accepted a transfer to the throne of Spain. His successor, King Joachim I (once a simple cavalryman named Joachim Murat), decided it would be an insult to his new subjects to allow foreigners in his army, so the plan was never put into practice. (Schaller, pp. 43–4.)

King Joachim, however, had no objection to the continued use of the 1st Swiss in the vanguard of his military endeavours. The Grenadiers, Voltigeurs and artillerymen of the Regiment were consequently included in the élite force that stormed the island of Capri in October 1808 and captured the British garrison commanded by Sir Hudson Lowe, the man who would become Napoleon's jailer on St Helena. (Schaller, pp. 45–6.) The Swiss also played a prominent part in the defence of Capri and nearby coastal targets the following year. They suffered some combat casualties as a result of these endeavours, but the real enemy turned out to be the malaria that was endemic around the Bay of Naples, since it killed nearly 800 men (including some who became so depressed by the disease that they committed suicide). (Schaller, pp. 47–8.)

In 1810 the 1st and 2nd Battalions, the élite companies of the 3rd and 4th Battalions and the regimental artillery company were all assigned to the force that King Joachim concentrated at the toe of Italy in August for the purpose of launching an invasion of Sicily. That plan was abandoned after two Neapolitan battalions made their way to the shores of Sicily and were captured *en masse*, and the various components of the 1st Swiss were dispersed to a variety of garrisons and duties in lower Calabria. Finally, in July 1811 the Regiment received a reprieve from its hard labours in the form of a summons to re-join the main French armies after an absence of over five years. (Schaller, p. 49.)

2nd Swiss Regiment

The 2nd, 3rd and 4th Swiss Regiments were formed by a decree dated 12 September 1806. The 2nd was based in Provence and, according to one of its officers, 'the process of organising the Regiment was relatively difficult because most of the officers and men were conscripts who had no prior military experience'. (Begos, p. 133.)

Commanders *Creation to 30 March 1812*: Colonel Nicolas Xavier Antoine, Count Castella de Berlens (1767–1830). He was wounded at Polotsk and promoted to the rank of General in the spring of 1813. *31 March 1812 to final transformation*: Major Placide Abyberg, who spent the Russian campaign in command of the regimental depot.

Operational History (Pre-1812) The first operational experience for the 2nd Swiss involved a great deal of travel but little action. The 1,200-man-strong 2nd Battalion under Battalion Chief Octave de Laharpe (but accompanied by Lieutenant-Colonel Joseph de Segesser) was assigned to General Androche Junot's expedition to Portugal in October and November 1807. Junot executed a forced march to Lisbon under difficult conditions and just missed capturing the Portuguese royal family before it escaped with the Portuguese fleet. Portuguese resistance was otherwise so feeble that the country effectively came entirely under control of the French, who disbanded the Portuguese Army and deported the best of its soldiers to form the Portuguese Legion (see separate entry).

It is a measure of Napoleon's lackadaisical approach to affairs in Spain that when two other battalions of the Regiment were also assigned to the Peninsula they were split up from each and from the 2nd Battalion. The 1st Battalion (Battalion Chief Joachim de Castelberg with Colonel Castella in tow) was attached to Marshal Moncey's Coast Observation Corps which entered Old Castille in January 1808. The 3rd Battalion (mustering only 600 men), under the command of Battalion Chief Ignace de Flue, was attached to General Duhesme's force destined for the occupation of Catalonia and arrived at Barcelona on 13 February. (Schaller, pp. 72–3.) To complete the dispersion, Laharpe's 2nd Battalion, which had been stationed near Lisbon, was moved south in April 1808 when the Spanish government withdrew the troops it had committed to assist their French 'allies' in the occupation of the neighbouring kingdom. The battalion, minus its Grenadier company, which was retained by Junot, was detailed to garrison the important border fortress of Elvas in the province of the Alentejo not far from Badajoz. (Schaller, p. 70.)

The 3rd Battalion in Catalonia was the first to suffer combat losses in the Peninsula. On 6 June it participated in a sortie from Barcelona intended to disperse some of the insurgent forces threatening the city. After some initial success, the French column found itself surrounded and had to cut its way to safety, with the 3rd taking heavy casualties along the way. (Schaller, pp. 73–4 and 90.) In July, still another detachment of the 2nd Swiss, this time a mixed half-battalion under Adjutant-Major Claude de Tschudy, entered Catalonia as part of a force under General Reille intended to open communications with General Duhesme's troops in Barcelona. This unit suffered officer casualties at the fortress of Rosas on 11 and 18 July, and others near the fortress of Figueras. It eventually broke through to Barcelona, where the two detachments of the Regiment were combined for operational purposes. (Maag, *Spanien*, Vol. 1, pp. 522–4.)

Back in the centre of Spain, Castelberg's 1st Battalion avoided the dangerous fate of being assigned to Dupont's force for the invasion of Andalusia. Instead, it was first used to put down an uprising at Segovia and then it participated in an abortive advance by Marshal Moncey from Madrid towards Valencia. The battalion was then recalled to Madrid where it assisted on 26 July at the arrival of the new Spanish monarch, Napoleon's brother Joseph. (Maag, *Spanien*, Vol. 1, p. 257.) Six days later the battalion served as part of the French rearguard when King Joseph was forced to abandon his new capital and retreat to the Ebro River because of the news of Bailen. (Maag, *Spanien*, Vol. 1, p. 510.)

In Portugal, a large force of Portuguese and Spanish troops gathered at Evora in July and threatened both Lisbon and the French garrison at Elvas. In response, Junot formed an élite unit under General Loison from detached grenadier companies, including that of the 2nd Battalion, which was then sent to disperse the insurgents. The Swiss led the assault on the town, which was captured and put to the sack. (Schaller, p. 86.) No sooner had that threat been disposed of, however, when another, more dangerous one arrived from the sea in the form of a British force under a general named Wellesley. The Grenadiers returned to Junot's main force and fought at the Battle of Vimeiro on 20 August as part of General Kellerman's reserve. (Schaller, pp. 87–8; Oman, Vol. 1, p. 246, n. 1, states, on the other hand, that there were no Grenadiers of foreign regiments in the reserve.)

The rest of the 2nd Battalion had meanwhile remained in Elvas and the adjoining citadel of Fort La Lippe. The town was invested in early September by a strong Spanish force under Galluzo, the Captain General of Estremadura. Since there was not much scope for the deployment of infantry, the Voltigeurs of the Swiss battalion, along with one company of Fusiliers, were assigned to artillery service for the duration of the siege. (Bégos, p. 151.) Although news of the Convention of Cintra arrived in mid-September, the French commander continued to resist and Galluzo for his own reasons also declined to recognise a cessation of hostilities. The Spaniards therefore continued a heavy, but ineffective, bombardment until Junot sent a direct order to the garrison to end its resistance. Ironically, it was not until British troops approached the town that the garrison was allowed to march out with honours of war on 1 October 1807. They were embarked at Lisbon on 7 October in accordance with the Convention, but the sea voyage back to France ending up taking over four months, including an unscheduled return to Lisbon because of bad weather *en route*. (Schaller, pp. 89–0.)

By the autumn of 1808, therefore, the 2nd Swiss had two units still in Spain. The reinforced 3rd Battalion (Flue and Tschudy) was still in garrison at Barcelona. The 1st Battalion (Castelberg), reduced to a strength of 644 men on 15 November, was combined with the 2nd Battalion of the 3rd Swiss Regiment (Graffenreid) in a provisional regiment commanded by Colonel Castella of the 2nd. (Schaller, p. 93.) This unit was then attached to General Pierre Merle's division of the II Corps of the new army organised by Napoleon for the reconquest of Spain. Early in November command of the II Corps passed from Marshal Bessières to Marshal Soult, who led the main advance of the French on the road to Madrid. After the Battle of Gamonal near Burgos on 10 November, however, Soult's corps was detached on a sweeping march around the flank of General Blake and the Spanish forces occupying the provinces bordering the Bay of Biscay. Before it left, there was time for both Napoleon and Marshal Jean Lannes, lately appointed Colonel-General of all the Swiss Regiments, to review the unit on 12 November. They are said to have been very satisfied with its appearance. (Maag, *Spanien*, Vol. 2, pp. 17–18.)

At the end of November General Julien Mermet replaced General Merle at the head of Marshal Soult's 1st Division and the Swiss were brigaded with the 31st Light Regiment and the élite companies and first battalion of the 9th Line Regiment under the command of General Joseph Yves Manigault-Gaulois. (Order of Marshal Soult, 30 November 1808, reproduced in Balagny, Vol. 2, pp. 503–4.) They did not play a featured role in Soult's activities, however, because the *ad hoc* combined unit had suffered significant attrition (Soult to Berthier, 13 December 1808, reproduced in Balagny, Vol. 3, pp. 551–3) :

> The two Swiss battalions with my Army Corps have been reduced to 350 men and 230 men, respectively; they have many sick and they have left detachments scattered all over the place which I have not been able to recover since I took command of this Corps.

The Swiss were actually left behind in the latter stages of the pursuit of Sir John Moore's British army so that they were not present at the Battle of Corunna on 16 January 1809 (although they did suffer one officer casualty in the person of Lieutenant

D'Armhyn of the 2nd Swiss Regiment). (Balagny, Vol. 4, p. 341, n. 1.) The Swiss rejoined Mermet's division in time to participate in an attack on Ferrol on 24 January, an action that cost the 2nd Regiment two more wounded officers but led to the capitulation of the fortress one day later. Other action followed in the next month as the French temporarily cleared Galicia of its last organised Spanish defenders.

The Swiss were reorganised again for Marshal Soult's advance into Portugal towards Oporto. This time the 1st Battalion of the 4th Regiment was added to Mermet's division, thus bringing elements of the 2nd, 3rd and 4th Swiss together in the same unit. Colonel Castella of the 2nd, who had been the senior field officer, was sent back to France to look after the rest of his Regiment, and he was replaced by Lieutenant-Colonel Thomasset of the 3rd Regiment. (Maag, *Spanien*, Vol. 2, p. 47; see also the order of battle in Le Noble, pp. 549–53.) In the campaign that followed, the Swiss faced an unusual foe in the form of hordes of untrained Portuguese militia who fought fiercely but ineffectively in defence of their homeland. The force defending the city of Oporto itself may have outnumbered Soult's army, but it was routed with relative ease on 29 March and the city was taken by storm. The élite companies of the Swiss battalions were in the forefront of the attack, and Lieutenant Graff of the 2nd Swiss earned the Legion of Honour by being the first man in the breach in the city walls. The decoration was also awarded to Captain Hartmann Fussli of the Voltigeurs of the 2nd Swiss, who suffered a wound in the action. (Maag, *Spanien*, Vol. 2, pp. 87–8.)

Soult had thus attained his initial objective, but he was in no position to make the attempt on Lisbon that Napoleon had contemplated when he set the second French invasion of Portugal into motion. His men were worn out by incessant campaigning and the Portuguese troops he had easily brushed aside during his advance had reformed in his rear to cut off communications with the nearest French forces in Galicia. Some Swiss, mainly sick and stragglers, were captured when Chaves surrendered to a Portuguese force on 25 March, and the paychest of the 2nd Corps was captured when a weak French garrison, including some Swiss, was forced to capitulate at Vigo on 27 March 1809. Another post at Tuy was closely besieged, but was saved by a timely relief expedition. Soult was also distracted from his appointed task by his own efforts to be recognised as a potential ruler of northern Portugal and by the odd scheming, bordering on treason, it engendered within the ranks of his own generals.

The final blow came when the British Army under Wellesley effected a surprise assault on Oporto in broad daylight on 12 May 1809. The French were ousted in disorder, covered by the Swiss and other troops of Mermet's division. That defeat left no option to Marshal Soult but to retreat, but the main roads north were cut by the ever-present Portuguese militia, so he was forced to lead his men along a little-used route back to Spain. Marshal Soult's retreat through the mountains of northern Portugal back to Galicia was admirably conducted from a tactical standpoint, but his soldiers suffered great privations and hardships. Many sick and wounded, as well as much baggage and equipment, had to be abandoned *en route*.

The Swiss regiments continued to serve together through 1809 but saw no significant action. They were now in General Thomières brigade, which was eventually transferred out of the 2nd Corps and attached to General Kellerman's command in Leon for the purpose of fighting guerrillas. This type of warfare was hard and thankless, leading to constant attrition. By the year's end, the 1st Battalion of the 2nd Swiss Regiment had fewer than 400 fit men (Schaller, p. 103). There was, however, no relief for the Swiss, who were called upon to carry out the same duties in 1810. The élite companies of all the Swiss battalions were sometimes formed in a separate force to serve as General Kellerman's bodyguard. (Schaller, p. 104) In a typical action, 2nd Lieutenant Henri Gerbex was shot in the neck on 2 February during an action in which 330 men of the 2nd Swiss held off double theat number of guerrillas until help arrived. (Schaller, pp. 104–5.)

The combined regiment received some reinforcements during the course of the year, both from France and from the escape of a number of Swiss soldiers who had been made prisoner at Bailen, but none of them were for the 2nd Regiment. In October 1810 the pick of the officers and men from the 1st Battalion were sent back to France, leaving only a skeleton unit to serve in Spain.

Ironically, it was shortly after this departure that the soldiers who remained behind gave the 2nd Regiment its most heroic moment in the Peninsula. A detachment of 50 men of the 2nd Swiss under Captain Anton von Salis-Samaden was occupying the village of Puente-el-Santo on the road from Toro to Salamanca on 21 November when it was attacked by the guerrilla band of Don Julian Sanchez. The Swiss barricaded themselves in a fortified house but left five men posted in the steeple of a nearby church. When the Spaniards tried to burn out both forces they failed in their primary objective, but the men in the church were left trapped because the stairway to the steeple burned through. This mini-epic lasted 66 hours, during which the Swiss had no more food and water than that on their persons when the attack commenced, but it ended happily for the defenders when the appearance of a relief force drove off the guerrillas. The five men in the steeple were unharmed. (Maag, *Spanien*, Vol. 2, pp. 323–4.)

The year 1812 was one of dramatic upheaval for the French armies in Spain, but there were only 127 men from the 1st Battalion to witness all the developments. (Schaller, p. 113.) For all practical purposes they were considered to be part of the 4th Swiss Regiment, which provided the largest component of men and the commander for the mixed Swiss unit. The few remaining men of the Battalion still in action were finally allowed to return to their depot in France only in April 1813.

During all the years the 1st Battalion was fighting and dying in northern Spain, the 3rd Battalion of the 2nd Regiment remained part of the garrison of Barcelona. Out of fear that the morale of the unit might be adversely affected by the number of Swiss who were fighting on the side of the Spanish patriots in Catalonia (including, at one time, General Theodore Reding, the Spanish commander), the unit was kept on fortress guard duty most of the time. For that reason, they were on duty in the important fort of Mont-Juich when the Spaniards tried to capture it by surprise on 19 March 1811 with the help of a traitor paid to open the gates from within. The French authorities learned of the attack in advance, but allowed it to go ahead in order to have the opportunity inflict a bloody reverse on the attackers when they found themselves trapped in the ditch of the fortress before the door that they had expected to find open. (Schaller, p. 115.) By the end of 1811 there were only 156 men of the 3rd Battalion still with the colours. They must have been a tough lot because there were still many of them left when the French finally evacuated Catalonia in 1814.

3rd Swiss Regiment

The 3rd Regiment was formed in Flanders in 1806 and 1807 pursuant to the same decree as the 2nd and 4th Regiments.

Commanders *Creation to 22 July 1808:* Colonel Louis de May (1764–1833), another Bourbon veteran who served in the military forces of his home canton of Berne from 1792 to 1806. He became a prisoner of war upon General Dupont's surrender at Bailen, and spent three years in Majorca and England before he was allowed to return to Switzerland on parole. He remained titular commander of the 3rd Regiment straight through to 1814, although others led the unit in the field. *1808–26 June 1812:* Lieutenant-Colonel Frédéric Georges Thomasset (1764–1812), who began his career in the Dutch Army and took over field command of the 3rd Regiment after Colonel de May was taken prisoner. He left the Regiment in late June 1812 to take a staff position and disappeared at the crossing of the Beresina in November. (Belhomme Vol. 4, p. 176.) *June–6 December 1812:* Battalion Chief Jonathan von Graffenreid, a veteran of service in Spain took command after Colonel Thomasset and held it until the was wounded and captured by Cossacks on 6 December. (Belhomme Vol. 4, p. 177 and 212.) *1813:* Battalion Chief Jean Baptiste Bucher. (Schaller, p. 224.)

Operational History (Pre-1812) The 3rd Swiss Regiment was also committed to action in the Peninsula without any particular co-ordination between its battalions. The 1st Battalion, with Colonel May accompanying Battalion Chief Charles Philippe d'Affry, crossed into Spain with General Vedel's division of General Dupont's Corps in December 1807. The 2nd Battalion under Battalion Chief von Graffenreid followed in February as part of General Mouton's division of Marshal Moncey's corps.

Despite the fact that it was itself a relatively new unit, the 1st Battalion was probably the most reliable unit in General Dominique Vedel's division, the rest being Reserve Legions raised specifically for service in Spain. Vedel's force was initially excluded from Dupont's expedition into Andalusia, but as concern for the safety of the original force mounted, the division was dispatched to reopen communications with Dupont, a task that it accomplished on 27 June. Vedel's men, including the Swiss, had their first taste of warfare in Spain when they captured and sacked Jaen on 2 July. (Maag, *Spanien*, Vol. 1, pp. 325–6.)

When the Spaniards under Theodore Reding seized Bailen on 18 July Vedel's division was cut off from the rest of Dupont's force, but at least it had a clear line of retreat back toward Madrid. Nevertheless, after some vacillation and confusion, Vedel marched on the 19th to the sound of Dupont's guns, arriving just after Dupont had conceded his failure to break through the Spanish force blocking his path to freedom. Vedel at first refused to accept the situation and launched an impetuous attack on the Spanish forces in his way, capturing nearly 1,000 men. The 1st Battalion seems to have been heavily engaged in this action, because Martinien reveals that the 3rd Swiss Regiment had six officers killed and eight wounded on the day, but those casualties seem out of line with the amount of fighting that took place. Finally, under direct orders from Dupont, Vedel ceased fire and the negotiations for capitulation began. (Maag, *Spanien*, Vol. 1, pp. 347–8.)

The French made one last bid to save some shred of honour on night of 20–21 July when Dupont ordered Vedel to slip away with his undefeated force and return to Madrid. Vedel's division got away without interference, but when the Spaniards realised what had happened they threatened vengeance on the divisions of Dupont still in their power. When that news reached Vedel, he was placed in a terrible quandary—to ignore the Spanish summons might consign his comrades to a terrible fate, but to surrender without having been defeated would seem dishonourable. He eventually chose the latter course, but now the 1st Battalion of the 3rd Swiss took some action on its own. Battalion Chief d'Affry was leading the vanguard of the division and he had already reached the passes of the Sierra Moreno. On his own initiative, he decided to ignore orders recalling him to Bailen and he pressed on to Madrid with part of his men, preserving the 1st Battalion's Eagle and 122 men. (Maag, *Spanien*, Vol. 1, pp. 358–9.)

The surrender did, however, include Colonel May and 960 other men of the 1st Battalion of the 3rd Swiss, and after the Spaniards reneged on the terms of the original capitulation they were marched off to captivity. The Colonel and some officers were eventually exchanged, but the vast majority of the prisoners were consigned to the floating prison ships in the harbour of Cadiz and, later, to the infamous island prison of Cabrera. Except for a small number who escaped from the hulks when the French armies arrived to besiege Cadiz, virtually none of these prisoners lived to see Switzerland again.

Elsewhere in Spain von Graffenreid's 2nd Battalion of the 3rd Swiss, commanded in person by Lieutenant-Colonel Thomasset, had only progressed as far as Burgos in its travels, arriving there after serving in Marshal Bessières' reserve at the Battle of Medina del Rio Seco on 14 July. In November, this unit absorbed the few men of the 1st Battalion who had escaped from Bailen, then combined with Castelberg's Battalion of the 2nd Swiss in a provisional all-Swiss regiment in Marshal Soult's Corps. (Schaller, p. 94.) During the pursuit of the British army in December and January, the battalion belonging to the 3rd Swiss was given the unglamorous task of escorting the artillery and baggage trains and it consequently missed the Battle of Corunna. (Order of Marshal Soult, 29 December 1808, reproduced in Balagny, Vol. 4, p. 158, n. 1.) As the New Year began, the 3rd Swiss Battalion mustered 25 officers and 236 other ranks. (Balagny, Vol. 4, p. 341, n. 1.)

The experience of the combined Swiss unit under Soult after the embarkation of the British army and during the second invasion of Portugal in the spring of 1809 has been detailed above in the section relating to the 2nd Swiss. The noteworthy events in that story with respect to the 3rd Regiment were few and far between. One was a personal tragedy in that three officers of the Regiment were 'assassinated' by brigands while *en route* to Corunna in January 1809. Lieutenant Hermann of the 3rd was wounded twice in the defence of Tuy, while paymaster Adelmann of the 2nd Battalion was captured along with his papers and funds at Vigo and was sent off to England as a prisoner of war. (Schaller, p. 101.) Finally, the unit was involved in some of the heaviest fighting during the British assault on Oporto on 12 May and had three officers killed and two who 'disappeared.'

The retreat from Portugal was painful for the 3rd, because they were forced to abandon sick and wounded, including three officers who ended up as British prisoners of war. It may have provided some psychic revenge at least in that, on 19 May 1809, the red coats of the Swiss fooled the inhabitants of the village of Allaris as to the identity of the troops entering their home (Naylies, p. 132–3):

> . . . [T]he inhabitants mistook the men of the 3rd Swiss for British soldiers. They pressed food and wine on them, hailed them as liberators, and hurled thousands of curses on the French. One of the inhabitants, armed with a musket, boasted of having assassinated many Frenchmen and expressed a desire to march with the regiment against the common enemy. The arrival of our infantry caused the people to discover their error, and they thereupon hid their enthusiasm for a better occasion.

(No information is given about the fate of the self-incriminated assassin, but one suspects that he did not live long to regret his mistake.) Not all the soldiers of the 3rd who survived the retreat still had red coats. Voltigeur Jean Bussy of the 3rd later recorded in his memoirs (Bussy, p. 245):

> I arrived with bare feet, wearing a badly worn pair of cloth trousers and a ill-fitting overcoat I took from the English. . . . I went twelve days without the shirt on my back ever being dry and I went five days without food.

In the aftermath of the Oporto campaign, Lieutenant-Colonel Thomasset, who had earned the Legion of Honour for his performance during the retreat, took command of the three Swiss battalions. This ensemble, which numbered just over 1,000 men, was treated as a provisional regiment. (Schaller, p. 102.) It continued to serve in the northern Spain through 1809 into 1810.

During the night of 7 June 1810 von Graffenreid's 2nd Battalion of the 3rd Swiss was part of the French garrison of the town of León when a Spanish patriot in the town opened a door in the walls to admit a waiting force of guerrillas. Although taken by surprise, the Swiss rallied quickly, many of them fighting in their shirtsleeves because they had not had time to dress properly. Captain von Hundbliss cleared the main square with his Voltigeur company but was killed in the process. His actions, however, gave the Swiss the initiative and they routed the enemy, taking many prisoners. (De Vallière, p. 682; Bussy, pp. 253–4.)

In August, however, the Battalion's luck ran out. While serving under General Séras, von Graffenreid and 333 of his men were detached to defend the small town of Puebla de Sanabria in Galicia near the border with Portugal. They took post in a large fortified house in the upper part of the town, where they soon found themselves besieged by a large Portuguese/Spanish force. A volunteer named Corporal Tinguely was dispatched to bring help, but the enemy pressed the siege with vigour. With little ammunition and a dwindling water supply, the morale of the Swiss plummeted and 48 men of the garrison, including twenty grenadiers, deserted after being subverted by a Swiss deserter serving with the enemy who promised them safe passage back to Switzerland. The end came on 9 August 1810 when the enemy managed to explode two mines and open a breach in the Swiss defences. Despite his desperate situation, however, von Graffenreid managed to negotiate an honourable capitulation that included transport back to France in return for a promise that the prisoners would not serve again in Spain. (Bussy, pp. 255–61.) Unlike the case of Bailen, this time the terms were honoured for the most part, although the British made a concerted and relatively successful effort to entice men to desert and join their army. In November the remaining 133 officers and men of the Battalion was deposited back in France by British ships. (Schaller, pp. 107–10.)

Napoleon was infuriated by von Graffenreid's course of action because a relief column arrived the day after the surrender and because the unit lost one of his Eagle standards. The latter fact was apparently much denied at the time, but there is no reason to doubt the testimony of a British officer who saw the Eagle after the siege (Letter dated 22 August 1810, in Warre, p. 160):

> The Eagle which Silveira took at Pueblo de Sanabria arrived here. It is an imitation of the Roman Eagles, and I think an ugly one. It has, however, its effect upon the volatile courage and vanity of the French. To them a cap of liberty, or emblem of slavery, is equal, so long as it flatters the self-sufficiency and vainglory of the grand nation. The [Swiss] Battalion is gone to Corunna to embark for England. They will almost to a man enlist with us.

Battalion Chief von Graffenreid was court-martialled on 2 February 1811. Contrary to Imperial expectations, he was acquitted with honour, but the men who deserted during the siege were condemned to death *in absentia*. The results of the inquiry were distributed to the Swiss Diet and to all the other Swiss Regiments.

In the wake of the capture of von Graffenreid's force, Lieutenant-Colonel Thomasset was recalled to France in October 1810 with the few remaining officers and NCOs of the 3rd Swiss still on active service in Spain. (Schaller, p. 110.) These included a number of men from the 1st Battalion captured at Bailen who had escaped from the prison ships in Cadiz harbour in July 1810 and been able to re-join the 2nd Battalion. The remaining soldiers were left to serve under Battalion Chief Goeldin of the 4th

Swiss. Their numbers dwindled continuously, so that by the end of 1811 there were only 70 soldiers of the 3rd Swiss still in action. Those who survived the events of 1812 were finally recalled to France in April of 1813.

4th Swiss Regiment

The 4th Regiment was formed under the same circumstances as the 2nd and the 3rd Regiments, but its depot was in Brittany.

Commanders *Creation to March 1810*: Colonel Perrier, formerly commander of the 1st Swiss Demi-brigade (see separate entry). He was too old to support the rigours of his command and was allowed to retire on 20 March 1810. *29 June 1810 to final transformation:* Colonel Charles Philippe d'Affry (1772–1818). Having escaped the massacre of his first unit, the Swiss Guards of Louis XVI, he served briefly in the Austrian Army and then served in the militia of the Canton of Fribourg until he joined the 3rd Swiss. He served with that unit as a Battalion Chief up to the time he was promoted and transferred to the 4th Regiment. (Maag, *Spanien*, Vol. 2, p. 476.)

Operational History (Pre-1812) The 4th Swiss was called to the Spanish Peninsula in two contingents. The first, composed of the Regiment's 1st Battalion under Battalion Chief Béat Felber and half of the 2nd under Adjutant-Major Salomon Bleuler, was attached to the Junot's expedition against Portugal. The second contingent consisted of the 3rd Battalion under Battalion Chief Christen, but it was commanded in person by Lieutenant-Colonel Joseph de Freuler. This battalion, 947 men strong, entered Spain in December 1807 as part of General Dupont's Corps.

After reaching Lisbon in November 1807 the contingent in Portugal was given a number of different garrison assignments, ending up for a long stretch at Almeida on the Spanish frontier. Along the way they saw minor action against insurgents. As the situation of Junot's force became critical following the uprising in Spain, an improvised depot of 200 men (mainly sick and noncombatants) was left at Almeida, but all other elements of the 1st and 2nd Battalions were recalled to the Fortress of Peniche on the coast, one of the four strongpoints (along with Setubal, Elvas and Almeida) Junot had chosen to hold in the face of a possible English invasion. (Maag, *Spanien*, Vol. 1, pp. 279–80.) The élite companies of the 4th were formed into a provisional unit under Adjutant-Major Bleuler that formed part of General Thomières' Brigade of General Henri François DeLaborde's division. (Maag, *Spanien*, Vol. 1, p. 284.)

The 3rd Battalion had, in the meanwhile, advanced in to Andalusia as part of General Pierre Dupont's force, which also included two regiments (commanded by de Preux and Charles Reding the Younger) of the Swiss troops that had been in service to the Spanish Bourbons. On 7 June 1808 it participated in a relatively insignificant skirmish at Bridge of Alcolea outside of the city of Cordoba which cost the unit one officer killed and one wounded. (Maag, *Spanien*, Vol. 1, p. 302.) The Spanish defenders of the city were easily routed, but the pursuit of the French took them into the city itself and, for reasons that will probably never be entirely clear, they turned on the unfortunate inhabitants. The ensuing sack of Cordoba was to become an immensely significant event because it set a horrific precedent for the type of cruelty and brutality that subsequently characterised so much of the fighting between Frenchmen and Spaniards during the rest of the war.

The capture of Cordoba was the high-water mark for the French advance. Spanish resistance stiffened and Dupont realised that his force was too weak to proceed any farther. He retired to Andujar to await reinforcements, but the Spanish forces increased proportionately more than the French. The Spanish made the decisive move of the campaign on 18 July when they occupied the town of Bailen, cut Dupont's line of communication back to Madrid and left the French general on the verge of being attacked from two directions at once. Ironically, one of the Spanish commanders was Colonel Theodore Reding, the commander of the senior Swiss regiment in Spanish service who had sided with the insurgents supporting the legitimate Bourbon monarchy.

Dupont resolved to cut his way through the blocking force to safety, and called upon the 4th Swiss and the two Hispano-Swiss regiments to be among the leaders in his all-out attack on 19 July. Almost immediately the men of the regiment of Charles Reding found themselves face to face with men from the Regiment of Theodore Reding. At first both units seemed inclined to put down their arms and become mere observers of the action, but at a crucial moment one of officers serving with the French persuaded his men to begin fighting again. They immediately took prisoner some of the opposing Swiss. According to some sources, orders were given to shoot these prisoners but they were saved by the intervention of still another Swiss officer. (Maag, *Spanien*, Vol. 1, pp. 335–6 and 337–8.)

The prospects for the French at this point seemed bright, but in three more hours of fighting they failed to make any significant headway against the Spaniards. Then came disaster. General Jean Adam Schramm, the French commander of the two Hispano-Swiss regiments who had himself risen from the ranks of the Diesbach Regiment in French service, was wounded in the cheek and forced to leave the field. His troops were exhausted from their efforts and uncertain of success. In these circumstances the Hispano-Swiss once again came into contact with old comrades fighting for the Spaniards, and this time there was no one to save the day for the French. Just after noon what was left of the two regiments—probably close to 1,400 men—went over to the enemy, leaving a gaping hole in the French line of battle. (Maag, *Spanien*, Vol. 1, pp. 341-2.)

This betrayal, plus the general exhaustion of his best troops after the exertions of the morning in oppressive heat, led Dupont to seek the best terms he could from the enemy. (The 3rd Battalion of the 4th Swiss alone had lost over 300 men—although, curiously, no officers—in the fighting on 19 July.) (Maag, *Spanien*, Vol. 1, p. 360.) There were tense negotiations complicated by the arrival of Vedel's division late in the day—see 3rd Swiss Operational History (Pre-1812)—but ultimately the French decided that a quick repatriation to France would be a good enough outcome to justify the indignity of surrender. That calculus might have been correct in theory, but it proved drastically wrong in practice as the Spaniards reneged on their promises. What lay ahead was years of imprisonment in prison ships or on the island of Cabrera. Some of the officers and men of the 3rd Battalion who were captured at Bailen escaped from their prison ships in Cadiz harbour when Soult laid siege to the town in 1810, but most did not live to see Switzerland again.

The contingent of the 4th Swiss in Portugal was represented at the Battle of Roliça on 17 August by its élite companies. The 29th English Regiment of Foot took a leading role in the attack by Wellesley on Delaborde, and it managed to advance unchecked deep into the heart of the French position. Once there, it encountered the 4th Swiss with consequences that illustrate the difficulty of reconstructing past events even with the help of primary sources. What happened next, according to the memoirs of an officer of the 29th, is not flattering to the Swiss (Leslie, p. 43):

> Some of the enemy in front of the extreme right, either as a ruse or in earnest, called out that they were poor Swiss, and did not wish to fight against the English; some were actually shaking hands, and a parley ensued, during which the enemy's troops, who had been posted on this side of the ravine, finding that we had forced it, and that they were likely to be cut off, began to retire, and coming in the rear of our right dashed through, carrying off with them one Major [Wray], who was dismounted, as before stated, five officers and about 25 privates.

Swiss sources, on the other hand, mention hand-to-hand fighting with the 20th (not the 29th) Foot and also record an incident of 'friendly fire' in which the French 70th Line was unable to distinguish between the red uniforms of the British and those of their Swiss comrades and fired on both. The Swiss casualties were 37 dead and 27 wounded, including one officer killed and two wounded. (These facts, based on Bleuler's diary, come from Maag, *Spanien*, Vol. 1, pp. 462 and 464.) The élite companies of the 4th Swiss were also in action at Vimeiro on the 20th when they lost 30 men killed or taken prisoner and 45 wounded. (Maag, *Spanien*, Vol. 1, p. 473.)

The remaining Swiss of the 1st and 2nd Battalions of the 4th Regiment were included in the Convention of Cintra and were transported back to France in British ships. These units, along with the grenadiers of the 2nd Battalion of the 2nd Swiss, who were repatriated at the same time, were used to reconstitute the 1st Battalion of the 4th, the command of which was awarded to Bleuler while Felber was on detached service. As an ironic reward for its services, this new 1st Battalion was immediately marched back to the Peninsula in December 1808 as part of Delaborde's division. Shortly thereafter, yet another detachment from the 4th Swiss, this one equal to about half the 2nd Battalion, was sent off to Spain under the command of Battalion Chief Ludwig von Ernst to supplement the effort of the re-formed 1st Battalion. (Maag, *Spanien*, Vol. 2, pp. 5–6.) Von Ernst's detachment was inspected by Napoleon himself at Valladolid on 11 January 1809. (Schaller, p. 97.)

The 1st Battalion of the 4th Swiss, which mustered at this point only nineteen officers and 168 other ranks, did play a minor role in the pursuit of General Moore at the end of 1808 and the beginning of 1809, but was not present at the Battle of Corunna. (Balagny, Vol. 4, p. 341, n. 1.) Shortly thereafter both detachments of the 4th Swiss were combined into a single battalion under the command of Battalion Chief von Ernst, and that unit was then added to Mermet's division so that all the Swiss Battalions then serving in north-western Spain were united in a single formation. The 4th accordingly saw action during Soult's invasion of Portugal, taking officer casualties near Chaves on 11 March, at the siege of Tuy on 16 March and at the capture of Oporto itself on 29 March. By the end of 1809 the strength of the remaining Battalion had been reduced from an original 1,156 men to a total of 587, of which 364 were present under arms, 49 were on detached service, 92 were in hospital, nineteen were stragglers and 63 were prisoners of war. Seventy-nine of the men of the Battalion had deserted during the year. (Schaller, p. 104.)

The surprise of the New Year 1810 was the arrival of the 4th Regiment's 4th Battalion in northern Spain in February under the command of Battalion Chief Jean Baptiste Goeldin. This 800-man unit was assigned along with all the other Swiss battalions to General Lauberdière's brigade of General Séras' division of the Army of the North and instantly became the largest of the Swiss battalions. The Grenadier companies of the three Battalions that had served longest in Spain were sometimes combined to provide a special élite guard for General Kellerman. (Schaller, p. 104.) At the end of 1810 the excess officers and men of all the Swiss battalions were sent back to their depots, leaving behind Goeldin's 4th Battalion reinforced to a strength of 1,008 men by the incorporation of the rank-and-file from the battalions of the 2nd, 3rd Swiss and 4th Swiss Regiments that lost their separate identity from that point forward. (Schaller, p. 110.)

After another year of thankless duty, only 680 men were left in the Battalion, 127 of whom were originally from the 2nd Swiss, 70 from the 3rd Regiment and the rest from the 4th. (Schaller, p. 113.) During 1812 the Battalion came under the command of General Vandermaesen. Following Marshal Marmont's defeat at Salamanca, a small detachment of the 4th under Lieutenant Bremi served as part of the escort for the badly wounded Marshal on his return to France. (Maag, *Spanien*, vol. 2, p. 372.) The rest of the Battalion was involved in the counter-offensive launched against Wellington by General Clauzel and Marshal Soult after the failure of the siege of Burgos. The strength of the Battalion was so reduced by this further campaigning without reinforcements that it was finally sent home early in 1813 to help make good the losses suffered by the battalions that had participated in the Russian campaign.

Operational History (all Regiments,1812 onwards) The Swiss battalions that did not serve in either Spain or Italy during the years prior to the Russian campaign led relatively sedate existences in a variety of garrison posts, often on the coasts of the Empire. One of the few noteworthy events in which they were involved was the British attack on Walcheren Island in 1809, which led to a number of battalions being deployed temporarily as part of the French forces that observed the invaders until the local fevers caused them to re-embark voluntarily. One situation that might have been significant had it not ended in farce rather than tragedy arose when the 4th Swiss Regiment was garrisoning the post of Belle-Isle-en-Mer. One of its officers, Lieutenant Samuel Lauper, borrowed money from a British naval officer named Cunliffe Owen who was living on parole in France. The former apparently offered to arrange for his unit to turn over its post to the British in return for forgiveness of his indebtedness. When the Lieutenant failed to deliver on his promises, Owen published their correspondence and the Swiss officer was thrown into prison, only regaining his freedom in 1815. (Schaller, p. 142.)

When Napoleon began in 1811 to consider preparations for a future war with Russia, his thoughts turned to his Swiss mercenaries: 'We must pay serious attention to the Swiss regiments.' (N. to Minister of War, 7 March 1811, N. *P&T*, No 5137, Vol. 4, pp. 99–100.) Having noted that the sixteen battalions called for by the Franco-Swiss convention of 1803 were spread all over Europe—'four remain in Naples, three are employed in defence of the Mediterranean coast, two are used for the defence of Walcheren Island, three for the defence of Brest, one is at Valladolid, one is in Catalonia, two more companies are at Valladolid and one battalion has been captured and exists only on paper'—the Emperor went on to call for a major effort to recruit the regiments up to strength and bring about their organisation. As a result, during the course of the next year the Regiments were gradually reassembled and each received a new regimental artillery company (Decision of 7 December 1811, N. *P&T*, No 6461, Vol. 4, p. 839):

> You will organise an artillery company for each Swiss regiment so that each will have two 3-pound. cannon, three munitions caissons, two caissons for infantry baggage, two caissons for military transport [and] one for medical supplies . . .

This initiative also resulted in a renegotiation of the convention governing the four regiments. Having decided that he ultimately preferred to have four smaller regiments that were full-strength than four larger ones that never came close to their prescribed establishment, Napoleon reduced the overall size of the contingent to 12,000 men and changed the composition of each regiment (Convention of 28 March 1812, reprinted in Margueron, Vol. 4, pp. 544–50):

> *Article 2*: Each regiment will be composed of a staff, three active-service battalions, a depot demi-battalion and a company of artillery.
>
> *Article 3*: Each active-service battalion will consist of six companies of 140 men each categorised as follows: one company of grenadiers, one of voltigeurs, four of fusiliers. . . .

The new convention had three other noteworthy new provisions. The Swiss government was required to produce a steady stream of 2,000 replacements a year to

TABLE 15: SWISS COMMANDERS, 1812

Regiment	Commander	Battalions	Strength
1st	Col. Raguettly	Scheuzer Dulliker	2,103
2nd	Col. von Castella	Vonderweid v. Seedorf von Flüe Füssli	1,822
3rd	Lt-Col. Thomasset	Peyer-Imhof Weltner von Graffenreid	1,743
4th	Col. von Affry	Bleuler von Maillardoz Imthurn	1,597

keep up with attrition, with an extra 1,000 per annum required in the case of the outbreak of war in Germany or Italy. (Article 9.) In order to reduce competition for recruits, the convention prohibited the Swiss government from providing Swiss regiments to any other country, and further required the authorities to 'recall all Swiss currently in foreign service and to use all the means of persuasion and authority in their power to induce them to return home'. (Article 11.) Finally, Article 15, which was never executed, called for the creation of a special Swiss grenadier battalion to be admitted to the Imperial Guard.

As a result of all this attention, the Swiss Regiments were well staffed, equipped and organised when Napoleon began to assemble his Grand Army for the invasion of Russia. Contrary to prior practice, he now decided to let all the Regiments serve together, although he stopped short of forming them into a single integrated brigade or division. They were all assigned to Marshal Oudinot's 2nd Corps, and in early 1812 the regimental contingents were organised as seen in Table 15 (Maag, *Russland*, p. 32). The Regiments were all assigned to a division commanded by General Merle, who had already seen the Swiss in action in Spain. They were brigaded as shown below, in Table 16.

On most levels, Napoleon's campaign against Russia was a hugely complex series of events. For the Swiss Regiments it was much simpler–it consisted of three major

TABLE 16: SWISS BRIGADES, 1812

Brigade Commander	Units
General Candras	1st and 2nd Swiss
General Coutard	3rd Swiss and 128th Line
General Amey	4th Swiss and 3rd Provisional Croats

engagements separated by long stretches of inactivity. The First and Second Battles of Polotsk are among the least-known actions of the campaign because they took place far from the watchful eye of Napoleon. The Battle of the Beresina is better known, but the role played by the Swiss in that engagement is not always clearly described. In all three instances, however, the Swiss covered themselves with glory and provided some of the most heroic episodes in the story of Napoleon's foreign troops.

Marshal Oudinot's corps was detached early in the campaign along with that of Marshal MacDonald to guard the northern flank of the Grand Army's advance, which generally followed the line of the Dvina River. After encountering stiff resistance from Russian forces under General Wittgenstein early in August, Oudinot fell back and took up a defensive position in and about the town of Polotsk, a town of 5–6,000 inhabitants on the north, or right, bank of the Dvina just upstream from its confluence with the River Polota, where he was joined by General St-Cyr and the 6th Corps, composed exclusively of Bavarian troops.

On 17 August Wittgenstein attacked the French in force, inflicting a sharp reverse on the Bavarians and wounding Marshal Oudinot, who turned over command to St-Cyr. The latter earned his Marshal's baton on the 18th by counter-attacking and driving off the Russians. The Swiss were not engaged on the 17th, and on the 18th St-Cyr initially placed them in reserve as a precaution in case the action went against the French (Maag, *Russland*, p. 85):

> I know the Swiss. I had a battalion of the 1st Regiment under my orders at Castelfranco in Italy. The French are more impetuous in an advance, but if it comes to a retreat, we can count of the calm and courage of the Swiss.

In the afternoon, the 1st, 2nd and 3rd Regiments were called upon to play a small but important role in the action when Wittgenstein launched a bold cavalry charge in an attempt to stabilise his deteriorating position. The Russian horsemen overran a French brigade but were brought up short of their full objective by several squares of Swiss. St-Cyr, who was riding in a carriage because of a wound he had suffered, was nearly captured when his transport was upset, but was saved by the 3rd Swiss. (Marbot, p. 537). The casualties of the Swiss were, fortunately, very light.

For the next two months the Swiss led a relatively calm existence in and around Polotsk despite the relative proximity of the enemy. The fact that all the Regiments were serving together for the first time since they were formed meant that there was much occasion for socialising among relatives and old comrades-in-arms who had not seen each other for a long time. The men built sturdy huts for themselves and entrenchments and field fortifications wherever the approaches to the town were not already covered by the rivers. Meanwhile the officers hunted and fought duels. (Bégos, pp. 179–80.) Life was far from perfect, however, because a lack of fresh food and clean water led to outbreaks of dysentery and other diseases that ravaged the strength of the Regiments. (De Vallière, p. 692.)

The Russians finally returned to the offensive on 17 October 1812. Wittgenstein deployed some 40,000 men in a concentric attack against the positions held by less than 30,000 men under St-Cyr, while another 12,000 Russians under General Stengel advanced along the south bank on the Dvina in a flanking attack designed to cut off the French retreat. The 1st and 2nd Swiss were on the left of the French position, the 4th was in garrison in Polotsk itself and the 3rd Swiss was on the extreme right of the French some way down the road to Witepsk with some cuirassiers and the 3rd Light Horse Lancers of the Line. (Report of d'Affry, 2 January 1813, Hellmüller, p. 271.) On that first day of fighting the 1st Swiss had the most noteworthy role. The Regiment had formed its Voltigeurs and Grenadiers into two separate élite battalions and, on the 17th, the Grenadiers under Captains Jean Gilly and Jean Pierre Druey were posted in the chapel of Rostna and an adjoining walled cemetery that had been turned into a strongpoint. At 7 p.m. the battalion was assailed by two Russian regiments. The Swiss fought until their ammunition was gone, then broke through the surrounding enemy forces in a desperate bayonet charge, leaving 150 dead behind, but not abandoning a single wounded man. When the remaining Grenadiers were safely back within French lines, all of the officers of the Regiment gathered to assist in the midnight burial of the two Grenadier Captains, who had not survived the battle. (*Ibid.*, p. 272.)

The fighting became more general on the 18th. The Russians first assaulted the French right, but were finally driven off in see-saw action that lasted most of the day. Then Wittgenstein launched a late attack on the French left. This gesture should have had little consequence, but the 1st and 2nd Swiss Regiments and the 3rd Provisional Croats (see separate entry) were then posted somewhat in advance of the French entrenchments. Before they could be withdrawn from harm's way, however, they came under fire and responded with a few volleys of their own followed by a bayonet charge that repulsed the enemy. Prudent withdrawal was still a possibility, but the passions of combat instead led the Swiss into disaster and the annals of history. The Eagle-bearer of the 2nd Regiment was wounded, and he passed his burden to Captain Louis Bégos. That officer was then confronted by Captain Leonard Müller, one of the biggest men in the Regiment, who demanded the honour of defending the regimental standard. To Bégos' amazement, however, no sooner did Müller take the Eagle than he ran directly toward the enemy yelling 'Forward the 2nd!' All orders for disengagement were ignored and the Swiss swept forward after the Captain. (Bégos, p. 182.)

It was magnificent, but it was also folly. The Swiss pushed forward unsupported in the face of Russian infantry and artillery fire, and the casualties were appalling. When it was impossible to advance further, they gave ground only grudgingly, withdrawing with parade-ground precision that inspired admiration in friend and foe alike. Wittgenstein attempted to administer a *coup de grâce* by launching his cavalry, including some elements of the Russian Imperial Guard, at the embattled redcoats, but they never lost their courage or composure as Colonel Raguettly of the 1st urged the men of both units to keep to their ranks, hold firm and not give up. (Maag, *Russland*, pp.

124–5.) Their steadiness is demonstrated by the following passage from a memoir by an officer who participated in the action (Memoir of Rosselet, reproduced in Hellmüller, pp. 287–9 at 288):

> [T]he resistance stubborn: I mention the 1st Swiss Regiment, which deployed, began firing by platoons, advanced, stopped and began firing again, this time by files. Ceasing fire, the unit performed an about-face and retreated at a normal pace, then stopped, faced around and began firing again.

By the time they returned to the French lines, the two Regiments had suffered casualties of over 60 officers and 1,100 men. As an example to illustrate the carnage, at the end of the day one company was commanded by a Sergeant-Major named Bornand who had been wounded three times (a sabre-cut to the head, a musket ball in the arm and a wound in the leg) and mustered only three privates and a single corporal. (De Vallière, p. 694.) Colonel Castella of the 2nd Regiment reported that 33 of the 50 officers of his unit present with the colours at the start of the day were killed or wounded. (Report dated 4 November 1812, reproduced in Hellmüller, p. 269.)

The Swiss preserved their standards as well as their honour. Captain Müller was shot dead shortly after he started his charge, leaving the Eagle of the 2nd at the mercy of the Russians. Captain Bégos rushed forward to save it, but found that the flag was pinned underneath Müller's corpse, which he was at first unable to budge because of Müller's great weight. Bégos got down on his knees and, undoubtedly with the help of some adrenalin, was finally able to pull the colour clear. He gave the Eagle and the colour to an NCO to carry to safety, then took his place again at the head of his troops. (Bégos, p. 183) The Eagle of the 1st Regiment was preserved by Lieutenant Legler and Sergeant Kaa, but we have no intimate details of that feat. (Schaller, p. 177.)

On 19 October, the very day that Napoleon began his retreat from Moscow, the battered Russians rested for the most part, waiting for their flanking movement to develop and provide more decisive results than they had been able to achieve on the battlefield. St-Cyr realised what was happening, and also realised that he had to withdraw to avoid encirclement. The French retirement through the town of Polotsk and across the bridges over the Dvina was favoured by a thick fog and was handled so discreetly that the Russians at first failed to notice what was happening. Unfortunately, in the early evening some of the retreating soldiers set fire to their abandoned barracks, and the flames brought on an immediate Russian assault. The 3rd and 4th Swiss were among the troops ordered to hold the town at all costs until the rest of the army had escaped. (Maillard, pp. 203–4.)

The fight for Polotsk was one of the most savage battles of the campaign, conducted at night in a town of full of blazing wooden buildings. Once the outer perimeter was breached, the fighting became hand-to-hand in the streets and houses, but the Swiss maintained their discipline and organisation throughout. Captain Schumacher of the 4th wrote in his memoirs about the end of the fighting (Schumacher, p. 88):

> On the 20th, at 4.00 a.m. in the morning, we abandoned our positions and retired under an uninterrupted rain of bullets through the streets lighted by burning buildings. The houses on fire collapsed around us as we fought against the advancing enemy. Covering fire from the French artillery on the south bank of the Dvina finally enabled us to retreat across the river. As soon as the last of us crossed the bridges, they were destroyed and Polotsk was lost.

Captain Beuler, commander of the combined élite companies of the 4th Swiss, was the last man out. The Russians were so close that he was forced to jump into the river and swim to safety. St-Cyr decorated the sodden Beuler on the spot with the Marshal's own cross of the Legion of Honour. (De Vallière, p. 695.) The 4th lost 400 men plus ten officers killed and 27 wounded; the 3rd Swiss had seven officer casualties.

The performance of the Swiss Regiments at the Second Battle of Polotsk was one of the finest by foreign troops during the whole of the Napoleonic wars. St-Cyr recognised in his report that he owed the escape of his baggage and all of his guns to the Swiss, although he did chide them for the 'excessive' courage that had led to such fearful losses on the 18th. (Maag, *Russland*, p. 303.) Napoleon himself mentioned the stalwart performance of the Swiss in the 28th Bulletin published on 1 November and the four regiments were awarded 34 Legion of Honour decorations. (De Vallière, p. 695.)

After Polotsk the Swiss and the other remaining units of the 2nd Corps retired slowly towards the French main body returning from Moscow. Although reduced in numbers, the Swiss were in relatively good condition since many had warm overcoats and new shoes they had found at Polotsk. (Bégos, p. 188.) They were stunned when they finally met up with the ragged remains of the Grand Army on the banks of the Beresina accompanied by a tired-looking Napoleon wearing his traditional grey overcoat. (Bégos, p. 190.) The Emperor subjected the Swiss to an impromptu review on 27 November, then dispatched them across the improvised bridges with the all-important mission of protecting the French line of retreat from the forces of Russian Admiral Tchichagov. After a restless night spent bivouacked in a gloomy forest, they awoke to the unexpected sound of a traditional Swiss patriotic hymn sung by Lieutenant David Legler of the 1st and a chorus of officers and men. This song of voyage and homecoming, known thereafter as the 'Song of the Beresina', must have seemed both poignant and ironic to men who knew that few of them would survive the day. (De Vallière, p. 697.)

The thin line of battle that was formed that morning of 28 November to face the Russian onslaught consisted of the four Swiss regiments, the Vistula Legion, the 123rd Line (formed from disbanded regiments of the Kingdom of Holland) and the 3rd Provisional Croats, plus General Jean Pierre Doumerc's heavy cavalry division, all under the command of Marshals Ney and Oudinot. The understrength units mustered perhaps 7,000 men, and were heavily outnumbered by the enemy. The Swiss commanders let their men know what was expected of them (de Valliére, p. 698):

> Soldiers! We have been given a post of honour that we must defend while the rest of the army retires along the road to Zembin. We are certain that you will live up to your well-deserved reputation. Today we must die for the honour of Switzerland!

And die they did—as part of an epic struggle that lasted the whole of the day. Attacked by eight full regiments of light infantry, the Swiss fired off all their ammunition and then, under direct orders from General Merle, advanced with cold steel to drive back the enemy. (Maag, *Russland*, p. 194.) Having won some breathing room, they retired, found more ammunition, then repeated the same sequence again—something they were to do a remarkable total of eight times during the day. The men who were not wounded were exhausted and had no opportunity to eat, but they fought on, never offering a complaint and mustering the same vigour for their bayonet attacks as they had throughout the day. (Bégos, p. 194.) By the end, all the drummers had been killed or wounded and Captain Rey of the 1st Regiment had to pick up an abandoned drum to beat the charge himself. (Bégos, p. 195.)

The astonishing effort of the Swiss alone might not have been enough to win the day for the French, but it was matched by those of the other foreign troops in action and surpassed by that of Doumerc's cavalry. The 400 men of the 4th, 7th and 14th Cuirassiers, representing almost the last organised cavalry in the whole of the French Army, routed an entire Russian division and forced over 2,000 Russians to surrender. As soldiers on both sides collapsed from exhaustion at 10.00 p.m., the French knew that they had held their position and had prevented the Russians from trapping the Emperor and the last remnants of his army.

The cost for the Swiss in human lives was severe, particularly in terms of the many officers who were still mounted and therefore made easy targets. Battalion Chief Blattman of the 1st was knocked from his horse and killed by a bullet in the forehead. General Amey was surrounded by Russians when his horse was killed, but Captain Gaspard Schumacher of the 4th dashed forward with some men to save his commanding officer. Vonderweid, a 28-year-old Battalion Chief of the 2nd Regiment, gave his horse to another wounded officer, grabbed a musket and joined the firing line like a simple soldier. Mortally wounded by a shot through his stomach, Vonderweid urged the men coming to his aid to return to their companies and keep up the fight. Captain Bégos called him 'the most courageous of soldiers and the most humane of commanders'. (Bégos, p. 199.)

No exact count of casualties was possible in the circumstances, but the Swiss were virtually wiped out as a fighting force, although each of the four regiments had preserved its Eagle standard. At roll-call the next day, the 2nd Swiss had two officers and twelve men present, while the 3rd had 60 men and the 4th only 67. (Maag, *Russland*, pp. 203–4.) Counting stragglers and detachments, there were perhaps 300 men left in the division. Even those that had survived were hardly unscathed, if Captain Schumacher is any example (Schumacher, p. 97):

> For my part, I was hit five times: two musket balls went through my shako; one ball hit my portfolio of papers, where I found it stuck in a packet of letters; a fourth shot grazed the sole of my boot and a piece of a howitzer shell tore off my right epaulette. I thus returned from peril without a wound to speak of, a fact that seems incredible. A Russian lancer did prick my right hand, but it was nothing serious.

Some detachments of the 3rd and 4th Swiss must have survived relatively intact, however, because the former lost five officers killed and ten wounded in fighting around Vilna from 6 to 10 December, while the latter lost seven killed and three wounded on 9 and 10 December alone.

General Merle told Napoleon that he thought that every Swiss soldier deserved to be decorated for the Battle of the Beresina, and he persuaded the Emperor to award the Swiss 62 crosses of the Legion of Honour (Schaller, p. 204.) Unfortunately, the order to that effect was lost and so the deserving officers and men of the Swiss Regiments never received any official recompense for their valour. Their performance was, however, accorded proper recognition by their countrymen, who viewed them as heroes whose actions were a source of national pride. This attitude is expressed in a letter from the father of Captain Louis Dulliker of Lucerne, an officer of the 1st Regiment killed during the campaign, to the Swiss government (quoted in de Vallière, p. 702):

> The death of my son, who fell on the battlefield of Polotsk, is a heavy blow for me, but the reports of the brilliant conduct of the Swiss regiments in that action and the sympathy you have shown me are a consolation. My heart is filled with pride and gratitude.

The Swiss regiments had suffered such stupendous casualties during the Russian campaign that they had to be completely reorganised for the 1813 campaign. Through the accumulation of men in the regimental depots, survivors of the Russian campaign, new recruits, recovering wounded, soldiers returning from Spain and other odds and ends, each Regiment was able to field a single battalion for active service. These units were organised in April 1813 as shown in Table 17 (Schaller, pp. 223–5). There were also small detachments of Swiss serving in several of the fortresses (including, most notably, Custrin) left occupied by the French when their main force retreated from the Duchy of Warsaw and eastern Prussia.

TABLE 17: SWISS FORMATIONS, 1813

Regiment	Field Battalion Chief	Strength	No of 1812 veterans
1st	Dufresne	587	210
2nd	Abyberg	786	295
3rd	Bucher	629	350
4th	Bleuler	912	211

Colonel Castella of the 2nd Regiment was promoted to the rank of General and he tried to have all the remaining Swiss put under his command. His request was denied, but the Swiss were all assigned in the spring to the army corps of General Molitor charged with defending the Dutch departments of the French empire, where they were formed into a provisional regiment under the command of Major Abyberg of the 2nd Regiment. The battalion belonging to the 4th Regiment eventually became part of the garrison of Groningen, but the other three were advanced into Germany in October to take up a position at Minden in Westphalia. (Schaller, pp. 225–6.)

On 10 October Dufresne's Battalion of the 1st Regiment and 50 recruits of the 4th Regiment joined the garrison of Bremen, a town of 30,000 inhabitants of dubious loyalty to the Emperor. Their arrival was quite timely for the French commandant, Colonel Thuillier, because on 13 October the town was assaulted by a mixed force of 4-5,000 Russian Cossacks and Prussian volunteers under General Tettenborn. The Voltigeur company of the 1st under Captain Segesser was assigned to dispute the possession of the eastern suburb of the town and a French official who observed the combat noted that the Swiss 'shot with such marvellous accuracy that any enemy soldier who showed himself was soon dead or wounded.' (Anon., 'Rélation', p. 11.) The enemy retired, however, and the Swiss made the mistake of pursuing them into open country. When a cloud of Cossacks appeared, a supporting French cavalry unit fled, leaving the Voltigeurs surrounded. The Swiss chose to fight rather than surrender, but it was not a fair contest and 86 out of the 97 men were killed, captured or wounded. Captain Segesser himself, badly wounded, is said to have fired two last pistol shots before he died, killing two Cossacks. (Schaller, pp. 227–8.)

The next day saw more fighting and more Swiss casualties, but resistance faltered when Colonel Thuillier was killed and Major Dufresne wounded. The new commander was able to negotiate an honourable capitulation on 15 October which allowed the garrison to leave with the honours of war but bound them not to fight against the allies again anywhere north of the Rhine River. Recruiters for the Russo-German Legion then being raised to fight for the allies descended on the Swiss to try to persuade them to desert and enlist in that unit. Schaller notes proudly that the Swiss disdained these advances with indignation. (Schaller, p. 229.) By a decree of 22 December 1813 four Swiss officers and two other ranks received the Legion of Honour for their part in the defence of the town.

All the Swiss fell back towards French territory in the aftermath of the Battle of Leipzig, and the different battalions experienced different fates. The Battalion of the 4th Regiment stationed in northern Holland was split into two parts, one of which was besieged in the fortress of Delfzil and the other of which found itself defending the town of Coeverden. The Delfzil contingent was commanded by Salomon Bleuler, a veteran of Portugal, Spain and Russia, and under his leadership the Swiss sustained a siege by Russian troops that lasted from November 1813 until the abdication of Napoleon. They were still making active sorties in March. The troops at Coeverden were less steadfast, and over half the companies there deserted to the enemy and joined the Russo-German Legion, but the rest still held out until the end. (Schaller, pp. 231–2, 234.)

After its defeat at Bremen, the Battalion of the 1st Regiment was pulled back to the Rhine, where it was incorporated into the garrison of Maestricht. It remained there until the end of the war, ravaged by typhus rather than warfare. The Battalions of the 2nd and 3rd Regiments went to Wesel with detachments in other nearby strongpoints. All of these also held out until peace came. Swiss detachments were also found in many other fortresses. A force of 271 mixed Swiss stragglers and wounded ended up in Mainz, while a small marching battalion of men of all the regiments intended as reinforcements for the active-service battalions was caught in Landau and besieged by some of the same Bavarians who had fought with the Swiss at Polotsk. Depot units of the four regiments were also blockaded in Besançon and Metz by the advance of the Allies against Paris. (Schaller, pp. 234–7.) The portion of the 1st Regiment besieged in Metz suffered a small mutiny when a number of men refused to work on the fortifications until they had received all the pay due to them. The instigator of the trouble was quickly tried and shot. (Guye, pp. 201–2.)

Final Transformation The Swiss government had tried to recall the Swiss Regiments at the end of December 1813 by invoking a clause in the Convention with Napoleon that permitted such an action if the Swiss homeland was invaded, but circumstances prevented that initiative from having any practical outcome. The Bourbons wanted to keep the Convention in effect, and so under the First Restoration the status of the Swiss Regiments remained unchanged, although life was hardly normal as released prisoners, recovered wounded and missing detachments returned to their depots from all over Europe. When Napoleon returned from Elba, the Swiss Regiments found themselves in a serious dilemma. They were now bound by their home government to serve the Bourbons, and the Swiss authorities refused to switch the benefit of the contract back to Napoleon. When Napoleon called upon the Swiss to defy their own government and serve again with him, most of them took the path of patriotism (and, possibly, disgust with war) and returned home. They were commended by the Swiss Diet for having 'remained faithful at the decisive moment to their oaths and to the wishes of the supreme authority of their country.' (Schaller, pp. 246–50; resolution of Diet quoted at p. 248.)

Some Swiss did decide to join Napoleon, and they were formed into a regiment under the command of Colonel Christopher Stoeffel, who had been a Captain in the 3rd Swiss in 1807 but had served exclusively in staff posts thereafter. A single battalion of that regiment served in Vandamme's Third Corps during the Waterloo campaign.

Uniforms In addition to the sources discussed below, there is a significant collection of portraits of officers of the Swiss Regiments reproduced in black-and-white in Hellmüller.

1st Swiss Regiment The 1st Regiment, which was formed in large part from the *3ème Demi-brigade Helvétique* (see separate entry), seems to have retained the uniforms of the latter unit, which were red with yellow lapels, cuffs (with red cuff flaps) and turnbacks, sky blue trim around the collar, the cuff flaps and the yellow facings and white turnbacks. This colour scheme is confirmed by the following portraits and uniform jackets that are known to have existed in museum collections until at least the start of the Second World War:

1. Officer Jacket, 1807, from Montreux Museum
2. Two Officer portraits, 1807
2. Grenadier Jacket,1808, in Dresden Museum
3. Portrait of Sergeant-Major in Swiss National Museum

All of these are reproduced in either Forthoffer's *Fiche Documentaire*, No 241 (*Le 1er Regiment Suisse*), or Jürgen Olmes' *Heere der Vergangenheit*, Print No 73. These artefacts and portraits evidence variety as to the colour of the collar (sometimes yellow); the form of the pockets in the skirts of the jacket (sometimes horizontal, sometimes vertical); and the colour of the cuff flap (sometimes yellow).

Forthoffer's plate includes an illustration of a plain red, single-breasted jacket with long tails and red turnbacks ornamented with gold grenades on a sky blue cloth background that is said to be in something called the Landolt Collection. Forthoffer also depicts other types of Swiss soldiers (such as a drummer and a sapper) for the purposes of his plate, but none of these figures can be traced to primary sources. Plate No 140 of the Weiland MS shows the Regiment's uniform from the period 1809–12. The figure depicted is a Fusilier who is wearing a shako with white cords, yellow shoulder straps, yellow collar and white piping all around (perhaps an omission by the colourist?).

The 1st Regiment uniforms were modified in style and detail by the 1812 dress regulations (see Decree on Uniforms of 19 January 1812). The jackets now had yellow collars and closed yellow lapels, both with red piping, while white piping was prescribed for the cuff flaps. The Fusiliers were assigned red shoulder straps piped yellow while the Grenadiers were now supposed to have red epaulettes. These details are borne out by the evidence of (a) Martinet Plate No 2 (alternate) depicting a 1st Regiment Grenadier in a bearskin cap with a copper plate adorned with a grenade, (b) a Grenadier officer coat from the Military Museum of Vaud, and (c) a portrait of Lieutenant Legler in the Museum of the Swiss in Foreign Service near Geneva.

The 1st Regiment had a full band that participated in the Russian campaign. (Decision of 16 April 1812, Nap. *P&T*, Vol. 5, No 7127, p. 305.) In 1805 the uniform jacket of the Regimental drummers appears to have been adapted from that for the 3rd Swiss Demi-brigade—blue with yellow collar, cuffs, cuff flaps and lapels, all trimmed with gold laced and piped with sky blue. (Ganier-Tanconville, 'Les Légions et Demi-Brigades Helvétiques', *Le Passepoil*, Vol. 10 (1930), pp. 49–52 and 79–80.) The drummers also wore red 'swallow's-nest' ornaments, trimmed yellow, on their shoulders.

2nd Swiss Regiment The 2nd Swiss wore the normal red uniform with dark blue facings piped red, although the piping in the portrait of Colonel Segesser reproduced in black-and-white in de Vallière, p. 671, seems to be white instead. The unit received jackets with closed lapels in 1812 or later and a surviving example in the French Army Museum has an unusual collar that features a scallop-edged patch of red with a button on each side of the opening of the blue collar and an embroidered gold grenade ornament on the blue portion itself. The turnbacks are red instead of white, piped blue, and the jacket has 'soubise'-style pockets. Another jacket, this one from the Military Museum of Vaud, has blue turnbacks. The Gaudard, or Berne, Manuscript from 1813–14 depicts two soldiers of the 2nd Swiss with yellow piping on their lapels.

3rd Swiss Regiment There is a very rich iconography for this unit, starting with a figure in a painting from the Rovatti MS who is wearing a bicorne hat and a red collar but black facings piped white. The rest of our knowledge of the Regiment's dress comes from a series of prints published in Berne in 1808 by an artist named Lang. The figures from this series have been reproduced many times by many different artists, but it is very difficult to find a set of the originals. Perhaps the cleanest and most complete set of reproductions is that found in Prints No 74 and 75 of the *Heere der Vergangenheit* series published by Jürgen Olmes.

The recurring elements in the uniforms of the Lang figures are red coats with black collars, cuffs and lapels, all piped white; scallop-edged red cuff flap piped white; white vest and trousers; yellow metal buttons; and shakos with eagle plates, the cockade positioned on the upper left (from the perspective of the wearer) side of the shako, and cords looped from the cockade around the whole circumference of the shako. Blondieau specifies that the shako plate was of a design unique to all the Swiss regiments, consisting of a brass eagle without a base surmounted by a separate brass crown. (Blondieau, p. 26.)

The specific features illustrated by particular figures in the Lang series are as follows:

Fusilier private: White cords and flounders and a flat circular pompom with a white stripe around the circumference and a black '3' on a central red field.

Fusilier officer (in campaign dress): Pompom as for private; black cloth cover for shako, gold chin straps and trim to brim; speckled kerchief visible within collar; gold gorget with silver regimental device incorporating the arms of the Swiss cantons; lapels arranged so that only the uppermost portion of black facings is visible; and grey overalls. This figure is reproduced in *Le Plumet*, Plate No 29 (*Infanterie de Ligne, 3e Rég Suisse, Drapeau 1804–1812*). The rear view of this figure can be supplied by a photograph of the back of a surviving Fusilier officer jacket in the Military Museum of Vaudois that appears in Pigeard, *L'Armée*, p. 473. That jacket has vertical pockets outlined in white and white turnbacks, each pair of which is held in place by a single embroidered gold star placed at the point of juncture.

(Fusilier) officer (in second uniform): Large bicorne with pompom as for privates and gold tassels; entirely dark blue single-breasted jacket with gold buttons; gold fringed

epaulette on left shoulder, counter epaulette on right (no gorget); broad white waist-belt for sword; white gloves; dark blue trousers; and gaiters below the knee.
Grenadier private: Black bearskin with brass chinscales, a brass eagle on the front, white-tipped red plume on the left side and white flounders, also on the left side; white epaulettes; and sabre with red sword knot.
Grenadier officer: Same bearskin as grenadier private, but gold flounders and gold cords around the whole of the cap; gold fringed epaulette on left shoulder, counter epaulette on right; gold gorget; and boots with gold trim and tassel.
Voltigeur private: Shako as for Fusilier private but tall, yellow-tipped green plume in place of pompom; yellow collar piped white, green epaulettes; and sabre with green sword knot.
Voltigeur officer: Shako as for Voltigeur private, but gold cords, gold band around top, gold trim to band and gold chinscales; gold gorget; gold fringed epaulette on left shoulder, counter epaulette on right; buff gloves without cuffs; crossed shoulder-belts with gold crown, chains and shield device on cartridge box belt; short musket (rifle?) as side arm; and knee-length black gaiters. This figure is reproduced in Bertin, 'Tenue d'un Officier', together with a letter dated 1812 from 2nd Lieutenant J. N. Perret of a Voltigeur company of the 3rd Swiss. The article includes a photograph of the regimental model of gorget and the letter specifies that Lieutenant Perret owned the following items of clothing and equipment:

Two pairs of boots
Two pairs of white trousers
One uniform jacket
One fur bonnet
One shako
One blue frockcoat and vest
One pair of blue trousers for undress wear
Epaulettes
Sword and sabre
Carbine and cartridge box
Blue overcoat
Five shirts
Six white handkerchiefs
Two black handkerchiefs
Eight pocket handkerchiefs
One portmanteau

Sapper: Bearskin as for Grenadier private but red-tipped black plume; no eagle plate or chinscales and small white tassel at top of the front of the bonnet; gold epaulettes with metal scales and crossed-axes devices on the shoulder pieces; beard; four golden crossed-axe ornaments on the outside of each sleeve; wooden axe handle with small brass medallion bearing the number '3'; and a leather apron. This figure has been reproduced by Job in his *Tenues de Troupes de France* and by Rigo in *Le Plumet*, Plate No 191 (*Infanterie Légère et Étrangere, Sapeurs de 10e et 16e Régiments, Bataillon de Neufchatel, 3e Suisse 1808–1812*).

Drummer: Shako as for Fusilier private but yellow band around top; thick yellow lace outlining lapels and cuffs but white piping still visible; 'swallow's-nest' shoulder ornaments consisting of a red shoulder piece trimmed white and a black 'nest' with yellow trim and stripes; five(?) yellow chevrons equally spaced up each sleeve; and a brass drum with red and black diagonal edging. This figure (and the other musicians depicted by Lang) are also reproduced in *Le Plumet*, Plate No 87 (*Infanterie de Ligne, 3e Rég. Suisse, Tambour-Major, Tambour et Musicien 1807–1809*).

Drum Major: Large bicorne hat with gold, scalloped-shaped trim and white feather edging and the same pompom as for the fusilier private except for no red centre; regimental with thick gold lace instead of piping, gold buttonhole laces with tassels and gold lace on all seams; black 'swallow's-nest' trimmed with gold, gold shoulder strap; thick black leather baldric with elaborate gold braid; silver mace with golden knob; and black boots with double gold trim along top.

Musician: Large bicorne hat with white feather trim and the same pompom as for the Drum Major; sky blue single-breasted coat with crimson collar and cuffs trimmed with gold lace, white turnbacks and unusual upside-down trident-shaped gold lace decoration in lieu of pockets in the coat-tails; gold trefoil shoulder straps on each shoulder; three rows of buttons on breast joined by strips of gold braid and tassels off the end buttons in each horizontal line; gold counter epaulettes; white trousers; and black boots with gold trim.

Other known depictions of the pre-1812 uniforms of soldiers of the 3rd Swiss are a portrait of Battalion Chief Charles d'Affry wearing a large bicorne adorned only with a cockade and retaining strap (de Vallière, p. 673); a naive self-portrait of a Voltigeur named Jean Marc Bussy (Bussy, p. 221) wearing a more standard shako with diamond-shaped plate; and an accomplished watercolour self-portrait of an officer named Ott wearing black gauntlet gloves and a shako with a tall white plume in front illustrated on Plate XXV of the auction catalogue for the sale of the Charles Delacre Collection of Prints and Artwork Relating to Military Costume in Paris on 31 May 1961.

The 1812 Uniform Regulations specifiy that the facings were to be of black velvet and the piping was to be red instead of white, but there is little way of knowing how widely those changes were made. An 1813 drawing of a 3rd Regiment Grenadier from the Domitz Manuscript depicts the standard pre-1812 uniform with white piping and white epaulettes, but the buttons are silver and the figure is wearing grey overalls. He has a black shako with a black cockade, red plume, red lace around the top and bottom and in a 'V' shape on the side and an indistinguishable, but small, silver device in front. The figure also has three chevrons point down above the elbow on his right sleeve, which could be a rank distinction or a Swiss version of the long-service stripes worn in the French Army.

The Regiment is represented by six figures in the Berne MS, some of which have 1812-style uniforms and some not. There is also variety in the piping, since some have red piping on the black facings, some white and some none at all. The most unusual figure is a Voltigeur in a pre-1812 style uniform wearing a busby with a visor and a black bag. The Voltigeur's collar is yellow with red piping, his epaulettes are yellow, and his lapels are black with red piping. The cuffs are yellow piped red and the cuff flap is red.

4th Swiss Regiment

The only verifiable information about the pre-1812 uniforms of this Regiment comes from surviving artefacts. The first is an unusual brass shako plate in the National Army Museum in London that has a right-facing eagle atop a rectangular base with the following inscription in large and small letters with spaces in between: '4m Rt Se.' (This plate is illustrated in Blondieau, p. 46.) The second artefact is the jacket of an 1810 Grenadier officer in the collections of the Museum of Lucerne. The coat is red with sky blue collar, lapels and cuffs, all piped white. It has horizontal pockets, also piped white, and white turnbacks with a crowned eagle ornament in the outer turnback of each pair and a grenade ornament in the inner one. The buttons all bear the number '4'.

A contemporary print of Salomon Bleuler, who commanded the contingents of the 4th Swiss in Portugal, depicts an alternative uniform that may have been the service dress for officers. It features a red coat with no visible lapels but instead merely two vertical lines of gold buttons. (See reproduction in Pigeard, *L'Armée*, p. 473.) The collar and cuffs are dark blue rather than sky blue (an error of the colourist of the print?) and there is one button one either side of the opening of the collar and two buttons on each cuff, which do not seem to have cuff flaps. The men of the 4th who served in Portugal also had to make adaptations in their dress. When they were inspected at Astorga at the beginning of 1809, most were wearing their greatcoats because their red uniforms were in shreds. (Schaller, p. 96.)

Bory, whose work is generally unreliable because it is based primarily on the paper soldiers of the 'Alsatian collections' with no further detail given, depicts a Grenadier in a bearskin with sky blue facings piped with black, citing a drawing by an artist named Bovard in the possession of P. de Vallière. Grenadiers of the 4th Swiss wearing bearskins (with a red back patch) can also be seen in a painting of the Battle of Polotsk by Wilhelm von Kobell which is now in the Residenzmuseum in Munich.

The use of an 1812-style uniform with closed lapels by the 4th Swiss is demonstrated by a number of sources. The most important of these is a Fusilier uniform coat in the Museum of Swiss in Foreign Service which has the requisite sky blue facings and piping that was probably white originally but now appears yellowish. The coat does not have actual cuff flaps—they are merely suggested by a line of three buttons paralleled with a line of piping that curves over the top button. The narrow turnbacks are white, piped sky blue, and devoid of ornaments, and the shape of the horizontal pockets in the coat-tails is rectangular, with four buttons in a line under the flap.

The Brunon Collection has a painting of a Grenadier wearing a shako with a red plume and red lace trim top and bottom and forming a red 'V' on each side. His uniform conforms to the 1812 Uniform Regulations except that there is no piping at all around the collar, cuffs and lapels, the cuff flap is red piped sky blue rather than the other way around and the grenades in the turnbacks are sky blue instead of red. The Gaudard/Berne MS depicts a number of figures from the Regiment:

Grenadier officer: Shako without a plate, no piping on any facings, sky blue trousers with a red side stripe.

(Fusilier?) Officer: Bicorne with gold cords, lapels closed to show red side only, grey trousers.

Voltigeur Officer: Shako with yellow pompom but no plate, yellow collar, piping on lapels and cuffs, cuffs without flaps but with two buttons, and grey trousers with red side stripe.

Fusiliers: Shakos with a plate, white piping on facings, white shoulder straps.

(Grenadier?): red pompom, no plate on shako; sabre with red sword knot.

Bory cites the 'Pelet Collection' as the source for both a figure of a mounted officer in the 1812 uniform with a gorget, a sky blue saddle cloth and bearskin pistol covers and one of a Fusilier with a shako with a standard 1812-style plate and a red pompom. Based on figures in the Wurtz Collection of paper soldiers, Rigo gives several different musician figures from 1813–14 in blue uniforms with sky blue facings, but the source may be unreliable. (*Le Plumet*, No 162 [*Infanterie, 4e Régiment Suisse, Cornet de Voltigeurs, Tambour de Fusiliers, Tambour-Major and Musiciens 1813–1814*].)

Standard Each of the Swiss regiments received an Eagle and a Model 1804 standard of the same type used by French line troops when it was formed. According to Charrié (p. 168), however, they were never issued Model 1812 standards.

1st Swiss Regiment The Helvetian Demi-brigades that were used to create this Regiment had possessed their own Eagles and colours, but they were replaced when the new unit was formed. The Regiment received one Eagle and one standard for each battalion, which were distributed during the course of the first trimester of 1806. (Charrié, p. 168.) A wing was broken off the Eagle in action at the First Battle of Polotsk and Sergeant Kaa had to save it from being captured at the 2nd Battle of that name. It was preserved during the retreat from Russia by Lieutenant Legler and is mentioned as having been at Maestricht in January 1814. (Charrié, p. 168.) Some officers preserved both the colour and the Eagle in safekeeping after Napoleon's abdication and they were used briefly by the 2nd Foreign Regiment in 1815.

2nd Swiss Regiment This regiment received three Eagles and colours at Avignon on 19 March 1807. All three were in Portugal, but seem to have returned safely. By 1812 only one of the original Eagles was still in service. As described above, it was fought over and saved at the 2nd Battle of Polotsk, and was then preserved by Colonel Castella during the retreat from Russia.

3rd Swiss Regiment This unit received one Eagle and one colour for each of its three battalions from General Antoine Morlot in March of 1807. That of the 1st Battalion is illustrated in *Le Plumet*, Plate No 29 (*Infanterie de Ligne, 3e Rég. Suisse, Drapeau 1804–1812*). As noted above, one Eagle of this Regiment was saved from capture at Bailen by one of its officers, but that of the 2nd Battalion was captured at Pueblo de Sanabria in 1810. One Eagle was taken into Russia and was brought back safely.

4th Swiss Regiment This unit also received one Eagle per battalion. That of the 3rd Battalion may have been captured at Bailen, but many of these trophies were recaptured by the French in 1810. The Regiment had one Eagle in Russia, which returned safely.

Sapeurs Espagnols

(Spanish Sappers)

Date of Creation Formed by decree of 18 February 1812. (Lienhart & Humbert, Vol. 4, p. 349.)

Circumstances of Creation This unit represents another manifestation of Napoleon's desire to find uses for his many Spanish prisoners of war. In this case, he intended to combine Spanish manpower with French cadres to add an additional force to support the engineering efforts of the Grand Army.

Composition The Battalion was identical in composition to all other French battalions of Sappers. It was ultimately accepted as a regular Sapper unit and became the 8th of such Battalions in the French Army.

Commanders *Formation to final transformation:* Battalion Chief Grandjean, who was wounded at the Battle of Lützen on 2 May 1813.

Operational History The Battalion was not organised until September 1812, when a number of prisoners of goodwill who had been earmarked for Napoleon's project to create a *Régiment de Catalogne* (see separate entry) became available. (Aymes, p. 247.) It remained at its depot at Metz until November. It saw active service in the spring campaign in 1813, six officers being wounded at Lützen. Captain Ximenez was wounded at the Battle of the Katzbach on 26 August 1813 and 2nd Lieutenant Decamps, who had been a casualty at Lützen, was wounded again in an outpost skirmish in Saxony on the 29th.

Final Transformation The Battalion was reorganised as a single company in December 1813 due to casualties and attrition. It was dissolved the following May. (Fieffé, Vol. 2, p. 149.)

Uniforms According to Lienhart & Humbert, the Spanish Sappers wore the same uniforms as French Sappers. (Lienhart & Humbert, Vol. 4, p. 349.)

Standard No information found.

Sapeurs Ioniens

(Ionian Sappers)

Date of Creation 7 August 1812 (Index for SHA Carton X[l]37 in Ministry of War, Inventaire, p. 239.)
Circumstances of Creation This unit was formed by combining the original 9th company of *Pionniers Blancs* (see separate entry) with the remnants of the *Bataillon Septinsulaire* (see separate entry). (Index for SHA Carton X[l]37 in Ministry of War, *Inventaire*, p. 239.)
Composition The strength of the unit was one company.
Commanders No information found.
Operational History No information found.
Final Transformation The unit was repatriated to France after Napoleon's abdication and finally disbanded at Lyon on 5 September 1814. (Index for SHA Carton X[l]37 in Ministry of War, *Inventaire*, p. 239.)
Uniforms No information found, but it would most likely have been similar to that of the *Bataillon Septinsulaire* (see separate entry).
Standard No information found, but a unit this small is unlikely to have had a colour.

Sbires

(Sbires; also known as *Compagnies de Police*)

Date of Creation 19 May 1808.
Circumstances of Creation These troops were formed by a decree of Napoleon's sister Elisa, the Grand Duchess of Tuscany, for service in the three departments of her realm of Tuscany as an adjunct to the local rural constabulary. (Fieffé, Vol. 2, p. 119.) To emphasise that role, within one month after formation of the Sbires they were given the new name of *Compagnies de police*. There was also a separate but similar company of Sbires formed in the Department of Rome by a decree of 11 July 1811. (Fieffé, Vol. 2, p. 120.)
Composition There were four companies of Sbires which Napoleon referred to as the *Bataillon de Police*. (Decision of 11 June 1809, Nap. *O&A*, No 3892, Vol. 3, p. 221.)
Commanders No information found.
Operational History No information found.
Final Transformation No information found.
Uniforms For an obscure unit, there is a surprising amount of information about its uniforms, albeit none of it primary. According to Bucquoy, the unit wore a grey uniform with black belts and a tall felt hat with a broad brim cocked on one side only. (Bucquoy, *Troupes Étrangères*, p. 125.)
Standard No information found.

Serezaners

Date of Creation 1809.

Circumstances of Creation The six regiments of Illyrian Chasseurs (see separate entry) transferred from Austrian to French service at the end of the 1809 War each had an attached company of irregular troops known as Serezaners used to police quarantine and customs laws along the border between Croatia and the Ottoman Empire. The Serezaners are reported to have had the right to kill any person crossing the border from Turkey who attempted to avoid visiting a quarantine station. (P. Boppe, p. 43.)

Composition As irregular troops, these companies do not seem to have had a formal organisation and, in fact, initially did not have any officers above the non-commissioned level. (P. Boppe, p. 225.) They served without pay, but were exempt from all taxes and other service obligations, and had some special privileges as well. (P. Boppe, p. 14.) They committed so many offences against public order themselves that Governor Bertrand proposed in late 1811 that two retired officers should be assigned to each company to provide a proper disciplinary framework. (P. Boppe, p. 225.)

Commanders No information found.

Operational History No information found

Final Transformation No information found.

Uniforms No primary source has been found that depicts a soldier of this type during the French rule of Illyria, but the uniform of this corps probably reflected prevailing local dress. Two illustrations of Serezaners that are contemporary to an earlier period of Austrian rule suggest that the uniform would, at a minimum, have included a red skull cap, a red cloak and a collection of knives and pistols worn in a waistband. (See Hollins, illustrations on pp. 5 and 6, plus text on p. 10.) Boppe's work on the Croatian troops contains a reproduction of a picture of a mounted Serezaner that originally appeared in *K. K. Oesterreichische Armee nach der neuen Adjustirung* by M. Trentschensky (Vienna, 1848), but that source is not contemporary to the Napoleonic era. (P. Boppe, p. 43, n. 1.)

Standard No information found, but it is unlikely that these companies had standards.

Tatars Lithuaniens

(Lithuanian Tatars)

Date of Creation October 1812.

Circumstances of Creation The ancient territory of Lithuania in Russia had a significant Moslem population descended from the Tatar (often spelled 'Tartar') tribesmen who had invaded Russia in the Middle Ages. On 24 August 1812 General Dirk Hogendorp, the military governor appointed for that territory by Napoleon, took note of the expressed desire of that population to contribute to the efforts to free their country from Russian rule and authorised the formation of a volunteer corps of Tatar cavalry. (Date in report of Captain Ulan quoted in Brunon, *Tatars*, p. 7.) Napoleon himself authorised his subordinates to 'spare nothing' to bring that project to fruition as quickly as possible (N. to Maret, 29 September 1812, Nap. *Corr.*, No 19234, Vol. 24, pp. 233–4), but it was not until 23 October that the following proclamation was published to the Moslems at Vilna by Mustapha Murza Achmatowicz, the individual designated to command the new unit (Brunon, *Tatars*, p. 5):

> People, Brothers and Friends! I want to let you know that in order to prove our zeal to serve Poland, our dear homeland, and to justify our ancient reputation in this kingdom [of Lithuania] that has just been re-established under the protection of the great Emperor and King, Napoleon, I and other comrades in arms who share the same views demanded permission from the government of Lithuania to form a Tatar regiment. That demand has now happily been granted by his excellency, Division General Hogendorp, adjutant [*sic*] to his Majesty the Emperor, in the form of an Imperial decree that gives us assurance of financial support and recompense commensurate with our services, sacrifices and military conduct. I consequently resolved, in concert with two Captains, Abraham Mursa Korycki and . . . Samuel [Murza Ulan], to offer our personal services to raise a regiment of lancers of the finest quality possible. I also resolved to devote a portion of my own fortune to defray the administrative costs of raising such a unit. The formation of this regiment will begin with the organisation of the first squadron, which will be assembled at Vilna and dressed at government expense.

Composition Since the French retreat from Moscow had already begun by the time the organisation of the unit commenced, only the first squadron was ever organised. The Tatars had four captains and seven lieutenants and 2nd lieutenants in addition to the Squadron Chief.

Commanders *Formation to 11 December 1812*: Squadron Chief Mustapha Murza Achmatowicz, the primary organiser of the unit, who was killed in action. *12 December 1812 to final transformation*: Captain Samuel Ulan.

Operational History The first combat duty of the Lithuanian Tatars was nearly its last, since during the defence of Vilna on 10–12 December the Tatars lost ten officers (including Squadron Chief Achmatowicz) and 80 men killed or wounded. (Brunon, *Tatars*, p. 5.) Captain Ulan led the 46 remaining men back to Germany, assisted by Lieutenants Ibrahim and Assan Alay. They were briefly attached to the surviving portion of the 3rd Guard Lancers, but that was offensive to the Tatars from the point of view of 'customs, practices, uniform and, most of all, religion', so they obtained permission to serve independently again. While part of the unit remained with the headquarters of the Grand Army, Ulan returned to France to carry out an ambitious plan to return the unit to full strength using Moslems who had been captured while serving in the Russian Army and who had been recruited from the prisoner-of-war camps for service in the 1st (Tour d'Auvergne) and 2nd (Isembourg) Foreign Regiments in Italy. (Ulan to Minister of War, 13 April 1813, quoted in Brunon, *Tatars*, pp. 6–7.) Amazingly, a number of Moslems were identified and transferred to the Tatar squadron, though far too few to make a difference in the unit's status. (Brunon, *Tatars*, p. 7.)

The Tatars who remained with headquarters saw action during the spring campaign in 1813. These were reunited with Captain Ulan for the autumn fighting, when the unit (with a strength of about 50 men) was attached to the 1st Light Horse Lancers of the Guard. During this period the Tatars were treated as members of the Middle Guard. (Note of General Dautancourt, Vanson, 'Tartares', p. 231.) When the Polish Lancers were reorganised in December, the Tatars mustered just 46 men, only 23 of whom were available for duty. (Note of General Dautancourt, Vanson, 'Tartares', p. 232.) It is unclear whether thereafter the Tatars remained attached to the main regiment of Lancers or were attached instead to the 3rd Scout Lancers created from the 1st Regiment.

Final Transformation By April 1814 there were only one officer and fourteen troopers left in the unit. (Text to Forthoffer, *Fiches Documentaires*, Nos. 264/265, 'Les Tatares Lithuaniens de la Garde Impériale'.) They were repatriated back to Lithuania after the abdication of Napoleon.

Uniforms There are probably as many representations of the uniforms of the Lithuanian Tatars as there were men in the unit, but only a very few of them can be considered reliable. Two things are certain: (a) the Tatars undoubtedly wore ethnic clothing rather than a true a French-style uniform, and (b) the unit wore at least two different versions of uniform during its short existence since it is known to have received a 'new' pattern uniform in June of 1813. There is also a surviving artefact from the unit in the form of an officer's shako in the collections of the Sikorski Institute in London.

There is no definitive information available about initial dress of the Tatars beyond the fact that it was stylistically similar to the uniform worn by the Mamelukes of the Imperial Guard since it consisted of a shirt, a vest without sleeves, a sash and trousers with very full-cut legs. Many secondary sources have suggested that this uniform may have consisted of a crimson vest worn over a green shirt and trousers, but none has produced conclusive evidence supporting that proposition. The unique and relatively tall shako of the Tatars was made of leather covered with black lamb's fleece and had a black visor trimmed with a broad yellow metal strip and metal chinscales. It also had a thick (stuffed?) sash (turban?) around its bottom and a cloth bag covering the top of the shako and hanging down to the side like those worn on the busbies of élite hussars. The bag on the surviving shako is dark green trimmed with thin gold piping and a large red tassel with green threads mixed in. The original colour of the sash around the base of the shako cannot be identified. The front of the shako was adorned with a yellow metal crescent and four metal stars, three positioned above the crescent and one below.

According to report dated 11 June 1813 from General Pierre D'Autancourt, who was Major of the 1st Guard Lancers in 1813, whatever uniform the Tatars wore initially was changed in that month (Vanson, 'Tatares', p. 230): '. . . As for the squadron of Tatars, I have dressed, equipped, armed and mounted them according to the uniform models adopted by General Krasinski.' The results were not perfect, however, because D'Autancourt noted on 11 July that six out of a detachment of 26 Tatars he was sending to the front were still dressed in the unit's 'old uniform'. D'Autancourt unfortunately does not give any details of either the new or the old uniform, other than to mention in several places the expense of the shakos. Given that the Tatars had by this time become attached to the Polish Lancers, who wore blue uniforms with crimson facings, it may be that the uniform prescribed by General Krasinski had complementary colours.

This latter theory is buttressed by the evidence of an undated, but probably first-hand, painting of a Tatar in the Brunon Collection that is reproduced in Brunon, p. 2. The figure is wearing a black shako with a visor (but no crescent or stars), a yellow turban and a green bag trimmed with crimson piping and a crimson tassel. The figure's shirt is blue and his vest is crimson, and both articles are decorated with intricate yellow embroidery. The uniform is completed by a yellow sash, billowing blue trousers, a green cartridge box belt and black sword belt. The figure is carrying a lance with a white over green pennon, and his white horse has a black light cavalry bridle, a blue saddle cloth bordered with a band of white between two lines of crimson piping and a crimson portmanteau with a circle of white lace on each end. (This figure is also reproduced in Forthoffer, *Fiches Documentaires*, Nos. 264/265.)

Unfortunately for those who prefer straightforward answers to questions about uniforms, the only other two contemporary pictures of the Lithuanian Tatars contradict this source and each other. The first source is an anonymous watercolour that depicts Napoleon and his staff at the Battle of Leipzig (reproduced in Tulard, pp. 254–5.) The relevant figure is quite close to the Emperor and is dressed in an exotic costume consisting of a red shako (without a visor or a visible bag) with a green turban and gold crescent, a yellow vest trimmed with black embroidery worn over a green shirt with yellow embroidery, a light blue (?) sash and red mameluke trousers. The figure is wearing black gauntlet gloves and is mounted on a black horse with a magnificent yellow saddle cloth with red wolf's-teeth trim and with numerous long decorative gold strings hanging off various parts of the bridle and saddle straps. There is nothing that definitively identifies this figure as a Tatar, but that is a reasonable conclusion given the fact that his dress does not resemble any known Mameluke costume, including those of the men who served as Napoleon's personal servants. Rigo goes even further in that view when claims in *Le Plumet*, No 228 (*Garde Impériale: Tartares Lithuaniens, Officier 1813*), that the figure is a portrait of Captain Ulan at Leipzig.

The other important primary source is a painting of a Tatar that appears in the Freiburg Manuscript from 1813. The painting depicts a dismounted lancer dressed blue grey narrow leg trousers, a red shirt with black embroidery and a blue vest with red trim. The headwear is a black shako with a visor, a white turban, a yellow metal crescent ornament and a green bag with a yellow tassel. The lancer is holding a lance with a green-over-white pennon and has two pistols stuck into a black sash or waist-belt. To complete the confusion, there is also a picture of a Tatar in the normally reliable

Vernet & Lami series of prints that depicts a uniform consisting of a black fur busby with white cords and a red plume, red shirt, yellow vest and blue mameluke trousers.

There are no less than seven different representations of the uniforms of the Tatars (including three of trumpeters) in the Marckolsheim Manuscript purportedly found, copied and then lost by Roger Forthoffer. Such a variety for such a small unit is one of the reasons that the authenticity of this manuscript must remain highly questionable.

Standard No information found.

Tirailleurs du Po

(Po Tirailleurs [Sharpshooters])

Date of Creation 20 April 1803.

Circumstances of Creation This unit was created to make use of the disbanded soldiers of the King of Piedmont. It was labelled at creation as the *Bataillon Expéditionnaire Piémontais*, but its name was changed on 24 September. (Belhomme, Vol. 4, p. 268.) The unit was recruited exclusively by means of voluntary enlistments in the former territories of Piedmont (N. to Berthier, 27 July 1804, Nap. *Corr.*, No 7875, Vol. 9, p. 434):

> . . . [T]his Battalion [of Po Tirailleurs] must have a recruiting centre at Turin. Its establishment calls for over 1,000 men, but today it has only 700. Order that measures be taken to bring this unit up to full strength, and that it should enlist only men who have previously served in the army of the King of Sardinia. Order a special review of the Battalion to eliminate any soldiers who were not born in Piedmont; one of the main purposes of this unit is to enable me to rid Piedmont of soldiers of the former regime who might favour their old prince.

Composition The unit was intended to consist of nine companies of 100 men each, one of which was a Carabinier company. (Belhomme, Vol. 4, p. 268.)

Commanders *4 February 1803–24 January 1804*: Battalion Chief Jean Dominique Borghese (1769–1832), a Piedmontese native. He left the Battalion as a result of his retirement from active service. *24 January 1804–15 June 1805*: Battalion Chief Bernard Cattanéo (*État Militaire Pour An XIII*). Cattanéo was an amnestied emigré who had been an officer in the Royal Corsican Regiment. In a coincidental development, he left the Po Tirailleurs when he was promoted to the rank of Major in the Corsican Legion. (Text to *Le Plumet*, Plate No 248 [*Infanterie Légère, Batailon de Tirailleurs du Po*].) *June 1805–October 1805*: Battalion Chief Brun-Cussan. *1 November 1805–22 March 1807*: Battalion Chief Étienne Hulot de Mazerny (1774–1850), a volunteer of '93 who was serving as ADC to Marshal Soult when he was chosen to command the Battalion. *March 1807–May 1809*: Battalion Chief Chenaud. *May 1809–5 July 1809*: Battalion Chief Gassa, who was killed at Wagram. He was succeeded by Battalion Chief Falguières, who was mortally wounded the next day. *October 1809 to final transformation:*

Battalion Chief Mano, who had risen from the rank of Lieutenant in the Battalion.

Operational History The most productive period in the Battalion's history started with an abrupt change of command. When he reviewed the Battalion outside Ulm at the end of October 1805 Napoleon noticed that the unit was in a serious state of disorganisation and he decided to take some swift remedial action (Hulot, *Souvenirs*, p. xi, n. 1):

> [Napoleon] turned brusquely towards Marshal Soult, the commander of the army corps in which the Battalion was serving, and asked him if he knew an officer with enough experience and good will to make a success of reorganising the Battalion. 'Sire, I know just the man—take Hulot,' responded Soult, pointing out Hulot, one of his ADCs who had recently been promoted to the rank of Battalion Chief. Napoleon knew that Soult's ADC was in fact a spirited and active officer, but he nevertheless raised objections because of his age. Soult insisted, pointing out the services Hulot had rendered in Italy and Switzerland and noting further that Hulot would be a good choice because he able to speak the same kind of Italian as the men of the unit. This last point overcame all Napoleon's objections . . . Several weeks later the Emperor reviewed the Battalion again and was unable to hide his amazement and satisfaction at the excellent appearance of the unit and the transformation of the men. Soult's ADC had changed the unit's spirit as well as its appearance. He had made himself very popular with his Italian men by speaking their language and even arranging for them to receive distributions of *polenta* [a favourite food] from time to time.

The Tirailleurs fought extremely well under their new commander. Brigaded with the Corsican Tirailleurs and the 26th Light under General Charles Juste Alexandre Legrand in Soult's 4th Corps, the Tirailleurs helped create the success of Austerlitz by tenaciously defending the château of Sokolnitz against the Austro-Russian flank attack. The unit suffered casualties of 29 killed and 154 wounded out of a total strength of only 340. (Detaille, p. 38; Bowden, p. 494.)

The Battalion remained part of Soult's Corps for the 1806 campaign. This meant that it was present, though not heavily engaged, at the Battle of Jena, but it did play an active role in the pursuit of the Prussians thereafter. The Battalion was particularly distinguished in the final action at Lübeck when the remains of Marshal Blücher's forces were brought to bay. At Hof on 6 February, during the winter campaign in Poland in 1807, the Tirailleurs were caught in skirmish order by a charge of Russian cavalry but avoided disaster through the quick thinking of Commandant Hulot (Hulot, *Souvenirs*, pp. xiv–xv):

> All my Battalion was deployed as skirmishers, except for one company guarding our colour, when I suddenly saw several squadrons of Russian cavalry galloping towards us. Luckily, the cavalry was still far enough off so that I had a minute and I took advantage of that time to have the drummers and fifers beat and play recall, rally my brave children around me, tell them not to fire until we could touch the noses of the enemy horses and order the first rank to 'Fix bayonets!' and the other ranks to 'Ready their muskets!' The charge came as close as twenty paces, but then the cavalry turned their backs to us.

The Battalion suffered heavy casualties over the next two days at the Battle of Eylau. In the spring campaign, the unit lost one officer killed and four wounded (two mortally) at Heilsberg on 10 June 1807.

The Tirailleurs stayed in Germany when Soult's 4th Corps went off to Spain. For the 1809 campaign the unit found itself in Marshal Jean Lannes' 2nd Corps, still brigaded with the Corsicans and the 26th Light but now under the command of General Louis Jacques Coehorn. Two officers of the Tirailleurs were wounded at Ertingen on 29 April and one was killed at Ried on 1 May, but the first significant fighting for the Battalion took place at Ebersberg on 3 May. There General Coehorn led his brigade in a wild charge across a bridge and up a hill in the face of heavy Austrian resistance. The Tirailleurs had three officers killed outright and five wounded (one mortally). The unit continued to be in the thick of the action, fighting at Essling on 22 May and Wagram on 5 and 6 July. The Battalion suffered nine officer casualties in the two battles.

The Tirailleurs were never again in action after 1809. The only official recognition of the unit during the next years was an attempt to purge it of soldiers who were born elsewhere than Piedmont. Those that did not fit the geographic criteria were to be sent to the 3rd Battalion of the 18th Regiment of Light Infantry. (Decision of 24 October 1810, Nap. *Inédits*, No 428, Vol. 1, p. 122.)

Final Transformation The Po Tirailleurs were formally disbanded in August 1811 because of the inefficiency of sustaining their existence as an independent unit, but the unit effectively continued intact as one of the component battalions of the 11th Light Infantry Regiment that was re-formed that same month (Decision of 11 August 1811, Nap. *Inédits*, No 479, Vol. 1, p. 135):

> The Battalion of Corsican Tirailleurs and the Battalion of Tirailleurs of the Po will form a new regiment under the name of the 11th Light Infantry Regiment. The depot of this regiment will be at Trèves. The Corsican Tirailleurs will form the bulk of the 1st Battalion of the new regiment and the Po Tirailleurs will form the bulk of the 2nd Battalion.

Uniforms Most sources agree that the Po Tirailleurs wore the same general uniform as all other light infantry troops of the Grand Army, but some sources are adamant that the unit had red lapels as a distinguishing feature. The definitive word on this point is provided by a letter written by a former commander of the Battalion to correct the depiction of his unit in a painting by Colonel Langlois (E. Hulot to Tholozé, 15 March 1847, quoted in Anon., *Hulot*, p. 64–65):

> You have asked me to write to you to describe the uniforms worn by the Po Tirailleurs and the Corsican Chasseurs so that these two corps can be accurately depicted in a painting concerning the Battle of Hof, 6 February 1807, that is being created by Colonel Langlois. These two corps had the exact same uniform as all other light infantry of the period and the same organisation–nine companies (including one of carabiniers) and no voltigeurs. My battalion differed from the other only in the dress of the drummers.

> Both a drummer and a fifer were attached to each company; they carried a small carbine suspended from a sling and were commanded by a Drum Major. Their uniform was different from that of all the other drummers and fifers in the army because the lapels were red and were cut to a point in light infantry style.

One other point about the dress of the Battalion can be verified from primary sources: the Carabiniers wore bearskins. 'I have agreed to give bearskin bonnets to the Carabiniers of this Battalion. Make sure they are furnished.' (N. to Berthier, 27 July 1804, Nap. *Corr.*, No 7875, Vol. 9, p. 434.)

Standard The Battalion received an Eagle with an 1804 Model colour sometime early in 1805. (Regnault, p. 30.) These items are illustrated in *Le Plumet*, Plate No 248.

Vélites de Turin et Florence

(Vélites of Turin and Florence)

Date of Creation 24 March 1809.

Circumstances of Creation In his never-ending search for manpower, Napoleon created these units to provide security for his relatives in Italy while adding two new Battalions to the Imperial Guard. The Vélites of Turin served as a guard for Prince Camille Borghese, Napoleon's brother-in-law (married to Pauline), who served as Governor-General of the French departments in northern Italy (as opposed to the territory of the Kingdom of Italy), while those of Florence guarded Napoleon's sister Elisa, the Grand Duchess of Tuscany. (Rigo, 'Vélites', p. 23.)

Composition The two Vélite Battalions were created by separate but nearly identical decrees. Both units were to be recruited from men living in the departments of the 27th (headquarters Turin), 28th (headquarters Genoa) and 29th (headquarters Florence) Military Divisions who could demonstrate an annual allowance of 200 francs. Each Battalion was to have 21 officers, but the Turin Battalion was larger by one company. (Titeux, p. 777.) A depot company was formed at Paris for each Battalion in January 1814. (Decision of 18 January 1814, Nap. *O&A*, No 6397, Vol. 4, p. 427.)

Commanders

Vélites of Turin *Formation to final transformation:* Battalion Chief Jean Baptiste Antoine Hyacinte Cicéron (1778–1840), a former Captain of the Tirailleur Grenadiers who had been decorated by Napoleon himslef for his heroic conduct at the Battle of Essling. (Rigo, 'Vélites', p. 30.)

Vélites of Florence *Formation to June 1812*: Battalion Chief Dufour. (All information in this section comes from Fieffé, Vol. 2, pp. 116–17.) *June 1813–September 1813*: Battalion Chief Barrois. *September 1813–November 1813*: Battalion Chief Ardouzel (or, possibly, Ardourel), who was disabled by wounds suffered at Leipzig. *20 November 1813–25 January 1814*: Battalion Chief Delaire (1774–1813), who had been Captain Adjutant-Major of the Vélites of Turin until he was transferred to command of the sibling Battalion. He was killed at the combat of Fontaine in 1814. (Rigo, 'Vélites', p. 30.)

Operational History The Battalions were not fully organised until 1810 and even then they had only ceremonial duties. They were moved as far as Poland in 1812 but missed the horrors of the Russian campaign. They formed a prominent part of the infantry strength of the re-formed Imperial Guard in the winter and spring of 1813. On 25 April 1813 the two Battalions were serving in the 2nd Brigade of General François Roguet's Old Guard Division, with the Turin Vélites mustering sixteen officers and 303 men and the Florence Vélites seventeen officers and 202 men. (Bowden, *1813*, p. 221.) The Battalions lost one officer each at the Battle of Lützen on 2 May 1813.

The Vélites continued to form part of the Old Guard Division for the autumn campaign, but the composition of that force was changed pursuant to an Imperial order dated 14 September 1813 (reproduced in Nap. *1813*, No 443, pp. 163–4):

1st Division (General Louis Friant)
1st Brigade Chasseurs
2nd Brigade Grenadiers

2nd Division (General Curial)
1st Brigade Fusiliers
2nd Brigade Vélites of Turin
Vélites of Florence
Saxon Guard Battalion
Polish Battalion

Article 4 of the order specifies that the Vélites were to be topped up to a strength of 800 men each by a draft of 'robust, Italian-speaking men' from the remaining regiments of the Young Guard. It seems unlikely that this draft would ever have taken place.

The Vélites finally got into serious combat during the Battle of Leipzig in the autumn campaign. The Florence Battalion had one officer killed and eleven wounded; the Turin Battalion only had four non-fatal officer casualties at Leipzig itself, but had two officers wounded during the retreat. The Battalions survived intact to fight actively during the 1814 campaign, albeit with a much reduced strength. The Vélites of Florence had one officer killed and four wounded at the combat of Fontaine on 25 January, while the two Battalions had nine officer casualties combined at Montmirail on 11 February. Some officers were particularly unlucky when it came to combat. Second Lieutenant Dutreuil of the Florence Vélites was wounded at Leipzig, Fontaine, Montmirail and a skirmish near Meaux (although he was promoted to Lieutenant for his troubles). Captain Gavignet of the Vélites of Turin was hit at Leipzig, Laon and the last battles in front of Paris, while his colleague 2nd Lieutenant Desalines was wounded at Leipzig, Montmirail and the same action near Meaux as Dutreuil of the Florence Vélites.

Final Transformation Both Battalions of Vélites were disbanded on 15 July 1814. On the last day, the Vélites of Turin had only 49 Italians in its ranks; the other 137 soldiers were French and were transferred to the 14th Line. (Rigo, 'Vélites', p. 31.)
Uniforms The Organisational Decree for the Vélites specifies that they were to wear the same uniform as the Fusilier-Grenadiers of the Guard, namely a shako, dark blue jacket with white fringed epaulettes, blue collar, white lapels, red cuffs and white cuff flaps. (See, generally, Rigo, 'Vélites', pp. 24–9.)
Standard The Vélites of Turin received an 1804 Model standard with gold grenades on the corner circles and the following legends: obverse–'L'Empereur/des Français/A u B.ion de Vélites/de Turin'; reverse–'Garde/Impériale/Valeur/et Discipline'. This colour can be seen in the collections of the Museum of Turin and is reproduced photographically in Rigo, 'Vélites', p. 31.

No information has been found about the standard, if any, carried by the Vélites of Florence, but they served so much with the Turin Vélites that it seems likely that they would have requested and received the same kind of colour.

Vétérans Espagnols

(Spanish Veterans)

Date of Creation Decree of 1 July 1811. (Belhomme, Vol. 4, p. 521).
Circumstances of Creation This unit was formed to provide a means of dealing with the soldiers of the Joseph Napoleon Regiment who became too old or too weak to remain on active service. (Fieffé, Vol. 2, p. 147.)
Composition The unit had a strength of one company.
Commanders No information found.
Operational History The Spanish Veteran Company formed part of the garrison of Namur.
Final Transformation No information found.
Uniforms The unit was uniformed and equipped in the same manner as a unit of French Veterans, but most likely kept their own uniform buttons.
Standard No information found.

Vétérans Ioniens

(Ionian Veterans)

This unit is noted in Fieffé (Vol. 2, p. 154) and Chartrand, Napoleon's Army (p. 128), but no other details of its existence have been found. It was undoubtedly formed to provide a home for aged and decrepit soldiers from the other Ionian and Septinsular formations.

Appendices

A. Organisation of Piedmontese Troops, 1798–1801

Following the ratification of the Armistice of Cherasco on 15 May 1796, the Kingdom of Piedmont-Sardinia was still theoretically an independent state allied with the French Republic, but for all practical purposes King Charles Emmanuel IV was subservient to the French occupiers of his territory. He was also engaged in a long internal struggle with Piedmont's own revolutionaries, who hoped to transform their country into a republic. The French eventually tired of this ambiguous state of affairs and on 5–6 December 1798 General Joubert accused the King of plotting with the Austrians and Russians and ordered a military occupation of the Piedmont. Shortly thereafter the King renounced his rights to Piedmont and retired to Sardinia. As a result, the part of northern Italy that formed the mainland half of the Kingdom of Piedmont-Sardinia went into a state of political limbo.

As a result of these developments, all Piedmontese troops were declared to be part of the French Army and were required to wear French cockades. (Belhomme, Vol. 4, p. 182.) At the moment of transition, these troops consisted of two regiments of Dragoons, one regiment of Hussars, five line infantry regiments, five Swiss infantry regiments and several artillery batteries. In March 1799 the five line regiments were transformed into three numbered Legions of three battalions each and the Swiss were reorganised into two Legions of three battalions each, one commanded by Andermatt and the other by Bellemont. (Belhomme, Vol. 4, pp. 185–6.) The Swiss Legions were destroyed at the Battle of Verona and the subsequent siege of Mantua. The line Legions saw little active service.

After the campaign, the debris of the Piedmontese infantry was reorganised into two line demi-brigades. The first of these eventually became the 111th French Line Regiment on 26 August 1801; the other became the 112th of the Line on the same date but was disbanded on 6 April 1803, its first battalion being attached to the 11th Line and its second and third battalions being added to the 31st Light. (Belhomme, Vol. 4, pp. 246 and 268.) Another unit associated with Piedmont was the *Légion Vaudoise*, which became the 1st Piedmontese Light Demi-brigade on 20 August 1800. On 26 August 1801 it became the 31st Light Regiment. (Fieffé, Vol. 2, pp. 27–8.) A battalion of Piedmontese veterans eventually became the 9th Veteran Battalion.

As for the cavalry regiments, the Piedmontese Hussars became the 17th Mounted Chasseurs of the Line on 26 August 1801, changing to the 26th of that arm in May 1802. The single remaining Piedmontese Dragoon regiment became the 21st Dragoons of the Line on that same date. (Fieffé, Vol. 2, p. 30.)

B. Organisation of Lithuanian Forces, 1812

The troops raised by Napoleon in the region of Lithuania during the 1812 campaign present a challenge in terms of the definition adopted for this study because it is clear that Napoleon intended them to be part of the armed forces of a new state that would be allied with France, either independently or as part of a revived Polish-Lithuanian nation incorporating the Grand Duchy of Warsaw, and not to be *'troupes étrangères'*. Of course, the outcome of the campaign meant that the new state never came into being, so their status remained ambiguous to the end other than for two units that definitely qualify for inclusion in this study because they were formally incorporated into the French Army—the *3ème Lanciers de la Garde* and the *Tatars Lithuaniennes*. Nevertheless, I have decided to include this Appendix on the Lithuanian forces for the sake of completeness.

On 1 July 1812 Napoleon established a provisional government for a Principality of Lithuania that he created from the four Russian administrative territories centred on the cities of Vilna, Grodno, Minsk and Bialystock. (Most of the information from this Appendix is taken from Dundulis—which is based on archival sources—supplemented by Chabanier.) One of the first tasks it was assigned was that of forming its own army to protect the rear areas of the Grand Army during its advance to Moscow. The establishment called for five infantry regiments and four cavalry regiments, all of them numbered sequentially to the regiments of the Army of the Grand Duchy of Warsaw but operating independently from that force. A decree of 13 July provided commanders from the Lithuanian aristocracy for all the planned units:

Unit	Commander	Location
18th Infantry	Alexander Chodkiewocz	Vilna
19th Infantry	Constantin Tyzenhauz	Raseinai
20th Infantry	Adam Bisping	Slonim
21st Infantry	Charles Przezdziecki	Bialystock
22nd Infantry	Stanislas Czapski	Minsk
17th Lancers	Michel Tyszkiewicz	Kupischkis
18th Lancers	Joseph Wawrzecki (replaced end Aug. by Charles Przezdziecki)	Nevizh
19th Lancers	Constantin Rajecki	Novogrudek

20th Lancers	Xavier Obuchowicz	Pinsk

In addition to these regular troops, the population of Lithuania was also called upon to support a national guard for each of the four departments and 33 companies of gendarmes.

Recruiting proceeded slowly at first, but then picked up speed as Napoleon put General Dirk Hogendorp, one of his own aides-de-camp, in charge of the organisation of all the Lithuanian forces. He was aided by the formation of a Lithuanian general staff that included an Inspector General (Romuald Giedroyc), an Inspector of Infantry (Xavier Niesolowski) and an Inspector of Cavalry (Joseph Wawrzecki). Their efforts were ultimately so successful that there were enough recruits left over to begin the formation of a 23rd Infantry Regiment.

In the meanwhile, on 12 August, the government ordered the formation of six battalions of light infantry (called foot chasseurs) with the following commanders:

Battalion	Commander
1st	Joseph Dominique Kossakowski
2nd	Rokicki
3rd	Casimir Plater
4th	Kurczewski
5th	Obukowicz
6th	Lochowski

Each battalion had six companies of 139 officers and men. The men were all volunteers at first and were mainly foresters and gamekeepers from large estates. Recruiting became mandatory after the government decided to turn these battalions into two regiments of light infantry. The first two battalions were consequently formed into a regiment under the command of Colonel Kossakowski of the 1st Battalion, but the 3rd and 4th Battalions operated independently until the end of the campaign. No information has been found about the destiny of the last two battalions.

The Lithuanian military effort also included some proprietary elements. In October, after Napoleon had reached Moscow and the success of his invasion seemed assured, a wealthy landowner named Ignace Moniuszko received permission from the government to raise a regiment of volunteer cavalry at his own expense that was denominated as the 21st Regiment (even though no more than a squadron was ever raised). Another patriot, Rudolph Tysenhauz, formed a horse artillery battery as a gift to the state. Prince Gabriel Oginski formed an Honour Guard for Napoleon of twenty or so sons from the wealthiest families, and this small force actually accompanied Napoleon to Moscow and back. There were also some initiatives that did not come to fruition such as Prince Sapieha's proposal for the formation of volunteer infantry regiment, which failed when the Prince died unexpectedly.

The best estimate of the total military force raised in Lithuania in 1812 is 19,000 men (or 16,000, not including the national guard and gendarmes). Their military contribution to the French effort was minimal, however, because very few of the new units ever reached a state of organisation that allowed them to be committed to combat. A force of several thousand men under General Kossecki (consisting of the 22nd Infantry Regiment and part of the 23rd, the 1st Chasseur Battalion and the 18th Lancers) was committed to the defence of Minsk on 13 November and suffered severe casualties. The 18th and 19th Lancers both fought in the battles at the Beresina later that month and the national guard and gendarmes both fought in the defence of Vilna in December.

Given the magnitude of the French defeat, the Lithuanians who had sided with Napoleon had little choice but to dissolve their forces or to accompany the Emperor into an open-ended exile. The 18th, 20th and 21st Infantry Regiments chose the latter course and were assigned to the garrison of the fortress of Modlin, where they remained until it surrendered on Christmas Day 1813. The 20th Lancers ended up in Danzig while the single squadron of the 21st Cavalry Regiment was incorporated into the 5th Mounted Chasseurs of the Grand Duchy of Warsaw and Tysenhauz's battery joined the Duchy's artillery corps. The remaining men of the light infantry regiment, Plater's battalion of Chasseurs and the 19th Infantry Regiment made it to Königsberg, where they were given new French uniforms. Those units were eventually disbanded, however, and the men transferred to regiments of the Grand Duchy. The 17th and 19th Lancers retreated under the command of Colonel Rajecki of the latter unit. They suffered so heavily in several rearguard actions, including one on 12 February 1813 in which the 17th was severely mauled, that they eventually came to be treated as a single unit for practical purposes. The combined regiments ultimately became part of Marshal Davout's forces that defended Hamburg and the Lower Elbe until the abdication of Napoleon in April 1814, making them the last surviving element of the Lithuanian military contribution to the Napoleonic wars.

C. Foreign Troops in 1815

When Napoleon returned to power in the spring of 1815 he found that Louis XVIII had preserved the four Swiss Regiments and three of the four *Régiments Étrangers* (the Tour d'Auvergne, Isembourg and Irish Regiments). The Swiss were so punctilious about the legalities of the new contract that they had signed with the Bourbons, however, that they refused to recognise him as their replacement employer. Napoleon was consequently forced to dissolve the existing units, although he then tried to get the individual soldiers to re-enlist in a new Swiss Regiment he intended to form that would not be subject to control of the Swiss government (Decree of 2 April 1815, Nap. *O&A*, No 6594, Vol. 4, p. 517):

I. The Swiss Regiments contracted for service in the French Army are hereby dissolved . . . .

II. The officers and men who have served in our armies and under our eagles will be admitted if they wish to a new Swiss Regiment to be created and organised by the Minister of War.

Several days later Napoleon unveiled his new grand scheme for the use of foreign troops (Decree of 11 April 1815, Nap. *O&A*, No 6634, Vol. 4, p. 534):

I. There will be five foreign regiments:
The 1st, composed of Piedmontese and Italians.
The 2nd, composed of Swiss.
The 3rd, composed of Poles.
The 4th, composed of Germans.
The 5th, composed of Belgians.

II. Each of the regiments will have three battalions, each of which will have the same composition as a regiment of line infantry.

III. These regiments will have the same pay, financial arrangements and furnishings as a regiment of line infantry.

IV. The uniform of each regiment will be the same colour and style as that used by troops of that country. The clothing allowance will be determined after the price of the chosen uniform is established.

As for foreign cavalry during the Hundred Days, Napoleon only resurrected two of his old units. On 13 April he recreated the 7th Line Lancers as a Polish regiment. (Nap. *O&A*, No 6640, Vol. 4, p. 537.) On 22 April he used the squadron of Polish Lancers that had accompanied him to Elba as the nucleus to re-form the 1st Light Horse Lancers of the Guard. However, only the first squadron of that regiment was intended to be composed exclusively of men of Polish descent. (Nap. *O&A*, No 6679, Vol. 4, p. 550.)

Although he was in power for only a short time in 1815, Napoleon made a large number of changes to this basic organisation. On 15 April he added a 6th Foreign Regiment composed of Spaniards. (Nap. *O&A*, No 6651, Vol. 4, p. 540.) The decree for that new unit specified that the regiment would be dressed in white and would have an artillery company if enough Spanish artillerymen could be found. Since the Emperor's approach now focused on a strict differentiation among foreign troops on the basis of nationality, he decided to do away with the two holdover foreign regiments that did not have a national identity. He dealt with the old Irish Regiment by re-designating it as the 7th Foreign Regiment and ordering that it was to be recruited exclusively from Irish and English soldiers. (Decree of 2 May 1815, Nap. *O&A*, No 6724, Vol. 4, p. 567.) Napoleon then split the new 1st Foreign Regiment in two, creating an 8th Foreign Regiment of Italians other than Piedmontese to be uniformed in green jackets with red facings. (Decree of 20 May 1815, Nap. *O&A*, No 6791, Vol. 4, p. 596.) As a final afterthought, he created a battalion of 'men of colour' to be dressed in blue light infantry-style uniforms. (Decree of 26 May 1815, Nap. *O&A*, No 6818, Vol. 4, p. 608.)

Of all these troops, only the 2nd Foreign Regiment and the Polish Lancers of the Guard are known to have participated in the Waterloo campaign. The 2nd Regiment, wearing red uniforms, fought at Ligny and Wavre. The Lancers were at Waterloo itself. They, and all the other foreign regiments, were disbanded after the second Bourbon restoration.

Bibliography

A surprisingly large number of books and articles have been written about Napoleon's *troupes étrangères*, with Fieffé's work leading the way by its breadth of information (though not its quality). The key source for the study of these units, however, remains the archives of the French Service Historique de l'Armée de Terre (SHA) at Vincennes, near Paris. An invaluable guide to that material is provided by France, *Inventaire*. The most essential printed sources for this work were the various compilations of Napoleon's letters and orders. In this regard, the selections presented in Nap. *P&T* and *O&A* were more important than the letters in the volumes of his official correspondence because of the extraordinary detail they provide about the organisation of Napoleon's armies. (One cannot help but be amazed at the wholly insignificant matters handled by Napoleon himself on a daily basis. He may have been a genius, but that is not evident from his management style, which was marked by his inability to delegate.) Napoleon's own writings are complemented nicely by the official documents printed in the *Journal Militaire*, a publication of the Ministry of War.

Four other works were essential for the completion of this study (and, indeed, are essential for any research concerning units of the French Army during this period). Although they are only secondary sources as a technical matter, they are practically primary in content because their authors have worked directly from archival sources. These works are Six's dictionary of French generals, Quentin's complementary work on French colonels, Martinien's listing of officer casualties and Belhomme's history of the French infantry. This last is almost impossible to find, but it provides an astonishing amount of information about the evolution of infantry units during the Napoleonic wars.

The present work would also not have been possible except for the existence of three important Napoleonic bibliographies. Ronald Caldwell's magnificent two volume opus, *The Era of Napoleon: A Bibliography of the History of Western Civilization, 1799–1815* (New York and London, 1991), is the definitive bibliography of the period, but is daunting to work with. Victor Sutcliffe's catalogue *The Sandler Collection* (Cambridge, 1996) is the least comprehensive of the three, but the easiest to use because it is organised alphabetically and provides useful annotations about the books covered. In the middle is the bibliography of *Napoleonic Military History* (New York and London, 1986), edited by Donald Horward, which has very helpful essays from the contributors but lacks an index.

Achard, Claude, 'Organisation Militaires des Prisonniers de Guerre Espagnols 1808-1814', *Le Briquet* (1980), No 2, pp. 1-8.

Adjutant I. . ., 'Souvenirs de la Guerre d'Espagne (1809-1812)', *Revue Retrospective*, Vol. 18 (January-June 1893), pp. 1-48, 97-149, 169-216, 241-88, 313-60 and 385-432; Vol. 19 (July-December 1893) pp. 49-65.

Alia Plana, Jesus Maria, et al., *Documentos del Ejército de José Napoleon*, (n.l., 1997).

Alombert, Paul C., and Colin, Jean, *La Campagne de 1805 en Allemagne* (6 vols, Paris, 1902-08).

Andolenko, C. R., *Aigles de Napoléon Contre Drapeaux du Tsar*, (Paris, 1969).

Anon. (Julius Wichede, ed.), *Aus Tagebüchern und Lebenserinnerungen: Ein Soldaten Leben* (Stuttgart, 1854).

Anon., 'La Siége de Hambourg [Bremen] 1813: Relation d'un Assiégé', *Revue Retrospective*, Vol. 3 (May-Dec 1885), pp. 9-36.

——, 'La Légion Grecque', *S.C.F.H. [Société des Collectionneurs des Figurines Historiques] Bulletin*, 2nd Trimetser (1961).

——, 'La Légion Maltaise', *S.C.F.H. [Société des Collectionneurs des Figurines Historiques] Bulletin*, 2nd Trimester (1961).

——, *Le Lt. Général Baron Étienne Hulot (1774-1850)* (Paris, 1884).

Auguste, C. B., *La Participation Étrangère à l'Expédition Française de St. Domingue* (Ottawa, 1980).

——, *Les Déportés de Saint-Domingue* (Quebec, 1979).

Aymes, Jean René, *La Déportation sous le Premier Empire: Les Espagnols en France (1808-1814)* (Paris, 1983).

Baeyens, Jacques, *Les Français à Corfou* (Athens, 1973).

Balagny, D. E. P., *Campagne de l'Empereur en Espagne (1808-1809)* (4 vols, Paris, 1902-06).

Begos, Louis, 'Souvenirs de ses Campagnes', *Soldats Suisses au Service Étranger* (8 vols, Geneva, 1909-19); Vol. 2 (1909), pp. 111-233.

Bernegg, Sprecher von, *Histoire Militaire de la Suisse* (Berne, 1921).

Bertin, G., 'La Tenue d'un Officier du 3e Régiment Suisse en 1812', *Carnet de la Sabretache* (1903), pp. 387-92.

Bethke, Martin, 'Das Fürstentum Isenburg im Rheinbund', *Zeitschrift für Heereskunde*, Vol. XLVI, No 302/303 (July-October 1982), pp. 94-9.

Bielecki, Robert, 'L'Effort Militaire Polonais 1806-1815', *Revue de l'Institut Napoléon*, No 132 (1976), pp. 148-64.

Bjelovucic, Harriet, *The Ragusan Republic: Victim of Napoleon and Its Own Conservatism* (Leiden, 1970).

Blondieau, Christian, *Aigles et Shakos du Premier Empire* (Paris, 1980).

Böck, August, *Leben und Schicksale des ehemaligen Musikmeisters im Königl. Preuss. 24sten Infanterie-Regiment August Böck* (Halle, 1838).

Boeri, Giancarlo, 'La Cronaca Rovatti', *Revista Militare Europea* (May-June 1989).

Boisselier, Henri, 'La Cavalerie de la Légion Hanovrienne 1805–1811', *Bulletin de la Société des Collectioneurs des Figurines Historiques* (1956).

Bonaparte, Joseph, (A. Du Casse, ed.), *Mémoires et Correspondance Politique et Militaire du Roi Joseph* (10 vols, Paris, 1854–55).

Bond, Gordon, *The Grand Expedition: The British Invasion of Holland in 1809* (Athens, GA, 1979).

Bonnal, Henri, *La Vie Militaire du Maréchal Ney* (3 vols, Paris, 1910–14).

Boppe, Auguste, *L'Albanie et Napoléon (1797–1814)* (Paris, 1914).

——, *Le Régiment Albanais (1807–1814)* (Paris, 1902).

——, 'Le Colonel Nicolas Papas Oglou et le Bataillon des Chasseurs d'Orient', *Carnet de la Sabretache*, Vol. VIII (1900), pp. 13–30 and 112–27.

Boppe, Pierre, *La Croatie Militaire (1809–1813)* (Paris, 1900; reprint Paris, 1989).

——, *La Légion Portuguais 1807–1813* (Paris, 189; reprint 1994).

——, *Les Espagnols à la Grande-Armée* (Paris, 1899; reprint 1986).

Bory, Jean René, *Régiments Suisses Au Service de France (1800–1814)* (Fribourg, Switzerland, 1975).

Bouillé, Louis Joseph de, *Souvenirs et Fragments pour Servir aux Mémoires de ma Vie* (3 vols, Paris, 1911).

Bowden, Scott, *Napoleon and Austerlitz* (Chicago, 1997).

——, *Napoleon's Grande Armée of 1813* (Chicago, 1990).

Brancacico, N., *L'Esercito de Vecchio Piemonte: Gli Ordinamenti. Pt 1: 1560–1814* (Rome, 1923).

Brandt, Henri, (J. North, trans. and ed.), *In the Legions of Napoleon: The Memoirs of a Polish Officer in Spain and Russia 1808–1813* (London, 1999). Based on Baron Ernouf, ed., *Souvenirs d'un Officier Polonais: Scènes de la Vie Militaire en Espagne et Russie (1808–1812)* (Paris, 1877).

Brethon, Paul le (ed.), *Lettres et Documents pour Servir à l'Histoire de Joachim Murat 1767–1815* (8 vols, Paris, 1908–14).

Brosse, J., and Lachouque, Henri, *Uniformes et Costumes du 1er Empire* (Paris, 1972).

Brun, Jean François, *Les Oubliés du Fleuve: Glogau-sur-Oder, un Siège sous le Premier Empire* (St-Julien-Chapteuil, 1997).

Brun de Villeret, Louis, *Les Cahiers du General Brun, Baron de Villeret* (Paris, 1953).

Brunon, Jean, *Des Légions de Dombrowski à l'Escadron des Chevau-Légers Polonais à l'ile d'Elbe* (Marseilles, n.d. [1940?]).

——, *Des Tatars au Service de Napoléon (1812–1814)* (Marseilles, n.d.).

Brunon, Jean and Raoul, *Les Éclaireurs de la Garde Impériale 1813–1814* (Marseilles, n.d.).

——, *Les Mamelukes d'Égypte* (Marseilles, 1963).

Bucquoy, E.-L., *Les Uniformes du Premier Empire: Gardes d'Honneur et Troupes Étrangères* (Paris, 1977).

——, *Les Uniformes du Premier Empire: L'Infanterie de Ligne et l'Infanterie Légère* (Paris, 1979).

——, 'Le Bataillon Valaisan', *Le Passepoil*, Vol. 7, No 6 (1927), pp. 80–1.

Bueno, José Maria, *Los Franceses Y Sus Aliados en España 1808–14*, Vol. 1 (Madrid, 1966).

Byrne, Miles, *Memoirs* (Paris 1863; reprint Dublin, 1972).

Bussell, Peter, *The Diary of Peter Bussell (1810–1814)* (London, 1931).

Bussy, J. M., 'Notes d'un Appointé de Voltigeurs', *Soldats Suisses au Service Étranger* (8 vols, Geneva, 1909–19), Vol. 5 (1913), pp. 219–312.

Calmon-Maison, Jean Joseph Robert, *Le Général Maison et le 1er Corps de la Grande Armée: Campagne de Belgique (Décembre 1813–Avril 1814)*, (Paris, 1914).

Carles, Pierre, ('Carles I'), 'Le Corps Irlandais au Service de la France sous le Consulat et l'Empire', *Revue Historique de l'Armée,* No 2 (1976), pp. 25–54.

——, ('Carles II'), 'Les Derniers Jours des Régiments Étrangers au Service de Napoléon', *Revue Historique de l'Armée*, No 4 (1972), pp. 55–74.

——, 'Un Régiment Noir sous le Premier Empire', *Carnet de la Sabretache*, No 434 (1967), pp. 342–51.

Castellane, Boniface de, *Journal du Maréchal de Castellane 1804–1862* (5 vols, Paris, 1895).

Cayron, J. R., 'La Carrière Militaire de Cosme Ramaeckers Après 1810', *Carnet de la Fourragère*, 12th Series (1956–57), pp. 270–82.

——, 'Note sur le Régiment d'Isembourg (2e Étranger)', *Carnet de la Fourragère*, 12th Series (1956–57), pp. 270–82.

Chabanier, Jean, 'La Grande Armée en Lituanie et en Courlande', *Revue Historique de l'Armée* (1973).

Chambers, G. L., *Bussaco* (London, 1910; reprint 1994).

Champeaux, ?, *État Militaire de l'Empire Français, Pour L'An Treize* (Paris, Year XIII [1805]).

Charrié, Pierre, *Drapeaux et Étendards de la Révolution et de l'Empire* (Paris, 1982).

——, ('Charrié II') 'Les Aigles et Drapeaux du Régiment d'Irlande', *Carnet de la Sabretache* (1972), p. 93 and Plate No 103.

Chartrand, Réné *Napoleonic Wars: Napoleon's Army* (London, 1996).

Chelminski, Jan V., and Malibran, A., *L'Armée du Duché de Varsovie* (Paris, 1913).

Chesney, A.G. 'The Negro Troops of Murat's Army', *United Service Magazine*, N.S. 48 (1913–14), pp. 198–202.

Chlapowski, Désiré, *Mémoires sur les Guerres de Napoléon 1806–1813* (Paris, 1908).

Chodzko, Leonard, *Histoire des Légions Polonaises en Italie sous le Commandement du Général Dombrowski* (2 vols, Paris, 1829).

Ciejka, Stephan, 'Trois Pistolets de Mamelucks', *Tradition*, No 49 (March 1991), pp. 10–14.

Clark, Brian 'Napoleon's Irish Legion, 1803–1815: The Historical Record', *The Irish Sword*, Vol. XII, No 48 (Summer 1976), pp. 165–72.

Coignet, J.-R., *Aux Vieux de la Vieille! Souvenirs de J.-R. Coignet* (n.l., 1851; reprint Paris, 1965).

Coppens, Bernard, *Légion du Nord 1807* (text to Coppens Plate No G.T.4) (Beauvechain, Belgium, 1992).

Coqueugniot, L.-C., *Histoire de la Légion du Nord 1806–1808* (Beauvechain, Belgium 1992).

Courcelle, Patrice, 'La Légion du Nord . . . Variations sur un Thème peu Exploité', *Carnet de La Sabretache*, N.S. 113 (3rd Trimester, 1992), pp. 79–80.

Courvoisier, J., *Le Maréchal Berthier et la Principauté de Neufchatel 1806–1814* (Neufchatel, 1959).

Couvreur, H. J., 'Le Régiment des Chevau-Légers Belges du Duc d'Arenberg et le 27eme Régiment de Chasseurs à Cheval', *La Revue Belge d'Histoire Militaire*, Vol. XVII (1968), pp. 563–75.

Crusius, Peter, (ed.), *Die Französische Revolutionsarmee Moreaus* (Osnabrück, 1985).

Darbou, René, 'Tenues des Troupes du Corps Expéditionnaire de Saint-Domingue 1801–1804' (MS in Library of the French Army Museum, illustrated by Henri Boisselier).

Dard, E., 'Le Général Descorches de Sainte-Croix', *Dans L'Entourage de Napoléon* (Paris, 1940).

Davin, Didier, 'L'Archipel Toscan et Piombino sous le Drapeaux Français (1800–1815). 3ème Épisode: Les Robinsons del la Pianosa (1805–1814)', *Le Briquet* (1998), No 1, pp. 29–32 and Plate 8.

Depreaux, Albert, 'A Propos d'un Tableau: Les Trompettes des Gardes d'Honneur', *Carnet de la Sabretache* (1931), pp. 64–7.

Despreaux, Fringet, *Le Maréchal Mortier, Duc de Trevise* (3 vols, Paris, 1913–20).

Detaille, Edouard, *L'Armée Française: An Illustrated History of the French Army 1790–1885* (New York, 1992).

Dundulis, Bronius, *Napoléon et la Lithuanie en 1812* (Paris, 1940).

Duplan, Victor M., *La Vie Militaire: Mémoires et Campagnes* (Paris, 1901).

Ede-Borett, Stephen, 'The Eagle and Colour of the Légion Irlandaise, 1804–1812', *First Empire*, No 46 (May/June 1999), pp. 20–3.

Espinchal, Hippolyte d', *Souvenirs Militaires 1792–1814* (2 vols, Paris, 1901).

Feldmann, M., and Wirz, H. G., *Histoire Militaire de La Suisse* (Berne, 1921)

Fieffé, E., *Histoire des Troupes Étrangères au Service de France* (2 vols, Paris, 1854; reprint Paris, 1995).

Finley, Milton, *The Most Monstrous of Wars: The Napoleonic Guerilla War in Southern Italy, 1806–1811* (Columbia, SC, 1994).

Forde, F., 'Napoleon's Irish Legion', *Au Consantoir*, Vol. 34, No 3 (March 1974), pp. 71–6.

Fortescue, John W., *A History of the British Army*, Vol. 5: 1803–1807 (London, 1910).

Fosten, D. S. V. 'First French Empire: Regiment de Prusse', *Tradition*, No 7, pp. 18–23.

Fosten, Don and Bryan, 'The Portuguese Legion 1808–1813', *Campaigns*, No 9 (March/April 1977), pp. 48–9.

Foy, Maximilian, *Junot's Invasion of Portugal 1807–1808* (Felling, UK, 2000). Translated excerpt from Foy's *Histoire de la Guerre de la Peninsule* (Paris, 1829).

France, Ministère de la Guerre, *Inventaire des Archives Conservées au Service Historique de l'État-Major de l'Armée (Château de Vincennes) (Archives Modernes)* (Paris, 1954).

Frasca, Francesco, 'Les Italiens dans l'Armée Napoléonienne'. Posted on the Internet January 2001 in the Reference Section for the *Napoleon Series* (www.napoleonseries.org).

——, 'Official Returns of the Republic of Italy Armed Forces 1802'. Posted on the Internet January 2001 in the Reference Section for the *Napoleon Series* (www.napoleonseries.org).

Friedrich, J.-C., *Mémoires d'un Mort (1805–1828): Faits de Guerre et Exploits d'Alcove* (3 vols, Paris, 1913).

Gachot, Edouard, *La Troisième Campagne d'Italie* (Paris, 1911).

Gallaher, John G., *Napoleon's Irish Legion* (Carbondale, IL, 1993).

——, ('Gallaher II') 'Conflict and Tragedy in Napoleon's Irish Legion: The Corbet/Sweeney Affair', *The Irish Sword*, Vol. XVI, No 64 (Summer 1986), pp. 145–56.

Ganier, Henri. See Tanconville.

Gärtner, Markus, 'Die Hannoveransche Legion: Die Kavallerie das Regiment Jäger zu Pferd 1803–1810', *Die Depesche* (1998).

Gembarzewski, Bronislaw, *Wojsko Polskie: Ksiestvoo Warszawskie (1807–1814)* (Warsaw, 1905).

Girod de L'Ain, M., *La Vie Militaire du Général Foy* (Paris, 1903).

Godechot, Jacques, *Les Espagnols du Marquis de la Romana 1807–1808* (Paris, 1924).

Gomez Ruiz, M., and Alonso Juanola, V., *El Ejercito de los Borbones. Vol. 5: Reinado de Fernando VII 1808–1833. Part 1: La Guerra de la Independencia 1808–1814* (Madrid, 1999).

Grabowski, Joseph, *Mémoires Militaires de Joseph Grabowski* (Paris, 1907).

Gross, Senateur, *Souvenirs Inédits sur Napoléon* (Paris, n.d.).

Guye, Alfred, *Le Bataillon de Neufchatel (Dit Des Canaris): Au Service de Napoléon 1807–1814* (Neufchatel, 1964).

Hatzopoulos, Konstantinos K., 'Greek Volunteers from Wallachia in the Military Corps "Les Chasseurs d'Orient" during the Campaign of the French Army in Dalmatia (1808–1809)', *Balkan Studies*, No 2 (1983), pp. 425–35.

Haussadis, Jean M. 'La Collection Wurtz du Musée de l'Armée [I]', *Uniformes*, No 108 (November 1987), pp. 50–1.

——, 'La Collection Wurtz du Musée de l'Armée [II]', *Uniformes*, No 119 (October 1988), pp. 46–7.

Hollins, David, *Austrian Auxiliary Troops 1792–1815* (London, 1996).

Homsy, Gaston, *Le Général Jacob et l'Expédition de Bonaparte en Égypte (1798–1801)* (Marseilles, 1921).

Horward, Donald, *Napoleon and Iberia: The Twin Sieges of Ciudad Rodrigo and Almeida, 1810* (Tallahassee, FL, 1984).

Houdaille, Jacques 'Pertes de l'Armée de Terre Sous le Premier Empire d'Après les Registres Matricules', *Population* (1972), pp. 27–50.

Hulot, Jean Jacques, *Souvenirs Militaires du Baron Jean Jacques Hulot, Général d'Artillerie 1773–1843* (Paris, 1886).

Humbert, René 'Notice sur le Bataillon Italique', *La Giberne*, Vol. 13 (1911–12), pp. 63–6.

Jalabert, D.-J., *Documents des Archives Communales de Grenoble Concernant La Légion Portuguaise (1808–1814)* (Paris, 1969).

John, Wilhelm, *Erzherzog Carl der Feldheer und Seine Armee* (Vienna, 1913).

Juhel, Pierre, 'La Légion Portuguaise Pendant la Campagne de Russie (1812)', *Tradition*, No 111 (June 1996), pp. 11–15.

Kann, Roger, *Les Portugais de la Grande Armée* (Paris, 1969).

Kirkor, Stanislaw, *Legia Nadwislanska 1808–1814* (London, 1981).

Koch, F., *Mémoires d'André Masséna, Duc de Rivoli, Prince d'Essling, Maréchal d'Empire* (7 vols, Paris, 1849–50; reprint Paris 1967).

Lamon, Siméon, 'Souvenirs d'un Chasseur de la Vieille Garde', *Soldats Suisses au Service Étranger* (8 vols, Geneva, 1909–19), Vol. 7 (1916), pp. 1–159.

Leclerc, Victor, *Lettres du Général Leclerc* (Paris, 1937).

Leconte, Louis, 'A Propos d'Un Portrait du Bruxellois Charles-Joseph Evers, Commandant la Cavalerie de la Légion Hanovrienne au Service de la France, 1803–1811', *Carnet de la Fourragère* (1937), pp. 97–110.

Lemonnier-Delafosse, M., *La Seconde Campagne de St-Domingue de 1er Décembre en 15 Juillet 1809* (Havre, 1846).

[Le Noble, Pierre], *Mémoires sur les Operations Militaires des Français . . . en 1809* (Paris, 1821).

Leslei, ?, *Military Journal of Colonel Leslie* (Aberdeen, 1887).

Lienhart, ?, and Humbert, R., *Les Uniformes de l'Armée Française* (Leipzig, 1900).

L'Invalide, 'Les Hussards Croates', *La Giberne*, Vol. XII (1910–11), pp. 139–43 and 149–58.

——, 'Les Régiments Croates et Leur Uniformes (1809-1814)', *La Giberne*, Vol. XII (1910–11), pp. 129–39.

Lumbroso, A., *Miscellanea Napoleonica.*

Luraghi, Sergio, 'Les Chroniques Italiennes (1796–1814)', *Carnet de La Sabretache*, New Series No 132 (2nd Trimester, 1997), pp. 47–54).

Maag, Albert, *Geschichte der Schweizertruppen im Kriege Napoleons I in Spanien und Portugal (1807–1814)* (2 vols, Biel, 1892).

——, *Die Schicksale der Schweizer-Regimenter in Napoleons I Feldzug nach Russland 1812* (Biel, 1890).

Mackesy, Piers, *British Victory in Egypt, 1801* (London, 1995)

[Maempfel, J. C.], *Adventures of a Young Rifleman in the French and English Armies during the War in Spain and Portugal* (London, 1826).

Maillard, J. P., 'Mémoires d'un Lieutenant au Service de France', *Soldats Suisses au Service Étranger* (8 vols, Geneva, 1909–19), Vol. 5 (1913), pp. 1–218.

Malhet, Elzear, 'Lettres de Elzear de Malhet', *Carnet de la Sabretache*, No 469 (March 1966), pp. 65–90.

Marbot, Jean-Baptiste, *The Memoirs of Baron de Marbot* (London, 1893).

Marbot, Alfred de, and Noirmont, Dunyoyer de, *Costumes Militaires Français de 1789 à 1815* (Paris, n.d.).

Margerand, J., 'Le 7e Chevau-Légers Lanciers', *Carnet de la Sabretache* (1925), pp. 237–8.

Marmottan, Paul, 'Le Bataillon Piombino', *Carnet de la Sabretache*, No 337 (December 1929), pp. 513–25.

——, 'Notes sur le Bataillon de Neufchatel (A propos du Portrait d'un de ses Capitaines)', *Carnet de La Sabretache* (1894), pp. 175–81.

Martin, Emmanuel, *La Gendarmerie Française en Espagne et Portugal (Campagnes de 1807 à 1814)* (Paris, 1898; reprint Paris, 1998).

——, 'Le Bataillon Valaisan (1806–1811)', *Carnet de la Sabretache* (1906), pp. 321–36.

Martinien, Aristide, 'Les Generaux du Grand-Duché de Varsovie de 1812 à 1814', *Carnet de la Sabretache*, Vol. 14 (1906), pp. 257–71 and 415–33.

——, *Tableaux Par Corps et Par Batailles des Officiers Tués et Blessés Pendant les Guerres de l'Empire (1805–1815)* (Paris, 1899; reprint Paris, n.d. [1986?]).

Masson, Frédéric Masson, *Les Cavaliers de Napoleon* (Paris, 1896).

Mercador Riba, Juan, *Barcelona Durante la Occupacion Francesa (1808–1814)* (Madrid, 1946).

Morawski, Richard and Wielecki, Henryk, *Wojsko Ksiestwa Warszawskiego: Kawaleria* (n.l., n.d.)

Morvan, Jean, (pseud.), *Le Soldat Imperial 1804–1815* (2 vols, Paris, 1904).

Murat, Joachim, *Lettres et Documents pour Servir a l'Histoire de Joachim Murat 1767–1815* (8 vols, Paris, 1908–14).

Nafziger, George, *Lützen & Bautzen: Napoleon's Spring Campaign of 1813* (Chicago, 1992).

——, *Napoleon at Dresden: The Battles of August 1813* (Chicago, 1994).

——, *Napoleon at Leipzig* (Chicago, 1996).

——, ('Nafziger IV'), 'The Irish Legion or The 3ème Régiment Étranger', *First Empire*, No 7 (1992), pp. 24–7.

——, *Poles and Saxons of the Napoleonic Wars* (Chicago, 19??)

Napoleon I, ('Nap. *Confidential*'), *The Confidential Correspondence of Napoleon Bonaparte with his Brother Joseph, Sometime King of Spain* (2 vols, NY, 1856).

——, ('Nap. *Corr.*'), *Correspondance de Napoléon I* (32 vols, Paris, 1858–69).

——, ('Nap. *P&T*'), (Ernest Picard and Louis Tuetey, eds.), *Correspondance Inédite de Napoléon I Conservée aux Archives de Guerre* (5 vols, Paris, 1911–14).

——, ('Nap. *Dernier Lettres*'), *Dernières Lettres Inédites de Napoléon 1er* (2 vols, Paris, 1903).
——, ('Nap. *Inédits*'), (Arthur Chuquet, ed.), *Inédits Napoléoniens* (2 vols, Paris, 1914–19).
——, ('Nap. *1813*'), *Lettres de L'Empereur Napoléon du 1er Août au 18 Octobre 1813 Non-insérées dans la Correspondance* (published by ?) (Paris, 1909).
——, ('Nap. *O&A*'), (Arthur Chuquet, ed.), *Ordres et Apostilles de Napoléon, 1799–1815* (4 vols, Paris, 1911–12).
Naylies, Joseph Jacques, *Mémoires sur la Guerre d'Espagne* (Paris, 1817).
Niegolewski, André, *Les Polonais à Somosierra* (Paris, 1854; reprint 2001).
Nieuwazny, Andrei, and Pattyn, J.-J., 'Le Bataillon Polonais de la Deuxième Division de la Vielle Garde Impériale Septembre-Octobre 1813', *Carnet de la Sabretache*, N.S. 111-E (1st Trimester, 1992), pp. 1–15.
Oman, Charles, *History of the Peninsular War* (7 vols, Oxford, 1902–30).
——, *Studies in The Napoleonic Wars* (London, 1929; reprint 1987).
Pachonski, Jan, and Wilson, Reuel, *Poland's Caribbean Tragedy: A Study of Polish Legions in the Haitian War of Independence 1802–1803* (New York, 1986).
Pattyn, Jacques 'Notes sur Deux Portraits d'Officiers du 27ème Régiment de Chasseurs à Cheval', *La Figurine*, Vol. 43 (4th Trimester, 1981), pp. 27–9.
Pelet, Jean Jacques, *The French Campaign in Portugal, 1810–1811* (Minneapolis, 1973).
Perconte, Jean-Pierre, *L'Infanterie de Ligne Italienne 1799–1814* (privately printed, n.l., n.d.).
Perrot, Maurice, *Surprise de Jersey en 1781; Prise de Capri en 1808* (Paris, 1929).
Pétard, Michel, 'Le Chevau-Léger-Lancier Polonais en 1812', *Tradition*, No 59 (December 1991), pp. 4–12.
——, 'Le Lancier Polonais', *Uniformes*, No 50 (July/August 1979), pp. 23–7.
Petiet, Auguste, (Nicole Gotteri, ed.), *Mémoires du Général Auguste Petiet, Hussard de l'Empire* (Paris, 1996).
Picard, Ernest, *Hohenlinden* (Paris, 1909).
Pigeard, Alain, *L'Armée Napoléonienne* (Paris 1993).
——, 'Le Bataillon Valaisan', *Tradition*, No 35 (December 1989), pp. 26–30.
——, 'Le Régiment de Prusse, 1806–1813', *Tradition*, No 85 (February 1994), pp. 17–21.
——, *Les Étoiles de Napoléon: Maréchaux, Amiraux et Généraux 1792–1815* (Paris, 1996).
——, 'Les Pionniers Sous le Consulat et L'Empire', *Tradition*, No 161 (November 2000), pp. 11–16.
——, 'Napoléon et les Troupes Polonaises 1797–1815' (Paris, n.d.).
Pisani, Paul, *La Dalmatie de 1797 à 1815* (Paris, 1893).
Pivka, Otto von, *Armies of 1812*, Vol. I (only volume published), (London, 1977).
Pouvesle, Frédéric, *Uniformes de l'Armée de Westphalie* (n.l., 2000).
Poyen de Belle-Isle, ?, *Histoire Militaire de la Révolution de Saint-Domingue* (Paris, 1899).
Rambaud, Jacques, *Naples Sous Joseph Bonaparte 1806–1808* (Paris, 1911).

Regnault, Jean, *Les Aigles Impériales 1804–1815* (Paris, 1967).

Reitzel, Christian, *Ein Schweizerbattalion im franzosizchen Kriegdienste und dessen Kampfe gegan die neapolitanischen Briganten* (Berne, 1864).

Rembowski, Alexandre, *Histoire du Régiment de Chevau-légers de la Garde de Napoléon 1er* (Warsaw/Paris, 1899).

Rigo (Albert Rigondaud) 'Drapeau [de la Légion Irlandaise] 1803–1804', *Carnet de la Sabretache* (1972), p. 93 and Plate No 103.

——, 'Le Régiment Joseph Napoléon: Les Espagnols dans la Tourmente', *Tradition*, No 88 (May 1994), pp. 22-30.

——, 'Les Vélites de Turin 1809–1814', *Tradition*, No 83 (December 1993), pp. 23-31.

——, 'Quelques Bizarreries dans l'Uniforme des Officiers de Chevau-Légers Lanciers Polonais 1811–1814', *Uniformes*, No 77 (February 1984), pp. 33-4.

——, 'The Lancers of the Vistula in Spain 1808–1812', *Tradition*, No 55 (1970), pp. 8–11.

——, 'Un Chevauléger à la Main Lourde: Le Général Baron Ameil', *Gazette des Uniformes*, No 28 (November/December 1975), pp. 29–32.

Robinson, R. E. R., *The Bloody Eleventh: A History of the Devonshire Regiment. Vol. 1 (1685–1815)* (Exeter 1988) .

Rosselet, Abraham, *Souvenirs* (Neufchatel, 1857).

Rousseau, François, *La Carrière du Maréchal Suchet, Duc d'Albufera* (Paris, 1898).

Sarramon, Jean, *La Bataille des Arapiles (22 Juillet 1812)* (Toulouse, 1978).

Sauzey, Camille, *Les Allemands Sous Les Aigles Françaises: Essai sur les Troupes de la Confédération du Rhin 1806–1813* (Paris, 1912).

Savant, Jean, *Sous les Aigles Impériales: Napoléon et les Grecs* (Paris, 1946).

Schaller, H. de, *Histoire des Troupes Suisses Au Service de France Sous le Règne de Napoléon 1er* (Paris, 1883; reprint 1995).

Schmeisser, Georg, *Le Régiment de Prusse* (Landsberg, 1885).

——, *Die Spanischen und Portugiesische Kontingente in de Armee des erstens Kaiserreichs* (Landsberg, 1886).

Schumacher, Gaspard, *Journal et Souvenirs de Gaspard Schumacher . . . 1798–1830* (Paris, n.d.).

Six, Georges, *Dictionnaire Biographique des Généraux et Amiraux Français de la Révolution et de l'Empire (1792–1814)* (2 vols, Paris, 1934; reprint 1989).

——, *Les Généraux de la Révolution et de l'Empire* (Paris n.d.).

Sorando Muzas, Luis, 'Aragonese al Servicio del Imperio', *Guerra de la Independencia Espanola*. Website http://members.tripod.com/˜gie2808a1814/colabora/soran5.html (6/25/99).

Spillman, Georges 'La Création de Corps Auxiliaires Égyptiens et Syriens', *Souvenir Napoleon*, No 304 (1979), pp. 7–15.

——, 'Les Égyptiens et les Syriens Dans la Grande Armée', *Souvenir Napoleon*, No 304 (1979), pp. 16–21.

Suchet, Gabriel, *Mémoires du Maréchal Suchet* (2 vols, Paris, 1834).
Suckow, K. von, *Fragments de ma Vie: d'Iéna à Moscou* (Paris, 1901).
Tanconville (pseud. of Henri Ganier), 'Les Légions et Demi-brigades Helvétiques', *Le Passepoil*, Vol. 10 (1930), pp. 49–52 and 79–80.
Teulière, Jean François, 'Le Sabre "à l'Orientale" d'un Empire à l'Autre', *Tradition*, No 95 (December 1994), pp. 6–11.
Thiébault, Paul, *Mémoires du Général Bacon Thiébault* (5 vols, Paris, 1895–97).
Titeux, Eugène, 'Un Officier des Gardes d'Honneur Italiens', *Carnet de La Sabretache*, Vol. X (1902), pp. 777–81.
Tranié, J., and Carmigniani, J. C., *Les Polonais de Napoléon* (Paris, 1982).
Tulard, Jean, *Histoire de Napoleon par la Peinture* (Paris, 1991).
Vallière, P. de, *Honneur et Fidelité: Histoire de Suisses au Service Étranger* (Lausanne, 1940).
Van Brock, F. W., 'A Proposed Irish Regiment and Standard, 1796', *Irish Sword*, Vol. XI (1975), pp. 226–33.
Vanson, General 'Soldats d'Autrefois: Tenues Oubliées. Les Chevau-Légers Polonais de la Garde Impériales', *Carnet de la Sabretache*, Vol. 4, pp. 12–21.
Vanson, General, 'Note Concernant l'Escadron de Tatares', *Carnet de la Sabretache*, Vol. VI, pp. 228–32.
Vernet, Horace, and Lami, Eugene, *Collection des Uniformes des Armées Françaises de 1789 à 1815* (Paris, n.d. [1820?])
Vignolles, M. de, *Précis Historique de Opérations Militaires de l'Armée d'Italie, en 1813 et 1814* (Paris, 1817).
Warre, William, *Letters from the Peninsula 1808–1812* (London, 1909).
Wielecki, Henryk 'Les Krakus (1812–1939)', *Uniformes*, No 95 (May/June 1988), pp. 7–9.
Wielhorski, Janusz, and Zaremba, Andrew, 'The 113th and 114th Polish Demi-brigades in San Domingo, 1802–1804', *Military Collector and Historian*, Vol. XIII, No 4 (Winter 1961), p. 116.
Woringer, R. August, 'Das Regiment Westfalen', *Zeitschrift für Heereskunde* (1932), pp. 393–6.
Zaremba, Andrew, 'The 1st and 2nd Regiments of Polish Lancers in the 1814 Campaign', *Adjutant's Call*, Vol. 6 (1969), No 4, pp. 52–5.
——, 'The Polish Legions of the Napoleonic Period, 1797–1815', *Adjutant's Call*, Vol. 4 (1966), No 4, pp. 53–5 and 64–5.
Zygulski, Zdzislaw, and Wielecki, Henry, *Polski Mundur Wojskowy* (Cracow, 1988).

Index

N

T